Telecommunications in Latin America

Telecommunications in Latin America

EDITED BY

ELI M. NOAM

New York   Oxford

OXFORD UNIVERSITY PRESS

1998

Oxford University Press

Cau   Oxford   New York

Athens   Auckland   Bangkok   Bogota   Bombay   Buenos Aires
Calcutta   Cape Town   Dar es Salaam   Delhi   Florence   Hong Kong
Istanbul   Karachi   Kuala Lumpur   Madras   Madrid   Melbourne
Mexico City   Nairobi   Paris   Singapore   Taipei   Tokyo   Toronto   Warsaw

Cau   and associated companies in
Berlin   Ibadan

Copyright © 1998 by Oxford University Press, Inc.

Published by Oxford University Press, Inc.
198 Madison Avenue, New York, New York 10016

Oxford is a registered trademark of Oxford University Press

Library of Congress Cataloging–in–Publication Data
Telecommunications in Latin America / Eli M. Noam. [editor]
p.   cm.
Includes bibliographical references and index.
ISBN 0–19–510200–2
1. Telecommunication—Latin America. 2. Telecommunication policy—
Latin America. I. Noam, Eli M.
HE7820.5.T45   1997
384'.098—dc20   96–36073

1 3 5 7 9 8 6 4 2

Printed in the United States of America
on acid-free paper

Contents

Contributors

Antonio José J. Botelho is a Ph.D. candidate in political science at M.I.T. and has done extensive research on the political economy of high technology in both developed and developing countries, focusing on the computer (hardware and software), semiconductor, and telecommunications industries.

Percy Cornejo is with the Dirección de Investigacion, Instituto de Investigacion y Capacitacion en Telecomunicaciones in Peru.

Ramón Morales Cortés is with New Era Technologies, Inc.

Juan Ernesto Barreda Delgado is with the Dirección de Investigacion, Instituto de Investigacion y Capacitacion en Telecommunicaciones in Peru.

Hopeton S. Dunn is a communications policy analyst and lecturer at the Caribbean Institute of Mass Communication (CARIMAC) at the University of the West Indies, Jamaica. He also serves as president of the Caribbean Association for Communication Research (CACR), based in Kingston, Jamaica.

Ivan N. Espinoza graduated in 1981 as an electronic and telecommunications engineer and works at the National Polytechnic School in Quito, Ecuador.

José Roberto Ferro is a professor at the School of Business Administration of São Paulo–Getulio Vargas Foundation and Federal University of São Carlos, Brazil.

Winston S. Gooden is president and chief executive officer of Export Investment Financial Services Ltd., based in Kingston, Jamaica.

Kathleen A. Griffith is the president of Informatica, a Washington D.C.-based communications consulting firm. She has since 1981 specialized in information technology regulatory policy, commercial markets, and social applications in Latin America.

Graciela Pérez Montero Gotusso has been director of the Public Enterprises Division for the Planning and Budgeting Office, which reports to the president of Uruguay, since 1990.

Alejandra Herrera is associated with the Universidad de Buenos Aires in Argentina.

Margot Lise Hooley works for the Strategic Planning Department of the New York Times. While conducting research in Colombia, she developed a model to forecast future demand in the long-distance telecommunications sector for Bell Canada International.

Lee McKnight is a research associate at the M.I.T. Center for Technology, Policy and Industrial Development.

José Ricardo Melo is professor of telecommunication systems at the University of Chile in Santiago and a consultant for several Chilean and foreign institutions on telecommunications policy, regulation, and economics.

John Spicer Nichols is associate professor of communications at Pennsylvania State University, where he teaches international communications. As a specialist in Cuban communications issues, Nichols has met with President Fidel Castro (most recently in 1994) and most of his top media policy makers and has testified frequently before U.S. congressional committees.

Eli M. Noam is professor of finance and economics at the Columbia University Graduate School of Business. He is currently director of the Columbia Institute for Tele-Information.

Felipe M. Noguera has served as secretary general/managing director of the Caribbean Association of National Telecommunication Organizations (CANTO) since its formation in April 1985. He has taken CANTO from a seven-member-nation association to a thirty-member national trade consortium.

Antonio C. Manfredini Oliveira is professor of economics at EAESP–Getulio Vargas Foundation in São Paulo, Brazil.

Michael Chong Pineda is an expert in telecommunications in Ecuador.

Sheryl Russell provides strategic consulting services to both end users and suppliers. With twenty years of experience in telecommunications, her expertise is recognized internationally.

Edgar Saravia is associated with the Ministry of Planning and Coordination in Bolivia.

Alicia M. Torres is the executive director of the Cuban American Committee Research and Education Fund and is a consultant in Washington, D.C. In 1978, she was the youngest participant in a series of conversations between the Cuban government and sectors of the Cuban American community held under the auspices of the Carter Administration.

Márcio Wohlers is a professor in telecommunications at the State University of Campinas in Brazil.

Natan Zaidman served as director of the board and chief of the legal department of the National Telephone Company of Venezuela (CANTV) from 1984 to 1989.

Introduction

ELI M. NOAM AND CYNTHIA BAUR

This volume documents and analyzes the historical dimensions and contemporary transformations of the telecommunication systems of forty-one countries in Latin America and the Caribbean. The studies do not single out technology as the cause of underdevelopment and change but the social, economic, and political factors that have shaped technology's uses. Regulatory, economic, and social change are examined in light of technological evolution, marketplace developments, and institutional reorganization. The unique histories of each country's network growth are also reviewed.

Current trends in the region are a shift from the state as the supplier of telecommunication services to regulator of network operations and services; the gradual introduction of competition at all levels of the system; the growth of private, limited access networks; and the modernization of public networks with digital and fiber-optic technologies.

Traditionally, Latin America and the Caribbean have been characterized by major inequalities in access to telecommunication services: inequalities in comparison to developed countries and inequalities within the region and within individual countries. The regional average of telephone access lines per 100 persons is 7.19,[1] but this figure masks the concentration of services in a few countries. Two-thirds of installed lines in Latin America are located in three countries: Argentina, Brazil, and Mexico. Contributors to this volume amply record the internal imbalances in domestic systems; the middle class received preferred access over the poor, and business users were favored over residential subscribers. Universal service was a distant achievement for societies with widespread poverty and underfinanced telecommunication systems with expensive connection fees and monthly charges.

System inadequacies have been the other hallmark of Latin American telecommunication networks. National telecom monopolies owned and operated partially or fully by the state were the norm in the region during the postwar period. Despite numerous modernization programs, domestic monopolies failed to build widely accessible, reliable public networks. Common complaints included insufficient lines to meet demand, poor-quality equipment, outdated technologies, and infrequent maintenance and repairs. Decade-long, "official" waiting lists for line installation only scratched the surface of the pent-up demand for basic service.

The systems were also financially inadequate. Artificially high equipment prices at several times the international average and direct payments to national treasuries transferred surpluses from network investment (often supplied directly by new subscribers who were expected to bear the full cost of line installation) to large equipment manufacturers and the national treasury. Although a lack of capital and poor and/or highly politicized management of national telecom companies deserve blame for past failures, these problems were as much a manifestation of general political crises as direct causes. In many countries in the region, chronic political instability, reflected by the alternation between authoritarian and democratic regimes and political violence, has had an enormous impact on the ability of national telecommunication administrations to set long-term policy goals and to carry out mandates that changed frequently.

Although the recent evolution of telecommunication systems in the United States and other countries did illustrate the feasibility of institutional arrangements other than monopoly, these examples were not the sole or even the primary cause of change in Latin America; neither was trade pressure from Washington, London, or Brussels. The widespread changes in policy and industry throughout Latin America are part of a broad transition caused by diverse forces, both international and domestic.

Two of the most important factors are the emergence of global telecommunication carriers and the processes of state reform and market liberalization in Latin American countries. A generalized financial crisis precipitated by the threat of widespread loan defaults gripped the region in the early 1980s, and public-sector investment dried up in many countries. As a partial response, governments throughout Latin America instituted orthodox economic stabilization programs with the twin goals of reducing inflation and public spending and debt. (Authoritarian governments in Argentina and Chile began these programs in the late 1970s.) Governments focused on changing domestic market conditions to stimulate private-sector economic activity. They actively promoted the sale of state-owned companies, courted foreign and private investment, and encouraged production for export to accomplish their goals.

The reorganization of national telecom sectors is enmeshed in these processes of sweeping reform of state responsibilities. The capital intensive telecom sector was a prime candidate for sell-off, especially as subscribers (business and residential) were unwilling or unable to assume the full burden to finance necessary network upgrades and expansion. In examples from Caribbean countries, change began in the late 1970s when governments recognized the demand for necessary infrastructure to support service based economies of data processing and tourism. The transfer of responsibility from the state to the private sector for network management and investment has ranged from complete privatization of the public switched network to the parceling out of value-added services and the so-called new technologies, such as mobile cellular and data transmission. The impact of telephone company privatization on state finances seems to have been most direct in providing large infusions of cash and/or foreign debt forgiveness.

In general, telecom system reorganization in Latin America and the Caribbean has been a top-down, government-led phenomenon. The policies for change were generated by the inner circles of advisers to the presidents and had full presidential support. This definitely was true in the first wave of privatizations in Argentina, Chile, Mexico, and Venezuela; policies of privatization of state companies, as well as liberalization of national market operations, are closely associated with Menem (Argentina), Pinochet (Chile), Salinas de Gortari (Mexico), and Pérez (Venezuela). In particular, the privatization of telecom companies served to mark political commitment to change and to anchor budding national stock markets.

Commitment at the highest levels of government meant that opposition to change from entrenched interests was rarely successful. The role of the telephone workers unions is alluded to by several of the authors. In Argentina, telecom reform was carried out against the vehement protests of the telephone workers, many of whom were fired when they went on strike. President Menem brought in the military to operate the network, and front-page newspaper photographs of military occupation of telephone offices were powerful reminders of the power of the executive. The telephone workers' union in Mexico also was initially against the privatization of Telmex, the national phone company, but a pact between the government and the union prior to the privatization co-opted the union and muted resistance. In Colombia, however, opposition of the union blocked privatization of the national company, Telecom Colombia, and forced a more modest restructuring of ownership.

As in developed countries, established multinational equipment manufacturers with subsidiaries in Latin America were opposed to sector reorganization. They had developed highly profitable supply relations with postal and telecommunications agencies (PTTs) and privatization plans threatened to disrupt the comfortable situation. Equipment suppliers anticipated new entrants and downward pressure on prices from new owners. To mollify the old guard, governments struck political deals to extend supply contracts into the postprivatization period.

Fundamental change at the domestic level has coincided with changes in the international telecom sector. Liberalization in domestic telecom systems is also transforming the international system of telecommunication. Specifically, liberalization leads to the emergence of global telecommunication network alliances and carriers and the end of the traditional idea of telecommunication as primarily a domestic concern.

The emergence of transnational carriers and alliances can be traced to the maturation of the most technically advanced domestic telecom markets. As the markets for basic services in their respective countries become saturated, Public Telecommunications Operators (PTOs) of developed countries expand their sights geographically to find markets with low teledensities and great potential for expansion. Moreover, they look abroad to newly liberalized markets to escape residual domestic restrictions, such as prohibitions against the provision of video and long-distance services. Transnational telecom operators also are responding to the globalization of corporate activity and new market opportunities, such as outsourcing. Greater customer sophistication and the growing multinational business market fuel an increasing global demand for advanced and specialized end-to-end telecommunication services. Provision of these services becomes even more financially lucrative as cost becomes less sensitive to distance.

Transnational carriers reap numerous benefits from cooperative arrangements across borders. Through alliances with other providers, carriers compensate for their lack of global presence, adequate financial resources, or technical and managerial expertise, at the same time they expand their customer base for new services. Affiliations spread the risk of investments in new services or activities, which is especially desirable when carriers enter unknown markets with uncertain demand. Partnerships may also give carriers indirect access to monopoly markets reserved for a local operator. When confronted with political obstacles, such as difficulty in obtaining necessary licenses and permits, a consortium of carriers can pool their clout to influence the decision-making process. Lastly, affiliations provide a defense against the entry of other foreign carriers into domestic markets.

For the countries that are the recipients of foreign investment, the trend of supranational carriers and ventures leads to pressure on the traditional controls of telecommunication networks. A primary means that governments have long used is to regulate company structures. Governments can either devolve or consolidate traditional postal and telecommunication monopolies. Devolution entails the dismantling of PTT monoliths into several units. Further, the dismantling can entail the full structural separation of various entities into distinct legal, operational, and functional units. The major example of devolution was the divestiture of AT&T in the United States. Consolidation is the opposite strategy. To capture economies of scale and scope, existing operators continue as a single, large firm. Recent examples are Denmark, Italy, and Portugal. In Latin America, where decentralized models existed more than in any other region of the world other than North America, devolution occurred in Argentina; consolidation was implemented in Mexico, Puerto Rico, and Uruguay.

Until the late 1980s, most developed countries combined postal and telecommunication functions under the same roof (PTTs) and typically owned, operated, and controlled PTTs through state agencies such as Ministries of Post and Communications. PTTs held a monopoly over all postal and telecommunication services and were closely allied with domestic manufacturers of telecommunication equipment. Although direct government civil service status maximized control, its bureaucratized structure reduced efficiency. As a remedy for inefficiency, governments experimented with corporatization.

Corporatization is the transformation of the PTT into a semiautonomous government entity. It may still be state-owned, but it controls its own managerial and administrative functions. Although the monopoly is left intact, the separation of the PTT from government sets in motion processes that make further changes more likely. The loosening of direct administrative controls usually is accompanied by the creation or the strengthening of a government regulatory mechanism.

Privatization, which is the full or partial transfer of state-owned company operations from the public to the private sector, also presents a challenge to traditional control of domestic networks, especially if the domestic monopoly is preserved. Although privatization may encourage efficiencies in operation, quality of service may fall if an unrestrained monopolist seeks cost reductions without regard for its captive customers. Furthermore, private monopolies generate their own constituencies that seek to preserve monopoly status.

In developed countries, privatization and corporatization aim to overcome restrictions on the borrowing or investment requirements of state operations and to provide a means to shake up bureaucratized enterprises. In developing countries, privatization derives from a need to raise capital to reduce the heavy national debt burden and to attract foreign capital and expertise to telecommunication. Even with a complete transfer of operations to the private sector, governments often reserve the right to nationalize vital infrastructure to safeguard national sovereignty. Historic examples include the United Kingdom, Sweden, Chile, and Spain. Additionally, governments may place restrictions on the permissible level of foreign ownership of the telecommunication infrastructure, as in the United States

Clearly, privatization provides an opening for supranational carriers and alliances to enter formerly closed markets, and, in theory, governments still have a wide assortment of regulatory tools to achieve national goals.

Once governments make the decision to liberalize markets and to permit multiple providers, they can organize domestic telecom markets to allow various amounts and types of competition. The licensing of operators can be used both to limit the number of competitors and services and to impose obligations on providers. Licenses for spectrum access can be allocated according to specific use or assigned according to specific users. Once multiple providers are permitted in domestic markets, governments can restrict the extent of collaboration among competitors with limits on vertical and horizontal integration and separation of territories of operation. Whereas price and profit regulation are tools to replicate competition, structural antimonopoly rules (antitrust) can be invoked to help achieve conditions of a competitive market or to prevent or correct for the development of market imperfections.

There are numerous ways to control the participation of foreign PTOs. They can be regulated as common carriers and required to meet minimum quality of service and investment criteria specified by the regulatory entity. Particularly important in developing countries with low teledensities is the mandate to strive for universal connectivity. Traditionally, in developed countries, universal service was financed from the profits of national monopolists. Monopolies were able to favor certain customers, namely residential and rural, by cross-subsidizing them. Transfers can occur between customers within a carrier, between carriers, and from the government to carriers. In the first case, carriers may institute higher subscription charges for business than residential lines; price business-oriented services, such as leased lines, or special services, such as touchtone service, above cost; or average access charges and rates. In the second instance, access charges of carriers may function as contributory subsidies.

As noted earlier, however, this model of cross-subsidization does not describe completely the situation in Latin American and Caribbean countries. In theory, the presence of national state-owned telecom monopolies should have meant they could accomplish redistribution in favor of universal access. Equally typical, however, was the use of telephone companies' profits to subsidize other nontelecommunication government activities.

The contemporary situation in the region is complicated by the fact that, as a result of privatization, private monopolies, sometimes foreign-owned, have, in many countries, replaced the old state monopolies. In the first privatizations, the new private owners were guaranteed periods of monopoly on all basic voice services and preferences in the provision of other services. Governments argued that, despite the international trend away from monopoly, this policy was necessary to provide sufficient incentive in the form of monopoly rents to promote high levels of investment and greatly expanded network coverage. Also, the policy contributed to a high price realized by the state for the privatizations.

A central problem amply documented by contributors to this volume is that adequate, consistent regulatory controls of private monopolies have yet to be instituted. Moreover, as part of the initial sale agreements, purchasers of telephone companies demanded policy changes that undercut many of the supposed benefits to the public of sector reorganization.

For example, in Caribbean countries, purchasers demanded that governments remove rate of return caps and not impose any conditions on equipment compatibility, technology transfer, or obligation to serve. In Argentina, the government increased tariffs prior to the sale of ENTel to increase the basic rates from which future increases would be calculated. Also in Argentina, entrenched suppliers were able to secure continuance of existing contracts in order not to lose market share. In Venezuela, the government and the state telecom company, CANTV, renegotiated the company's contract prior to the privatization to ensure CANTV's monopoly for the first 9 years after its sale and its continued contribution to the National Treasury; this policy was supported by the major political parties in Venezuela.

Although fundamental change is occurring in the region, it is at different rates and in different parts of each country's telecom system. The countries covered in this volume are organized according to the stage of evolution of their public networks.

- Cost-sharing networks, whose growth is based on the sharing of costs and increasing the value of interconnectivity. Countries such as Cuba, Nicaragua, Guatemala, and Ecuador are presently in this stage.
- Redistributory stage networks, which grow through politically directed expansion and through transfers from some users to others. In this stage, although at various levels of development and moving toward the third stage, are Argentina, Mexico, Puerto Rico, and Uruguay.
- Pluralistic stage networks, which are not necessarily more advanced technologically than redistributory stage networks, but they have progressed institutionally. They are not a uniform system but a federation of subnetworks. The United States and Japan are in this stage. Chile is moving toward it. Other Latin American countries are affected by pluralism in other countries whose companies invest in Latin America.

The analysis of cost-sharing stage countries begins with the Caribbean. The narrative of Caribbean telecommunication development is divided among four sets of authors. The dramatic changes in Cuban telecommunication are recounted by John Spicer Nichols and Alicia M. Torres. Hopeton S. Dunn and Winston S. Gooden review the struggles to develop Jamaican telecommunication capacities. Ramón

Morales Cortés focuses on the evolution of Puerto Rican telecommunication systems. Felipe M. Noguera, secretary-general of the Caribbean Association of National Telecommunication Organizations (CANTO), covers the rest of the countries in the Caribbean. A notable commonality in the region is the impact that strong demand for international service has had on telecom sector development and change. The need for technically advanced networks to support business applications is complemented by demand from the large expatriate Caribbean populations who now live in the United States and want to maintain contacts with home.

Noguera connects the story of telecommunication in the Caribbean to the long history of colonization and postcolonial dependence in the region. Private monopolies invested in the development of services to sustain export production for the metropole and left local systems underdeveloped; all equipment was imported. After independence in the 1960s, governments nationalized domestic telecommunication systems and invested heavily in state-of-the-art systems. By the 1980s, 75 percent of networks in the area were digital, but state-owned telcos had incurred large debts to achieve these results.

Carriage of international traffic was assigned to Cable & Wireless (C&W), the U.K.-based operator. C&W was the telecom arm of the British empire, which made it the operator of choice in many Caribbean countries. Later, it became a private and far-flung carrier with innovative global strategies. Noguera notes that C&W's profitability was greatly enhanced because of the improvements that governments had made in domestic systems. When, in the late 1980s, governments decided to privatize the debt-laden state telcos, C&W parlayed its familiarity with domestic systems into a favored position to become the new PTO. Although the shedding of debt was an important criterion for the selection of private investors, access to state-of-the-art technology, as well as the pressure from international institutions to liberalize local economies, propelled privatization of state-owned telcos. Notably, Belize has been the exception to the trend toward C&W management; it bought out C&W and brought in British Telecom (BT), replaced by MCI as part of its partnership with BT, as minority partner and kept a majority stake for the state.

Noguera identifies several unique features of telecommunication systems in the Caribbean. The small size of domestic markets for basic services and equipment is counterbalanced by governments' strong emphasis on the development of telecommunication networks and services for the tourist and international business services sectors. Despite uneven access to basic services, the high rates of digitalization in the national networks are evidence of the specialized demand for the latest technologies. Moreover, the absence of an indigenous manufacturing capacity has left Caribbean countries without alternatives to foreign suppliers. Noguera advocates a regional approach to telecom management and development, particularly in the areas of equipment manufacturing and technical training.

The unique political relationship that Cuba has with the United States has been a defining factor in the trajectory of Cuban telecommunication. The U.S.-led political and economic blockade of Cuba forced a form of self-reliance in Cuban telecommunication development. Notable was Cuba's limited access to international calling, despite its participation in Intersputnik and Intelsat.

The collapse of the Soviet Union, Cuba's most important ally, has forced a reconsideration of the fundamentals of development in Cuba. The Cuban Revolution in 1959 replaced the dominance of U.S. investment in all parts of the Cuban economy with the state as the central economic and planning unit. State control of all communication media was an important part of the socialist project, and nationalization of the country's communication system was one of the new regime's main accomplishments, according to Spicer Nichols and Torres. Initially, direct political management paid off with the extension of affordable basic telegraph and telephone service to all parts of the country. Although most equipment was imported from Communist bloc countries, Cuba also developed some equipment manufacturing capacity.

Limited investment funds throughout the 1980s resulted in a badly deteriorating system by the early 1990s. A major fire and a lack of electricity compounded the financial problems, causing hard-won gains toward universal service to be in jeopardy. In an unprecedented move, the Cuban government responded with a series of measures to attract new, private investment. In 1992, the government approved a joint venture with a group of Mexican investors to build a bypass cellular network for use by foreign businesses, diplomatic missions, international organizations, foreign news agencies, and government offices in Havana. This was followed by a 1994 billion-dollar joint venture agreement between the Cuban phone company, EMTELCUBA, and a Mexican holding company, Grupo Domos, to install a million new lines by the year 2000; Grupo Domos has brought in Stet International of Italy as a technical partner. The agreement guarantees EMTELCUBA's monopoly of local and long distance service for fifty-five years.

In the area of international calling, pent-up demand for international service between Cuba and the United States is forcing a gradual improvement in the antiquated and highly limited system in Cuba. Bypass services based in Canada, U.S.-based companies that are taking advantage of a slight thaw in U.S.-Cuban relations in the telecom sector, and a joint venture between the Cuban government and ItalCable, part of the semigovernmental Stet group, all are reconfiguring the Cuban international telecom sector.

Jamaica has not had an explicit policy in favor of extension of universal service, and according to Dunn and Gooden, the result is a system skewed in favor of urban households and business users. Urban corporate centers enjoy access to advanced telecom networks and services while poor, rural areas remain unserved. Moreover, the situation in the near future is unlikely to change, argue Dunn and Gooden. Government policy requires both cross-subsidization to expand the local network and a guaranteed rate of return of 17.5 to 20 percent for the monopoly provider, Telecommunications of Jamaica (TOJ), a 79 percent-owned subsidiary of C&W. Sustained government regulation of the monopoly, however, has been lacking. The situation is unstable, the authors conclude, because influential sectors of public opinion and potential competitors are set to challenge TOJ's position.

Guatemala and Nicaragua represent two approaches to the same problem: a heavily indebted state, an inadequate basic telecom infrastructure, and large populations of rural poor. In Guatemala, liberalization at the margins best describes the current situation, according to Sheryl Russell. Despite the state's recent fiscal crisis, the state-owned monopoly, Guatel, has ambitious plans to continue technical upgrades, extend service to rural areas, and expand existing services. Russell anticipates private-sector investment in private networks, value-added services, and rural telephony.

Alejandra Herrera reports that Nicaragua is pursuing privatization of the state-owned telco but has yet to define many of the basic conditions for private, and most likely foreign, PTO management. Notably, the areas reserved for monopoly and those open to competition are still unspecified. Also, the means to regulate the new environment and to extend minimal service to all parts of the country have not been clarified. Moreover, debate of telecom reform has become caught up in the more general debate in the country about constitutional reform, of which privatization of the state-owned telco is a part. Herrera concludes that serious discussion of the parameters of reform is necessary to clarify the goals and intentions of the proposed changes.

In Ecuador and Peru, separation of the operation and regulation functions of state-owned PTOs preceded partial privatization. In their chapter on Peru, Percy Cornejo and Juan Ernesto Barreda Delgado recount the gradual move toward privatization of public telecommunication that is reshaping the country's telecom sector. Since 1969, the government has operated the national telecommunication monopoly, and subscribers have financed the system with the purchase of company shares. Technical upgrades have been slow in an admittedly limited system. In the 1980s, the PTO introduced new services, such as mobile telephony and data transmission.

Since 1990, as part of a philosophical commitment to reduce the participation of the state in the economy, the government of Alberto Fujimori has led the drive to induce more private investment. In 1993, the government began this process with the creation of a separate regulatory agency to report directly to the president. It followed this with the sale of a 35 percent stake in the national PTO, based in Lima, the capital, to a consortium led by Telefónica Internacional de España. The private operators have a twenty-year concession. Since the transfer, line installation is up and installation charges are down, although tariffs have increased. At the same time, the government is levying a tax on telecom service providers to be used for the expansion of rural service. Cornejo and Barreda Delgado are optimistic that telecom sector reform is sufficient to lead the country's general economic revitalization.

Michael Chong Pineda and Ivan Espinoza cover Ecuador, in which partial privatization is under way. The regionalism of telecommunication in Ecuador can be attributed to the distinctive geographic (and consequently, political and economic) zones that characterize the country. Telephone service is unevenly distributed, particularly between urban and rural areas. Although local rates have been kept low through subsidies from international service, telephone penetration via the public network also is low, and official estimates of unmet demand are high. This situation accounts for the popularity of private networks and mobile cellular telephony. Technical upgrades in the public network, however, have digitized two-thirds of the switching system and 90 percent of the transmission system. Services competition is slowly being introduced in domestic long distance, cellular, public coin-

operated telephones, and satellite transmission for data and video. The local public network is in a state of transition with partial privatization under way as a
means to infuse capital into the system. Pineda and Espinoza note that serious
political opposition in the National Congress to privatization, along with disputes
between the regulatory agency and other state agencies, has slowed reform, but
they foresee sufficient momentum to support ongoing change.

In Bolivia and Colombia, telecom sector reform is occurring at different rates
within the systems because of their diffuse organizational structures, report Edgar
Saravia and Margot Lise Hooley. In Bolivia, until 1995, Saravia notes, telecommunication operations were split between local operating companies run by
municipal governments and ENTel Bolivia, the centralized state company in
charge of long distance and international services, telex, telegraph, and data and
broadcast transmission. To finance operations, municipalities forced subscribers to
become investors in the local telcos, but subscribers did not have representation
on the boards of the companies nor could they transfer their investment from one
company to another if they relocated outside the original service area. In an
attempt to make the companies more responsive to user needs, the national government compelled the companies to restructure as cooperatives in 1985. Also,
competition from mobile cellular telephone operators has been in effect since
1990, and there are multiple carriers for international calling.

Saravia is not optimistic that the restructuring will decrease the power of the
municipalities to direct telco operations because board members elected since the
reorganization still have strong ties to the government and political parties. He also
projects that the local loop will remain the bottleneck in the system, causing further
imbalance in local and long-distance network modernization and expansion.

As an alternative to privatization of ENTel Bolivia, the national government
has pursued company reorganization and "capitalization" to remake part of the
public network. The government began the reform process in the mid-1980s when
it required cost-based accounting, streamlined procedures, and raised quality-of-
service goals. In 1995, the government created a new regulatory agency to supervise the telecom sector and made it legal for ENTel and the cooperatives to merge,
buy, or transfer shares among themselves. In 1994, the government instituted a
policy of capitalization, which split interest in the company between a new
investor and local pension funds. The government required an investor to set aside
a predetermined amount of capital to be invested in the network.

In 1995, Stet International won the right to invest $610 million in ENTel in
exchange for a six-year monopoly of long distance and international services and
a forty-year nonexclusive concession in mobile cellular, rural and local telephony,
satellite, data transmission, telex, telegraph, and public telephones. The company
must meet expansion and quality targets to maintain its concession. Saravia argues
that this approach is a creative solution for governments faced with political opposition to outright privatization and a shortage of cash to invest in public networks.

Colombia also has a system divided between the state-owned company, Telecom
Colombia, which provides national and international long-distance telephone service, telex and telegraph service, and local telephone service to rural areas, and the
regional and municipal telephone companies that provide local telephone service.

Hooley states that liberalization at the national level began in 1989 when the Congress passed a law to separate regulatory and operating functions and to allow concessions to private companies to provide telecommunication services. This act was followed by a decree-law that called for a threefold increase in telephone density by the year 2000, a regionalization of municipal telephone company operations, and an increase in the number of services offered, as well as areas served. As a result, competition in value-added and data services and mobile cellular telephony exists; the long-distance market is scheduled to open to competition in 1997. The former Gaviria administration proposed the privatization of Telecom Colombia but was opposed by the telephone workers' union, one of the most powerful in the country. Congress approved the use of joint ventures as an alternative to privatization. In anticipation of competition, Telecom Colombia is reducing its costs, planning to enter new lines of business and expand its geographic coverage, and building a fiber-optic backbone. At the local level, the popularity of cellular telephony, despite its high prices for subscribers, is challenging the monopoly of municipal operators. Hooley notes that there is a considerable demand for all types of telecommunication services that the new operators are only beginning to tap.

Oversight of telephone company operations remains a test for the government. In 1991, the Colombian government created a Telecommunication Regulatory Commission to regulate and promote competition, tariffs, and concessions for national and international telephony. Previously, there was no national system of price regulation; each company set its own rates. The government has tried to rectify this with decrees to standardize rates. The issue of interconnection charges has also been a matter of dispute between Telecom Colombia and the municipal companies. The government, however, may have a credibility problem when it tries to play the role of enforcer. It has been in conflict with mobile cellular operators regarding a tax that the government levied to fund the development of rural telecommunication services; revenues, however, were diverted to the national treasury.

In the chapter on Venezuela, Natan Zaidman argues that political consensus to reform the public sector, including telecommunications, permitted the 1991 privatization of CANTV, the formerly state-owned telecommunication monopoly. An inadequate and inefficient public network had led many users, especially the petroleum companies at the center of Venezuela's export economy, to bypass the public system. Residential users also faced eight-year delays to receive a connection for basic service. The inability of CANTV to satisfy demand made the company an easy target when the government committed itself to restructuring state-owned companies.

Privatization introduced a management consortium that held 40 percent of CANTV's shares. The new owners are obligated to maintain this stake until 1997. As part of the reorganization, the government granted CANTV a thirty-five-year concession with the possibility of competition at all service levels after nine years. In exchange, the company pays 5.5 percent of total revenue to the government. Mobile cellular telephony and value-added service, among others, are open to competition in which CANTV can participate. CANTV is obligated to meet quality standards that are set and regulated by CONATEL, the national regulatory

body. Technical upgrades have already been completed, including a digital backbone that connects all major cities.

Despite the initial support from the political and business sectors in Venezuela
for telecom reform, Zaidman notes a public backlash against foreign participation
in the domestic economy. Riots and an attempted coup indicate the extent of the
discontent with restructuring of the public sector. This political unrest has affected
economic growth along with CANTV's stock price. Disagreements with the regulatory authority have also restrained CANTV's progress. As a result, cellular service provided by private companies other than CANTV has become a popular
alternative to the wired public network. Zaidman is only cautiously optimistic that
CANTV's situation will improve in the near future.

The countries in the second and redistributory stage have gone well beyond the
early developmental stages and have begun to expand their networks through a
redistributory process, though most operations are still closely controlled by a
monopoly carrier.

Alejandra Herrera analyzes Argentina, which since the introduction of the telegraph has had one of the more advanced telecommunication networks in Latin
America. Prior to the 1940s, telephone networks were built with U.S. and British
investment capital. From the 1940s until 1990, the state centralized 90 percent of
domestic and international telecom services in a state owned enterprise, Empresa
Nacional de Telecomunicaciones (ENTel); the remaining 10 percent was provided
by an L. M. Ericsson affiliate. Subsidiaries of international telecom equipment
companies manufactured locally. Beginning in the late 1970s, military governments began to open the domestic equipment markets to international bidding, but
this process ended with the transition to democracy in 1983. The new Radical
government proposed partial privatization of ENTel in 1987, but the opposition
Peronist party defeated the plan in the National Congress. Eventually, ENTel's
inability to meet subscriber demand for lines and services, to maintain network
integrity, and to sustain coherent investment and technical plans, combined with
the indebtedness of the state, led to its full privatization in 1990.

The government of Peronist President Carlos Menem divided the national
monopoly into two regional monopolies (north and south) with Buenos Aires, the
political and financial hub of the country, as the point of intersection. Two international consortia composed of international banks, domestic investment companies, and foreign PTOs bought 60 percent of ENTel, as part of a debt equity swap.
Each consortium was guaranteed a monopoly on basic local, long-distance, and
international services (voice, data, and video) in its respective territory for a minimum of seven years, with the possibility of a three-year extension. Also, the two
companies are partners to provide "services open to competition"—mobile cellular telephony, mobile maritime, telex, and domestic data transmission. Competitors can provide urban telephony if the duopolists fail to provide requested services within six months; the government requires interconnection on terms
negotiated by the duopolists and their potential competitors. After the period of
exclusivity, the duopolists are free to provide services outside their regions. As
part of the sale, the government did not mandate minimum investment require-

ments but did specify minimum rates of expansion and service requirements that must be met to keep the monopolies.

Herrera concludes that the postprivatization period in Argentina is inherently unstable because of the institutional weaknesses of the national telecom regulatory agency; the two regional monopolies are virtually unregulated. The agency has been excluded from all major disputes among companies and between the companies and the government since privatization. The companies have used the regulatory vacuum to their advantage to consolidate their position in the major service areas. Although the new owners have exceeded their service goals so far, they also have increased and kept prices for many services (e.g., international and data) at very high levels. Users of these services, potential competitors, and nonfavored equipment suppliers already have challenged the monopoly. Herrera proposes that the development of a trading bloc in the Southern Cone and the privatization of the Brazilian telecom company could change firms' strategies in Argentina and lead to further industry consolidation.

Graciela Pérez Montero Gotusso relates that lack of public support rebuffed the privatization of the state-owned PTO in Uruguay. Recent governments had proposed privatization of the company as part of a plan to increase export production and to turn Montevideo, the capital, into the financial hub of the Southern Cone. With the defeat of the privatization package, the state monopoly, ANTel, is in charge of the reformation of the public network. During the 1980s, ANTel began an ambitious investment program, but it has yet to catch up with demand. In frustration with ANTel's poor service, business users have resorted to private networks and other means of communication, such as courier services, to bypass the public network. In name, there is a separate planning body, but it has done little in policy development and oversight of ANTel operations. Competition is permitted in some sectors, including value-added services, electronic mail, and mobile cellular telephony. Packet-switched data transmission remains an ANTel monopoly. Despite the monopoly, Montero Gotusso finds a new customer orientation in the company's approach to operations, and she anticipates that the high profitability of many services will provide sufficient investment funds for the future.

Mexico's integration into regional and global markets has been both cause and effect of liberalization in the country's telecommunication sector, argues Kathleen Griffith. Telecom reform was preceded by Mexico's adherence to the General Agreement on Tariffs and Trade (GATT) and reinforced by Mexico's commitment to the North American Free Trade Agreement (NAFTA) with the United States and Canada. Business-sector demand for specialized services, notably along the border with the United States, continues to drive change.

Prior to the opening of the Mexican economy in the late 1980s, Teléfonos de México (Telmex), the partially state-owned national monopoly, had made important gains in the extension of service and the introduction of modern transmission technologies, specifically microwave and satellite communication. The domestic credit crisis that began in the early 1980s, however, put a brake on public-sector borrowing, and Telmex was unable to invest to meet users' needs, particularly those of the business sector.

As part of its plan to modernize the Mexican economy with foreign investment and export promotion, the government of President Carlos Salinas de Gortari began a rapid restructuring of the telecom sector. Restrictions of the importation of telecom equipment were reduced or eliminated, and new international carriers were authorized. Private networks, mobile cellular telephony and very small aperture terminals (VSATs) were permitted as alternatives to the public network. In preparation for Telmex's privatization, the government restructured the regulatory agency, the Secretary of Communications and Transportation (SCT), and authorized the SCT to license competitors to Telmex. Public fax, data, satellite, and electronic mail services were spun off into a separate company. In 1990, a consortium of Grupo Carso, Southwestern Bell (now SBC Communications), and France Telecom bought controlling interest of Telmex. Liberalization of the domestic long-distance market is set for 1997.

The new ownership has significantly increased investment and profitability. Wait times for new lines has decreased from three years to three months, and the number of public pay telephones has tripled. The company is expanding into new services, such as cable television. Even though Telmex loses its monopoly of long distance in 1997, it retains its virtual monopoly of the local network through 2026. Although the financial crisis of 1994 was a severe blow to Telmex's stock price, Griffith observes that the company may be able to use the decline to its advantage to convince government officials to slow the introduction of competition. Moreover, Telmex may also be able to benefit from internal divisions in the government regarding the goals of reform. Despite these concerns, Griffith predicts that reforms in Mexico are sufficiently substantial to position the country as the gateway to Latin America for the Global Information Infrastructure (GII).

In Puerto Rico, close political and economic ties with the United States since the turn of the century have promoted the construction of one of the most extensive and technologically advanced telecommunication systems in Latin America and the Caribbean. A mix of government and private operators built and operated both telegraph and telephone services; International Telephone and Telegraph (ITT) was the main force behind the development of the island's telephone system, the Puerto Rico Telephone Company (PRTC). On several occasions, national disasters destroyed the basic telecom infrastructure, and each time, it was rebuilt. In the 1940s, the government committed to a policy of universal service and became the provider of last resort.

Rapid economic expansion and a demand for business services have driven much of the network's growth. In the 1960s and 1970s, economic activity fueled a demand for phone service, but ITT did not reinvest sufficiently to meet demand. In response, the government bought out ITT and placed the PRTC under a newly created government Telephone Authority. The company invested heavily in technology and increased installed lines by 71 percent in six years. In the 1980s, continued demand from U.S. corporations and international banks caused the PRTC to invest in digitalization and fiber optics to provide advanced business services.

Notably, Puerto Rico is one of the few examples of public opinion defeating the proposed privatization of the national telecommunication network; Uruguay is another example. To finance future investment, in 1990, the government proposed the sale of the long-distance network and local networks not under the PRTC's control, as well the mobile cellular service, but there was little public support. In 1992, the government did reorganize the telecom sector with the sale of the long-distance network to Telefónica Internacional de España and the consolidation of all local service into the PRTC. Ramón Morales Cortés predicts that the advanced state of the island's network, including the recent introduction of business and residential ISDN (Integrated Services Digital Network), will support future rapid growth and expansion to all users.

Despite political uncertainties and opposition from many quarters, liberalization ultimately will take hold in Brazil and replace the state ownership and import substitution policies of the past with foreign, private investment and competition, predict Antonio José J. Botelho, José Roberto Ferro, Lee McKnight, and Antonio C. Manfredini Oliveira. More than in any other country in Latin America, Brazil in the postwar period had attempted to develop an integrated telecommunication sector based on centralized operation of domestic networks, indigenous research and development, and a local equipment manufacturing industry. High taxes on local and long-distance calls and high up-front subscriber line charges financed considerable network expansion and modernization in the late 1960s and 1970s. Economic crises in the late 1970s and 1980s, however, wiped out investment funds and eroded the successes of previous years. The chapter's authors claim that a significant decline in network quality and operations was the inevitable result, which provided the opening for reform in the 1990s.

Former President Fernando Collor introduced the possibility of liberalization of Brazilian telecom markets in 1991 as part of his plan to restructure completely the domestic economy. The first hurdle was the legal telecom monopoly that the state has held since 1962. Removing the state as monopoly operator required rewriting both the national constitution and telecommunication code, and political opposition to privatization managed to stall such efforts. Collor's resignation in 1992 further slowed the reform process, although it has picked up momentum again under current President Cardoso.

The regional operating companies and Embratel, the national long-distance and international operating company, have been preparing for eventual competition, if not privatization. They are seeking to provide new services, such as private lines, data communications, mobile telephony, and maintenance functions previously supplied by the national telco, and to incorporate elements of the intelligent network into existing systems. As in other countries throughout Latin America, cellular telephony has become an important alternative to the public network.

Botelho and his fellow authors foresee a difficult transition period for the public telcos in Brazil. They argue that although pricing of service is completely distorted in the current system, it is politically untenable to raise tariffs sufficiently to cover operating costs and to provide the necessary capital for future investment. Lack of capital remains the central weakness of the current arrangement in Brazil. The authors anticipate that the benefits of competition in cellular telephony, satellite and cable television, Internet service, and equipment markets that have occurred because of reform eventually will lead the way to reorganization of all levels of the domestic public telecom system.

Moving toward the third stage, the pluralistic network, is Chile, which has been at the forefront of liberalization efforts in Latin America. Reform of the telecom sector in Chile has been under way since the late 1970s, according to José Ricardo Melo. As part of its commitment to free-market ideology, the military government of General Augusto Pinochet instituted a policy based on competition in the telecommunication sector. The policy was grounded in laws barring monopolies and periods of exclusivity. Foreign attachment to the network was approved in 1977, resale of private lines began in 1979, and the first services competition was in mobile cellular telephony and the local loop in 1981. The state holding company, CORFO, began to divest itself of telephone company operations as early as 1982.

Moreover, rivalry between the two main formerly state-owned telephone operating companies, Compañía de Teléfonos de Chile (CTC), the provider of the majority of local services, and ENTel Chile, the long-distance and international services company, has been intense. SUBTel, the national regulatory and policy agency, was charged with coordination of company activities. Despite their previously separate bases of operation, both CTC and ENTel have fought to become the leader in Chilean telecommunication. Privatization of CTC (1985–87) and ENTel (1986–89) has fueled the conflict. In the last years, CTC has expanded into mobile cellular telephony, information and business services, and long-distance signal transmission, and ENTel participates in commercial services and equipment sales, international consulting, data services, mobile cellular telephony, and satellite transmission.

Melo notes that regulation of private operators has fallen to the state antimonopoly commission and the courts rather than SUBTel, which concentrates on the resolution of technical matters. In several instances, the commission and the courts have been called on to settle disputes regarding interconnection and monopolistic practices, and a consequence has been de facto policy making in the sector. Although privatization has resulted in a tremendous increase in the quality, variety, and quantity of services, it has also exposed the problem of the institutional weakness of the regulatory regime. Power is being transferred from executive and administrative action to the judiciary. This transfer has consequences for the government's ability to promote social objectives in the sector, particularly in the extension of service to rural areas and cross-subsidies. Melo worries that there are many unresolved questions about the proper role of government and the means to achieve universal service and to structure competitive markets.

Conclusion

The contributions in this volume represent a unique attempt to survey both the historical origins of public telecommunication systems in Latin America and the Caribbean and the fundamental transformations that currently are remaking the region's telecommunication environment. Although each country has shaped the reform process to accommodate its own political, economic, and cultural circumstances, three themes emerge from the analyses: the sublimation of telecom sector reorganization to the powerful dynamic of economic reform programs, the lack of universal service, and the inadequacy of current regulatory mechanisms to police a competitive environment of private telecom operators.

First, throughout the region, economic reform provided the basic policy platform from which telecom sector reform was launched. This connection has contributed to the apparent irreversibility of telecom reform and the momentum driving continued change.

The specifics of economic crises in the 1980s varied, but the impact was the same. Governments ran out of external credit sources to finance state operations, including telecommunication. Although in some cases state telcos may actually have been sources of revenue for the national treasury, countries' general indebtedness led to the sell-off of state enterprises, and particularly those such as monopoly telecommunication operators that promised to bring a high price and to retire some of the outstanding national debt. In exchange, in some instances, governments received political credit for bringing in badly needed foreign investors and technical expertise. In other countries, governments were criticized by the political opposition for turning over a vital sector of the economy to foreign management. Regardless, the contributors to the volume are clear that the national debates of telecom reform had less to do with remaking the sector according to Information Age strategy and more to do with a lack of cash to fund government functions and the immediate demands of creditors and potential lenders.

Second, the descriptions of inadequate, outdated telecom facilities and low teledensities in each country demonstrate the pressing need for basic telephone service in the region. Unlike developed countries in which advanced services are being layered on existing infrastructures that make it possible to provide universal service, all the countries in the Latin American and Caribbean region have yet to bring their populations in easy reach of a dial tone for voice service. The lengthy waiting times and expensive connection fees made telephone service an impossible achievement for many.

This fact affected the dynamic of reform in the region. Not only did large users stand to benefit from liberalization, but the promise that privatization of state-owned telcos would make it possible to have access to a telephone exerted enormous pressure from below, that is, from residential and small business users. Even when it was difficult or impossible to achieve consensus for full privatization, there was agreement that at least some type of reform was necessary to alter an untenable situation.

A lack of basic telephone service via the public network also has had a significant impact on the speed of introduction and acceptance of "new technologies," which has important consequences for network evolution. Despite high prices and limited coverage, mobile cellular telephony has been enormously popular, and penetration rates have far exceeded initial projections. Several authors indicate that cellular service is often a replacement for, rather than an add-on to, the public network. Bypass is also a notable phenomenon, with satellite-based and private line services a viable alternative for heavy telecommunication users. Given the variety of choices and intensity of demand, the authors are uncertain about how these developments will be integrated into a full-service public network.

Finally, the lack of precedent in Latin American and Caribbean countries to regulate private telecommunication operations is a common concern of the volume's contributors. They note that governments have pledged to regulate private companies in a way that will expand and modernize the public network and eventually to extend service to all who want it, but to date, the authors have found little evidence that government officials have made the necessary political and financial commitments to create and to sustain credible regulatory agencies. In some cases, regulatory agencies were supposed to have been established prior to the sale of state companies but either became entangled in domestic political disputes or, according to the cynical view, were purposefully not created and/or not funded in order to give the new owners a free hand. Several authors predict a bleak future of ever higher prices for the majority of subscribers, especially low-income residential users who have yet to be brought onto the public network, if regulatory agencies with real enforcement power are not established.

In short, the authors are only cautiously optimistic that this first round of change will fulfill all the promises of liberalization. They remain skeptical that the new monopoly providers will not abuse their positions, and they foresee the need for vigilant governments to ensure that the private operators of public networks meet investment, service, and quality targets. The dynamic of change, however, appears to be unstoppable, and the volume's contributors remain hopeful that continued change eventually will produce a pluralistic network environment, a network of networks, in which universal connectivity becomes reality.

The information contained in this volume and the series on regional telecommunications as a whole is the result of the cooperation and collaboration of twenty-three authors, each of whom contributed their research, knowledge, and expertise of particular countries. Invariably, it proved quite complex to get so many authors to completion.

Besides the contributing authors, many others were involved in the compilation of this volume. Thanks to Guillermo Guzmán-Barrón, who reviewed the original submissions, and Cynthia Baur and Lisa Domonkos, who coordinated the updates. I am also grateful for the assistance of Larry Meissner, who completed the developmental editing of the project, and John E. Kollar, who prepared the manuscript for publication.

Note

1. *Americas Telecommunication Indicators* (Geneva: International Telecommunications Union, May 1994), A-4.

Telecommunications in Latin America

1
The Caribbean

FELIPE M. NOGUERA

Revolutionary changes in information technologies have left few economic sectors untouched, and the much-touted global information village has brought the earth's inhabitants closer. Access to, and control of, information is replacing access to natural resources as a determinant of the socioeconomic position of nations. Although this holds great promise for eradicating poverty and underdevelopment, the dichotomy between rich and poor, the metropolitan and the peripheral, the developed and the underdeveloped, instead could be widened by these same technologies.

The Caribbean is a microcosm of this worldwide phenomenon. It consists mainly of tropical island nations, many quite small in both size and population, which were fought over and colonized by Europeans since they first reached them. The region's pre-Columbian peoples were long ago lost to genocide and disease or largely mixed with the newcomers, including—mostly as slaves or indentured workers—Africans, Chinese, East Indians, and Javanese. Spanish, French, English, and Dutch are official languages in various places. All this makes the Caribbean incredibly diverse in customs and ancestral homelands, as well as in the diffusion and overall level of economic development. About half of the region's population of just over 35 million (July 1994 estimate) live in its two poorest countries: Cuba, with 11.1 million people, and Haiti, with 6.5 million.

Although the Caribbean is not a populous or rich region, it is nonetheless a major telecom market. Indeed, parts of it have telecom infrastructures as advanced as any in the world. Proximity to North America and a heavily service-oriented economy, with particular emphasis on tourism, is the principal reason for this. At the same time, the poor in general, and those in rural areas in particular, often do not even have convenient access to pay phones, let alone their own lines. One of the major challenges for the region is balancing the business sector's demand for enhanced services with demand for basic services for ordinary citizens.

The activities of CANTO (the Caribbean Association of National Telecommunication Organizations) are extensively discussed because of the organization's importance to its members and, by extension, to telecom development in the region and because it offers lessons for smaller telcos and governments both directly and as a model of regional cooperation.[1]

Table 1.1. Indicators of Tele-Accessibility, 1991

Country	Population	GNP per Capita	Total No. Main Lines	Telephones per 100 Population	Telephones per Capita	Total No. PBIs	Total No. Public Phones
Antigua/Barbuda	70,000	2,788.0	10,870	15.5	3.90	91	108
Bahamas	254,685	11,767.0	65,009	25.5	5.52	316	573
Barbados	250,000	5,637.0	76,478	30.6	13.57	240	365
Belize	160,000	1,269.0	21,320	13.3	16.80	98	35
Bermuda	57,784	2,100.0	37,142	64.3	17.69	229	704
Curaçao	171,000		42,116	24.6		316	235
Dominican Republic	6,500,000	1,014.0	442,521	6.8	436.41	801	2,655
Grenada	90,000	1,128.0	13,634	15.1	12.09	43	139
Guadeloupe	330,000		119,445	36.2		1,765	622
Haiti	6,000,000	250.0	45,000	0.8	180.0	141	42
Jamaica	2,360,000	1,188.0	88,348	3.7	74.37	1,004	1,006
Puerto Rico	3,254,000	6,801.8	815,898	25.1	119.95	19,530	15,997
Suriname	400,000	2,328.0	36,714	9.2	15.77	731	175
Trinidad and Tobago	1,234,388	3,856.0	216,040	17.5	56.03	5,586	669
U.S. Virgin Islands	112,000		46,769	41.8		1,136	615
Total/Average	21,243.857		2,077,304	9.8		32,027	23,940
Bolivia	6,808,824	796.1	277,800	4.08	348.93		
Colombia	28,940,390	1,200.0	3,038,741	10.50	2,532.28		
Ecuador	9,930,599	1,049.0	696,135	7.01	663.62		
Peru	20,750,197	1,600.0	630,806	3.04	394.25		
Venezuela	18,292,683	2,481.0	2,100,000	11.48	846.43		

Sources: CANTO Secretariat (C.L.E.R.C.), Copyright FN 1990–1991; Aseta 1990, Ing. Ricardo Herrera Alliot.

As is often the case, the Caribbean as a region is not quite the same as its name-sake, the Caribbean Sea. Although most of the islands lie in a chain forming the sea's northern and eastern edge, three are in the North Atlantic (Bermuda, the Bahamas, Turk and Caicos Islands). The shores of Jamaica, the Cayman Islands, Aruba, and the Netherlands Antilles are washed on all sides by the Caribbean. The region covers 1,000 square kilometers. Table 1.1 provides data on the region.

Cuba is covered in a separate chapter, but Belize and three small nations on the northeast coast of South America are included here because, like many of the islands, they were colonies of countries other than Spain and thus have more in common with parts of the Caribbean than with the mainland. Additional material on Jamaica and Cable & Wireless are in Chapter 3.

1.1 Service Providers

Telecom services were introduced into the region not long after Bell's invention of the telephone had become commercially available in North America and Europe. Owned by private, government-regulated monopolies based in the Euro-pean metropole, international services were developed to support mercantile inter-ests. Local public services, offered under monopoly franchises by the colonial governments, were invariably less developed.

Although Haiti and the Dominican Republic ended colonial status with the anti-slavery revolution of Toussaint L'Ouverture in the 1790s, they did not formally declare independence until later, and by the mid–nineteenth century both had been reduced to an extremely dependent neocolonial status relative both to their former colonial patrons—France and Spain, respectively—and to the United States, their powerful neighbor to the north. The Dominican Republic integrated domestic and international services under Codetel, a subsidiary of U.S.-based General Tele-phone (GTE) in 1930. This succeeded an antiquated system. Codetel and govern-ment-owned Corporation Teleco d'Haiti operated as tele-mercantile monopolies. Evidence of this is Haiti's telephone penetration rate of 0.07 per 100 inhabitants some 200 years after nominal independence.

The 1960s was a decade of worldwide decolonialization, and the Caribbean was part of this as the most populous English-speaking Caribbean nations became independent. At this time, a U.S. company, Continental Telephone (Contel), bought the telcos providing domestic service in Barbados, Jamaica, and Trinidad and Tobago, and the provider of both domestic and international service in the Bahamas. Contel installed new electromechanical switching and transmission sys-tems. Cable & Wireless (C&W), then owned by the U.K. government, continued to provide service elsewhere. (Privatized in 1985, C&W owns communications companies in the Caribbean, United Kingdom, and Hong Kong.)

As part of the philosophy of nationalism, state ownership of the "commanding heights of the economy" was prevalent in what was then referrred to as the Third World. In the countries discussed here, the consequences were mild by compari-son to the more radical socialist policies pursued by Fidel Castro in Cuba. Still, popular pressure from black-power and trade union movements was primarily responsible for the nationalization of Contel's telephone companies. Contel was compensated and was quite happy to divest its holdings.

In the late 1960s, U.K.-based Cable & Wireless signed Heads of Agreements with the governments of Barbados, Jamaica, and Trinidad and Tobago to provide international service through subsidiaries (Barbados External Telecoms, Jamintel, and Textel), and in the mid-1980s the company acquired interests in the domestic Barbados, Jamaica, and Trinidad and Tobago systems. Governments of the Caribbean had already invested billions of tax dollars to make the systems state-of-the-art. C&W's further upgrading increased external capacity 60 percent, to 960 circuits, although the new circuits were not needed at the time.

1.1.1 Privatization in the 1980s

The ongoing inability of state-owned telcos to satisfy rapidly increasing demand for business telephone systems in the early 1980s led to allowing a variety of locally based suppliers to provide equipment directly to users for attachment to the public switched network. Trinidad and Tobago was the first to liberalize, establishing technical standards and specifications for interconnecting subscriber terminal equipment in 1984. By the early 1990s, Jamaica, Barbados, the Bahamas, and Belize had followed. Northern Telecom, Mitel, Ericsson, and Rolm have been the major sellers of Public Automated Broadcast Exchange (PABX) and key business switches.

Network privatizations took place in several countries. Already the provider of international service in most cases, Cable & Wireless had an intimate familiarity with the networks and policy makers. This made it easy for them to become the investor of choice in privatizations in the English-speaking Caribbean. It is difficult to analyze the terms of the deals Caribbean governments made, and continue to make, with C&W because they have never been made public (see Dunn 1995). Indeed, many negotiations took place clandestinely. Certainly "bad deals" were made in at least some instances.

Ironically, heavy investment by state-owned telcos in extending and improving their networks, which had become more than 75 percent digital during the 1980s, was an important factor leading to government divestment. The state-owned telcos had trouble servicing their debt, which led to pressure from international lenders—the International Monetary Fund and World Bank in particular—to privatize the systems as a way to reduce debt. This was specifically relevant in Grenada, Guyana, Jamaica, and Trinidad and Tobago—all former British possessions.

Debt, however, was not the only incentive: access to state-of-the-art technology was also an important criterion. For the Bahamas, Barbados, Belize, the Netherlands Antilles, and Puerto Rico it has been a major factor in the privatization debate. Another factor has been the need to conform to the trend toward trade liberalization and privatization (as per GATT and NAFTA discussions) as a prerequisite for obtaining foreign investment capital for other sectors of the economy.

Those investing in the region's telecommunications systems requested removal of statutory limits on returns on investment in Barbados, Grenada, Jamaica, and Trinidad and Tobago. At the time of privatization, governments by and large did not impose conditions on setting standards or technology transfer, and extending service into rural areas was not a requirement. In general, the former state monopoly has simply been replaced by a private one, which, since it has an important foreign element, has implications for the erosion of sovereignty. Belize seems to have been the only exception to this. However, rate hearings presided over by various Caribbean public utilities commissions remain a form of regulatory pressure.

For example, the failure of the government of Guyana to approve rates for Atlantic TeleNetwork, which owns Guyana Telephone and Telegraph (GT&T), has resulted in a vexing liquidity problem for the company. The company has been unable to charge for local cellular calls but is collecting activation and basic monthly fees. In mid-1995, hearings were under way regarding GT&T rates.

In 1985 the Belize government wholly owned the local telco, but Cable & Wireless (West Indies Ltd.) wholly owned the external system. Cable & Wireless retained 87 percent of revenue on international calls, compared to just 50 percent in Jamaica, 65 percent in Barbados, and 70 percent in Trinidad and Tobago. Extensive negotiations led to the government securing British Telecom (BT) as a minority investor. The government sold BT 24 percent of a new company, Belize Telecom, and sold 25 percent to employees, keeping 51 percent. The new firm then purchased C&W's external service and merged with the local service. Since the formation of the British Telecom-MCI alliance in 1994, MCI has taken over all BT holdings in the Americas, including the minority share of Belize Telecom Ltd. Table 1.2 shows the providers of telecom services in the major Caribbean nations.

1.2 CANTO

The Caribbean Association of National Telecommunication Organizations (CANTO) is the region's telecom trade association and lobby. Among other things, it acts as an information clearinghouse for Caribbean operating telcos and carriers. A major goal has been to help the region see itself as a whole, regardless of differences in size, language, and colonial experience. The great shared resource for this is information. By creating innovative means to share data on equipment, technology, suppliers, training, and finance, CANTO seeks to assist its members, which include most of the telecom service providers in the region.

CANTO was formed in 1985 by seven operating telcos whose executives felt the need to establish an independent forum through which regional telecom organizations could exchange information, set a Caribbean telecom agenda, and influence regional policy. The inaugural meeting took place in April in Port of Spain, Trinidad, and was keynoted by Richard Butler, former secretary-general of the ITU (International Telecommunication Union). He encouraged the CANTO initiative as being consistent with ITU objectives of fostering technical cooperation and information sharing among developing countries.

One factor leading the seven then state-owned telcos to establish CANTO was the discrepancy they saw between the high levels of investment they were making in domestic infrastructure and the capital expenditures for international calling

Table 1.2. Telecom Providers in the Caribbean and CANTO Members, 1995

Country	CANTO Member Since	Company	Private Ownership (%)	Company (based in)
Anguilla	1991	Cable & Wireless West Indies Ltd.	100	Cable & Wireless (U.K.)
Antigua and Barbuda	1985	APUA[1,2]	0	—
Antigua and Barbuda	1991	C&W[3]	100	Cable & Wireless (U.K.)
Aruba	1988	SETAR	0	—
The Bahamas	1985	Batelco	0	—
Barbados	1985	Bartelco	100	C&W (85%); others (15%)
British Virgin Islands	1989	Ministry of Telecommunications[2]	0	—
British Virgin Islands	1991	C&W[3]	100	Cable & Wireless (U.K.)
Cayman Islands	1991	Cable & Wireless West Indies Ltd.	100	Cable & Wireless (U.K.)
Cuba	1992	Ministeriod de Comunicaciones	0	—
Dominica	1991	Cable & Wireless West Indies Ltd.	100	Cable & Wireless (U.K.)
Dominican Republic	1987	Codetel	100	GTE (U.S.)
Grenada	1985	Grentel	80	Cable & Wireless (U.K.)
Guadalupe	1987	France Telecom	0	—
Haiti	1988	Teleco d'Haiti	0	—
Jamaica	1989	Telecom of Jamaica	79	Cable & Wireless (U.K.); workers own 11%
Martinique	1992	France Telecom	0	—
Montserrat	1991	Cable & Wireless West Indies Ltd.	100	Cable & Wireless (U.K.)

Country	Company	Year	%	Foreign partners
Netherland Antilles	Setel de Curacao	1986	0	—
Netherland Antilles	Telbo Bonaire	1994	0	—
Puerto Rico	PRTC	1986	0	—
Puerto Rico	Telefónica Larga Distancia (TLD)	—	100	Telefónica de España[4]
St. Kitts and Nevis	Skantel	1991	100	Cable & Wireless (U.K.)
St. Lucia	Cable & Wireless West Indies Ltd.	1991	100	Cable & Wireless (U.K.)
St Vincent and the Grenadines	Cable & Wireless West Indies Ltd.	1991	100	Cable & Wireless (U.K.)
Trinidad and Tobago	Telecom Services of Trinidad & Tobago	1985	49	Cable & Wireless (U.K.)
Turks and Caicos	Cable & Wireless West Indies Ltd.	1991	100	Cable & Wireless (U.K.)
Virgin Islands (U.S.)	U.S. Vitelco	1990	100	Atlantic TeleNet (U.S.)
Belize	Belize Telecom	1985	25	British Telecom, MCI; workers own 24%
Mexico	Telecomunicaciones de Mexico	1992	0	—
Mexico	Iusacell	1993	100	Bell Atlantic (U.S.) (42%); Grupo Iusacell (58%)
Guyana	GT&T	1985	0	GTE (U.S.) (30%); AT&T (U.S.) (5%);
Suriname	Telesur	1989	0	—
Venezuela	CANTV	1992	50	Telefónica de España (3%); trade unions (12%)

[1]Antigua and Barbuda Public Utilities Authority.
[2]Company provides only domestic service.
[3]Company provides only foreign service.
[4]TLD provides only long-distance service within Puerto Rico. Telefónica de España is 34% owned by the Spanish government and state agencies.

made by Cable & Wireless, which was making much higher returns. In most instances, C&W had only to react to increases in demand, rather than try to stimulate growth or generate traffic.

CANTO members had plans to—and did—spend U.S.$1 billion on telecom plant and equipment in the 1985–90 period. This action raised the question of how such an expenditure—virtually all of which would be for imported technology and equipment—would provide macroeconomic benefits to the region.

In the early 1990s, CANTO began to work with the newly formed CTU (Caribbean Telecommunications Union), the ITU, the CBU (Caribbean Broadcasting Union), and the region's communications ministries to formulate regulatory policy.

CANTO also has actively worked to improve human resource development in the region. It has attempted to anticipate training and workforce requirements so that, through cooperative efforts in mounting seminars, symposia, and courses, they can be met more efficiently and comprehensively within the region at reduced costs.

Based on the fact that the Caribbean is technologically a generation ahead of many developing countries, CANTO established a Human Resources Skills Bank in 1989 to market its telecom expertise to other countries. Uruguay, Venezuela, Botswana, Swaziland, Tanzania, and Zimbabwe indicated early interest in the consulting services but were constrained by finances in pursuing them.

The Bank was superseded in 1992 when CANTO established a Consultancy Assistance Bureau (CCAB) to provide technical assistance and advice to its members and other developing countries. Jamaica has provided technical expertise to Suriname in digital central office switching installation and maintenance. The Curacao and Jamaica members of CANTO were part of an ITU fact-finding and technical assistance mission to restore Haiti's telecom network in January 1995. Outside the region, the fifty-two-member Organization of African Unity (OAU) and fifteen-member South Pacific Forum (SPF) Secretariat have requested assistance from CANTO regarding such topics as bulk purchases of equipment and technology and negotiating international call accounting rates.

CANTO signed an agreement in 1994 formalizing the exchange of technical expertise, documentation, invitations to seminars and meetings, and the like, with AHCIET (the Asóciacion Hispana de Centros de Investigación y Estudios de Telecomunicacions), the largest regional telecom organization in Latin America.

Headquartered in Port of Spain, Trinidad, CANTO has a staff of seven (full-time equivalents) and an annual budget of about U.S.$1 million. Funding comes from members (about 65 percent) and internal initiatives such as consulting, publications, and conferences.

1.3 Level of Service

Most Caribbean countries compare favorably with other developing countries in terms of teledensity measured in lines per 100 population. However, this is a crude measure that says little about accessibility to phone service. Many Caribbean phone lines are at businesses, and specifically at tourist and financial services facilities, so density significantly overstates accessibility for most individual residents. Moreover, as Eric Williams, once prime minister of Trinidad and Tobago, observed, "What good is it for me to have a telephone on my desk when it doesn't work or the number I am calling does not work?"

Access to working telephones as a form of "social justice" was first popularized by Rajiv Gandhi when he was prime minister of India. He was, more generally, attempting to improve the infrastructure of rural areas, ending the pattern of technological advances being concentrated in urban centers. His goals included improving rural education, health, and other social services, as well as telecommunications. As befits a large, poor country, the initial telephone goal for India was modest: a public phone in each village. This has proven difficult to achieve even in small, poor countries: as of 1995, it had yet to be done in the Dominican Republic, Guyana, Haiti, Jamaica, Mexico, Suriname, Trinidad and Tobago, and Venezuela. Table 1.1 provides data on various measures of service.

By the early 1990s, over 75 percent of phone lines in the region were digital, with Dominica Telco (owned by Cable & Wireless) being heralded as the first fully digitalized network in the world, although with only some 5,000 lines that is a small-scale boast.

Whereas in the United States and United Kingdom, divestment by AT&T and British Telecom was geared toward promoting competition in the provision of long distance and value-added services, the Caribbean's largely unmet demand for basic telephone service—plain old telephone service, or POTS—requires that operating telcos be committed to providing public network use and access to subscribers at "reasonable" prices. Although rate structures should in general cover specific costs, I feel it is appropriate to subsidize provision of service to low-revenue-yielding rural areas. This does not, however, mitigate the fact that, unlike the United States and United Kingdom, competition in the provision of basic and value-added services—with the exception of equal access in Puerto Rico—is nonexistent in the Caribbean telecom sector. Callback services are the new exception to this. Although outlawed in many Caribbean territories, they continue to thrive because of the existing rate structures.

1.3.1 Wait Lists

Demand for telephone service in all these countries has been generally strong, with the result that there are wait lists for services. These vary in size. In Jamaica in 1990, unsatisfied demand for new lines almost equaled the installed base of 88,000 lines. In Trinidad and Tobago, the wait list was over 40 percent of the installed base of 216,000 lines and over 7 percent of the population in the same year.

1.3.2 Rates

Telephone charges vary widely among countries in the region, which reflects both government policy and the quality and extent of service available. All of these factors are continually changing. In general, in the early 1990s, English-speaking countries had relatively higher rates than elsewhere in the Caribbean, with Belize and Guyana being low-cost exceptions. Countries with higher rates also generally had better—more varied and reliable—service.

1.3.3 Satellite Services

There are few data on satellite services. Most satellite transmission systems facilitate broadcasting services. Many of the countries have at least one Intelsat link, sometimes as a nonsignatory user rather than as a member. The Bahamas and Cuba are members of Inmarsat, and Cuba is a member of Intersputnik.

In 1987 the Trinidad & Tobago Telephone Company, together with Intelsat, Textel, Trinidad and Tobago Television (TTT), and CANTO, initiated Project SHARE (Satellites for Health and Rural Education). This for the first time linked by satellite two developing nations—Tanzania and Trinidad and Tobago—facilitating a dynamic exchange among health care professionals on nutrition, public health, and sexually transmitted diseases.

The University of the West Indies, which has campuses in Mona, Jamaica; Bridgetown, Barbados; and St. Augustine, Trinidad, utilizes the UWI Distance Teaching Experiment (UWIDITE) satellite system to reach St. Lucia, Grenada, Dominica, and other noncampus sites.

1.4 Telecom Equipment

Subject to meeting technical specifications, subscribers can obtain equipment from sources other than the operating telco. There are a number of companies offering equipment as retailers and distributors. There are no import-substitution policies in the region for telecom products; no government policies encourage local technology development. There were discussions in the early 1990s about developing a science park in cooperation with the University of the West Indies, but these have yet to yield concrete results. The talks' focus has been on assembling telephone and cellular equipment in the region. Where to locate the park has been one of the stumbling blocks. In 1990 Northern Telecom indicated it would apply its volume discount rebate to establish a Distance Learning Centre, but CANTO members could not agree on where it would be headquartered.

Northern Telecom (NT), based in Canada, is the dominant supplier of central office equipment to the Caribbean region, with over half the installed base in 1994. This is larger than its world-wide share, but consistent with its generally strong position globally. L. M. Ericsson, a Swedish company, is a distant second, with AT&T and NEC trailing in the distance. Other product lines, including PABX and cellular systems, have a larger number of players, although again Northern Telecom is dominant, with 40 percent of the PABX and subscriber terminal equipment base in 1994. Mitel, a Canadian-based supplier of PABX and key systems, is a distant second. Northern Telecom is particularly strong in cellular switching equipment. It is also supplying the region's first major high-capacity synchronous digital hierarchy (SDH) fiber-optic network. Announced in January

1995, it will serve over 500 business customers of a Cable & Wireless subsidiary in the Cayman Islands.

In earlier technological eras, ITT—once a major factor in the hemisphere's telecommunications—was instrumental in introducing step-by-step and crossbar analog switches. NEC analog switches were sold to the Bahamas, Barbados, Jamaica, and Trinidad in the late 1970s and early 1980s, but the Japanese company provided poor maintenance support, exacerbated by language problems. The appearance of digital switches led to the displacement of NEC equipment everywhere except Jamaica.

1.4.1 Local Producers

In the mid-1980s two government-owned telcos—the Trinidad and Tobago Telephone Company Ltd. (T&T) and Telesur, in Suriname, became the only two equipment manufacturers in the region.

T&T's then director of research and development, Dr. Stephan Gift, developed a device, dubbed the subscriber pair identifier, to identify local faults on the main distribution frame. It was subsequently patented. A Canadian distributor has made it available to the small, regional telco operating companies in that country, and it has been sold to other Caribbean telcos. Influenced by Cable & Wireless, which became a 49 percent owner in 1991, T&T has since eliminated research and development. The stated rationale is that it is too costly for a small country to undertake effectively.

In Suriname, which has had a relatively undeveloped telephone system, Telesur came to equipment production as a result of the financial constraints on expanding and upgrading the system. The telco's training center began to make minor adaptations to equipment, which led to producing a wireless, solar-powered public phone to provide service in rural areas. Telesur has also manufactured a PABX handling two external trunk lines and sixteen internal extensions. It has been used throughout Suriname, and CANTO has been attempting to market it elsewhere in the Caribbean. The center's fundamental objective is to reduce dependence on foreign technology and expertise and to foster local capacity, while keeping abreast of new technologies available internationally.

Every new recruit to Telesur works in the research and training center for nine months prior to being deployed elsewhere in the company. Research has been incorporated into the training process, including ongoing training for experienced technicians. This has meant continuous upgrading of instructors' knowledge, shorter adjustment periods for new job environments, and reduced staff needs (in comparison to separate training and research departments, as all researchers are instructors).

A number of companies in Suriname use Telesur's center to train their employees. In the early 1990s, the ITU studied the feasibility of making the center a regional one. The ITU's support of Telesur's Training and Resource Center continues, including holding a training seminar on signaling attended by CANTO members from eighteen countries in November 1994. Telesur hosted an ITU network planning and management software training symposium (PLANITU) for Latin America and the Caribbean in April and May 1995.

Tariffs on parts are considered by some to be a barrier to the emergence of more local production. In any case, no local private capital has made any effort to invest in production or even assembling telecom equipment thus far. With transnationals having significant stakes in many of the region's operating telcos, it is unlikely there will be much encouragement from them to change this situation.

1.4.2 Cooperation vis-à-vis Transnational Suppliers

In 1988 CANTO negotiated a volume discount agreement with Mitel. The agreement provided for rebates or credits once CANTO members had purchased a specified aggregate amount of Mitel PABXs. These discounts would be prorata among the members. That year there were U.S.$70,000 in discounts based on U.S.$1.4 million in purchases. In 1989 Northern Telecom signed a similar agreement for the same product lines, giving CANTO members over U.S.$1 million in credits toward future purchases based on U.S.$18 million in purchases that year.

The number of suppliers and product lines covered by volume discount agreements has subsequently grown steadily. In 1994 agreements were in place wtih AT&T, Ericsson, MER Communications Systems, Mitel, Newbridge Networks, Northern Telecom, Quebecor Printing, Southwestern Bell, Tellabs International, and Teleco Systems. By combining analysis of previous purchases with forecasts from individual companies, CANTO can negotiate with aggregate numbers that do not compromise specific buyers, as well as cross-reference suppliers' reported sales with purchases recorded by members' invoices.

Many, including myself, feel this should be a first step toward joint regional purchases of equipment by CANTO acting as a single purchasing body. In the early 1990s CANTO members began reviewing their tender procedures with a view toward this goal. Joint purchasing can serve as the foundation for regional manufacturing, which I feel very strongly is something that should be done to strengthen the economic base of the Caribbean in the information-media age. At a minimum, it can help justify customization of equipment for the specific circumstances of the region. However, joint purchasing has not yet occurred.

CANTO has created a Products and Standards Evaluation Team that has carried out preliminary feasibility studies to identify several product lines for which it was felt the technical means and economies exist to support regional assembly or manufacture. However, it will take impeccable planning and firm resolve to overcome the obstacles to realize this goal. A CANTO Standards Bureau, created in the mid-1990s, is attempting to deepen this process. Each of the telcos, governments, and current suppliers (including both local representatives and the transnationals themselves) has different needs and goals. Even leaving aside the opposition one can expect from existing vendors, reconciling the diverse interests is a major problem.

CANTO has also succeeded in persuading suppliers to provide financing for equipment purchases. In this and its other activities vis-à-vis vendors, CANTO has avoided becoming simply a sales agent for suppliers.

A CANTO-inspired ITU study on traffic routing patterns, authorized at ITU's Americas Telecom Development Conference in Acapulco in 1992, was completed in 1994. The sensitive traffic data generated will enable CANTO to negotiate volume discounts for regional traffic and optimize members' network capacity by rerouting transit traffic within the region. This study represents another new frontier in regional cooperation and the first step toward direct South-to-South telecoms.

1.4.3 Setting Technical Standards

The ITU appears to be bowing to pressure from commercial interests in the industrial countries for a more flexible, liberalized approach to defining standards for spectrum and orbital slot allocation. This is clearly so in direct broadcasting by satellite (DBS), high-definition television (HDTV), and broadband Integrated Services Digital Network (ISDN). Developing nations, including those in the Caribbean, may simply have to accept an international standards regime that they have no role in shaping. Caribbean and Latin American nations have been able to reserve space segments in the 12 Ghz band. However, prohibitive cost factors have prevented many of the region's countries from making effective use of this resource. (I was instrumental in getting the government of Trinidad and Tobago to license CaribSpace, the first Caribbean satellite to offer digital broadcast via satellite in the C band.)

I feel it is incumbent on the region to develop creative negotiating strategies that use rights to geosynchronous orbits as a bargaining chip to lease transponders dedicated to the region in order for Caribbean telcos to undertake their own tests. This will go a long way in helping them determine what standards are appropriate for regional telecommunications and broadcasting development.

1.4.4 Technology Transfer

Not only is there no production of sophisticated telecom equipment in the region, there is little in the way of technology transfer even at the level of training in maintenance of the equipment purchased from transnational suppliers. Although extended warranty programs are clearly a protection to equipment buyers, in practice they mean that anything beyond basic upkeep is done by foreign specialists or even remotely from Canada or the United States.

1.5 Strategy for Integration and Cooperation

Throughout this chapter I have expressed my feeling that cooperation and integration among the region's telcos and the development of local telecom equipment production are important goals. As secretary-general of CANTO I have worked to promote them.

To this end, CANTO sponsored, with the Trinidad Express Newspapers Ltd., from 1989 to 1992, a conference series entitled Caribbean Media and Telecommunications in the Information Age, also referred to as the Trincom Conference Series. Representatives from many organizations in these fields attended, including members of the Caribbean Broadcasters Union, CARIMAC (the Caribbean Institute of Mass Communications), CAMWORK (Caribbean Media Workers Association), CANA (Caribbean News Agency), and the Caribbean Telecommunications Union (CTU). Among the resolutions passed was a call that all of these organizations be recognized by the region's governments and afforded favors such as concessionary rates from telecom carriers to promote their operations. Delegates also resolved to organize a conference dealing specifically with the "Caribbeanization" of programs for the region, which was subsequently held. One important result of Trincom was that in 1992 the government of Barbados cracked open the door to ending monopoly in Caribbean telecommunications by providing both the CBU and CANA with licenses to uplink their programs via satellite, something that had until then been an exclusive franchise of Cable & Wireless. This move was a serious policy shift that could influence policy makers in the future.

Note

1. As strategic planning manager of the Trinidad & Tobago Telephone Company, I was the founding organizer of the inaugural CANTO conference, held in April 1985, and at the conference was appointed CANTO's secretary-general.

Reference

Dunn, Hopeton. 1995. "A One-Way Street Just off the Global Digital Superhighway." In *Globalization, Communications and Caribbean Identity.* Kingston, Jamaica: Ian Randle Publishers.

2
Cuba

JOHN SPICER NICHOLS AND ALICIA M. TORRES

The government of Fidel Castro, in an arduous struggle to survive the economic damage caused by the collapse of the Soviet Union and its trading bloc, has undertaken a radical restructuring of Cuba's economy and trade relations. In the early 1990s the Cuban leadership—for decades, the Latin American paragon of state ownership and central planning—has become more open to private enterprise and foreign investment while attempting to retain its vaunted social welfare programs and the existing political system.

To achieve this difficult transition to a hybrid political system and mixed economy, as well as to reenter the capitalist world, Cuba must modernize its crumbling telecommunications infrastructure. Without the necessary capital and know-how to do it alone, the Cuban government has had little choice but to enter joint ventures with foreign investors. This is significant because nationalization of the foreign-owned telephone company was among the highest priorities of the revolutionary government when it came to power in 1959. The issue of foreign control—along with the country's proximity to, and conflict with, the United States—has long dominated life on the Caribbean island and, similarly, has been a key factor in the development of the Cuban telecommunications system.[1]

The last of Spain's colonies in Latin America to gain independence, Cuba suffered under colonial control many decades longer than other nations in the region. Life on the island centered around growing and exporting sugar and other crops to fuel the colonial economy of Madrid. More than a half million slaves were imported to do the backbreaking field work, and slavery continued in Cuba twenty-one years after the end of the U.S. Civil War. As a slave-powered agricultural society dominated by a colonial master, Cuba had little opportunity to develop its own economic and political infrastructure. The result was grinding poverty and political instability.

The confluence of a strong Cuban independence movement, the decline of the Spanish empire, and the emergence of the United States as a global power led to the transfer of control over the island. As a result of the Spanish-American War, Cuba gained independence from Spain in 1898, only to become a political and economic dependency of the United States. As a condition for withdrawal of U.S. troops after the war, Cuba was forced to incorporate into its new constitution the so-called Platt Amendment, granting the United States the right to intervene in Cuba's domestic affairs. This was something the United States did routinely until the amendment was repealed in 1934. Consequently, the Platt Amendment has remained a powerful symbol of the history of U.S. intervention in Latin America and a rallying cry for Cuban nationalists and revolutionaries.

The 1959 revolution that brought Castro to power was, in large part, a reaction to U.S. control and a manifestation of years of economic hardship and instability. In the 1960s Cuba moved into the Soviet political and economic orbit and, as the first socialist state in Latin America, became the focus of Cold War tensions in the region.

With an area of 114,000 square kilometers, it is the largest of the Caribbean islands. A multiracial society, Cuba has a population of 11.5 million (July 1994 estimate). About 70 percent live in urban areas, including 20 percent in metro Havana. Highly educated by global standards, Cubans have remained poor by Latin American standards.

2.1 Early Development

The history of Cuban telecommunications is one of foreign control. Telegraph service began around 1851 when Cuba was still a colony of Spain. The system, which connected nineteen stations throughout the island, was initially used exclusively by the Spanish government and the railroads. Only years later was it opened to the general public (Gonzalez Porcell 1989, p. 152; Schroeder 1982, p. 338).

Cuba probably had the first telephone company in Latin America.[2] The Cuban Telephone Company (CUTELCO) was formed in 1881 by the Continental Telephone Company. A U.S.-based firm created by principals of the Bell Telephone Company, it held the Latin American rights to Bell's patents. By 1915 Cuba had a comparatively well-developed system. More than 67,000 miles of wire had been strung within and between 220 Cuban towns and cities and 60 sugar mills, and 19,876 telephones were in operation (Schroeder 1982, p. 335).

No later than 1906, and perhaps as early as 1904, the U.S. Navy was operating a high-power radio transmitter at Guantanamo Bay on the island's southeast coast. The Guantanamo naval base came under U.S. control at the conclusion of the Spanish-American War, and the United States later obtained perpetual treaty rights to lease the facility. For decades the base served as a coaling station for the U.S. fleet protecting sea lanes to the Panama Canal and as the hub of ship-to-shore military communications in the region (Brannigan 1994; Smith and Morales 1988, pp. 102–12).

Foremost among the U.S. companies that dominated the early development of Cuban telecommunications was Boston-based United Fruit Company (UFCO). Best known as a banana importer, UFCO entered the sugar business in Cuba at the turn of the century and by 1903 had established an extensive domestic telephone and telegraph network, primarily along railroad lines, to coordinate transportation between its cane fields, mills, and ports.

A reliable and speedy communications system connecting United Fruit's remote plantations in Central America with its railroads, coastal ports, transport ships, and destinations in the United States was necessary to a profitable banana business. Otherwise, large shipments of fruit would be left spoiling on some siding or dock in the supply line. Because of the rugged terrain, great distances over mostly water, and harsh weather and climate, wired telegraph was largely impossible. Consequently, United Fruit was a pioneer in radio telegraphy. In 1904 the company built the first wireless station in Latin America at Bocas del Toro, Panama, using the earliest equipment produced by American De Forest Wireless Company. UFCO was thus one of the very first commercial users of the then-emerging radio technology.

In 1908, barely a year after Reginald Aubrey Fessenden demonstrated the radiotelephone, UFCO was using the new technology for a relay station strategically erected at Cape San Antonio on the western tip of Cuba. It was not only the first radiotelephone station on the island, it was also a key component of the first commercial point-to-point radio network in the world (Mason 1922, p. 384).

In recognition of the importance of telecommunications to its operations, United Fruit incorporated the Tropical Radio Telegraph Company as a wholly owned subsidiary in 1913. With strong support from the U.S. government, which feared potential European control of telecommunications in Latin America, Tropical Radio rapidly expanded its network and dominated point-to-point radio communications in Central America and the Caribbean for decades (Wilson 1968, pp. 153–67; Fejes 1982, p. 21).

The early Cuban telecom system grew mostly in conjunction with the transportation system (primarily railroads), both of which had the financial backing of sometimes competing and sometimes collaborating U.S. companies. Some parts of the island had railroad, telegraph, or telephone service exclusively under the control, and primarily intended for the private use, of U.S. companies such as United Fruit. Other parts were served by common carriers, such as Cuba Railroad Company and Cuban Telephone Company, that were financed and operated by U.S. corporations under franchises from the Cuban government. Still other parts had overbuilt systems served by two or more companies, some public and some private. But most parts of the country—those that did not generate significant profits for U.S. companies—had no modern transportation or communications system at all. The 1920s was a period of rapid consolidation. Most parts of each sector fell under the control of one company, often a large U.S.-based multinational corporation, sometimes in joint ventures with the Cuban state (United Fruit Company 1976, pp. 299–302).

For example, the Cuban Telephone Company came under the financial control of International Telephone and Telegraph (ITT). Sosthenes and Hernand Behn, the founders of ITT, first invested in the financially shaky and inefficient Cuban phone company in 1916, and it was their success in wringing a profit out of that system that led them to expand into the global market. The Behn brothers' shares in Cuban Telephone were among the three original assets of ITT when it was created in 1920 and, within two years, the brothers' new company had gobbled up 90 percent of its shares, thereby controlling phone service on the island (Sobel 1982, pp. 29–36; Fejes 1982, p. 24).

Just as Cuba's domestic telecom system was one of the earliest in Latin America and was dominated by U.S. companies, so was its international system. The island's first telecommunications link to the outside world was a submarine cable laid between Florida and Havana in 1867. The company that built the system, International Ocean Telegraph Company, was acquired in 1878 by Western Union, which established Cuba as its gateway to Latin America. Radio telephone service to New York began in 1928 and to Madrid in 1929 (Rippy 1946, pp. 118–19; Schroeder 1982, p. 332).

An underwater telephone cable between Havana and Florida, established in 1949, was owned and operated by the Cuban American Telephone and Telegraph Company—a Cuban corporation owned by AT&T and ITT. The cable was supplemented in 1957 by an experimental over-the-air tropospheric scatter transmission system. The first of its kind in the world, the system was originally designed to relay television signals across the Straits of Florida, which separates Cuba and Florida. The channel, 145 kilometers at its narrowest, exceeded the maximum distance a television signal could then be transmitted. However, it apparently was used only for voice communications (Associated Press 1957).

Simultaneous with the addition of these new telecom services, United Fruit, which had dominated Cuban telecommunications for decades, phased out most of its radio operations on the island, relying instead on the less expensive common carriers for its business communications. Its relay stations, frequently damaged by hurricanes, were costly to maintain and no longer essential to the company. Further, UFCO faced ongoing bureaucratic conflict with the Cuban Ministry of Communications dating from the government's refusal to allow the company to enter the Cuban domestic radio broadcasting business in the 1930s. The result of UFCO's departure from the Cuban telecommunications market was yet more concentration under foreign control.

One of the most novel forms of international communications also had its debut across the Straits of Florida. In the fall of 1954 the four-year-old Cuban television system—eager to broadcast the World Series live—leased a DC-3 and fitted it with a transmitter and two antennas. During the series, the plane flew 8,500 feet above the straits relaying the programming from a Miami station to a Cuban ground station, from where it was distributed by microwave to the five-station Cuban television network. The following year the same method was used by NBC, a U.S. television network, to transmit the first live telecast from Cuba to the United States.[3]

2.2 Change from the Revolution

The Cuban revolution, at its core, sought a complete restructuring of the country's political and economic system, including the organization, financing, and control of telecommunications. On the eve of the revolution, U.S. investors controlled more than one-third of the country's public utilities, dominating domestic and international telecommunications and controlling 90 percent of electrical generating capacity. They also owned 22 percent of Cuban land, had a 30 percent stake in the sugar industry, and dominated the railroads, mining, and manufacturing (*Cuba at the Turning Point* 1977, pp. 16–17).

To the extent Fidel Castro had a coherent plan for his revolution, it was to extricate Cuba from the political and economic control of the United States. Within months of his guerrilla army seizing control of the Cuban government in January 1959, he began to nationalize U.S. properties. The primary focus was land. In May 1959 large agricultural tracts were expropriated from Cuban and U.S. owners, including the United Fruit Company. But even before tackling its major objective, the Castro government started tinkering with telecommunications.

On March 3, 1959, the Cuban government "intervened" (also called a "temporary" takeover) in the management of Cuban Telephone Company and revoked a rate increase authorized by the previous government. The revolutionary government also lowered the electrical power rates charged by U.S.-owned Cuban Electric Company. Finally, on August 6, 1960, Castro announced to a cheering crowd in the Havana sports stadium that he had nationalized U.S.\$132.9 million in CUTELCO assets from ITT, U.S.\$267.6 million from Cuban Electric (a subsidiary of Boise-Cascade), and U.S.\$85.1 million from United Brands (formerly United Fruit), as part of a total of U.S.\$2 billion seized from U.S. companies.

Castro's actions triggered a spiral of economic sanctions by the United States, Soviet assistance, Cuban retaliation against U.S. interests, additional U.S. measures, and so on. In January 1961 the United States broke diplomatic relations with Cuba and in 1962 imposed a trade embargo on the island, severing many long-standing communications links and heightening hostile relations between the two countries that would last for decades (Blaiser 1976, pp. 187–200; *Cuba at the Turning Point* 1977, pp. 22, 101–2).

The United States, in addition to imposing its own economic sanctions on Cuba, persuaded virtually all of Cuba's prerevolution trading partners to join the embargo. Almost all of them reestablished political and economic relations with Cuba during the subsequent three decades, but in the interim Cuba was forced to entirely transform its international trade and domestic economy. It had little choice in the 1960s but to establish trade relations with the Soviet Union and Eastern Europe. Given Cuba's geopolitical importance, the Soviet Union eagerly supplied and, to a considerable extent, subsidized the economy of its new ally. In 1958 about two-thirds of all Cuban trade was with the United States; three decades later, approximately three-quarters was with the Soviet Union. In effect, Cuba shifted its dependency from one superpower to another (*Cuba at the Turning Point* 1977, p. 19; Domínguez 1993).

2.2.1 Telecommunications under Castro

Economic control of Cuban telecommunications by the United States was largely replaced by state control. The new minister of communications was Jesús Montané, an original member of Castro's rebel army, a member of the central committee of the Cuban Communist Party, and one of the most trusted insiders in the regime. His appointment indicated the importance attached to controlling the telecommunications system and protecting it from the growing counterrevolutionary movement. Communications facilities were prime targets for sabotage by numerous paramilitary groups, including those backed by the U.S. Central Intelligence Agency as part of President Kennedy's aggressive policy against Castro and Cuba. Subsequent ministers of communications have been from the military.

But, in Castro's view, government control of telecommunications served important purposes beyond national security. "If we want to overcome the gap which separates us from the developed nations," he said, ". . . our resources [must be] used in a rational, organized way. There is no room for waste. We don't have the luxury of following the path of free competition to achieve economic development" (*Cuba and Fidel* 1976).

Castro considered the telecom system to be a precious resource that could not be left to the helter-skelter management of private owners under a capitalist system. He felt strongly that only central planning could bring the social and economic benefits of telecommunications to all Cubans, especially those living in the abject poverty of the island's isolated rural areas. For these reasons, investment in the communications infrastructure—especially in the countryside—was given priority during the early years of the Castro government. The result was expanded services, more widely distributed throughout the island.

In 1958, 73 percent of installed telephone service was in Havana, where about 20 percent of the population resided. By 1982, only 56 percent of new service was being installed in the capital, the rest was in the provinces. During the 1958–82 period, the number of telephones nationwide nearly doubled from 170,000 (2.4 per hundred inhabitants) to 447,000 (4.6 per hundred) ("Cuban Parliamentary Debate . . ." 1984, p. 2; Schroeder 1982, p. 335; *Statistical Abstract of Latin America* 1960, p. 28; Hunter 1991, p. 398).

In sum, although not matching the advances it achieved in health care and education, the revolutionary government made some significant improvements in Cuban telecommunications despite very meager resources. In the early 1990s, however, after the Soviet trading bloc collapsed, Castro's socialist ideology of a centrally planned and state-controlled economy became unsustainable.

2.3 Cuba in Transition

The disintegration of the socialist trading bloc in 1989 and the loss of an estimated U.S.$4 billion annually in Soviet subsidies in 1992 sent the Cuban economy into a tailspin. With its supply lines badly disrupted and without sufficient hard currency to purchase gasoline, fertilizer, and spare parts for farm machinery, the production of sugar—Cuba's primary cash crop—plummeted from 8.1 million tonnes in 1989 to 4.0 million in 1994. Projections for the 1995 crop were as low as 2.5 million tonnes. The gross domestic product of Cuba fell by nearly 50 percent between 1989 and 1993. Imports dropped from 8.1 billion pesos to 2.0 billion during the same period.

The purchasing power of a typical Cuban's income similarly dropped by half, and hundreds of thousands of workers—perhaps as much as one-fifth of the country's total workforce—are likely to have lost their jobs in the economic downturn. Daily consumption of calories per capita went from 2,845 in 1989 to 1,780 in 1993. As shortages of food and other basic goods cut deeply into Cubans' already meager existence, popular discontent and political tension increased (Mesa-Lago 1995; Domínguez 1993).

Analysts have been predicting the imminent demise of the Castro government for more than thirty-five years, and in the early 1990s the revolution has indeed faced a grave political and economic crisis. Without its Soviet patron, Cuba faced not only economic disaster but also international isolation. To avoid this fate, Cuba has been forced into the second complete restructuring of its national economy and international trade relations in little more than three decades. Although some experts have had serious questions as to whether it can succeed in this transformation, Cuba is in a somewhat better position than it had been during the 1960s. In the intervening decades, Cuba developed a relatively sophisticated infrastructure (by Caribbean standards) and a somewhat more diversified economy. Further, Cuba has been able to establish new trade relations with Western countries—with the obvious exception of the United States—an option not available to it in the 1960s (Griffin 1992; Zimbalist 1993).

While insisting that it is not forsaking socialism, Cuba has been steadily loosening state control over the economy and cautiously adopting capitalist measures in an effort to stem the economic free fall. Since 1993 the government has legalized the dollar, allowed self-employment and family businesses, permitted farmers to sell food at market prices, and begun to solicit foreign investment in Cuban industry. By the end of 1994, 185 foreign firms had signed joint-venture agreements with state-owned Cuban companies, resulting in a critical infusion of new capital, and some thirty more agreements were signed during the first eight months of 1995. Cuban law was amended in 1995 to allow foreign companies to own 100 percent of enterprises in all sectors except education, health care, and the military. Government control over foreign investment is still substantial, but these changes are remarkable in contrast to the early years of the revolution when foreign investments were nationalized. These and other economic measures appear to have stalled the rapid deterioration of the economy. But, although the economy apparently has bottomed out, there have been no signs of anything more than a slight recovery in the near term, and economic conditions remain grim.

After it came to power in 1959 the new government actively discouraged tourism (which had involved significant elements of gambling, prostitution, pornography, drugs, and organized crime). In the 1990s, seeking to capitalize on one of its greatest resources—some of the most beautiful beaches in the world—but lacking the funds and technical expertise to develop resorts, Cuba has aggressively sought foreign investors, primarily German and Spanish companies, to build and manage tourist hotels. As a result, many of the biggest foreign investments have been in the burgeoning tourist industry. From 1989 to 1994, the years of Cuba's steepest economic decline, gross revenues from tourism increased 406 percent to U.S.$850 million (Mesa-Lago 1995). There has been no stronger indication of Cuba's newfound economic pragmatism than its promotion of tourism.

2.4 The Domestic Telecommunications System

Reflecting the changes taking place in the overall economy, the Cuban telecommunications system was in transition in 1995 from a state monopoly to mixed public-private ownership. Prior to 1993 the Ministry of Communications operated all domestic telecom services through various state enterprises. The ministry, one of thirty major divisions of the Cuban government, was responsible for formulating policy recommendations on communications matters for the Council of State, over which Castro presides, and implementing the Council's decisions. Some operational decisions about domestic telecommunications, such as rates for services, were made by the Ministry of Communications in coordination with other government divisions; most were made by the local service providers under ministry supervision.

Cuban Telecommunications Enterprise (EMTELCUBA), the national telephone company, was a division of the ministry. The primary local operating unit was the Communications Enterprise for the City of Havana, which provided telephone service directly to homes and offices in the capital city. Local service outside Havana was similarly provided by provincial enterprises. Other divisions of the ministry handled international telephone, postal, telegraph, and radio and television service.

2.4.1 Technology and Services

Until the economic problems of the early 1990s, the Castro government provided rudimentary telecom services to a larger share of its population, at a far lower direct cost to the user, than most other Latin American countries at a similar level of economic development. In 1993 Cuba had 5.4 phones per hundred inhabitants. This compared favorably with other poor countries in the region, such as Guatemala (1.1), Nicaragua (1.6), and Ecuador (3.0), and was not far behind wealthier neighbors such as Colombia (5.7), Mexico (7.3), and Venezuela (7.3). Basic telephone and telegraph service reached almost all populated areas on the island. According to the vice minister of communications, a high percentage of the phones were either residential or public. Although hard data supporting the claim were not available, in-country observations generally verified that telephones are widely available for public use.

Consistent with its socialist ideology, the government heavily subsidized local service. In 1994 a residential phone cost 6.25 pesos per month for the average household plus a onetime installation fee of 100 pesos. Local calls on pay phones cost 5 centavos, the same as in 1959 (Marrero 1994; Lopez 1993; Luxner 1991, p. 17).[4]

The Cuban telephone system had become a hodgepodge of antiquated equipment by the 1990s. Analog technology was still being used for almost all of the domestic network. Of the 20,000 kilometers of phone lines, the vast majority were copper wire and pole mounted. Less than 1,000 kilometers of fiber optics were in use, mostly connecting switches in the Havana area. In 1993 there were more than 500,000 access lines in Cuba, 40 percent of them in the Havana area, where approximately 20 percent of the population resided. The majority of central offices—about 56 percent—still used electromechanical equipment, 1940s technology from the United States. Another 43 percent used step-by-step technology, primarily 1970s East European equipment. Only about 1 percent used digital technology. The switches in a few isolated rural areas were still manually operated.

Beginning in the late 1970s, the Ministry of Communications began to upgrade the national long-distance network with coaxial cable. It decided against introducing fiber optics after concluding the technology was too expensive, too sophisticated, and not sufficiently compatible with Cuba's old copper wire system, which the authorities recognized was not likely to be replaced soon. There were 15,000 kilometers of coaxial cable in Cuba by 1994. Because of the elongated shape of the island, the national network was relatively easy to build. A backbone extends east and west from Havana with short branches, usually of 80 kilometers or less, reaching all major population centers. The coaxial network also is used for television and other services. In addition, an analog microwave system carries domestic long-distance calls and radio and television signals. Electronic mail is in limited use (Marrero 1994; Lopez 1993; Roche and Blaine 1994).

Cuba does not have cable television service, nor is there direct satellite reception in Cuban homes. An estimated 200 satellite dishes were in use on the island in 1993, but all were for Cuban government or foreign entities, including tourist hotels in Havana and at beach resorts, which receive domestic and foreign television programming, including CNN (Coro 1994).

From 1962, when the United States imposed a trade embargo on Cuba, until the late 1980s, most communications equipment was imported from the Soviet Union and Eastern Europe. Some equipment was purchased from Japan, Canada, France, Sweden, and other Western countries that had ceased participating in the embargo. In an exercise of bad timing, Cuba launched a five-year plan in 1984 to increase the proportion of equipment from Eastern-bloc countries to 95 percent. With the embargo tightened during a peak in Cold War tensions, the Cuban government had sought to decrease its dependence on what it saw as less reliable Western suppliers ("Cuban Parliamentary Debate . . ." 1984).

Although most communications technology was imported, Cuba had developed a reasonably sophisticated electronics manufacturing industry, primarily in the 1970s and 1980s. The government had hoped to avoid the common practice in developing countries of importing all high technology. Radio and television receivers, semiconductors, and specialized medical equipment were assembled with foreign parts in Cuban factories. Believing that computer technology was important to the central planning of its economy, yet blocked from purchasing most Western-manufactured computers, Cuba also built domestically designed minicomputers using imported parts beginning in 1972 but has since abandoned those efforts (Barquin 1975; "Statistics on Computer Use . . ." 1989).

2.4.2 Deterioration

By the early 1990s the Cuban telecommunications system was rapidly deteriorating. The telephone system was particularly bad. Problems such as frequent interruptions in service, long delays in repairs and installations, network congestion, dialing difficulties, and scarcity of functioning public phones and even phone books were common in the dilapidated system. Much of the equipment had been cannibalized because of lack of replacement parts due to the U.S. embargo, and the few parts that were obtained were used primarily to maintain the military communications system. Most of the phone network was jerry-rigged to accommodate incompatible equipment imported from a variety of countries.

The already serious problems in the system were badly compounded in November 1988 when a mentally disturbed phone company worker set a fire that destroyed the main exchange in Havana. Preceded and followed by severe hurricanes that ravaged the national telephone network, the blaze caused an estimated U.S.$30 million damage and knocked out nearly 30,000 local lines, including those of key government offices, for as long as two years. An ambitious plan announced by Castro in 1989 to replace the lines lost in the fire, add 20,000 new lines in Havana, and begin installing high-technology equipment to restore the failing system was soon abandoned as the Cuban economy declined (Luxner 1991; "Fire Interrupts Telephone Service . . ." 1988; "Castro Speaks . . ." 1989; "$20 Million Planned . . ." 1989).

In 1993 U.S. technicians surveying the Cuban phone system reported that the deterioration was so serious that some interior cities could lose service by 1994 and predicted that the number of working lines would drop to 2.0 per 100 Cubans, from 5.4, within a year. They further reported that less than 18 percent of domestic calls were completed ("Phones Failing . . ." 1993). These predictions might have been exaggerated, but in-country observations and interviews in mid-1995 do indicate an estimated 30 percent of the country's access lines were inoperable.

2.4.3 Lack of Electricity

In the best of times Cuba had difficulty supplying enough electricity to meet basic demand. Virtually all its generating capacity is dependent on imported oil. Beginning in 1989 the Soviet Union, plagued by its own political and economic disruptions, terminated the barter arrangements that brought over 13 million tuns of oil and oil products to Cuba annually at far below market prices. In 1994 Cuba imported only 1.5 million tonnes of oil from the former Soviet republics, a nearly 90 percent drop (Mesa-Lago 1995).

Discovery of small amounts of low-quality domestic crude helped cover the shortfall somewhat, but the Cuban government had hoped to reduce its dependence on foreign oil by finishing construction of a nuclear power plant at Cienfuegos, a major southern port. However, because of frequent construction delays, design problems, huge cost overruns, and the dwindling supply of equipment and technical expertise from the Russian contractors, the project was halted in 1992. At that time, U.S.$1.1 billion had been spent and the project was 70 percent complete. Work resumed in late 1995. Completion is not anticipated in the near term.

The oil drought is one of Cuba's graver problems. As a result, electricity has been strictly rationed; work hours shortened; street lights and air conditioning to public buildings are frequently shut off; restaurants, nightclubs, and movie theaters close early; entire neighborhoods are blacked out for hours at a time; and bicycles have replaced automobiles on Cuban streets. In the late 1980s, the Cuban economy already was in decline, but without sufficient fuel to harvest and transport the sugar crop (Cuba's primary source of foreign exchange), there is little or no prospect for a significant economic recovery.

Electronic communications also have been hit: sufficient electricity is obviously important to effective operation of a telecommunications system. Although television was an extremely popular source of entertainment for Cubans living in increasingly bleak conditions (in 1986 Cuba had the second highest number of television receivers per capita, 202 per 1,000, in Latin America), it was an early casualty of the crushing energy shortage. Not only do transmitters require large amounts of power, but the Soviet-made television sets in widespread use are not energy efficient, consuming about three times the power of typical U.S. or Japanese sets. Television transmissions were cut to as little as five hours a day. Because radio receivers require very little energy, radio transmissions were not cut significantly. However, batteries were in very short supply (Marrero 1994). In mid-1995, as an indication of the stabilizing economy and the importance of television to the entertainment-starved Cuban population, television schedules were expanded to twelve hours a day. Blackouts also were far less frequent.

2.5 Partial Privatization

By the late 1980s the inability to operate the telecommunications system at full capacity had become a serious drain on the Cuban economy. According to the vice minister of communications, Cuba was faced with a stark, ideologically troubling dilemma: either most Cubans would continue to have the physical access and financial ability to make a call on a telephone system that did not work, or far fewer Cubans would be able to make calls on a system that did work (Marrero 1994). Further, Cuba was unlikely to attract the foreign investments essential to its economic survival plan without dependable telecommunications.

Faced with the necessity of modernizing telephone service, yet lacking sufficient capital to do so, the Cuban leadership was forced to compromise on its socialist principles. Ideology gave way to pragmatism, and EMTELCUBA, the state phone company, sought a foreign partner.

On June 13, 1994, Castro and then Mexican President Carlos Salinas de Gortari announced in Havana that Grupo Domos, a Mexican holding company, had signed a U.S.$1.1 billion joint-venture agreement to overhaul and operate the Cuban phone system. Domos acquired a 49 percent interest in EMTELCUBA, which was given a fifty-five-year monopoly concession on Cuban domestic and long-distance service, plus opportunities to expand into other services such as cable television.

Domos paid the Cuban government U.S.$700 million and pledged a U.S.$400 million capital infusion for EMTELCUBA. Because the Cuban government also will put U.S.$400 million into EMTELCUBA, the company has U.S.$800 million to refurbish the system. Allowing for its capital contribution, overall the government netted U.S.$300 million, consisting of U.S.$100 million cash and U.S.$200 million in Cuban debt to Mexico.

The agreement calls for installation of 1 million telephone lines, including replacement of 200,000 existing lines, by the year 2000. The government said priority would be given to social service providers such as hospitals, senior citizens' homes, and day care centers (Bardacke 1994; Whitefield 1994).

The venture was finalized in 1995 and Javier Garza Calderon, director general of Grupo Domos and member of a wealthy Monterrey family, became president of EMTELCUBA's council of stockholders. Domos was expected to take on a technical partner with telecommunications expertise to help defray its investment and manage the new enterprise. It did this in mid-1995 by selling a 25 percent stake in the venture to Stet International, a unit of Societa Finanziaria Telefonica, the Italian state-controlled telecom holding company, for U.S.$291 million. Garza Calderon, an unsuccessful bidder for the Mexican phone monopoly Telemex when it was privatized in 1990, was also reportedly negotiating with U.S. companies to launch a competitive long-distance service in Mexico (Torres 1994; "Italy's Stet Taps . . ." 1995).

Although foreign investment had been flowing into Cuba for several years, selling a partial stake in EMTELCUBA was the first privatization of a state enterprise since Castro came to power in 1959 and was the largest foreign investment of any type to date. Given the history of foreign control and nationalization of the Cuban phone system, the deal with Grupo Domos demonstrated the dramatic changes in Cuban economic conditions and the importance that the previously orthodox socialist government attached to telecommunications in those changes.

2.5.1 CUBACEL

In 1992 the Cuban government had approved another, albeit tiny by comparison, telecommunications joint venture with other Mexican investors. Telecomunicaciones de Mexico SA (TIMSA) paid U.S.$8 million for a 50 percent stake in the Cellular Telephone Company of Cuba (CUBACEL), a new enterprise created to construct a cellular network that bypasses the existing wired network. Connecting foreign businesses, diplomatic missions, international organizations, foreign news agencies, and government offices in the Havana area and offering direct-dial international service, the first stage of this elite network, which became operational in 1993, was intended as a stopgap measure until the wired system could be overhauled.

The CUBACEL system routes telephone traffic through its own switches, totally independent of the regular phone system. The infrastructure was built by L. M. Ericsson AB and the phones were primarily supplied by Japanese companies such as Toshiba. After eight months of operation, over 400 subscribers were paying U.S.$40 monthly plus 30 to 40 cents per minute in hard currency for the service. In 1995 cellular service was also available in Veradero, the primary beach resort. Expansion into other major population centers was planned ("Cuba's Cellular System" 1993; Luxner 1993; Colina 1993).

2.6 International Telecommunications

With about one-tenth of the Cuban population living in the United States, mostly in South Florida, there has been great demand for telecom services between the two countries. However, the U.S. embargo not only has prevented U.S. corporations from servicing or investing in the Cuban domestic telephone system, but it has for decades blocked upgrading the antiquated international telecommunications links between the two countries. Consequently, despite high demand, direct electronic communication between the United States and Cuba has been little more than a trickle since 1962 and was nearly impossible between 1987 and 1995.

Cuba has maintained some of its prerevolutionary telecom links with the outside world, such as the Cable & Wireless telegraph lines to the West Indies and a submarine cable to Spain, but virtually all development of Cuba's international telecommunications between 1959 and the early 1990s had been with the patronage of the former Soviet Union.

In 1973 Cuba joined the Soviet-led satellite consortium, Intersputnik, which linked the Cuban gateway at Jaruco, just outside Havana, to Moscow and Eastern European capitals. In 1991, with the disintegration of the Soviet Union and its economic and political bloc, Cuba and the other members of Intersputnik became stockholders in the reconfigured and considerably less relevant satellite system. Cuba began using Intelsat in 1979 with a Standard B ground station, also located at Jaruco. A more advanced Standard A station became operational in 1991 to handle television coverage of the Pan Am Games in Havana (Gonzalez Porcell 1989, p. 151).

2.6.1 Ending the Bottleneck in U.S.-Cuba Calling

Development of Cuba's telephone communications with the United States in essence froze in 1962 after the U.S. embargo was imposed on the island. At that time there were only two direct links—the 1949 underwater cable, which had 130 telephone circuits, and the troposcatter radiotelephone, with a maximum capacity of seventy-nine simultaneous phone calls.

The cable, owned by AT&T's Cuban American Telephone and Telegraph (after the revolution, ITT had sold its CATT shares to AT&T) and operated under a service agreement with EMTELCUBA, continued to carry telephone traffic despite the embargo. The U.S. Treasury Department, which enforces the embargo, allowed AT&T to operate it under a grandfather clause but prohibited upgrading the technology or expanding the number of circuits and blocked any payment to Cuba.

In 1987 the cable wore out, leaving only the troposcatter system. The U.S. Treasury permitted AT&T to install a replacement cable comparable to the old one. When AT&T was unable to locate a cable of an equivalent low capacity and level of technology, Treasury granted permission to use the oldest cable available, a mothballed segment of an old transatlantic copper-wire cable. The World War II–vintage replacement, with a capacity of 138 circuits (which can be expanded to over 300 with compression technology), was laid between Cojimar, Cuba, and West Palm Beach, Florida, in 1989 at a cost of U.S.$8 million.

However, AT&T could not activate it until EMTELCUBA signed a new service agreement, which Treasury had to approve. Given the long-standing hostility between the two governments, the three-party negotiations were politically charged, exceedingly complex, and glacial in pace. The major stumbling block was the U.S. government's reluctance to allow AT&T to pay Cuba its share of the revenues generated from the new cable. The U.S. administration did not want any hard-currency payments made to Cuba at the very time it was attempting to tighten the embargo in hopes of toppling the Castro government. Cuba not only wanted full compensation plus the usual installation and maintenance fees, it also demanded release of its past proceeds, which had been frozen in the United States. Under provisions of the embargo, since 1966 AT&T had been required to place Cuba's share of revenues in an escrow account. (Estimates of the amount range from U.S.$65 to U.S.$130 million; the Cuban foreign minister has put the actual figure at U.S.$100 million [Robaina 1993].) Over some five years, Cuba rejected several iterations of a U.S. government-approved formula before agreement was reached (Workman 1993; Robaina 1993; Luxner 1991).

Because AT&T was then the only authorized U.S. carrier to Cuba, the more than 1 million Cubans living in the United States had to squeeze their phone calls to relatives still on the island through a very narrow bottleneck—the aging seventy-nine troposcatter circuits. (For comparative purposes, the Dominican Republic, a Caribbean country with less than half the population of Cuba, had about 1,000 circuits to handle a much lower demand for calls with the United States.) Of the approximately 60 million phone calls attempted from the United States to Cuba in 1991, only about 500,000 were actually connected. Calling in the opposite direction was considerably easier because Cuba was not bound by the rules of the embargo and connected calls through third countries. Of all international telephone calls originated in Cuba in 1993, 72 percent were to the United States, immediately followed by the former Soviet Union (4 percent), Spain (3 percent), and Mexico (3 percent) (Lopez 1993; "Phones Failing . . ." 1993).

The problem was seriously compounded by Hurricane Andrew, which swept through south Florida in 1992, severely damaging the troposcatter facilities and toppling a microwave tower that linked it to Miami. Prior to the storm, the transmitter (the only one of its kind still in operation in the western hemisphere) was already in serious disrepair, and replacement parts to keep the system working were nearly impossible to find. AT&T decided not to repair the storm damage to this last remaining direct telephone link to Cuba. As a temporary measure, Cuba permitted AT&T to route a limited number of calls—about 2,000 per month—from the United States through ItalCable, Italy's intercontinental telco, with which EMTELCUBA had signed a joint venture agreement in 1991 (Workman 1993; "AT&T Says Cuban Government . . ." 1992).

Circuitous calling routes quickly developed. In 1992 several companies in Canada, which had direct-dial access to Cuba and were outside the jurisdiction of the U.S. Treasury Department, began to offer service. Popular with Cuban exiles, these companies typically charged U.S.$45 for a ten-minute call—U.S.$3 per minute plus a U.S.$15 handling fee—three and four times more than AT&T's rates. E-mail through Canada also was a reliable means of communicating with Cuba. These technical and legal end runs satisfied some of the demand for phone service to Cuba but resulted in lost revenues to AT&T, caused tension between the U.S. government and Canada, and reduced the possibilities that Cuba would relent in its dispute. Consequently, the U.S. government began to reconsider its telecommunications policy toward Cuba (Nordheimer 1994; Holmes 1993).

Enactment of the Cuban Democracy Act of 1992 set the stage for a reversal of U.S. policy. Intended to tighten the trade embargo on Cuba and facilitate the fall of the Castro government, the new law also required the president to permit adequate telecommunications services between the United States and Cuba and authorized him to license payments to Cuba for its portion of the service. The sponsors of the legislation were persuaded that more telephone traffic would undercut the Cuban leadership and were supported by Cuban-Americans eager to call relatives on the island. The legislation received broad, bipartisan congressional support. Then-presidential candidate Clinton endorsed it, and President Bush signed it into law (Gunn 1994; Skrzycki 1993).

Citing the new law as authority for powers it already had, but now with sufficient political cover to respond to lobbying by U.S. telecom companies upset over losing business opportunities in Cuba, the Clinton administration changed course and authorized U.S. telecom companies to share their proceeds with Cuba. In 1994, after extended and highly contentious haggling, Cuba dropped its demand for payment of the escrowed revenues and agreed to a standard bilateral arrangement for future compensation—a 50 percent split of toll calls up to a limit of U.S.$1.20 per minute plus a U.S.$1.00 surcharge for collect calls originating in Cuba. The Clinton administration approved the deal, and direct-dial service began in November 1994, ending the long drought in U.S.-Cuban telephone communications (Robaina 1993; "FCC Gives . . . Go-Ahead" 1994).

Despite continued hostile relations between the two countries in the 1990s, telecommunications was one of the very few areas in which the two governments had serious and sometimes productive negotiations, further indicating the importance of electronic communications even between adversaries.

As of 1995, five U.S. companies had either launched new telecommunications services to Cuba or were seeking approval from both governments for future services: AT&T, formerly the exclusive U.S. carrier to Cuba, had activated its undersea cable from Florida and was authorized to expand service to a predicted 10,000 calls daily, a volume severalfold larger than was previously allowed monthly; MCI Telecommunications was licensed to provide direct-dial telephone service to Cuba via satellite; IDB WorldCom Services was planning direct telex and telegraph services to the island; LDDS Communications had announced it would provide long-distance service to Cuba; and WilTel International had agreed with Cuba to lay a fiber-optic cable from Florida and was applying for U.S. permission. Other services by other companies were also anticipated.

2.6.2 International Telephone Joint Venture

Cuba's attempt to reestablish economic relations with the noncommunist world, its plans for continued development of tourism, and the rapidly growing number of foreign companies operating in the country require a modern, restructured international telecommunications system. The increasing international telephone traffic resulting from expanded tourism and trade has brought badly needed foreign exchange into the Cuban treasury because all international calls made by foreigners are paid for in hard currency.

In late 1991, lacking the start-up capital to restructure the system, Cuba sold a 50 percent share in a new international telephone venture to ItalCable, Italy's intercontinental telephone company, for U.S.$41 million. Under a multiyear agreement with the Ministry of Communications, ItalCable agreed to provide equipment, know-how, and the management necessary to establish a modern, computer-operated, direct-dial international telephone service to Europe and Cuba's new trading partners. The key component of the joint venture was the construction of a satellite earth station linking Cuba—especially its growing beach resorts—with ItalCable facilities in Rome, thus ending dependence on the increasingly irrelevant Intersputnik system. There were also plans to connect Cuba to ItalCable's optical fiber submarine cable under construction from Europe to North America (Luxner 1992; Lopez 1993).

2.7 Conclusion

The Castro government has viewed telecommunications as a lifeline needed to help save a badly leaking Cuban economy adrift in a turbulent sea. That the lifeline is partially owned by a foreign company is not of overriding importance to Cuba, given the gravity of the situation. It is, nevertheless, ironic that the Cuban revolution, predicated on liberating the nation from U.S. control and brought to the brink of extinction by its economic dependence on the former Soviet Union, had to seek massive foreign investment in hopes of surviving. Although the ideological foundations of the Castro government dictate that telecommunications and other parts of the Cuban infrastructure must be free of foreign control, the past, present, and the probable future of Cuba are for substantial foreign involvement in the organization, management, and financing of its domestic and international communications.

The Cuban revolution was a closely watched political and economic experiment. Fidel Castro's defiance of the United States and nationalization of vital industries was once viewed as a viable alternative by revolutionary movements in other poor countries in Latin America. In the dramatically changed world of the 1990s, that model is no longer seen as realistic. Cuba is now being carefully studied to see if it can navigate the difficult transition to a mixed economy and reenter the world marketplace without sacrificing its social and economic advances. What role will electronic communications play in this process? What are the implications of foreign investment in Cuban telecommunications? As often said, the one thing predictable about Castro's Cuba is the unpredictable.

Notes

The authors gratefully acknowledge the assistance and cooperation of the Cuban Ministry of Communications and Ministry of Foreign Relations; Terry L. Haines and Douglas A. Boyd, contributors to field research in Havana; Michael Krinsky of the law firm Rabinowitz, Boudin, Standard, Krinsky & Lieberman; and Penn State student researchers Sara Leipold, Krishna Kishore, and Michele Carlson.

1. Obtaining current and accurate information for this chapter was difficult because Cuba was undergoing rapid and unpredictable change and there has been continuing hostility between the U.S. and Cuban governments. During the period we were writing this chapter, U.S. researchers were prohibited by the Treasury Department from conducting academic research in Cuba without a license, and some Cuban officials were reluctant to release information about the telecommunications system because of national security implications.

2. The region's other early telephone companies—those in Mexico, Panama, and Uruguay—apparently were formed in 1882 and 1883 (Rippy 1946). The historical record is unclear on the exact founding dates and, therefore, on which telephone system was first. These conclusions are based on the best evidence available to the authors, but should be used with caution.

3. See "Game on Video" 1954; Salwen 1994; Shanley 1955. Airborne television relay, called Stratovision, was used on a limited scale in the United States by Westinghouse during the late 1940s. Prior to the introduction of coaxial cable, Stratovision was seen as a possible means of achieving the economic efficiencies of network television.

4. The monthly minimum wage in Cuba is 108 pesos (mid-1995). However, the value of the peso relative to the U.S. dollar has been quite volatile. According to Mesa-Lago (1995), the annual average black market exchange rate for Cuban pesos went from 7 per U.S.$1 in 1989 to 83 per U.S.$1 in 1994. Other sources, including in-country observations by the authors, indicate that the black market rate may have gone as high as 150 per U.S.$1 in late 1994 but dropped to as low as 10 per U.S.$1 in 1995 in response to the government's economic measures, such as legalizing the dollar and opening farmers' markets.

References

Associated Press. 1957. "Televising to Cuba Approved by FCC." *The New York Times,* June 1, p. 37.

"AT&T Says Cuban Government Is Frustrating Effort to Restore Service after Hurricane." 1992. *Telecommunications Reports,* September 7, p. 31.

Bardacke, Ted. 1994. "Mexico Venture Set to Get Cuba on the Line." *Financial Times,* June 16, p. 6.

Barquin, Ramon C. 1975. "Cuba: Cybernetic Era." *Cuban Studies/Estudios Cubanos* 5(July):1–23.

Bayer, Stephen D. 1992. "The Legal Aspects of TV Marti in Relation to the Law of Direct Broadcasting Satellites." *Emory Law Journal* 41(Spring):541–80.

Blaiser, Cole. 1976. *The Hovering Giant: U.S. Responses to Revolutionary Change in Latin America.* Pittsburgh, Pa.: University of Pittsburgh Press.

Brannigan, Alice. 1994. "Radio: The Old Days." *Popular Communications,* December, pp. 21–22.

"Castro Speaks to Communications Contingent." 1989. *Foreign Broadcast Information Service—Latin America,* November 2, pp. 3–4.

Colina, Cino. 1993. "Cuba Launches Cellular Phone System." *Granma,* March 7, p. 12.

Coro, Arnaldo. 1994. Radio Havana Cuba, interview. Havana, January 2.

Cuba and Fidel. 1976. Churchill Films.

Cuba at the Turning Point. 1977. New York: Business International Corporation.

"Cuban Parliamentary Debate on State Program for Communications." 1984. *Granma* (Havana), January 1, p. 2.

"Cuba's Cellular System." 1993. *CubaNews (Miami Herald),* November, p. 4.

Domínguez, Jorge I. 1993. "The Secrets of Castro's Staying Power." *Foreign Affairs* 72(Spring):97–107.

Edlund, Karin, Jon Elliston, and Peter Kornbluh. 1994. *U.S. Broadcasting to Cuba: Radio and TV Marti, a Historical Chronology.* Washington, D.C.: National Security Archive.

Europa. 1990. *South America, Central America and the Caribbean 1991.* London: Europa Publications Limited.

Falk, Pamela S. 1992. "Broadcasting from Enemy Territory and the First Amendment: The Importation of Informational Materials from Cuba under the Trading with the Enemy Act." *Columbia Law Review* 92(January):165–91.

"FCC Gives Five U.S. Phone Companies Go-Ahead." 1994. *CubaINFO* (Johns Hopkins University), October 13, pp. 2–3.

Federal Communications Commission. 1994. "Five Carriers Authorized to Provide Direct Telecommunications Services to Cuba." News release (Report no. CC-588), October 5.

Fejes, Fred Allan. 1982. Imperialism, Media, and the Good Neighbor: New Deal Foreign Policy and United States Shortwave Broadcasting. Ph.D. diss., University of Illinois at Urbana-Champaign.

"Fire Interrupts Telephone Service in Havana." 1988. *Foreign Broadcast Information Service—Latin America,* November 17, pp. 8–10.

"Game on Video in Havana." 1954. *The New York Times,* September 30, p. 41.

Golden, Tim. 1993a. "Castro's People Try to Absorb 'Terrible Blows.'" *The New York Times,* January 11, p. A1.

_____. 1993b. "Cuba's Economy, Cast Adrift, Grasps at Capitalist Solution." *The New York Times,* January 12, p. A1.

Gonzalez Porcell, Oscar. 1989. "Las Comunicaciones en Cuba." *Economia y Desarrollo* (Havana) 19(July/August):148–57.

Griffin, Clifford E. 1992. "Cuba: The Domino That Refuses to Fall. Can Castro Survive the 'Special Period'?" *Caribbean Affairs* 5(January–March):24–42.

Gunn, Gillian. 1994. "In Search of a Modern Cuba Policy." In Donald E. Schulz, ed., *Cuba and the Future.* Westport, Conn.: Greenwood Press, pp. 127–44.

Holmes, Steven A. 1993. "U.S. Studies Expansion of Phone Links to Cuba." *The New York Times,* May 29, p. 8.

Hunter, Brian, ed. 1991. *The Statesman's Year-Book.* New York: St. Martin's Press.

"Italy's Stet Taps in Cuba." 1995. *The Wall Street Journal,* April 13, p. A11.

Lopez, Enrique. 1993. "Cuba's Telecommunications Needs." *CubaNews (Miami Herald),* October, p. 5.

Luxner, Larry. 1991. "Out of Order—Indefinitely." *Telephony,* January 7, pp. 17–18.

_____. 1992. "ItalCable Buys 50% of Long-Distance Network." *Times of the Americas,* January 8, p. B2.

_____. 1993. "Mexicans Launch Cellular in Cuba." *Telephony,* June 28, p. 14.

Marrero, Rafael. 1994. Vice Minister of Communications, interview. Havana, March 4.

Mason, Roy. 1922. "The History of the Development of the United Fruit Company's Radio Telegraph System." *Radio Broadcasting,* September, pp. 377–98.

Mesa-Lago, Carmelo. 1995. "Balseros, the U.S., and the Cuban Economy." Speech to the 13th annual Journalists and Editors Workshop on Latin America and the Caribbean (Florida International University/*Miami Herald*), April 21.

"New Earth Station Named 'Caribbean Two.'" 1990. *Foreign Broadcast Information Service—Latin America,* March 29, pp. 15–16.

Nichols, John Spicer. 1990. "Broadcast Wars." *NACLA Report on the Americas,* November, pp. 30–33.

Nordheimer, Jon. 1994. "A Call to Cuba Is a Test of Patience." *The New York Times,* August 25, p. A18.

"Phones Failing as Talks Continue." 1993. *CubaNews (Miami Herald)*, November, p. 4.

Rippy, J. Fred. 1946. "Notes on the Early Telephone Companies of Latin America." *Hispanic American Historical Review* 26(1):116–118.

Robaina, Roberto. 1993. Foreign Minister, interview. Havana, December 30.

Roche, Edward M. and Michael Blaine. 1994. "Upgrading Cuba's Telecommunications Infrastructure: Technological Possibilities and Financial Realities." *Pacific Telecommunications Review* 15(June):11–23.

Román, Enrique. 1994. President, Cuban Radio and Television Institute, interview. Havana, March 4.

Salwen, Michael B. 1994. *Radio and Television in Cuba: The Pre-Castro Era.* Ames: Iowa State University Press.

Schroeder, Susan. 1982. *Cuba: A Handbook of Historical Statistics.* Boston: G. K. Hall & Co.

Shanley, J. P. 1955. "Cuba TV Program Relayed by Plane." *The New York Times,* November 14, p. 52.

Skrzycki, Cindy. 1993. "U.S. Allows Expanded Cuban Phone Service." *Washington Post,* July 24, p. F1.

Smith, Wayne S. and Esteban Morales Dominguez, eds. 1988. *Subject to Solution: Problems in Cuban-U.S. Relations.* Boulder, Colo.: Lynne Rienner Publishers.

Sobel, Robert. 1982. *ITT: The Management of Opportunity.* New York: Times Books.

Soley, Lawrence C. and John S. Nichols. 1987. *Clandestine Radio Broadcasting.* New York: Praeger.

Statistical Abstract of Latin America. 1960. Los Angeles: Center of Latin American Studies, University of California, Los Angeles.

"Statistics on Computer Use, Equipment Noted." 1989. *Foreign Broadcast Information Service—Latin America,* January 25, p. 3.

Szulc, Tad. 1987. *Fidel: A Critical Portrait.* New York: Avon Books.

Torres, Craig. 1994. "Investor Is Raising Funds to Challenge Mexico's Telefonos." *The Wall Street Journal,* June 23, p. A11.

"$20 Millon Planned for Communications Industry." 1989. *Foreign Broadcast Information Service—Latin America,* September 19, p. 4.

United Fruit Company: Un Caso del Dominio Imperialista en Cuba. 1976. Havana: Editorial de Ciencias Sociales.

"U.S. Rejects American Phone Companies' Bid to Expand Links to Cuba." 1993. *CubaINFO* (Johns Hopkins University), March 17, p. 1.

Whitefield, Mimi. 1994. "Mexicans Plan to Buy into Cuba Phones." *Miami Herald,* June 10, p. 22A.

Wilkie, James W., ed. 1990. *Statistical Abstract of Latin America,* Vol. 28. Los Angeles: UCLA Latin American Center Publications.

Wilson, Charles Morrow. 1968. *Empire in Green and Gold: The Story of the American Banana Trade.* New York: Greenwood Press.

Workman, Deborah. 1993. "U.S. Relaxes Terms on Services to Cuba." *Latinoamerica* (TelePress), November/December, pp. 38–39.

Zimbalist, Andrew. 1993. "Dateline Cuba: Hanging On in Havana." *Foreign Policy* 92(Fall):15–16.

3
Jamaica

HOPETON S. DUNN AND WINSTON S. GOODEN

Since the mid-1980s telecommunication in Jamaica has been marked by major restructuring in ownership and controversy over regulatory control. The government's majority ownership in the overall system moved from over 80 percent in 1987 to no equity ownership by 1990, while the British transnational Cable & Wireless moved from a total holding of 9 percent to 79 percent of the overall industry. The separate domestic telephone provider and the international carrier were merged into the single entity, Telecommunications of Jamaica Ltd, creating the Caribbean's largest company in terms of annual turnover.

The reorganization of the sector and the protracted debate it generated highlight the shortcomings of developing-country governments in the areas of telecommunications planning and regulation. The Jamaican debate focused attention on the extensive monopoly rights granted to Telecommunications of Jamaica (TOJ) and the limitations imposed on other local and foreign interests by the all-encompassing terms of the TOJ-C&W license. Because TOJ is 79 percent owned by C&W, the debate was also about the dominant role of external interests in Jamaica's communications sector.

3.1 Jamaica and the Regional Context

Jamaica is the largest of twelve independent, English-speaking Caribbean territories that together with the British colony of Montserrat are the membership of the Caribbean Community and Common Market (CARICOM). The combined population of this grouping is over 5 million, with Jamaica accounting for about half (July 1994 estimates). A mostly mountainous island with a discontinuous, narrow coastal plain, Jamaica has an area of almost 11,000 square kilometers.

Jamaica became independent in 1962. As a former British colony, the government is headed by a prime minister and there is a bicameral parliament. Members of the senate are appointed by the governor general, while the house is elected for a term of up to five years. The economy is based on bauxite, sugar, and tourism.

As a major tourist destination, Jamaica has a large volume of telephone traffic with North America and Europe. This volume is further augmented by a large expatriate Caribbean population living mainly in the United States, Canada, and Britain. Traffic balance figures from the U.S. Federal Communications Commission (FCC) indicated that in 1993 the United States-to-Jamaica route was among the most heavily used, accounting for a higher volume of calls than from the United States to a number of countries with which the United States has greater business relations, including Australia, India, and Nigeria.

Proximity to the large U.S. market and the availability of a literate, English-speaking workforce have stimulated the establishment of information-processing facilities in Jamaica in the form of the export processing zones (EPZs) in Montego Bay with a second one to be established in Portmore, near Kingston, in 1998. For this and other reasons, Jamaica and the wider Caribbean region are regarded by U.S. investors as an important and growing telecom market, with strong additional potential for the development of nonvoice services.

The urban corporate centers of Jamaica, like those elsewhere in the region, are well served by advanced telecom facilities. The main national trunk network is fiber optic and is linked regionally with the Eastern Caribbean Fibre System (ECFS). Both cable and satellite facilities provide alternative transmission modes to the rest of the world. Internally, digital exchanges, as well as mobile and cellular services, combine with the latest information technology applications to offer state-of-the-art services to the corporate sector.

Alongside this advanced, urban, corporate provisioning is an acute deficiency in services to the domestic sector and rural communities. A waiting list of potential subscribers extends many times beyond the existing list of subscribers, and a national penetration rate of about 12 telephones per 100 persons (1996) reflects a skewed pattern mainly in favor of urban households and business users. Despite efforts to increase the number of telephones in the rural areas, there remains a large unserved population. The absence of any explicit policy commitment to universal service has dictated priority attention for urban commercial users and for those subscribers willing to pay the high cost of cellular service.

3.2 Early Development

The British transnational company Cable & Wireless has been the major provider of telecom services in Jamaica and the anglophone Caribbean since the mid-nineteenth century. The company initially operated in the service of the British colonial government as the West India and Panama Telegraph Company, starting as early as in 1868. (For an analysis and history of C&W in the region, see Dunn 1991.) Despite changes, including in name, the company has remained largely unchallenged by external competition over these years.

In the 1960s, during the first decade of political independence in the region, the governments of the larger territories began to strengthen national control over the existing telecom resources. The measures taken included takeover of majority equity of the C&W-operated companies. In Jamaica and in Trinidad and Tobago, government shareholdings in the external telecommunications provider exceeded 51 percent, and in Barbados a 40 percent share was buttressed by the appointment of local managers.

Table 3.1. C&W Caribbean Ownership of Telecom

Country	Local Telco (%)	C&W Ownership in Overseas Carrier (%)
Anguilla	100	100
Bermuda	100	100
British Virgin Islands	100	100
Cayman Islands	100	100
Dominica	100	100
Montserrat	100	100
St. Lucia	100	100
St. Vincent	100	100
Turks Island	100	100
Antigua	0	100
Barbados	85*	85*
St. Kitts	80*	80*
Jamaica	79*	79*
Grenada	70*	70*
Trinidad and Tobago	49*	49*

*Single merged company.

Source: Compiled by H. S. Dunn, CARIMAC 1994.

Although such acquisitions were feasible propositions in the 1960s and early 1970s, when the basic technology of telecommunications was still a relatively stable body of knowledge, global changes in the late 1970s and 1980s have rendered the tasks of management, financing, and control of the national telecom systems more complex (Jonscher 1987; Hills 1986). Thus, during 1987–89 Cable & Wireless reacquired control of Telecommunications of Jamaica (TOJ). With a 79 percent interest, C&W directs overall policy from its corporate headquarters in London. This pattern of reversal in ownership arrangements has been replicated throughout the English-speaking Caribbean. As of early 1995, Cable & Wireless has exclusive licenses and mostly uncontested markets in fifteen Caribbean territories. In nine of these the company is a monopoly operator of both domestic and overseas services, as set out in Table 3.1. The company also controls the international cable and satellite gateway facilities linking the region with the rest of the world.

3.3 Challenges to Policy and Regulation

Analysts of public policy in Jamaica (Duncan 1993; Dunn 1991; Gooden 1994; Ritch 1993) have raised questions about the terms of the present licenses granted to TOJ and Cable & Wireless since 1988. The main license gives the company a twenty-five-year monopoly over all aspects of the local wired telephone network. This period is regarded as unduly generous in a global environment in which seven to ten years is the norm for investment recovery. Other sublicenses held by the company award it similar monopoly privileges in the areas of external telecommunications, wireless telephony, telegraphy, telex, and teleprinter services.

This comprehensive monopoly also included, until early 1995, the right to install or approve all attachments to the network and to levy undefined tariffs for such connections. An agreement before the Fair Trading Commission has required TOJ to allow interconnection of certain basic facilities to the network. However, major customer premises equipment remain within the supply and installation monopoly of the company.

The C&W license also granted the company an annual guaranteed return of between 17.5 and 20 percent on revalued assets, with a provision that "the rate charged for telephone services shall be adjustable annually as necessary to provide the permitted rate of return" (Telecommunications of Jamaica 1988, Section 27:1). "Revalued assets" are used because inflation has been substantial (15 to 80 percent annually since the late 1980s). The assets of the company are valued annually by C&W's independent auditors. These values, subject to the approval of the minster, become the basis for computing the return allowed. The speed with which various categories of equipment are depreciated is set forth in the license. Depreciation is at rates between about 4.5 and 22.5 percent per year, taken on the adjusted value of the asset.

The sole regulatory agency in Jamaica, a Public Utilities Commission, ceased to have oversight of rate setting in telecom services and was later abolished. The 1988 license vested sole regulatory control in the minister of public utilities. The current (1996) minister, who has been in office since 1989, has been closely associated with C&W. In effect, the company has been operating without any independent regulatory institution to represent or protect the public interest.

The controversial licenses were granted in 1988 when majority ownership of TOJ still resided with the government. However, after divestment to a foreign-majority company, the government failed to introduce the necessary regulatory review appropriate to the new ownership regime. Despite some research interventions (Dunn 1991), the matter did not enter the agenda of wider public debate until the closing months of 1993, some three years after the ownership transition. This is in part because telecom policy making in the Caribbean region has traditionally been treated as a private, almost secret arrangement between political and bureaucratic elites in government on the one hand, and the overseas or local operating company on the other. It only emerged as a public issue in this instance because certain documents were leaked to the press, disclosing demands by the company for new government legislation aimed at replacing the long outdated 1893 Telephone Act and at upgrading its monopoly license "to take account of advances in technology."

In response to this C&W demand, the government undertook "to make the necessary amendment to the Act and thereafter to make such amendment to the Telephone License as may be necessary to ensure that TOJ enjoys exclusive rights to provide public telecommunications services in, from and through Jamaica" (official letter from then Prime Minister Michael Manley to TOJ Chairman Mayer Matalon, November 2, 1990). It emerged that the proposed legislation was to be in return for further capital investment in the country by C&W. In the same letter, released only as part of the controversial public debate, TOJ-C&W was asked to "accept the good faith of the government" and to "proceed with its Capital Development Programme on the basis of the above assurances."

Such disclosures indicate the powerful influence of transnational financing in domestic policy making, particularly at a time when IMF-inspired economic policies favored a strong role for these companies. The disclosures, however, gave rise to intense, widespread public criticisms of the policy makers who presided over such secret undertakings and who allowed the company such unregulated privileges. Cable & Wireless itself was criticized for demanding restrictive monopoly rights in the Caribbean while spearheading, through its wholly owned subsidiary, Mercury, the breaking of British Telecom's monopoly in the United Kingdom.

In light of the controversy, the government, under Prime Minister Percival Patterson (who assumed office in March 1992), has undertaken a full review of existing arrangements and has promised greater public transparency in the drafting of a new Telecommunications Act. However, no significant changes in the introduction of competition and further liberalization are expected in this new legislation. The new law will update the outdated 1893 legislation and may further consolidate the hold of C&W on the Jamaican market until 2013, when the main operating license expires.

3.3.1 Tariff Structure

The merger between the domestic telephone company and the international carrier, formalized by an act of Parliament in February 1995, reflects the official policy of cross-subsidization of the costly internal network services by the traditionally lucrative overseas provider. This strategy aims to keep internal rates low even as the network expands to cover a wider range of users. However, there is no explicit acceptance of universal service as corporate strategy or as a national policy objective.

The operating company's guaranteed annual profit of 17.5 to 20 percent on revalued assets means it has the right to demand rate increases to meet this profitability level. During the late 1980s and early 1990s the company has achieved its expected profitability, except in 1988 when it fell short by a narrow margin because of network disruption caused by Hurricane Gilbert.

The tariff structure for international calls is based on the usual carrier ownership of half circuits. The system compensates carriers for interconnecting their half circuits to that of a counterpart carrier on the basis of a 50-50 split of the agreed accounting rate. The level of outpayment by the Jamaican carrier fluctuates, depending on the prevailing rate of exchange against the U.S. dollar.

In Jamaica, the monopoly company has been battling with a group of unauthorized operators attempting to provide users with cheaper overseas calls. In 1989, in an attempt to counter this, the company imposed an International Call Authorization (ICAS) system involving the use of individual ten-digit password codes for all outgoing calls. It also temporarily imposed a ban on collect calls to or from Jamaica as it put new, tighter arrangements into place.

In Jamaica—as in Trinidad and Tobago, Barbados, Japan, and other places— some network users have also resorted to call regeneration systems, under which a brief call is placed to high-tech collaborating firms in the United States, which employ advanced data-compression technologies. The computer-based callback system allows local users to place overseas calls at a fraction of the C&W rate without infringing the legal status of the monopoly operator. Such methods suggest that despite legal barriers, technology and public demand for alternative outlets can combine to circumvent the monopoly arrangements.

3.4 Replica of the Wider Caribbean

Many of the problems and undoubted benefits that have come to the public in the licensing and regulatory arrangements for TOJ also exist to varying degrees among other countries in the developing world. Where telecommunications are run with a free hand by large global transnationals, there is usually a wide range of available services and easy global connectivity. However, from the experience of Jamaica and the Caribbean, this is accompanied by a relative neglect of rural users as the company concentrates on the easily served business and urban sectors. The main variable likely to alter this pattern is systematic government monitoring and regulation of the quality and range of services against a publicly discussed development agenda.

Within the rest of the English-speaking Caribbean region, large telecom users, domestic consumers, and potential investors have been quite closely watching the events involving C&W, TOJ, and the Jamaican authorities.

In 1990 the Caribbean Telecommunications Union (CTU) was formed by state telecommunications authorities in the region.[1] The preamble of its charter "recognises the sovereign right of each State to regulate its telecommunications system." Based in Trinidad, CTU aims to promote information exchange among telecom operators; encourage the transfer of technology among member countries; coordinate standards and the planning, programming, and development of the regional and international network; harmonize Caribbean positions at international conferences; and foster greater awareness in the Caribbean of both telecommunications needs and the importance of the sector for social and economic development.

The region's national governments have, however, neglected to provide adequate resources for the effective operation of CTU, and they continue to rely heavily on C&W. However, the Jamaican debate, unprecedented for this sector, underlines the increasing importance with which telecommunication is being viewed both by influential sections of the wider public in the region and by potential U.S.-based competitors to the C&W monopoly. Information processing companies, cable television operators, cellular telephone operators, broadcasters, and domestic telephone users are just some of the diverse interest groups demanding a share of the tightly controlled market.

3.5 The Future: Regulatory Reform and Diversification

In response to criticisms about the need for institutional regulation of the sector, the Jamaican government has established a central Office of Utilities Regulation (OUR) with departments for electricity, water, public transport, aeronautical services, and telecommunications. The telecom division provides advice to the minister and serves as a central focus for national policy making and reform. This represents an important advance on the existing system, even if falling short of the "independent" institutions that exist in some countries.

The approach of combining the regulation of all utilities under a single agency is argued as a cost-saving measure. However, its scope runs counter to the more focused approach, which seeks to combine telecommunications, broadcasting, and information services as a dynamic growth sector having strategic implications for all other sectors of the economy (Dunn 1995).

3.6 Conclusion

The experiences of Jamaica and the Caribbean highlight the need for greater advisory support by the ITU's Development Bureau to small and developing countries negotiating with major transnational interests such as Cable & Wireless. After all, these countries are also ITU members, albeit with a different set of needs and support requirements than those being advanced by the powerful, industrialized members.

This assistance should be geared toward strengthening existing local research and regulatory institutions and encouraging regional joint bargaining, bulk purchasing, and skills development.

Many technological innovations are likely to play an important role in undermining the legislated monopoly arrangements of the traditional carriers. Continued refinements of satellite communication systems, cellular and other mobile technologies, and data compression and call regeneration services, as well as the increasing voice capacity of the Internet, are expected to lay the basis for increased network competition and improved access and diversity in rural and urban domestic services. At the same time, a major improvement in the systems of regulation and management of the technologies is an urgent requirement if the benefits of these innovations are to extend to all social classes in societies such as Jamaica and others in the global south.

Note

1. In this regard, CTU differs from the Caribbean Association of National Telecommunication Organizations (CANTO), discussed in chapter 1, which includes privately owned telecom companies as members.

References

Brock, Gerald W. 1981. *The Telecommunications Industry: Dynamics of Market Structure.* Cambridge, Mass.: Harvard University Press.

Duncan, Donald K. 1993. "Pickersgill, TOJ and Us." *Jamaica Herald,* November 28, p. 7A.

Dunn, Hopeton S. 1991. "Telecommunications and Underdevelopment: A Policy Analysis of the Historical Role of Cable and Wireless in the Caribbean." Ph.D. diss. City University, London.

_____. 1993. "Telecommunications Policy in the Caribbean." Paper presented at the 28th Annual Conference of the Caribbean Studies Association, Jamaica Pegasus Hotel, May 24–29.

_____, ed. 1995. *Globalization, Communication and Caribbean Identity.* New York and Kingston, Jamaica: St. Martin's Press and Ian Randle Publishers.

Gooden, Winston. 1994. "Lost Telecommunications Opportunities." *Sunday Gleaner,* June 19, p. 10B.

Hills, Jill. 1986. *Deregulating Telecoms: Competition and Control in the United States, Japan and Britain.* London: Frances Pinter.

International Telecommunications Union. 1993. "The Changing Role of Government in an Era of Telecom Deregulation—Report of a Colloquium." February 19–29. Geneva: ITU.

Jonscher, Charles. 1987. "Telecommunications Investments: Quantifying the Benefits." In *Telecommunications for Development—Exploring New Strategies.* Washington, D.C.: Intelsat.

Manley, Michael. 1990. Letter to TOJ Chairman, Mayer Matalon. Jamaica House, Kingston, November 2.

Ritch, Dawn. 1993. "A Telecommunications 'Plantation.'" *Sunday Gleaner,* November 14, p. 8A.

Spiller, Pablo T., and Cezley I. Sampson. 1992. *Regulation, Institutions and Commitment: The Jamaican Telecommunication Sector.* A World Bank Report. Washington, D.C., June 5.

Telecommunications of Jamaica. 1988. "All Island Telephone Licence." Kingston, Jamaica: TOJ.

_____. 1993. *Annual Report 1993.* Kingston, Jamaica: TOJ.

4

Guatemala

SHERYL RUSSELL

Guatemala, in the context of Central America, is best described with superlatives: the biggest population, the biggest economy, the fastest growing GDP, the biggest labor force, and the richest cultural legacy. However, a privileged few have long dominated a large underclass. A legacy of this rule by elites is a country riddled with social, political, and economic inequalities. Other problems relate to the country's position within the global economic system. Guatemala is a rural country with an agriculture-based economy. As such, it is heavily dependent on agricultural exports—principally coffee, bananas, and sugar—and suffers from fluctuations in the prices of these products.

Some 60 percent of the population of 10.8 million (July 1994 estimate) live in rural areas—the highest percentage of rural population for any country in Central America—and over half the labor force of 2.8 million work in the agricultural sector (July 1992 estimate). There is an extremely high population growth rate, despite emigration.

The country encompasses about 109,000 square kilometers. There is a narrow plain on the Pacific coast and a small lowland area on the Caribbean side. The rest of the southern half of the country is mountains and plateau. This highland area is where most of the population lives. Guatemala City, the capital, lies at about 1,500 meters in a valley surrounded by mountains and volcanos. It houses well over 20 percent of the population. Petén, one of twenty-two departments (provinces) makes up the northern part of the country. It is a lowland tropical area with few people.

Mayans, concentrated in the northern part of the highlands, account for almost half the population. Many speak only their Mayan dialect. Most of the rest of the population are *ladinos* (mestizos and Spanish-speaking Mayans). In rural areas, 80 percent of the inhabitants are illiterate.

4.1 Background

The Spanish arrived in the country in the early 1500s, and by 1700 the capital of Guatemala was the center of power for the Central American region. Independence initially came in 1821, but Guatemala was part of the Central American Federation until it broke up in 1838. The country was ruled by authoritarian leaders, many from the military, from then until 1944. After a ten-year period of civilian rule and reform, military governments returned to power for most of the next three decades.

As part of a shift from subsistence farming to a plantation-based economy, coffee became a major crop in the late nineteenth century and bananas in the early twentieth. Great Britain was a significant investor in Central America during the nineteenth century, but it was eventually surpassed by the United States and Germany. By 1929 U.S. investors in Guatemala were major land owners and held railroads and the principal electric utility company. United Fruit was a dominant force; its land holdings were expropriated in 1950 but returned in 1954.

The economy grew steadily during the 1960s and 1970s, with real GDP increases averaging about 6 percent a year. However, in the early 1980s GDP actually declined because of external economic conditions and internal policy failures. The civilian government elected in 1985 made initial progress in reducing inflation and restoring growth. However, in part because poor tax administration led to a decline in revenue, the government faced a series of crises throughout the decade and into the early 1990s. In order to offset internal fiscal crises, each new administration continued policies favoring competition, foreign trade, and investment (foreign and domestic).

Despite an open investment climate and steady GDP growth in the early 1990s, the government again faced a fiscal crisis in 1994. This was partly because of its failure to pass tax reforms. (Guatemala has one of the lowest income tax rates in the Western Hemisphere, due to resistance by its wealthy elite.) The political and economic instability led President Ramiro de Leon Carpio to call on the armed forces to take charge of internal security.

4.2 Early Telecommunications Development

In 1881 the country's first telecommunications lines were installed, linking the capital city with Antigua. By 1884 lines had been extended to Quetzaltenango. In 1890, a newly organized private company, Telefonos de Guatemala, assumed control of all telecommunications services.

The state intervened in 1916, taking over all Telefonos operations. Service, local and domestic long distance, was thereafter provided by La Direccion General de Telefonos y El Proyecto Telefonico (The General Directorate of Telephones and the Telephone Project). In 1927 the first automatic telephone exchange was introduced.

In 1926 a privately held foreign company, Tropical Radio and Telephone, was permitted to provide international telecommunications services. In 1966 the operation was nationalized.

4.2.1 Guatel

Empresa Guatemalteca de Telecomunicaciones (Guatel) was established on April 14, 1971, by Decree 14-71 as a government entity with a monopoly on local, national, and international telecommunications services.

A board of directors oversees the company, but the general manager and deputy general manager have a great deal of authority. Telecommunications are under the authority of the Ministry of Transport and Communications (MTC). The National Economic Planning Council (CONAPLAN) advises Guatel on tariff issues and investments. The Ministry of Finance provides guidelines for foreign borrowing.

4.3 The Present Situation

In the early 1990s the government began considering privatization and liberalization in the telecommunications sector, and the issue of privatizing Guatel has come before Congress several times. It is highly unlikely Guatel will be privatized any time soon, and the pace and timing of liberalization is indeterminate.

Private networks, value-added services, and rural telephony are the areas most likely to see liberalization. Two companies, Telepuerto SA and Empritel, won concessions in 1990 to provide IBS (Intelsat business service) for Guatemala City and the rest of the country. They offer point-to-point service on a nonexclusive basis for private commercial, agricultural, industrial, and tourism enterprises. Modes of transmission include FM, Single Channel Per Carrier (SCPC), and Time Division Multiple Access (TDMA).

Red tape and bureaucratic delays complicate business transactions in Guatemala. Purchases by government-owned entities are covered by the Government Procurement Law (Decree 35-80, modified by Decree 112-85). Purchases exceeding U.S.$65,000 must be made through public bidding, with a minimum of five bidders. Foreign bidders must have a locally registered representative, but wholly owned subsidiaries can be registered as local entities. For all foreign firms operating in Guatemala, managers must at least be temporary residents. Often, attorneys are used as local representatives or managers. Foreign investors are by law treated as nationals. There are no legal limits on repatriation of profits.

4.3.1 Telecommunications Services

In the metropolitan area (Guatemala City and its suburbs), 94,403 calls were received requesting repair service during 1993, against an installed base of about 179,000 lines. By the end of the year all but 0.11 percent had been resolved. Elsewhere in Guatemala, 10,075 calls were received, against an installed base of about 50,000 lines, with about 5 percent still pending at year-end. The capital has ten service bureaus, and another fifty-nine are located elsewhere in Guatemala. No new sales or service agencies have been added since 1991.

Guatel's revenue reached U.S.$168.3 million in 1993, 11 percent higher than 1992. International services provided over 74 percent of this, domestic long distance about 11 percent, and local service just over 4 percent (but it was up 20 percent). Telex and telegraph continued to decline, representing about 1 percent of revenue. Telex lines in service decreased from 1,131 to 948 between 1991 and 1993, and usage dropped by over half. Most telegraph traffic, about 124,846 words in 1993, is destined for Central America.

Table 4.1. Guatel's Labor Force, 1992

Categories	Number of Employees
Management	206
Planning and Design	123
Execution and Supervision	693
Maintenance	1,431
Marketing	1,341
Human Resources	579
Finance	201
IT and General Systems	96
International	269
Total	4,939

Source: Guatel, *Annual Report,* 1992.

Users are embracing newer technologies such as data transmission over leased lines. Guatel offers a service called Mayapaq that permits users to access e-mail, electronic funds transfer, international databases, and private virtual networks. Lines in service have gone from 247 in 1991 to 343 in 1992 to 628 in 1993, when they generated U.S.$1 million in revenues.

Intelsat business services is a high-speed data network offered since 1992. It can carry data, voice, fax, and video, and is provided via a terrestrial station at Jezriel linked to an Intelsat satellite. Comsat, based in Bethesda, Maryland, is working to provide high-speed data transfer, videoconferencing, fax, and private voice services using an eleven-meter earth station in Guatemala City. IBS pricing is based in part on contract length, although the breaks are not large: in 1994 the service ranged from U.S.$4,500 a month on a contract of up to four years to U.S.$4,000 a month on a ten-year contract. Installation was U.S.$3,000.

The project to provide cellular service to the capital and its environs, as well as to the Pacific port of San José, was more than 90 percent complete in early 1994.

4.3.2 Guatel's Labor Force

Guatel at first glance appears to be bucking the global trend toward downsizing, having increased its labor force from 4,939 in 1992 (Table 4.1) to 5,333 in 1993. However, the number of employees per thousand lines remained constant at about 23. This was a decided improvement over 1988, when the ratio was 36.

Guatel has been investing heavily in training. Courses were conducted for over 32 percent of its workforce in 1993.

4.4 The Network

Guatemala's network is very limited. In 1993 there were only 231,000 main lines, equivalent to 2.3 per 100 inhabitants (Table 4.2). However, too narrow a focus on

Table 4.2.   Guatemala's Telecommunications Network, 1987–1993

	1987	1988	1989	1990	1991	1992	1993
Density	1.56	1.56	1.59	1.77	2.06	2.25	2.30
Lines		138,222	158,840	190,218	202,209	214,409	231,090
Public Telephones	1,096	1,120	2,062	2,079	2,093	2,251	2,371
Telex	1,373	1,373	1,345	1,257	1,131	1,040	948

Source: Sheryl Russell, *Latin America Telecom Operators.* New York: CPG Research.

telecom development, relying only on the criterion of general teledensity, is apt to miss variations or imbalances favoring urban areas. Thus businesses, the elite, and even the middle class in Guatemala City have access to a fairly modern network. About 75 percent of subscribers are residential; the rest are industrial, commercial, and governmental.

Moreover, the system has been expanding: the number of lines increased over two-thirds from 1988 to 1993. Guatel is slowly but steadily increasing digitalization of its network, at the rate of about 2 percentage points annually. The overall percentage of digital lines had reached 46 percent in 1993. However, not all new lines are digital because they are being added to existing analog central office switches that had unused capacity.

The poor and rural areas have not been overlooked. The number of public telephones went from 1,096 in 1987 to 2,062 in 1989, an 88 percent increase. Of these, 73 percent are in Guatemala City. The country's ambitious expansion and modernization plans called for extending service to about 100 *poblaciones* (farms, villages, and country houses) per year from 1988 through 1992. Guatel defines basic service for each community as five telephones: two for the community and three for private or official use. However, such plans have repeatedly been stopped at various stages of completion because of political instability and lack of investment funds. Thus, after a strong start in 1988, with 172 *poblaciones* acquiring service, the next three years saw fewer than 100 get service. In 1992 another 166 were added, bringing the total to 436.

Guatel has a history of exploring relationships with foreign carriers. In 1994 it worked with AT&T to study the possibility of offering international toll-free service to the United States.

Telephone service extends to all twenty-two provinces in the country but not to all towns.

Guatel's domestic network consisted of 126 central office switches in service in 1993, up from 119 in 1992. Suppliers include Siemens, Italtel, NEC, and Ericsson. In the early 1990s Guatel invested U.S.$19.8 million to expand existing Ericsson AXE exchanges and add two new ones. In 1988 Bell South International provided consulting services for the installation of switches provided by Ericsson and Italtel.

In 1993 Guatel was in the final phase of a U.S.$17.1 million expansion of Italtel UT exchanges in urban and suburban areas. In another project, 50,000 lines were added in the capital in 1994. A total of U.S.$36.9 million was financed by U.S. entities. In addition, seven new exchanges were being installed to expand and interconnect metropolitan networks. This project includes a fiber-optic ring

Table 4.3. 1993 Project for Expansion of Exchanges

Location	Lines	Trunks
La Floresta		11,940
Reformita		21,030
Villa de Guadalupe	20,976	
El Pueblito	1,024	
La Pradera	3,000	
Centro I	15,000	
Lourdes		15,780
Lourdes III	6,114	
Parroquia III	6,114	

Source: Sheryl Russell, *Latin America Telecom Operators.* New York: CPG Research.

for the metropolitan area, 33,000 interurban trunk lines, 16,000 transit trunks, and 52,000 subscriber lines added to various exchanges, as illustrated in Table 4.3. The U.S.$25.7 million investment in this project is allocated among Siemens (U.S.$13.3 million), Alcatel (U.S.$3.4 million), and Italtel (U.S.$1.8 million). In April 1994 the project was about 24 percent complete.

In early 1994 Guatel was about 50 percent done with a project with MCI to install combined local-transit central offices in Monte Verde and Guarda Viejo (parts of metropolitan Guatemala City)—a total of about 40,000 lines. The project with AT&T to install about 13,200 local trunks, 2,800 interurban trunks, 1,000 international trunks, and 40,000 lines was about 58 percent complete. Both these projects were behind schedule, having originally been scheduled for completion in 1992 and August 1993, respectively.

In 1992, Alcatel was awarded a contract to digitalize the Intelsat Standard A earth station in Quetzal, which is jointly owned by Guatel and Comsat.

4.4.1 International Telecommunications

Guatel had 778 international circuits in service in 1993, up from 765 in 1992. Of these, 519 circuits are to the United States. All three major U.S. long-distance operators (AT&T, MCI, and Sprint) have circuits, as does Telécommunications, Radioélectriques et Teléphoniques (TRT). This is consistent with the fact the United States is the most-called country, receiving 17 million minutes out of 23 million (74 percent) of outgoing calling. Mexico, Canada, and South America account for most of the remaining calls; the rest of Central America is responsible for about 4 percent of outgoing call minutes.

In early 1995 Guatel was in the final phase of constructing its portion of the Central American microwave network. Capacity of up to 1,920 channels is being installed in Acatempa, Santa Elena Barillas, Torre de Guatel, Cerro Alux, Calderas, La Selva, and El Paraiso. The contractor for this U.S.$4.3 million project is Telesistemas (a venture of Telettra and Alcatel).

A digital microwave route to Petén and Mexico was begun in 1993. Intended to provide an alternative routing and to increase capacity (by 1,920 channels), it was about 24 percent complete in early 1994. Guatel is providing its own personnel to install the system, which has been supplied by Telettra and is being paid for by the government.

International calling from Guatemala is very expensive. In 1993 the cost of a three-minute (the minimum billing period) station-to-station call from Guatemala to Costa Rica was U.S.$3.60, with each additional minute U.S.$0.90. Calls to the United States were U.S.$3.00 a minute; to Europe, U.S.$7.50.

4.2.2 Rural Telephony

Rural telephony has been extended under a series of projects. In 1990 a grant agreement was signed between the United States Trade Development Program (TDP) and Guatel to finance the preparation of technical specifications and cost estimates.

The most recent rural telephony project, Phase III, cost U.S.$19.2 million and was financed by external sources. Contractors included Mitsui & Company, Ericsson de Guatemala, Italtel, Siemens, Mansilla, Mayorga, Metrotel, Telectro, Asaf, Sistec, Ruracom, and Conelca. The project was 70 percent complete at the end of 1992 and 90 percent complete at the end of 1993.

A national digital transmission network will be installed to create the backbone for Phase IV, which will install 17,700 lines in 154 municipal districts and 575 rural locations. Sources in the United States are providing a substantial part of the funding for this project. In another project, existing Italtel UT-20 exchanges in the provinces will be expanded.

Separately, a pilot plan to provide rural telephony via satellite led to at least ten stations being installed in isolated areas, including the tourist center of Tikal. Due to the success of the plan, Guatel is installing satellite service in another 100 towns. This project was about 16 percent complete in early 1994.

4.4.3 Equipment

Guatemala imports all of its telephone switching equipment. There is some local assembly of radio receivers, small VHF transceivers, television sets, and satellite television signal receiving antennas. Guatel used to assemble telephone sets to be sold to new subscribers but discontinued this practice in 1986. U.S. suppliers, such as AT&T, overtook Siemens and other German suppliers in 1992 to become the leading source of telephone systems, switching equipment, and accessories. Most foreign suppliers operate through domestically incorporated subsidiaries.

Guatemala's imports are subject to the General Treaty for Central American Economic Integration and the Central American convention of Equalization of Import Duties and Charges. Telephone and switching equipment are subject to an ad-valorem duty of 5 percent, based on Circuit Imprime Français (CIF) value, plus a value-added tax of 7 percent, plus an import tax surcharge of 3 percent. Telephone equipment can be imported without restrictions, provided the applicable duties are paid.

Guatel follows general Consultative Committee on International Telegraph and Telephone (CCITT) technical standards for purchasing equipment, and systems complying with these standards do not have to be altered technically for the local market.

4.5 Cable Television

There are about thirty-four registered cable television systems under the umbrella of one firm, Intercable SA. Another fifty to fifty-five nonregistered cable systems offer services that include programming originating in both Mexico and in the United States. Altogether, there are over 160,000 cable subscribers. Another 4,500 have imported and installed their own equipment. In 1992 Guatemala cracked down on commercial operators by prohibiting the pirated use of satellite television transmissions.

4.6 Conclusion

Guatemala recognizes that telecommunications infrastructure is essential to development, and the country has ambitious plans to modernize and expand services. Guatel has managed to make respectable progress since 1988. This includes an increase in lines of more than 67 percent (1988–93), which helped make the network 46 percent digital; introduction of Mayapaq in 1989; introduction of IBS in 1992; and a 100 percent increase in community telephones in 1993 (albeit from a small base).

Guatemala's low telephone density and continued economic development call out for investment in its telecommunications network. Pent-up demand will continue to drive telecommunications development in basic and enhanced services.

References

Cooper, Patricia and Jae Chung. 1994. "Guatemala: Telecommunications Market." Report prepared by Office of Telecommunications, U.S. Department of Commerce.

Crow, John A. 1992. *The Epic of Latin America.* Berkeley: University of California Press.

Empresa Guatemalteca de Telecomunicaciones (GUATEL). 1994. *Resumen Estadistico Guatel 1993.* Division de Planeamiento y Diseno, April.

Fundesa (Guatemalan Development Foundation). 1993. *Viva Guatemala: Investment Opportunities.*

"Guatemala: On the Brink." 1994. *The Economist,* April 9, p. 50.

"Guatemala: Out, Out." 1993. *The Economist,* June 5, p. 45.

LaFeber, Walter. 1993. *Inevitable Revolutions: The United States in Central America.* New York: W.W. Norton & Company.

Memoria de Labores 1992. 1992. Empresa Guatemalteca de Telecomunicaciones (GUATEL).

Russell, Sheryl. *Latin America: Telecom Operators.* New York: CPG Research.

Winn, Peter. 1995. *Americas: The Changing Face of Latin America and the Caribbean.* Berkeley: University of California Press.

5
Nicaragua

ALEJANDRA HERRERA

Telecommunications development in Nicaragua fell behind the general growth of telecommunications in Latin America and the Caribbean beginning in the 1970s, and particularly after the 1972 earthquake. Thus, between 1975 and 1980 the annual growth of lines was only 7.2 percent, compared with 10.8 percent in the region. In the 1980s this relative underdevelopment became even more pronounced: annual growth of just 4.7 percent against 6.6 percent. However, in the early 1990s the situation began to improve as a result of substantial state investment in both the expansion and modernization of the system.

This chapter looks briefly at the improvements in the network and then discusses the pending plan to privatize the state-owned operating telco, including the regulatory issues it raises.

5.1 Background

Nicaragua has a population of 4.1 million (July 1994 estimate) and a high birthrate. Migration to the cities in search of jobs and because of the dislocations of the civil war has made the country predominantly urban. The country has a total area of about 129,000 square kilometers. The low (generally under 2,000 meters) Sierra Amerique separates the Caribbean watershed from those of Lake Nicaragua and the Pacific Ocean.

As a republic, Nicaragua has a unicameral National Assembly and a president. During the 1980s the country was ruled by a junta dominated by the Sandinista National Liberation Front (FSLN), which had come to power in 1979 after a civil war that overthrew the Somoza government. The United States, which has a long history of intervention in Nicaraguan affairs, reacted to the Sandinistas' revolution by imposing a trade embargo.

The war and the embargo have increased the difficult socioeconomic situation in Nicaragua, given that the government has not found an adequate solution to the crisis, which has destabilized the economy and, in the second half of the 1980s, caused hyperinflation. During 1980–89 GDP per capita declined an average of 5 percent a year, real wages by 35 percent (World Bank 1991).

Because of its share of charges for calls made into the country from overseas, TELCOR, the state-owned phone company, became the main source of foreign currency for the Sandinista government. The government used the funds for its other needs. As a result of the embargo and lacking foreign exchange, TELCOR could not buy modern equipment on the international market. The technological changes spreading through the industry elsewhere in the world thus passed Nicaragua by.

Elections held in February 1990 brought Violeta Barrios de Chamorro to office as president and gave a majority to the UNO, a ten-party alliance. The Sandinistas (FSLN) became the major opposition party. The country has subsequently moved toward a more market-oriented economy, helped by substantial foreign aid, including amounts from the United States and the international banks like the World Bank and the International Monetary Fund. Many problems remain, including the significant gaps in wealth that contributed to the FSLN's success in the 1978–79 revolution and the power and influence the FSLN still has. In 1995 GDP per capita was only about U.S.$415, according to World Bank estimates (although on a purchasing-power basis it was substantially higher).

It should be stressed that Nicaragua's telephone density is eighth among the fifty-four countries with a 1992 per capita GDP of less than U.S.$635 per year (UIT 1994a). Underdevelopment of the telecommunications network is a reliable indicator of overall economic underdevelopment in Nicaragua.

5.2 Previous Structure

The evolution of telecom services supply was from the beginning closely linked to the military. From 1944 to August 1971 an administrative department of the Ministry of Defense, the Dirección General de Comunicaciones (DGC), was in charge of telecommunications. Then, under the presidency of Anastasio Somoza Debayle, the Dirección General de Telecomunicaciones y Correos (DGTC) was formed as a state corporate entity. DGTC supplied all postal and telecom services with the exception of the National Radio, and it could establish companies or acquire participation in domestic and foreign companies with similar goals. These companies could have the same franchises and privileges that TELCOR received.

When they came to power in 1979 the Sandinistas did not implement significant formal changes in the structure of the sector; it was, after all, already owned and controlled by the state.

In June 1982, the Instituto Nicaragüense de Telecomunicaciones y Correo (TELCOR) was founded, inheriting the powers and duties of the DGTC. This meant TELCOR was a state monopoly but was open to the possibility of an association with private capital to form new communications companies. An essential difference between TELCOR and DGTC was in matters of planning and project execution: TELCOR had greater decision-making power regarding organization and internal rules and could draft general regulation and tariffs subject to approval by the junta.

Although formally independent, both TELCOR and its predecessor DGTC were very dependent on the executive power, specifically three members of the Junta de Gobierno de Reconstrucción Nacional, which was the supreme power in the country, because their heads (who held the rank of minister) and three princi-pal deputies (ranked as vice ministers) all were appointed by the junta.

The regulatory framework of the sector was extremely weak. In addition to the omission of important procedures, such as a methodology for setting rates, the regulatory framework had been created before the spread of microelectronics and, consequently, is not able to face the challenges posed by new technology. The governing legislation also does not address such things as the conditions for inter-connection between domestic networks. The reasons are understandable: the issues did not have any importance when the only services that could be supplied were those of voice transmission, and the services were considered natural monopolies already in the hands of a totally state-owned company.

5.3 The Telephone System in the Early 1990s

At the end of 1993 the basic services network had an installed capacity of 93,026 lines, equal to a density of 1.6 telephones per 100 people. Behind this there are deep regional inequalities: metro Managua has 63 percent of installed lines and a density of 5.2, while the rest of the country has a density of only 0.7.[1]

The introduction of digital technology started in 1991, along with a policy of diversification of equipment suppliers. Of the 58,000 digital lines in 1993, 1,247 were installed in the metropolitan area in 1991 and the rest in 1992. This means over 60 percent of the country's total lines in 1993 were installed in 1992, and that 62 percent of total lines are digital. Digitalization was focused on two regions (the third and the fourth) and was almost completely nonexistent elsewhere. Informa-tion and data transportation services are completely digital.

Samsung and Alcatel have become the major suppliers. Prior to the Sandinista government, Siemens had been the almost exclusive source. During the Sandin-ista period, as a consequence of the economic embargo, TELCOR bought cross-bar exchanges from RFT, an East German company, for use in the second region.

There are no reliable data on the quality of services. From interviews it can be inferred that, even though the scope of services is very limited—basic wire and wireless telephony, fax, telex, and a very modest data transmission network—the quality is relatively high, as is appropriate for what has become in large part a rel-atively new system.

5.3.1 Pricing and Installation

Service applicants pay U.S.$33 for installation of an automatic telephone, U.S.$132 for a telex. (All calculations use the February 1995 exchange rate, approximately 7.55 córdobas per U.S. dollar.) The monthly tariff is U.S.$6.62, which includes 600 message units. Additional message units cost 0.73 U.S. cents. A one-minute call requires two units locally, six within a region, and twelve if interregional. These rates are not high, but a large part of the population does not have the means to afford them. The national public services offered from TELCOR branches or a phone booth cost U.S.$0.132 for the first three minutes of a local phone call.

These rates have been in effect since February 1, 1994, and represent a substantial price increase for domestic calls, but a major decrease for installation (the fee had been U.S.$182, so the charge dropped some 80 percent) and international calls (which fell by up to 27 percent). The previous monthly fee had been U.S.$1.75 and the cost of a message unit had been 0.22 U.S. cents, so the new rates were more than 278 and 233 percent higher, respectively.

5.4 Toward Privatization of TELCOR

The government headed by President Chamorro, which assumed office in April 1990, plans to expand the participation of private capital to every sector. Thus, in 1992 it allowed private parties to begin supplying wireless telephone services and public phone booths, as well as radio communications and television.

On October 15, 1992, a "bonds compensation system" (*sistema de compensación por medio de bonos*) was created. Its purpose is to compensate the owners of property that, in the judgment of the current government, was improperly seized by the Sandinistas. Payment is with fifteen-year bonds that will be redeemed from the proceeds of privatizing some state-owned companies, including TELCOR. The decree establishing the system provides for privatization of TELCOR within four years.

As a condition of receiving foreign assistance, the Nicaraguan government had agreed with the World Bank, the International Development Bank, and the International Monetary Fund to implement privatization within this period. Nicaragua has one of the highest per capita levels of external debt in the world and desperately needs external resources.

Immediately after approval of the compensation system, some important steps were taken toward privatizing companies. A temporary regulatory entity was created (DIGITEL) as a department of TELCOR. An evaluation of companies interested in becoming the main shareholder and administrator of TELCOR was begun. On January 12, 1994, it was announced that nine (of eleven) applicants fulfilled the requirements. These were AT&T, Cable & Wireless, France Telecom, GTE, Korea Telecom, Singapore Telecom, Sprint, Stet, and Telefónica International (a subsidiary of Telefónica España). The next step was to evaluate their bids.

5.4.1 Delay

The original schedule for privatization had to be modified because of passage of Law 169 of January 19, 1994. This law prevents privatization of services provided by the state unless the legislature has approved the specific proposed privatization, the creation of a regulatory entity, and the regulatory framework.

The consequence has been a freeze of the process for many months. The authorities had to; they could not continue until the National Assembly approved two laws introduced by the executive to meet the requirements of Law 169. Approval had become hostage to discussion regarding constitutional reforms. The executive earlier had refused to agree to changes to the National Constitution that had been approved by the Assembly. These changes have given the legislature power over some functions that have been exclusively under the authority of the executive. They have also made it impossible for the current president's brother-in-law to be a candidate in the next (November 1996) presidential election. This is intended to impede creation of family dynasties and is motivated by the country's memory of the Somoza family, which ruled from 1936 to 1979.

The circumstances in which the new telecommunications law will finally be approved (creating a new regulatory body), permitting the privatization of TEL-COR, will give rise to a political war over the passage of constitutional reforms. The specific questions concerning the sector that need regulation are relatively secondary to the discussion in the National Assembly.

5.5 The Draft Laws

In what follows, I analyze the main characteristics of the draft of the two laws introduced by the executive to meet the requirements of Law 169.

5.5.1 The Law of Telecommunications and Postal Services

The draft of this law (*Ley de Telecomunicaciones y Servicios Postales*) addresses only the development of telephone and related services; it is relatively incomplete regarding broadcasting. Still, it is adequate in everything related to the regulation of the convergence of telephony, television, and radio that will determine telecommunications development during the next decades.

An independent regulatory organization, named TELCOR (the same as the operating telco, which certainly can create confusion), will be created. Its structure, rules, and budget are not defined by the law, which means it is not possible to know if it will be able to effectively perform the functions for which it is being created. Its powers are to decide the level of competition for each type of service; to modify the classification of services created by the law (a classification that is very confusing); to authorize transfer of control and share ownership to private companies (that is, in effect, privatization); and to oversee transfers of licenses and of concessions (which will be granted by auction).

It is intended to create a competitive environment. Firms having more than one concession or license must manage the businesses independently, including separate accounting systems.

Regarding pricing, the law is imprecise, except that rates will be determined in a way that does not allow cross-subsidies. Charges for interconnection can be established by individual agreement between the companies and do not have to be published; regulators will intervene only if the parties cannot reach an agreement.

Foreign governments will not be allowed as shareholders in companies granted concessions or licenses. This could be interpreted as an obstacle to the participation of several European operators having their home state as an important shareholder. For example, subsidiaries of France Telecom and Telefónica de España both passed the prebid qualification process for purchasing TELCOR.

Based on available information, it is difficult to determine what the characteristics of the sector's structure will be and, in particular, what the possible levels of competition are. This is because these issues will be defined by decisions taken by the regulatory body once it begins functioning.

5.5.2 Privatization Ratification

The draft law ratifying privatization (*Ley de Ratificación del Instrumento Legal de Incorporación de Particulares en la Operación y Ampliación de los Servicios Telefónicos*) makes some specific points about the new company but leaves unanswered a number of others.

The new company is to provide nationwide basic telephone services, the maximum rates for which will be set by the regulatory authority. There are obligatory goals regarding expansion, modernization, and increase of service quality to be reached by the end of 1997. For one, the company must by then provide 6 telephones per 100 people. However, goals related to rural areas and additional public telephones have not been defined with precision.

The company will have monopoly rights to supply certain services, but it is not precisely specified which services these are. Indeed, there are inaccuracies regarding classification of services spread throughout the draft of the law. In addition, it can operate in areas open to competition. There is an obligation to permit interconnection of other networks, but the criteria regarding conditions and tariffs are not defined.

The state will retain a "golden share," giving it veto power on issues such as increases in capital or the company's liquidation, and initially it will hold 49 percent of the equity, with the probability of selling it later. Employees will be given 1 percent and have the option to buy an additional 10 percent. Administrative control and 40 percent of equity will be awarded in an international public auction. It is not explicit what type of shares each category of buyer will receive: in Mexico and Argentina, for example, different groups of buyers have received different classes of shares with different rights and restrictions.

The conditions regarding resale of shares by employees are not established. In particular, it is not clear how employees will participate in management. If participation is linked directly to share ownership, it is possible restrictions would be placed on marketability of the shares. It does seem that the general public will not be shareholders, at least initially.

5.6 Conclusion

The pending regulatory framework proposes that a privatized TELCOR hold monopolistic power in several services for seven years and, at the same time, grants it the possibility of supplying other, competitive services. This type of arrangement has a tremendous potential for abusive practices, and international experience shows it requires a sophisticated regulatory structure to prevent them. The regulator must be able to gather information, process it, and make decisions regarding such complex issues as predatory pricing and using profits from monopoly services to subsidize competitive ones. Moreover, in Nicaragua's case, where the administrator and principal owner of the operating telco will be foreign, regulators may face negotiations where the international companies' interests are supported by its home government through diplomatic pressure.

Indeed, this type of regulatory situation has generated difficulties even in developed countries. Therefore, in Nicaragua, given the imprecise way in which the scope of the monopoly has been demarcated and the indefiniteness regarding the conditions and costs of interconnection, this mix of monopoly and competition can easily become the source of ongoing conflict among the companies and between them and the regulatory entity.

Having a monopoly is what will allow the company to finance the investments needed to fulfill the agreed goals of expansion and quality improvement. This suggests the government's intention is to authorize rates that would not be possible in a competitive situation.

In addition, allowing a monopoly of international service with "excess" profits can be justified if the intention is to increase the price someone will pay for TEL-COR. It should be emphasized that accepting a lower price is a subsidy to the investment required of the buyer, which can make the granting of monopolistic power superfluous.

At the same time, one of the problems the country faces is the difficulty of part of the population to pay rates that reflect real costs, let alone generate profits that can be reinvested in the system. It can therefore be understood that the government is thinking of allowing cross-subsidies among customers who have different price elasticities. Some TELCOR officials have expressed opposition to the cross-subsidy alternative, and the draft Law of Telecommunications also expresses a philosophy contrary to such subsidies. So far, rate restructuring has presumably reduced cross-subsidies because the cost of long-distance calls has fallen relative to the cost of local service.

Granting a monopoly in international services to finance investment in local services and then saying you will not permit cross-subsidies among services are contradictory positions.

If international telephony is not going to be allowed to generate "excess" profits to finance investments in the domestic network, there is no reason not to permit immediate competition in this area, which has many potential players and relatively low capital costs to establish service.

If the drafts of these two laws are approved and implemented without substantial modifications, the issues of universal service and the level of resources available for it will be unresolved. Any intention to provide universal service would, almost inevitably, mean setting up an explicit system of public subsidy for the network expansion this entails. It is also possible the business sector will not be able to access special services at prices and quality that are internationally competitive.

The reasons the privatization of TELCOR has been delayed relate more to politics than to the substance of the proposed structure of telecommunications. But the draft laws are in serious need of debate in order to clarify not only basic regulatory procedures but also the actual goals and intentions of the government regarding telecommunications.

Notes

This chapter is extracted and updated from the author's "Telecomunicaciones en Nicaragua: El nuevo marco regulatorio y la privatización de TELCOR" (Telecommunications in Nicaragua: The New Regulatory Framework and the Privatization of TELCOR), which was written in 1994 for the "Privatization in Bolivia and Nicaragua" project (SUE/94/S18) under the auspices of the Comision Economica para America Latina (CEPAL) with financing from the Swedish Cooperation Agency (ASDI). The opinions expressed are exclusively those of the author and do not necessarily represent those of the sponsoring organizations.

1. Quantitative data are limited and were obtained primarily from interviews in the country and from *Anuario Estadistico TELCOR* 1993, TELCOR's data book (which unfortunately provides no historical data).

References

Castellòn, Avenda. 1994. *The Economy of Nicaragua.* NITLAPAN, CRIES.

CEPAL. 1990. Productive Transformation with Equity. LC/G. 1601 (Secs. 4 and 23).

De Franco, Mario A. 1996. "The Political Economy of Privatization in Nicaragua," CEPAL, unpublished manuscript.

Inter-American Development Bank. 1988. *Social and Economic Progress in Latin America.* Washington, D.C.

International Union of Telecommunications. 1994a. *World Telecommunications Development Report.*

_____. 1994b. *The New Function of the State in an Era of Liberalization.* Informative Document No. 2: Universal Service and Innovation.

Miller, N. P. 1994. "Regulation: Reconciling Policy Objectives," *Implementing Reforms in the Telecommunications Sector.* World Bank Regional and Sectoral Studies, Bjorn Wellenius, Peter A. Stern, and Michael Tyler, eds.

Nicaraguan Institute of Telecommunications and Carriers. 1994. *Panorama of Privatization: The Strategy and Actual Position of the Plan of Privatization.*

Pereira, Emilio. 1994. Statements made before the Legislative Assembly during the discussion on the Telecommunications Law project. *Latin American Weekly Report,* November 3, p. 503.

TELCOR. 1993. *Annual Report.*

_____. 1994. *TELCOR Speaks: Informative Bulletin on TELCOR,* special edition.

World Bank. 1991. *Information about World Development: The Diligent Task of the Development.*

6
Peru

PERCY CORNEJO AND
JUAN ERNESTO BARREDA DELGADO

Peru has several millennia of rich history—and political and economic instability. Despite significant silver and copper deposits, as well as plentiful fishing and some petroleum, it is a poor country. The population of almost 24 million (July 1994 estimate) is well over a third higher than in 1980. Over two-thirds live in cities with more than 5,000 inhabitants; Lima and its port, Callao, have a population of 7 million.

Sitting astride the Andes, the country has three distinct geographical regions in its total area of 1.3 million square kilometers. The lowlands along the Pacific (*costa*) are one of the world's driest and coolest low-altitude deserts. However, they are traversed by rivers fed by rain in the Andes that form extensively cultivated valleys. About a tenth of the country's total area, the *costa* is home to 55 percent of the population. The *sierra,* covering just over a quarter of the country, extends astride the Andes at altitudes ranging from 1,000 to over 6,000 meters. This is where the mineral resources are, as well as the cattle raising. It also has farmland and is where the centers of Inca culture once flourished. About 40 percent of the population live here. Both to escape guerrilla terrorists and to seek better economic opportunities, the population has steadily migrated from this region to the big cities of the *costa* and the highlands of the Amazon forest (where one attraction since the 1970s has been the coca culture promoted by narcotraffickers). Over half the country is in the *selva,* the lowland jungles of the Amazon and eastern foothills of the Andes. The native population of this region used to migrate seasonally looking for good lands for yuca culture and fishing. The area has seen several earlier waves of immigrants from other parts of the country: at the end of the nineteenth century there were rubber extractors; after 1920 there were miners seeking gold in the highland forest rivers; after 1940 there were loggers; in the 1960s there were palm oil and sugarcane growers (most of whose crops were destroyed by terrorists) who have attempted to convert the rain forest to plantation and farmland. For all that, only some 5 percent of the population live in the region.

A republic, Peru is led by a president who is elected for a five-year term. The legislature is unicameral. The constitution was adopted in 1993; before then, presidents could not succeed themselves. Until the 1990s the legislature had two chambers. For much of its history since independence from Spain in 1821, Peru has been controlled by military juntas or dictators, but there have been elected civilian governments since 1980.

The economy, particularly in per capita terms, was stagnant or declining from 1975 until the early 1990s. The 1985–90 government of Alán Garcia Pérez alienated foreign investors and creditors and pursued an expansionary fiscal policy. The inflation rate in 1989 was almost 3,400 percent and peaked at 12,000 percent for the fiscal year ending July 1990. The government of Alberto Fujimori, which took office on July 28, 1990, undertook dramatic fiscal action, drastically cutting the budget and moving to combat bureaucratic corruption and promote a free-market economy. Inflation was brought down to 15.38 percent in 1994, and was 10.2 percent in 1995. GDP grew by 6.5 percent in 1994 and is expected to grow by 4.5 percent annually through the year 2000.

6.1 History

The history of telecommunications in Peru as outlined here recounts the struggle of a people who desire to regain their place in history but who battle repeatedly with governments that do not understand the significance of this history. The account is a raw confession of frustrated triumphs and aspirations. While writing an account or making history for future generations, we assume a commitment to make up for lost time and to place our country where it belongs.

6.1.1 Telegraphy

A March 1857 law conferred on Augusto Goné the exclusive right to construct the lines from Lima to Callao, about 13 kilometers, and to Cerro de Pasco, a mining center in the mountains some 180 kilometers (in a straight line, 250 by road) to the northeast. This privilege was revoked ten years later, as only the connection to Callao had been built. The telegraph system was nationalized on June 25, 1867. Goné was paid compensation for the facilities he had built and assessed damages for breaching the contract for what he did not build. A public auction was set for the right to operate the services (*administracion*); the government would keep ownership and have ultimate control, including regulatory oversight. In the interim, the Army and Navy Communications Departments provided operators and a Treasury Ministry official was charged with management.

An offer by Carlos Paz Soldán was accepted. Then, in September of the same year, it was decided it would be more economical if the system was entirely in private hands. It was sold to Compañía Nacional de Telegrafos (CNT), which was established by Paz Soldán for this purpose and which set about connecting cities. However, in April 1875 the country's first civilian government, headed by Dr. Manuel Pardo (president, 1872–76), decided to take over all the lines Paz Soldán's company had already built because the company had not fulfilled its obligation to establish communication lines throughout the country. Thus, ownership and operation of the telegraph service returned to the state.

In July 1876 a new military government, headed by General Mariano Ignacio Prado (president, 1876–79), assumed power. Because of atrocious management and increasing costs, which became too much for the meager national budget, the new regime was willing to divest CNT. Paz Soldán had friendly relations with high-level members of the new government and was a logical choice to take it over. CNT thus returned to his ownership in 1877 with an eight-year concession that imposed conditions requiring improvements that would benefit the state. However, in 1878 the service was again nationalized, with Paz Soldán remaining as chief manager. By then the system had 2,525 kilometers of line, 53 offices, and 65 machines.

During the War of the Pacific (1879–83), in which Peru was allied with Bolivia against Chile, new lines were built to replace old ones in order to speed communications. Free schools were opened to provide trained personnel for the telegraph department. Shortly after the end of the war, in 1884, Paz Soldán retired from running the service. His successor was Melitón Carvajal, a high-level Navy officer and hero of the war. Carvajal faced the task of rebuilding the lines destroyed by the war and repairing damaged offices. The previous staff had almost entirely disappeared, so in 1884 a Telegraphy Training School was established in CNT's Lima headquarters. In 1895 Carvajal returned to Naval duty as part of the combining of the postal and telegraph services. The new institution, named Servicio Postal y Telegráfico del Peru, was under the charge of the chief manager of the postal service.

Augusto E. Tamayo, an engineer, established radiotelegraphy in Peru in 1904 under the government of Don José Pardo. In 1911 installation of the first station in Lima was completed by students of the Telegraph School. In 1912 President Leguía inaugurated the powerful Telefunken del Cerro San Cristobal station, opening communications between Lima and Iquitos in the Amazon basin.

A January 22, 1911, law consolidated the general administration of the postal, telegraph, and radiotelegraph services into the Dirección General de Correos y Telégrafos.

In January 1921 President Augusto B. Leguía's government contracted the Marconi Wireless Telegraph Company of the United Kingdom to operate the telegraph services under a management agreement with the government. According to the contract, Marconi was to receive 5 percent of the gross revenue plus 50 percent of net profits. The opposition parties criticized the contract. In rebuttal, the government pointed out such advantages as the reorganization of services, the modernization and development of the system, and the profits that would accrue to the state as owner of the system. In April 1935 the Oscar R. Benavides government signed a new contract with Marconi, with substantially the same terms as the 1921 agreement.

In July 1945, in his first message to the nation, President José Luis Bustamante y Rivero announced his intention to introduce legislation to cover telecommunications. As a result, in 1946 the Marconi contract was canceled and telegraph service was again placed under the management of the Dirección General de Correos y Telégrafos.

6.1.2 Telephone System

According to some authors, the Chimus, inhabitants of the sacred city of Chan-Chan near modern-day Trujillo, between A.D. 300 and 600 used a "telephone" system. The "sets" were the ends of gourd necks covered with leather; some 50 meters of cotton string, knotted on the inside of each gourd, connected the gourds. As many children who have done this with cans know, when the string is taut, the device can transmit voices. The first "modern" telephone line in Peru was established in 1888, connecting the House of Senators and the House of Representatives.

The same year, during the General Andrés Avelino Cáceres government, a public auction was called for the establishment of a telephone service in Lima. The only offer was from Casa Cohen, a trading and representatives firm, which bid in partnership with foreign investors and equipment makers. Its formal offer differed from what had previously been indicated, so the bid was refused. Soon after, a bid was accepted from Casa Bacigalupi, also a trading and representatives firm. With other Peruvian partners and technical and financial support from ITT, Casa Bacigalupi founded the Peruvian Telephone Company to accept the grant of the right to install telephone networks in Lima, the surrounding districts, and Callao.

On September 7, 1888, Lima was connected to Callao, and on September 13 the lines were opened for public service. A connection and five-minute conversation cost 10 silver centavos. Before long, competition appeared. Casa Cohen established the Compañía de Teléfonos del Peru, which laid cable to Callao and offered free calls while building its offices. Communication with Rimac, 3 kilometers to the northeast of central Lima, was made with an apparatus installed in the Backus and Johnston Beer Factory. In December 1888, ITT bought Compañía de Teléfonos and merged it into the Peruvian Telephone Company. By that time there were twenty telephone lines in Lima plus links to stations in Callao and various suburban districts; 30,000 meters of telephone cable had been laid. On January 13, 1889, a new line was opened between the Government Palace and the home of General Andrés Avelino Cáceres, the country's president, in suburban Miraflores, about 12 kilometers south of central Lima.

In 1910 cable was strung between Lima and Chosica, a spa village about 75 kilometers along the main road to the *sierra*. By the next year, the Postal Management had established service between Lima and Ancón, about 33 kilometers along the main road to the north, a beach resort and fishing village outside the area of Lima's concessionaire.

In 1920 Compañía Peruana de Teléfonos (CPT) was founded. It acquired the fixed assets of the Peruvian Telephone Company, which then had approximately 4,000 manual telephones in operation. This was not a matter of a mere change of an English to a Spanish name: facing the need to expand and modernize service, but lacking sufficient local capital, it was agreed that ITT would own 60 percent of the new company and Peruvian investors 40 percent. This allowed ITT to control management. CPT was the concessionaire for the cities of Lima and Callao and surrounding urban and suburban districts such as San Isidro, Miraflores, Barranco, and Chorrillos (most of which are within modern-day Lima).

In December 1930 Peru's first automatic switch went into operation at Jiron Washington in Lima with a capacity of 2,000 lines. This brought to 10,000 the number of telephones in metropolitan Lima, the others being on semiautomatic switches.

During the 1930s the government authorized telephone service in the interior of the country, granting concessions to several companies.

The Compañía Nacional de Teléfonos (CNT), a Swiss-Peruvian private company, started by providing service to Ancón, Pisco, Ica, and Huancayo. It then expanded to include the northern cities of Piura, Tumbes, and Lambayeque; Cusco and Abancay in the south; and Iquitos in the jungle. CNT also set up long-distance service by means of radiotelephone channels between the cities in which it had concessions and with Lima, where it interconnected with CPT.

Sociedad Telefónica de Arequipa (STA), owned entirely by private citizens in that district, served the southern part of the country, including Arequipa (long one of Peru's major cities), Mollendo (a Pacific port), Juliaca, Deseguadero, Puno (a port on Lake Titicaca), and all the towns along the railroad between Mollendo and Puno. The company provided radiotelephone links with CPT and CNT, as well as to the Bolivian network. STA received technical support from Swedish equipment-maker L. M. Ericsson.

All America Cable, by the late 1920s an ITT subsidiary, had been providing international radiotelegraphy service via a submarine cable from Callao to Panama since the beginning of the twentieth century. In 1930 it extended its service to include an eight-channel radio link for telephone or telegraph from Lima to New York, where it connected with ITT service to the principal cities of Europe. This led to its changing its name to All America Cable and Radio.

Cable West Coast, an Anglo-Canadian company, initially provided telegraph service by submarine cable from Callao to Valparaiso, Chile. From 1930 radiotelegraph and radiotelephone connections were provided with Buenos Aires, Santiago, and London.

In 1931 local telephone service in metropolitan Lima more than doubled, expanding by 10,800 telephones, all on automatic switches. Growth continued with installation of 25,000 lines in the San Isidro, Magdalena, and Miraflores central stations. By 1933 there was a total of 21,000 telephones, and the service became completely automatic.

6.1.3 Telex

In 1958 the All America Cable and Radio Company, a subsidiary of ITT, set up two circuits between Lima and New York exclusively for twenty international-traffic telex subscribers. In 1962 Cable West Coast also started to offer this service. It operated only eight hours a day until 1964, when it began to operate semi-automatically twenty-four hours a day.

In 1968 All America Cable implemented a completely automatic service with a Pentaconta switchboard connected as a subscriber exchange to the main switchboard in New York. In June 1969, Cable West Coast also opened an automatic station, linking thirteen correspondents. Both were exclusively for international service from the Lima metropolitan area.

6.1.4 Internet

In 1991, a small nonprofit organization was created with U.S.$7,000 in seed money from the United Nations Development Fund. Called the Peruvian Scientific Network, or RCP, the organization is dedicated to providing access to the information resources of the Internet to all Peruvians. RCP is growing rapidly from 40 subscribers in the beginning to 22,000 in 1996, with estimates of over 60,000 by 1998. For U.S.$15 a month, a subscriber not only gains access to the Internet but also to computers and classes on how to use them. All of the profits are reinvested in maintaining and expanding the network.

A setup like this is unique in South America; most of the other Internet providers, to date, have been government-funded and operate under the assumption that users would have access to computers. In some ways, RCP can be viewed as a role model for "universal net access," to provide Internet access to more than the few (5 percent in Peru) who can afford computers.

6.2 Nationalization and the Creation of ENTel-Peru

The All America Cable and Radio and Cable West Coast Company concessions ended in 1967, and the government notified them they would not be renewed, although they could continue operating until the expropriation process was complete. Beginning in 1969, CITI (Comité Interino de Telecomunicaciones Internacionales) took over operating the international telex service, and the companies were paid in 1970.

In 1968 the revolutionary military government of General Juan Velasco Alvarado began to nationalize companies. In 1969 the first steps were taken to expropriate CPT. By means of a Basic Conditions Treaty, on October 29, 1969, the government acquired ITT's shares, which had grown to 71 percent of the total because of continued acquisition, and those of the private Peruvian investors who held the rest. A formal transfer ceremony took place on March 25, 1970. Part of ITT's compensation was a piece of choice Lima real estate on which the company built a five-star Sheraton Hotel.

On November 9, 1969, the Empresa Nacional de Telecomunicaciones del Perú (ENTel-Peru) was created by Law 17881 as a 100 percent state-owned company to take charge of public telecom services. ENTel held 29 percent of the shares of CPT and, as provided by the law, 100 percent of the voting rights. It thus took over CPT's management, including designating the chair and members of the board of directors.

CPT was not fully nationalized: ITT's shares in CPT were distributed to some 37,500 existing telephone subscribers, who paid for them through a monthly charge on their phone bill. The reissued shares were transferable once paid for, but they carried no voting rights. In a sense, this is the reverse of the way telegraph service had been provided in the 1880s: then the government owned the service but contracted out its operation; with CPT after 1969, its subscribers owned (most of) its shares but a government-owned company operated it.

Immediately after the expropriation, CPT announced a 50,000 line expansion, primarily in the suburbs and area around Lima, putting a central station into operation in Chorrillos to provide service for the first time in the districts of San Juan de Miraflores, Villa Maria del Triunfo, and the area south of Surco, as well as to expand and upgrade with automatic equipment service in Chorrillos and Barranco. The costs were to be borne by new subscribers by obliging them to purchase newly issued shares in ENTel at the time of signing up for a phone line. These were paid for in installments while construction and installation was under way. Subsequent expansions have been financed in the same way. CPT shares were listed on Lima's stock exchange, and the government routinely bought shares, so that by 1994 its holdings had increased from 29 to 35 percent.

The company also set up the Magdalena Central, which serviced Magdalena, part of San Miguel and Pueblo Libre, and the Miraflores Central, which serviced the majority of Surquillo.

6.2.1 The 1970s and 1980s

In December 1971 a new General Telecommunications Law (Law 19020) was promulgated. Its stated purpose was to "make available to Peru the most modern methods of mass communication services and serve the needs of society as a whole, not just private interests." The law gave ENTel full authority over the exploitation of public communication services in the country and, more gradually, responsibility for the provision of services that private companies had been offering. Thus, in July 1972 the Swiss-Peruvian company Compañia Peruana de Teléfonos was folded into ENTel, and the Sociedad Telefónica de Arequipa followed in July 1973.

Immediately after formation, ENTel absorbed the international telex service that had been operated by CITI since its expropriation from its private owners in 1969. Service had been limited to the Lima area, but in 1975 the government implemented, under ENTel, a domestic telex network. On July 2, 1981, this domestic network was tied to the international service, called EDX.

The 1971 law put ENTel in charge of telegraph services, which had been operated by the Dirección General de Correos y Telégrafos since 1946. The actual transfer of facilities did not occur until December 22, 1976.

Under a telephone expansion plan, an automatic exchange providing national and international direct dialing was put into operation in Piura in April 1977. New exchanges were steadily introduced in other towns during 1977–78, when the pace of expansion slowed. By 1988 almost every town with a population of over 50,000 had automatic exchanges.

In February 1985 a DMS-10 exchange, the first digital switch in Peru, with 1,200 lines went into operation in Ayacucho. ENTel contracted Ericsson do Brasil in September 1983 to provide 40,000 lines in nineteen cities. This involved installation of nineteen AXE-10 exchanges. The same month, ENTel and the Italian company Telettra SPA, represented by Intertec SA, signed an agreement for the supply and installation of digital microwave systems and satellite links, with eight being installed.

In February 1992 Ericsson do Brasil was contracted to provide 65,000 new digital lines in thirty-two cities over a two-year period, and in March, Mitsui was awarded the contract for complementary equipment.

In February 1983 mobile telephone exchanges went into operation in Chimbote, a fishing port of about 300,000 people 350 kilometers north of Lima, and Huarás, a department capital of 90,000 located 320 kilometers northeast of Lima. ENTel earlier had begun using small-scale mobile exchanges to provide emergency service while permanent wireline facilities were being built, but these two exchanges were the first large-scale, permanent ones.

Traditionally, revenues from international long-distance services and business have subsidized local services. In 1992, a residential user paid U.S.$1.27 monthly for a line, while a commercial user paid U.S.$5.15. The installation of a residence line was U.S.$705, but the installation of a business line was U.S.$1,319. About 5 percent of ENTel's users accounted for 29 percent of its revenues. About 6 percent of CPT's users accounted for 28 percent of its revenues.

6.3 The Current Situation

ENTel now provides local telephone service directly or indirectly and operates the domestic and international long-distance network, as well as the telegraph system. CPT is the local-service provider in the metro Lima area, including Callao, as it has been since its formation in 1920. Since 1969 ENTel has operated CPT and, on behalf of the government, owned 29 percent, until 1994 when it increased its holdings to 35%.

Communication facilities are totally inadequate and do not meet demand. The majority of installations are analog, having been installed before 1980. Indeed, many cities are still served by manual exchanges. Installed capacity is in full use, which meant as of estimates in 1994 that only 44 percent of those wishing to make a call were able to get a dial tone immediately.

CPT and ENTel had bloated bureaucracies in 1993. The number of lines installed per employee was 48 in Peru; Mexico, by contrast, had 156 lines per employee. Operating costs per line neared U.S.$900 in 1992. In Brazil and Mexico, costs were only U.S.$230 and U.S.$270, respectively.

ENTel has facsimile machines available in its offices for public use, and private parties can offer fax services over their phone lines (including residential lines) if they obtain a municipal license and declare the revenue for tax purposes.

6.3.1 Infrastructure

In 1990 ENTel operated thirty-six automatic exchanges, mostly Philips PRX, with a capacity of 195,950 subscriber lines, out of a total of 563,000 lines nationwide. In 1992, CPT's digitalization reached 41 percent, but ENTel's reached only 18 percent. Over 60 percent of total lines are in the Lima area. Total lines were about 36 percent greater than in 1985.

A microwave network runs from Tumbes in the north through Lima and

Arequipa to Tacna and Puno in the south. Many branches run along the *costa* and *sierra* linking other communities. During 1995, Alcatel finished a 2,000-kilometer fiber-optic cable running from Piura through Lima and the other principal coastal cites to Arequipa. By 1993, CPT and ENTel's infrastructures were still outdated; CPT had 60,000 rotary lines in service, and ENTel still had 21,000 manual lines in service. The cabling for both companies was more than sixty years old in Lima and more than twenty years old in other areas. (This cable has a life expectancy of fifteen years.) Alcatel Standard Electric is an important fiber cable supplier. Two local manufacturers, Indeco and Ceper, are important copper cable suppliers.

Peru's first ground station for satellite communications, which is at Lurin, about 30 kilometers south of Lima, was put out for bid in December 1967. It went into operation on July 14, 1969, aimed at an Intelsat satellite, although Peru, through ENTel, did not join Intelsat until 1979. The station was under the administration of CITI until ENTel was created. The country joined Inmarsat in 1987. There are fourteen satellite ground stations for domestic long distance and ground stations for international service in Lurin and Huancayo (the latter built in 1980). Many of the domestic stations are in the Amazon area, where microwave links are impractical; the others reinforce the microwave backbone. This network is called Domsat.

By year-end 1994, Peru's cellular infrastructure was dominated by a duopoly: Moviline (part of Telefónica del Peru) and Cellular 2000 (part of Tele 2000), with a market share of 53.5 percent and 46.5 percent, respectively.

Two types of concessions—wired and wireless—have been created to operate cellular systems in two regions: Lima and Callao. Tele 2000 (previously named Telemovil) has operated wireless cellular since April 1990, and Telefónica del Peru has operated the same since April 1991. Tele 2000 offers telephony services via a joint venture with Empresa Difusoria Radio Tele (Radio Panamericana), with exclusive rights for twenty years to operate cellular and television services over cable. ENTel-Peru has the wired concession for the rest of Peru.

A license for wireless services has not yet been granted in the rest of Peru. Cellular 2000 provides traditional services via mobile cellular, connecting with CPT's network for calls in Lima—Callao and with ENTel for the rest of Peru. Tele 2000 charges about U.S.$0.35 a minute, and Moviline charges about U.S.$0.205 per minute.

In 1994, revenues for cellular services in Lima reached U.S.$22 million. The provinces accounted for U.S.$3.7 million and subscribers reached 49,000, divided as follows: CPT, 26,000; ENTel, 3,700; and Tele 2000, 20,000.

The Peruvian Data Transmission Network (PERUNET) permits the exchange of data between computers, or between terminals and a computer, including packet switching, via dedicated lines. Service started in July 1989. International connections are possible. The tariff is set in U.S. dollars and is paid monthly in local currency at the market rates at the time of payment. PERUSAT is an integrated digital service that provides private networks with voice, data, and facsimile transmission.

6.3.2 Research and Training

The National Institute of Research and Telecommunications Training (INICTEL) was established by the General Telecommunications Law of December 1971, as a result of a study undertaken in 1970 by the Transportation and Communication Ministry. It is separate from the Communications Sector of the Ministry. Scientific and technological research related to telecommunications are among the institute's objectives, as well as training specialized personnel for both the private and public sectors. In addition, INICTEL is responsible for the development of technical standards and their implementation, including certification of telecom equipment. It also conducts technical studies sponsored by public or private entities.

Despite limited financial resources, INICTEL has made significant strides. It has selected three broad priority areas for research and development programs, each involving several projects. The areas are radio and television, informatics, and telecommunication services.

ENTel also does research and development, both on its own and in partnership with INICITEL. Making use of advanced technology, during 1988–90 its engineers and technicians designed and built a prototype of a digital telephone exchange with 1,000 lines. Called Antara, it successfully passed laboratory and field testing and has been installed in Cañete. It allows urban and rural centers with low demand to be linked to the national network and provides national and international direct dialing as well as telematic services.

6.3.3 Regional Cooperation

The State Companies Association of Telecommunications of the Andean Sub-Regional Agreement (ASETA) was formed in July 1974 by five Andean countries (Bolivia, Colombia, Ecuador, Peru, and Venezuela). Headquartered in Quito, Ecuador, it coordinates programs related to the integration of networks and telecom services in the region.

The Hispanic-American Association for Centers of Research and Study of Telecommunications (AHCIET) works to increase coordination of company efforts toward the study of telecom development. ENTel (since 1984), INICTEL, and CPT are among the twenty-nine members.

6.4 The Move toward Privatization

The Fujimori government's commitment to privatization has been clear since it assumed office in July 1990, both reflecting and building a consensus that the state should have a significantly reduced role in the economy compared to the 1968–90 period.

In November 1991 Legislative Decree 702 (*Ley de la Promoción de la Inversión Privada en Telecomunicaciones*) acknowledged achievements that had taken place in telecommunications and set standards to regulate the development of private investment. The intention was for ENTel to become a modern, efficient, and productive company. The law requires that telecommunications move toward a digital network offering integrated services. Many specific projects were undertaken to implement this goal in terms of local and trunk service, as well as upgrading and expanding the PERUNET data network and international links. Cellular systems are also planned for the three largest urban areas (Lima-Callao, Trujillo, and Arequipa).

Under an August 1994 law, OSIPTEL (Organismo Supervisor de la Inversión Privada en Telecomunicaciones) was created as the regulatory body for the sector. Reporting directly to the president, the body is composed of representatives of service providers, users, and the state. Besides having oversight on tariffs, OSIPTEL's primary function is to promote a competitive environment, including assurance of interconnections, as part of furthering the rationalization of telecommunications.

In January 1994 Decree 26285 established "progressive monopolization" of telecom services. For five years (June 1994–June 1999) CPT and ENTel will control basic and long-distance services. Competition is allowed in telex, telegraph, public phones, cellular, cable television, value-added equipment, and other services.

FITEL (Fondo de Inversión de Telecomunicaciones) was created by the same law to finance telecom services in rural areas and other places that are marginal to private providers. FITEL is funded by a 1 percent levy on the annual gross revenues of telecom providers, with additional funds from the general sales tax (IGV) and other sources.

In 1994, twenty-eight companies were privatized, attracting investment of U.S.$2 billion. Telecommunications accounted for 46 percent of total foreign investments in newly privatized companies.

6.4.1 Telefónica Perú

In February 1994 the government sold 35 percent of CPT and ENTel. A number of international telecom players—AT&T, GTE, Southwestern Bell, France Telecom, Cable & Wireless, Telefónica International, Korean Telecom, and Stet—had joined with local interests to bid. The winner was a joint venture of Telefónica Internacional de España with the Peruvian firms Graña y Montero SA and Banco Wiese (the country's second-largest bank, it issued stock in a global underwriting in September 1994). The venture, Telefónica Perú, bid just over U.S.$2 billion in cash and investment commitments, 2.3 times the next highest bid and almost 3.6 times the minimum bid.

In connection with the privatization, new concession contracts were signed with ENTel and CPT. Running for twenty years, the agreement calls for tariffs to be rebalanced during the first five years so that they relate to costs. By 1998, the monthly rental for business and residence lines will be the same: U.S.$31.93. Installation for both types of lines will also be the same: U.S.$420. Costs per minute of long distance will fall. The companies are obligated to expand and improve service if they wish to retain their monopoly positions past June 1999.

Telefónica Perú assumed management of CPT and ENTel on May 1, 1994; in January 1995, CPT and ENTel merged to form Telefónica del Perú. The new company had 772,000 lines in service, equal to 3.4 per 100 inhabitants, 54 percent of which were digital. Imbalances existed between urban and rural areas. In 1993, Lima had 6.61 lines per 100 inhabitants, but the rest of Peru had only 1.23 lines. The goal is to have 1.75 million lines by 1998 with 96 percent digitalization. This includes bringing service to 1,514 small towns and increasing the number of public phones, particularly in the barrios, to 0.21 per 100 people as part of a plan to expand service to those who cannot afford their own lines. In 1993, there were only 0.41 public telephones per 1,000 inhabitants. Imbalances also existed between the wealthy and the poor populations. In 1993, only 1.6 percent of poor homes had a line, but 21.1 percent of the middle class and the wealthy had a line. In 1993, the average time to get a line was almost ten years.

From 1994 to 1998, CPT will modernize 125,000 lines and expand by 506,000 lines. ENTel will modernize 75,000 lines and expand by 472,000 lines. In April 1995 the company was installing 1,100 new lines a day. Some of those getting service had been waiting six years; the 1998 goal is fifteen days. Although the wait for lines has declined, the backlog has remained steady at about 250,000 as new people sign up. Increased efficiency and scale economies have reduced the cost per new line to U.S.$400 from U.S.$1,000. As part of this aggressive expansion plan, in July 1995 Telefónica del Perú announced a U.S.$800 million investment budget for its next fiscal year.

To finance its investments, Telefónica del Perú has been allowed rate increases that have generated substantial profits: it is estimated the company will have net profits of U.S.$280 million on revenues of U.S.$11.27 billion in 1995. Telefónica Internacional de España receives management fees from Telefónica del Perú, as well as a dividend.

Ericsson will continue to be an important supplier of equipment. In 1994, U.S.$40 million of equipment were imported from this supplier for various projects, including the installation of 120 central office projects in Lima and the provinces. As of March 31, 1996, Telefónica del Perú had roughly 1.2 million lines in service, with 79 percent of local and 100 percent of trunk connections being digitalized.[1]

6.5 Conclusion

Peru has been undergoing a major transformation in the 1990s. Although still fragile, the country is achieving political stability and economic growth despite the legacies of guerrilla movements and heavy government involvement in the economy. Telefónica del Perú is a major force in the country's revitalization.

Note

1. Telefónica del Perú, *Prospectus Survey*, 1996.

7

Ecuador

MICHAEL CHONG PINEDA AND IVAN N. ESPINOZA

Telecommunications in Ecuador has been almost entirely a state-provided service, such as it was, since the nineteenth century. International connections were the exception, and these were ultimately nationalized. In the 1990s Ecuador is another country moving toward privatization, motivated by the need to expand and improve its system.

7.1 Background

Ecuador sits astride the Andes mountains, which gives it three very different geographical regions despite being one of the smaller Latin American countries in terms of area (about 283,000 square kilometers). The tropical coast (*costa*) is home to about 49 percent of the country's 10.7 millions inhabitants (July 1994 estimate) while the mountain region (*sierra*) has 46 percent of the population. The tropical rain forest of the Amazon basin (*Oriente*) covers almost half of the area but has only 4.9 percent of the population. The Galápagos Islands, with 0.1 percent of the total population, are also part of Ecuador. Under a law of March 26, 1987, there are twenty-one provinces divided into 162 *cantones*.

Guayaquil, the principal port, is the largest city with 1.6 million inhabitants; Quito, in the *sierra,* is the capital and second largest city with 1.2 million. Long one of the poorest Latin American countries, Ecuador had petroleum discoveries in the *Oriente* in the 1970s that significantly affected its economy. Petroleum is now the principal export, having replaced bananas. Despite rapid growth population, per capita income has increased substantially, creating an urban middle class. The 1980s were more somber, however. The government significantly increased its involvement in the economy, generally running huge deficits. The situation was exacerbated by the abrupt halving of oil prices in early 1986 and a March 1987 earthquake that damaged the pipeline delivering oil for export. Inflation reached triple digits and per capita income fell. Agriculture still employs over a third of the labor force (1994).

During the twentieth century there has been a succession of military and civilian governments. In 1979 the junta allowed elections and a new constitution was adopted. All subsequent governments have been elected. The 1979 constitution mandates the direct election of the president, who serves a four-year term without the possibility of reelection, and a unicameral legislature elected every two years. There are many political parties; no single one has ever held a majority.

7.2 History

In 1871 the government granted a concession to All America Cable and Radio to provide international telegraphy services using its submarine cable. The cable ran along the west coast of South America linking Baltos (Panama) with Valparaiso (Chile) through stations in Buena Ventura (Colombia), Salinas (Ecuador), and Callao (Peru). Salinas, a beach resort, is about 100 kilometers west of Guayaquil.

The first domestic telegraphic message in Ecuador was transmitted on July 9, 1884, on a line between Quito and Guayaquil. A national organization to regulate telecommunications, the Direccion de Telegrafos, was created in the 1880s. The country's first central telephone exchange was installed in Quito in 1900 using a semiautomatic system.

Quito and Guayaquil were connected by wireless telegraph in 1920. By 1934 there were 7,000 kilometers of telegraph and telephone lines, 167 telegraph offices, 114 telephone offices, and 19 wireless stations collectively providing communications links to the principal towns and cities of the *costa* and *sierra*.

Radio Internacional del Ecuador was established in 1943 as an independent state organization for international telegraph and telephone services, as well as domestic long-distance telephone service. Until then these had been monopolized by All America Cable and Radio. The new company operated throughout the country.

Telecom authorities moved to begin replacing the manual telephone system with automatic switches in 1945 when the national government signed a contract with Ericsson for central exchanges in Quito and Guayaquil. Also in 1945, ETAPA, the telco owned by the municipality of Cuenca, contracted with Ericsson for its AGF switch. Subsequently, on July 15, 1949, Empresa de Telefonos Agua Polable y Alcantarillado (ETAPA) inaugurated the first automatic central urban telephone network in the country. The system had an initial capacity of 500 lines and 150 subscribers.

Empresa de Telefonos de Quito (ETQ) was created in 1949. It was placed in charge of installing and operating automatic service for the city, thus taking over responsibility for administering the equipment installed under the 1943 contract. In 1950 automatic service began in Quito using the Ericsson AGT switch in the Mariscal Sucre central. Initial capacity was 3,000 lines and 1,000 subscribers were served. In 1953 the Guayaquil Telephone Company (ETG) was created with a technical and an administrative framework similar to ETQ's. In 1955, also using the AGT switch, ETG began automatic service for 3,000 lines and 2,300 subscribers.

From the beginning of telecommunications in the country, both the planning and construction of networks were done under the direct administration of technical managers. Government departments were created to develop specific projects. Projects, and the skills required for installation, were determined on the basis of a population census of an area.

7.3 Service and Organizational Changes, 1957–1971

Empresa de Radio Telegrafos y Telefonos del Ecuador (ERTTE) was created in 1958 by merging the Direccion de Telegrafos and Radio Internacional del Ecuador. The main purpose of the new company was to update the international communications system. The national government in 1959 contracted British Marconi for a 48-channel VHF link between Quito and Guayaquil. Later, VHF links were used to connect the rest of the country's cities. International telephone circuits were established using the HFBLL 4-channel system.

In the 1960s the Quito and Guayaquil telephone companies began to extend their networks, initially into surrounding Pichincha (ETQ) and Guayas (ETG) provinces. ETG also moved into the neighboring Rios province.

Automated long-distance service between Quito and Guayaquil was begun in 1963 under a contract between ERTTE, ETQ, and ETG. In 1967 the Quito and Guayaquil telcos installed interurban transit exchanges. Utilizing these facilities, ETQ automated connections between Quito and Machachi, about 50 kilometers south on the main road to Guayaquil, and ETG automated connections between Guayaquil and Salinas.

ERTTE restructured itself in 1963 and changed its name to Empresa Nacional de Telecomunicaciones (ENTel). A national telecom advisory board was established and made responsible for coordinating the telecom activities of the three state companies (ENTel, ETQ, and ETG) and the various municipal companies. Raytheon, a U.S.-based company, was contracted to supply the country's first microwave system, with a capacity of 600 telephone channels plus a television channel, connecting Quito and Guayaquil. The system was installed along the coastal trunk route, an important communications corridor for the country. It went on line in 1968. In March 1969 direct dialing became possible between Quito, Guayaquil, and other population centers. Until then, other population centers were connected to each other only through Quito or Guayaquil in a hub-and-spoke network.

All America Cable and Radio was nationalized in 1970 and renamed Cables y Radio del Estado. Its principal function remained the operation of telex and the national and international public telegraph systems. The same year, four international telephone channels via satellite were initiated from the ground station at Choconta (Colombia).

In February 1971 the government combined ENTel, ETQ, ETG, and Cables y Radio del Estado into two regional companies under the Ministry of Public Works and Communications. The regional companies were Telecomunicaciones del Norte, with jurisdiction over Esmeraldas, Carchi, Imbaburaa, Pichincha (Quito), Cotopaxi, Tungurahua, Chimborazo, Bolivar, Napo, and Pastaza provinces; and Telecomunicaciones del Sur, covering Manabi, Los Rios, Guayas (Guayaquil), El Oro, Canar, Loja, Morona Santiago, and Zamora Chinchipe provinces, as well as Azuay outside the city of Cuenca. (ETAPA, Cuenca's provider, remained autonomous.)

To take advantage of joining Intelsat in 1971, the two regional companies set out to renovate and expand the national and international networks. They solicited bids for microwave trunk networks, telex-gentex networks, and a satellite ground station.

7.4 IETEL, 1972–1991

In October 1972 the national government created the Instituto Ecuatoriano de Telecomunicaciones (IETEL). The two regional companies were merged into this new body which, like its predecessors, was under the Ministry of Public Works and Communications. Thus, for the first time, a single government entity was responsible for regulating, planning, and operating all of the country's telecommunications (except in Cuenca). However, in part reflecting the historical development of the system, while IETEL had a central organization responsible for short- and long-term project planning and implementation for the entire country, operations were conducted by two regional units. Region 1 (IETEL R1) had jurisdiction over all services in the mountains and western provinces, while Region 2 covered the coast and inland provinces. These were essentially the previous regional companies, which in turn had been centered on ETQ and ETG.

During the late 1970s and early 1980s the economy's general malaise and huge level of foreign debt meant little was done to expand or upgrade the system. International telephone service was upgraded in July 1974 when calls became semiautomatic. Later, first incoming and then the outgoing calls were fully automated. With a loan from the Interamerican Development Bank (IDB), a project was started in 1982 to provide service to 460 rural towns.

The wiring necessary for the installation of primary (backbone) and secondary networks and international connections was carried out by domestic companies awarded contracts through bidding. These contractors followed technical specifications issued by IETEL, which had a department to inspect and accept projects. Digital centrals were installed in Quito and Guayaquil in 1987 and, in 1991, Ecuador became the first Latin American country to have a digital satellite ground station.

In 1990 there were 537,895 telephone lines installed, which was about 18 per 100 inhabitants. Service was 75 percent automated on a national level in 1991, with 156 cities connected to domestic direct dialing using 10,486 long-distance circuits.

In 1991 IETEL R1 had a primary capacity of 269,350 lines, of which 72,250 (27 percent) were digital. Some of these were installed by private companies under the technical supervision of IETEL. There were plans to add 47,000 lines in Region 1 during 1991, a 17 percent increase. Of these, 22,000 digital and 8,600 analog lines were for Quito and adjoining areas of Pichincha province. For 1992, IETEL was committed to 57,500 lines, 40,500 of them under contract within the various areas of Region 1. Region 1 also was installing cables of greater capacity to replace existing cables in order to alleviate saturation of channels for inter-central exchange connections. Some of this new cable was fiber optic, which helped pave the way for digital transmission.

The major cities have grown considerably since the 1970s, largely because of migration from rural areas. Municipal bylaws were amended to allow construction of low-income housing on the outskirts of cities, providing only basic services such as water, light, and sewer. At the same time, to accommodate a growing middle class, new areas have developed that provide housing with full facilities, including telephone service. In these upscale areas, the developers have at their own expense installed the cabling and other parts of the secondary telephone network, following technical norms and regulations issued by IETEL. In fact, housing developments and buildings that will have over ten subscribers were obligated to build their own telephone connections and submit them to the region's inspection department.

7.5 EMETEL, 1992–1994

Yet another restructuring of the telecom sector came in August 1992 when Congress passed a Special Telecommunications Law. Basic telecom services were maintained as an exclusive state monopoly, to be carried out by the newly created state-owned company Empresa Estatal de Telecomunicaciones (EMETEL).

EMETEL provides local and national and international long-distance telephone services in the country except in Ecuador's third largest city, Cuenca, where service continues to be provided by a local municipal operator, ETAPA. With this exception, EMETEL has a monopoly on all basic telephone and telegraph services, both national and international. In value-added services such as data transmission and mobile telecommunications services, EMETEL competes with the private sector.

Services such as cellular telephony, mobile radio, satellite communications, long distance, and paging may be operated by the private sector under concession arrangements regulated by the Superintendencia de Telecomunicaciones. Limited privatization of satellite, long distance, and mobile telephone services has already begun.

7.5.1 Regulation

The 1992 law established the Superintendencia de Telecomunicaciones as the sector's regulator, thereby separating operating and regulatory functions. (EMETEL's predecessor, IETEL, had been responsible for both.) Subject to oversight by the Congress, the office is responsible for the administration, regulation, and control of the entire telecom sector, including spectrum management, assignment of frequencies, approval of telephone tariffs, and authorization of final and carrier telecom services. In addition, the Superintendencia represents the Government of Ecuador before the International Telecommunication Union (ITU) and other international bodies (although EMETEL is considered the "signatory" to Intelsat). The office is headed by a *superintendente* appointed by the president for an indefinite term.

The duties of the Superintendencia are expected to change as reforms to the 1992 law are passed and privatization activities are initiated. Indeed, one argument in favor of modifying the 1992 law is that it provides too much power to one person, especially given the Superintendencia's authority to approve concessions and grant frequencies without any type of oversight.

7.6 Level and Nature of Service in the Early 1990s

Government support for the telecommunications sector in the early 1990s is often described as passive and highly politicized. Private-sector users complain of the lack of strong governmental support for expansion and a weighty bureaucracy.

Some companies have been forced to acquire independent systems in order to be able to use technologies unavailable from EMETEL. As a result of lack of government investment, an informal telecom sector has been expanding rapidly.

At the end of 1994 Ecuador's telecom network consisted of some 624,000 telephone lines, a penetration rate of just 5.6 percent. The average waiting period for a telephone line was six years, with over 160,000 customers on the waiting list. Demand is estimated at 2.2 million lines by the year 2000, and 2.7 million by 2010.

The current switching system is two-thirds digitized, with outside plant analog, but the transmission system is 90 percent digital. Only half of users have international direct dialing. Nearly 76 percent of nongovernmental lines are residential, 14 percent are for small and medium business, and 11 percent are for large industry. Through agreements with EMETEL, U.S. carriers providing telephone services to the United States include AT&T, Sprint, MCI, and IDB.

7.6.1 Domestic Long Distance

The Superintendencia issued regulations governing domestic long-distance systems on April 14, 1994. On the basis of these regulations, the Superintendencia then awarded concessions to six firms: Telemobil, Ramcomdes, Mottcashire, Eduardo Granda, Comovec, and Brunaci. These companies were expected to begin operations sometime in 1995 but did not. EMETEL argued that the government exclusively assigned domestic long distance to EMETEL, and it would not authorize any connections to its network under the current circumstances. As part of EMETEL's privatization, expected by the end of 1996, interconnection fees will be established and the new firms will be able to provide service.

7.6.2 Cellular Service

The Superintendencia issued regulations governing cellular telephone services in April 1993. Bids were submitted in May and the two top bidders, CONECEL and OTECEL, were awarded the right to negotiate contracts. CONECEL (Porta Cellular) started operations on the A band in December 1993 with Northern Telecom equipment, while OTECEL (Cellular Power) started operations on the B band in August 1994 with Ericsson equipment. Cellular telephony thus is the first case of private-sector provision of domestic telecom services in Ecuador. Original estimates were for 10,000 subscribers by year-end 1994. This was easily surpassed and, as of March 1995, there 27,870. Both CONECEL and OTECEL have domestic and international shareholders.

7.6.3 Public Telephones

Coin-operated telephones (*daruma*) developed in Brazil have been extensively installed in Ecuador's urban areas where there are few other phones. These phones allow long-distance calls. There were approximately 2,500 of them in the country at the end of 1994, but only 20 percent were operational. Most accept only coins, although magnetic card systems have been installed in several areas.

A call for bids was issued in mid-May 1995 by EMETEL and CONAM (the state modernization committee), offering a concession for a new public telephone system using either the coin or card method. Two independent companies each will install and operate 5,000 public telephones in any part of the country. There thus could be direct competition between the companies. The concession is for an initial operating period of ten years. Tenders were originally expected by mid-July 1995, with a final decision by September 1995. However, the Superintendencia is calling the tender illegal because it is based on the Modernization Law, which that office claims does not have precedence over the powers accorded the Superintendencia by the 1992 Special Telecommunications Law.

7.6.4 Rural Communications

Although about half the population live in rural areas, these people had only about a tenth of the telephone lines in 1991. IETEL, superseded by EMETEL, obtained funds from two foreign governments to promote expansion of rural telecom systems. Spain provided U.S.$15 million and Canada, U.S.$5 million. The Canadian money was a grant, although IETEL was committed to "repaying" it by supporting a social service foundation in rural areas.

The objective of the project was to provide rural telephone service in locations with easy access—such as police stations, churches, health centers, and schools—generally using radio communications. In areas where capacity is limited, preference was given community organizations and private subscribers such as banks, pharmacies, and shopping centers. The system is connected to the main network, allowing calls between subscribers anywhere in the country and internationally. The foreign money was only for transmission equipment; switches were acquired under other financing. So that the system will be especially reliable and not burdened with maintenance, the equipment is largely digital and computerized. Installation of more than 2,000 public telephones also was planned. The project was still under way in mid-1996. When complete, all towns with over 500 inhabitants will have telephone service.

7.6.5 Isolated Rural Areas

The Amazonian region is primarily a rain forest with scattered populations engaged in agriculture and in the country's main petroleum fields. One city, Nambija, has attracted many colonizers, including gold miners, due to its abundant mineral resources. Its population has grown substantially in spite of the lack of basic facilities.

As part of providing reliable high-quality telecom services in isolated rural areas located in the western region of the country, there are plans to introduce a domestic satellite system providing telephone, telegraph, facsimile, television, and low-speed data transmission. The network will have a hub-and-spoke configuration centered on Quito, with eleven remote stations. Intelsat will be used until the Andean satellite project is completed, at which time the Simon Bolivar satellite will be used. There will be eighty-one circuits. In Nambija, Zumba, and Analuza, where estimated demand is at a medium level, twenty-four, twelve, and twelve circuits are planned, respectively. The other eight settlements are considered to have a relatively low demand and will get three or six circuits, with emphasis on public phones. Implementation of this plan is under way, but as of mid-1996 it was not clear when it would be complete.

Areas near the borders with Peru and Colombia are provided services through high-frequency radio channels that have low quality and are not entirely reliable.

7.6.6 Satellite Communications

Ecuador joined Intelsat in 1971. Mitsubishi put up a ground station in Conocoto, a suburb of Quito, which went on line in 1972. With initial capacity of thirty-six channels and connections to Panama and Argentina, the station was upgraded in 1975, increasing the number of circuits to fifty-three lines and making later expansions easier. A station was later built in Guayaquil. Both are now digital. In 1991 the ground stations had 531 circuits, 70 percent of which were in use. Subsequently, new telephone circuits were opened giving EMETEL 1,000 international circuits at earth stations in Quito and Guayaquil. Ecuador also is a member of Inmarsat.

There are five satellites accessible from Ecuador: Intelsat, Panamsat, Anck (U.S.-based), Nawelsat (Argentina), and Solidaridad (Mexico). EMETEL operates exclusively through Intelsat for all public services (telephone, data transmission, television). The potential market is as high as 400 VSAT stations, 50 SCPC domestic stations, and 50 SCPC international stations.

In May 1994, the Superintendencia de Telecomunicaciones issued regulations governing use of satellite systems. That office granted licenses to three private companies: Impsatel del Ecuador SA, Americatel SA, and the cellular telephone operator Conecell SA. Their systems will have teleports in Quito and Guayaquil, and VSAT stations are being installed in many other cities. The earth stations in Quito and Guayaquil initially will operate with Intelsat or Panamsat satellites, but they are capable of operating with other satellites. Contracts are usually for five-year periods, renewable prior to expiration. Services will include domestic and international data transmission, videoconferencing and point-to-point teleconferencing, electronic mail, and other business services.

Ecuador had at least twenty private communications networks in 1994 operating through different satellite links, including a number of banks and petroleum companies using VSATs under contract with EMETEL or the Superintendencia. Vitacom (Canada), Mitsubishi, and Selena (Italy) have provided the VSAT equipment. The networks vary in size. Banco del Pacifico operates the largest, with four earth stations in Ecuador and one each in Miami and Panama.

Banco del Pacifico is currently (October 1995) the only entity providing Internet service to businesses and individuals, using its Ecuanet system. However, there are complaints that the system goes down several hours a day when the bank is transmitting its own data and that the service is too expensive. Other Internet access providers will probably emerge in 1996 because of the large, unsatisfied demand. Fundacyt, a nonprofit organization funded with a U.S.$35 million loan from the Interamerican Development Bank, is charged with expanding and promoting scientific and technological development in Ecuador. It has been seeking ways of offering Internet and satellite links to universities and students.

In 1995 EMETEL signed a U.S.$3.5 million contract with NEC for installation of a new earth station in Quito. A U.S.$13 million contract was also signed with U.S.-based Satellite Transmission Systems to install a domestic satellite system that includes one master station and stations in forty-four rural towns.

Ecuador and the four other members of the Andean Pact have been working together to upgrade their international telecommunications satellite capacity. Under the project, Bolivia, Colombia, Ecuador, Peru, and Venezuela will lease additional Intelsat transponders. Ecuador will rent two 36-Mhz transponders for ten years for domestic and international traffic. Andean Pact members have also discussed launching their own satellite, a project called "Simon Bolivar."

7.6.7 Telex

Radio Internacional del Ecuador introduced telex in 1957, replacing radiotelegraphic service for both international and national circuits between Quito and Guayaquil. As part of a general move to upgrade the country's telecommunications in the early 1970s, the task of installing telex-gentex service was given to Siemens in 1974. Central nodes were set up in Quito and Guayaquil and an international switch was installed in Quito for automatic international communications. Around then, the network had 945 subscriber lines, of which 700 were along the Quito-Guayaquil corridor. In 1994 there were 3,600 subscriber lines and almost 3 million international telex communications. Because of the pending privatization of EMETEL, there are no expansion plans. Subscribers may own their own machines or rent from EMETEL.

7.6.8 Cable Television

Three companies provide cable television services. TV Cable, with 50,000 subscribers, was formed by the 1995 merger of Satelcom (Quito) and Telesat (Guayaquil), which are the only licensed cable operators. Univisa started operations in October 1994 using satellite technology. Owned by Ecuavisa, which also owns a television station, Univisa provides eight channels to 1,500 subscribers in three major cities. Omnivision began operations in January 1995 using a combination of parabolic antennas and satellite dishes to receive signals that are redistributed by cable. It has 200 subscribers.

7.7 The 1995 Telecom Bill and Partial Privatization

The future and legal structure of the whole sector will again change significantly as a new telecommunications bill, approved on August 8, 1995, shapes the industry. Passed against strong opposition from labor unions and other politically important groups, it sets out the steps to privatize EMETEL.[1]

First, EMETEL will be changed into a limited-liability corporation through creation of a joint stock company, EMETEL SA, to which the personnel, assets, and obligations of EMETEL are transferred. Initially, 100 percent of the equity will belong to the state. This was done in late 1995.

Two subsidiaries will be created, EMETEL del Norte SA, headquartered in Quito, and EMETEL del Sur SA, based in Guayaquil. They will provide local telephone services in the *sierra* and *costa* regions, respectively, under exclusive concessions with an initial period of five years and will compete in domestic and international long distance. Rates are to be based on actual operating costs. The companies are obliged to submit plans for rural coverage, but costs are to be subsidized directly by the government if need be.

An international auction among prequalified and experienced operators will be held to sell 35 percent interests in each of the two companies. Employees will receive 5 percent of each company. The remaining 60 percent will remain in state hands, reserved for possible future sale. Some observers believe it will require twelve to fifteen months after December 1995 to complete the partial privatization.

Although no study has been conducted of the two operating companies' market value, published estimates range from U.S.$600 million to U.S.$2.2 billion. In the summer of 1994 the government hired consultants, led by GERASIN (which is based in Venezuela), to help set privatization guidelines and values.

ETAPA will remain separate, still owned by the municipality of Cuenca, which means there actually will be three local operating companies. However, some observers believe ETAPA will have difficulty surviving in a competitive environment.

Other value-added services, including cable television and satellite, are to be awarded on the basis of open competition. The Consejo Nacional de Telecomunicaciones (CONATEL) will be created to be in charge of awarding all concessions for the sector, taking these functions over from the Superintendencia de Telecomunicaciones. CONATEL's board is to include representatives of the president, the military, and the Escuela de Ingenieros (School of Engineers). The head of the Superintendencia would have a voice but not a vote in CONATEL's proceedings. The Superintendencia will otherwise remain as the controlling agency.

7.7.1 Complications and Critics

A complicating factor in privatization is Article 46 of the Constitution. It reserves "strategic sectors," including telecommunications, to the state; delegation of such services to the private sector is permissible only in exceptional circumstances. A debate is under way in Congress to liberalize the clause, but in any case most observers believe a sale of EMETEL can be justified as an appropriate exception because of the poor quality of service the company has provided and the limited funds the state has to modernize and upgrade the system. Still, if the Constitution is not amended, opponents of telecommunications privatization might use Article 46 to try to prevent transfer of control of EMETEL to the private sector.

Some critics of the 1995 law argue that EMETEL should not be divided into two companies because that decreases the overall market value of the assets. The critics claim that potential purchasers will have less interest in a divided market that is small by international standards. They also say that such a division reinforces the already strong regionalism present in Ecuador and creates problems of coordination. Additionally, it is argued that with two local operators, businesses with offices in both regions would face higher service costs.

In May 1994, CONAM (the State Modernization Committee) asked for bids for legal, financial, regulatory, and technical consulting services related to privatization of the sector. A consultant was tentatively selected in mid-1995 and CONAM is awaiting approval from the World Bank, which is providing funding. Nevertheless, some experts argue that until the new telecommunications reform bill is approved by Congress, the consulting contract should not be awarded. Others say the same consultants should have been contracted to provide advice on drafting the law, instead of having to work around it.

7.8 Conclusion

Telecom service in Ecuador's rural areas has improved since the late 1980s but remains very inadequate. EMETEL estimates basic services are now available to around 80 percent of the country but, due to the dispersion of the rural population, teledensity in rural areas is below 1 line per 100 people. Service in Quito is considered fair by Latin American standards, although overall service (repair, installation, completion rates, and so on) is poor. Service in Guayaquil has traditionally been much worse than in Quito. It is estimated that as of year-end 1994, EMETEL had a completion rate of 44 percent for international calls and 40 percent for local and domestic long-distance calls. Local and domestic long-distance service charges are extremely low, being subsidized by high international rates. Rebalancing the rate structure is expected during the latter part of the 1990s, making it more in line with international standards.

A partial privatization of EMETEL, the basic telephone services provider, is expected by the end of 1996 because the momentum is there. A suitable overall legal framework has been put in place (although not without controversy), and the winner of the May 1996 presidential election was Abdala Bucaram. Areas such as telex, satellite communications, public telephony, television, radio, cable television, and cellular telephone systems have been, or are soon to be, privatized. Thus the Ecuadorian telecommunications sector is transforming itself from a group of state-owned companies into private or semiprivate enterprises. The process has been slow, but it is sure to be completed.

Note

1. The State Modernization Committee, CONAM, is the government entity in charge of the overall privatization process. It has argued that under the terms of the Modernization Law approved in December 1993, concessions for basic telephone services already can be awarded to private firms without the need for the explicit permission granted by another special telecommunications law.

8
Bolivia

EDGAR SARAVIA

Bolivia has long been one of the least developed and poorest of Latin America's countries. The economy has been dependent on minerals, particularly tin, and, more recently, natural gas (which accounts for about 25 percent of the country's exports). Located in the heart of South America, it covers about 1.1 million square kilometers. The population of 7.7 million (July 1994 estimate) has increased almost 50 percent since 1979 and is growing at around 2.3 percent annually, a decrease from the 2.7 percent rate in the 1970s. In the late 1970s the population was only one-third urban, but by the mid-1980s over half were in cities or towns. The average life expectancy in Bolivia in 1994 was about fifty-four years, according to the World Bank.

Geographically, landlocked Bolivia is very diverse, with elevations ranging from 150 meters to well over 6,000 meters. There are three major areas: the Altiplano, the temperate valleys, and the plains.

The Altiplano is a plateau between the Cordillera Occidental and the Cordilleras Oriental and Real in the southwestern part of the country. It is about 140 kilometers wide and 840 kilometers long, with an average elevation of 3,600 meters. Most of the mining is in this region, so some of the largest and oldest cities are here, including the seat of government, La Paz, as well as Oruro and Potosí (where the Spanish began mining silver in 1545). About 50 percent of the population live in the Altiplano.

The temperate valleys *(Yungas)*, with elevations between 500 and 3,000 meters, are located in the eastern foothills of the Cordillera Real in the central part of the country. Cochabamba, the third largest city in the country; Sucre, the official capital and seat of the judiciary; and Tarija are the principal cities. Some 28 percent of the population are in this area.

The plains *(Llanos),* located in the north and east, slope from about 450 meters to as low as 150 meters in the southeast. Most of the *llanos* are in the Amazon basin; the southern part is in the Gran Chaco, an area of fairly dry grasslands and scrub brush. The plains account for over half of the country's total area, but only about 22 percent of the population live there. Santa Cruz, center of the natural gas discoveries, is Bolivia's second largest city.

Bolivia is a republic with a centralized government comprised of three independent branches. The president and members of the bicameral legislature are elected every four years by popular vote. Presidents cannot succeed themselves.

Since August 1985—under Paz Estenssoro (1985–89), Jaime Paz Zamora (1989–93), and Gonzalo Sanchez de Lozada (1993–), who was planning minister under Paz Estenssoro—the country has been following an open-market economic development model that has been successful in controlling hyperinflation, which had reached an annualized rate of 25,000 percent in July 1985. Annual inflation has generally been below 15 percent since 1986, and the economy has been growing since 1987, reversing a negative trend that started in 1980.

8.1 History

Telecommunications in Bolivia started when a telegraph line was built in 1874 between the mining center of Caracoles and the Pacific port of Antofagasta. This line was quickly followed by others, linking the principal cities.

Initially, telegraph lines were constructed and operated by the National Corps of Engineers, which reported directly to the Office of the Presidency. On September 8, 1892, the government created the General Directorate for State Telegraphs to construct new lines and operate all existing ones. Thus, since the very beginning, telegraph service has been a state monopoly.

8.1.1 Telephony

Telephone service has come late and slowly. Using operators and manual exchanges, people were able to make calls only within the same exchange. Municipalities had the authority to grant operating licenses, which went to local companies. The municipality was the largest shareholder in each case.

A customer seeking service was required to purchase a share in the telco for a price fixed by the company and approved by the municipality. The purchase entitled the customer to "own" a telephone number on the local exchange and to have a line connected, subject to space availability in the nearest telephone box. The assigned number stayed with the customer as long as the customer remained a shareholder of the company. This caused problems when a customer moved to an area of the city served by a different exchange.

Comparing the local telcos, one finds that service has developed at different rates, in many cases following separate paths. There were seventeen local telcos, and most towns in the Altiplano and *yungas* had service of some sort.

Truly automated service with direct-dial capability within a given exchange was first introduced in La Paz in April 1941. Other cities soon followed, and by the late 1950s the main cities—La Paz, Cochabamba, Santa Cruz, Oruro, Sucre, and Potosí—had this service. All the original automatic exchanges were electromechanical. Several were still in service as late as the early 1990s, in La Paz, Cochabamba, and Sucre; these had been installed in 1941, 1943, and 1950, respectively.

Despite the significant cash outlay required to purchase a share in the local telco in order to have access to a telephone, the number of users grew steadily. This was not only due to a growth in demand in cities already having telephone service but also because new cities were installing exchanges. By 1960, the number of users had reached 16,410. The next two decades saw dramatic growth, averaging close to 10 percent annually. From 1975 to 1980 the number of users more than doubled, reaching 129,800.

Bolivia entered a deep recession in the 1980s, with the economy shrinking at a yearly rate of over 2 percent. Spiraling inflation had reached hyperinflation status by 1984. The government maintained a policy of fixing the exchange rate to the U.S. dollar at an unsustainable level, well below the rate in the parallel market. The difference at times reached a 20 to 1 ratio. Because tariffs for all services were fixed at the official exchange rate and paid in Bolivian currency, companies providing services were greatly affected.

Local telcos were unable to continue the rapid expansion of their networks. The number of telephones increased only some 30 percent during the 1980s (Table 8.1). The slower growth was not so much from a decrease in demand as it was from the inability of local telcos to add capacity. Of the seventeen local telcos, only Santa Cruz and Cochabamba installed exchanges after the late 1970s or early 1980s. By the early 1990s Santa Cruz and La Paz had very significant waiting lists of people who had paid a deposit to secure a line once one became available. Tarija and Sucre also had relatively large lists, but ten telcos and the places where local service is provided by ENTel had no waiting lists. In March 1991 there were 172,423 users nationwide, and 52,675 people on waiting lists (44 percent of them in Santa Cruz and 43 percent in La Paz).

The lack of investment during the 1980s also meant most lines were on electromechanical (20 percent) or crossbar exchanges (72 percent). Fewer than 4 percent were digital. (Data are for 1991 and are not available on 4 percent of the lines, but they were analog of some sort.) Virtually all of the electromechanical switches were supplied by Ericsson; Oki supplied 77 percent of the crossbar exchanges, with Ericsson a distant second.

Table 8.1. Telephone Subscribers, 1955–1991

Year	Number of Telephones	Growth per Year (%)
1955	11,400	
1960	16,410	7.6
1966	25,235	7.4
1970	37,551	10.4
1975	62,630	10.7
1981	135,100	13.7
1984	158,308	5.4
1988	164,545	1.0
1991	172,423	1.6

Sources: AT&T, *The World's Telephones.* New York: AT&T, various years. Data for 1960, 1975, 1991 from ENTel, "Estado Actual de la Telefonía en Bolivia," and ENTel internal document, 1991.

8.1.2 International Long Distance

International calling first became available in the 1960s. Two foreign companies, as concessionaires of the government, operate the service, which still requires the use of an operator. Cable & Wireless (C&W), operating as Cable West Coast, linked Bolivia with Europe, while International Telephone and Telegraph, as All America Cable (AAC), provided connections to North America. As a requirement for the right to operate, the companies opened offices in the main cities where the public can place calls and send telegrams and telexes.

In the mid-1990s, three long-distance carriers—Sprint, MCI, and AT&T—entered the market with their long-distance services. By 1995, several North American companies were offering callback services in Bolivia. Also, a consortium consisting of Comsat and MCI, with ENTel, was offering international business services.

8.1.3 Telex

Telex was introduced in the early 1960s by Cable & Wireless and All America Cable. Subscribers paid a monthly fee that included rental of a telex machine; they could not use their own machines. The tariff was a fixed rate plus a variable rate depending on traffic.

In the early 1970s, as C&W and AAC's licenses to operate long-distance services expired, telex was taken over by ENTel. The network grew steadily through the decade, but by early 1980, with the introduction of facsimile, demand stabilized near 1,400 subscribers. In March 1991 active subscribers had reached 1,570, with over half in La Paz and almost a quarter in Santa Cruz.

8.2 ENTel

In December 1965 the military government then in power created ENTel (Empresa Nacional de Telecomunicaciones) through Decree 07441, as a joint private-public company. The intention was to establish a national telecom enterprise with which the local telcos would join in a united effort to modernize and further develop the sector. ENTel was given a number of responsibilities.

1. Provide public telecom services in certain urban areas and domestic and international long distance. Services would include telephone, telex, connections for radio and television, rental of circuits to state and private services, and all in-transit international traffic.
2. Promote and direct the modernization and expansion of public telecom services to keep up with technological change.
3. Advise and cooperate with the state and state-related agencies in matters related to telecommunications. This would be conducted through the Ministry of Public Works and Communications.

The decree specifically indicated that ENTel would not interfere with the international long-distance services provided by C&W and All America Cable or with national defense and national security services. Radio and television broadcasts and special systems defined as "mobile aeronautic" and "mobile maritime" were also excluded.

ENTel's board was to have ten members, five representing various ministries and five representing local telcos. The state would hold at least 51 percent of the company. Part of its funding included all payments made to date by the central and municipal governments and other state agencies in the telecom sector.

The local telcos did not agree with the creation of a single enterprise or with the participation of the state. To present a unified front against what was perceived as a threat from the government, they formed ABET (the Bolivian Association of Telephone Companies). This was the main reason for ENTel's inability to raise any funds from the private sector.

In February 1968, soon after taking office, a democratically elected government placed ENTel under the regulatory jurisdiction of the Ministry of Public Works and Communications. The ministry was, in particular, to oversee compliance with technical standards, tariffs, and any other requirements related to the operation of a concession.

In October 1968, Decree 08527 assigned priority to ENTel regarding the development and operation of telecom services in Bolivia. The decree also stated that no new concessions would be awarded if ENTel was capable of providing the necessary services. This did not include any existing concessions, and thus it did not affect the international long-distance and telex services provided by C&W and All America Cable.

The status of ENTel was changed in June 1970 by the military government to a state-owned enterprise (Decree 09250). At the same time the government decided not to renew the C&W and All America Cable concessions when they expired, and it placed all matters pertaining to the operation and development of domestic and international long distance in the hands of ENTel.

A year later, a new military government issued the General Law for Telecommunications confirming the decision not to renew the concessions. The companies were required to turn over their equipment without compensation. Some of the foreign managers, and most of the Bolivian staff, became employees of ENTel.

The June 1971 law also defined the functions of the General Directorate for Telecommunications (DGT) as a regulatory agency for the sector, with the authority to grant operating concessions, approve tariffs, and verify compliance with technical standards for all areas. This included local telcos, long-distance telephone, telex, radio and television broadcasting, cable television, and other related services. The DGT reported directly to the undersecretary for communications of the Ministry of Transportation, Communications and Civil Aviation. In other words, some of ENTel's original functions were transferred to the DGT.

In the early 1970s, after finally having in place all the legislation defining its role, as well as the resources from the state, ENTel set out to develop long-distance service. By 1976 it had constructed an analog microwave trunk network with 960 radio channels linking La Paz, Cochabamba, and Santa Cruz. By 1978 it had installed a satellite earth station in La Paz with a capacity of 292 circuits for international communications. A second 960-radio-channel microwave network had linked La Paz with Oruro, Sucre, Potosí, and Tarija by 1980. With demand for long-distance service growing, the analog microwave network underwent an expansion in 1989, using multiplexing to increase capacity to 2,100 channels on each route.

8.3 The 1985 Reorganization and Tariff Revision

In an attempt to alleviate the problems of the local telcos and to make services accessible to more users, the new Paz Estenssoro government in August 1985 reorganized all local telephone companies and established new practices for fixing tariffs. By law, the companies were converted into cooperatives. In addition, tariffs were fixed in U.S. dollars to be charged in local currency adjusted monthly to reflect the current exchange rate, a policy that remains in effect. In 1992 the average monthly rate was equivalent to U.S.$3.45.

Today, ENTel provides approximately 80 percent of the national and international telecommunications services in Bolivia with two large basic systems: transmission and the automatic telephone exchange systems. It is responsible for the operation of all telex and telegraphic services, data transmission services, television signal transmission, radio broadcasting, rent or lease of microwave channels within the industry, telecommunications, and other services. The phone industry is constructed as follows: ENTel handles long-distance calls; local co-ops own the lines within their areas, which correspond to the urban centers in most cases, with some limited service to rural areas (no numbers are available on the percentage of rural lines). Individual phone customers buy their lines from the co-op directly, if they are lucky to get an available line, or they purchase them from a current owner.

Another reason for the 1985 change in legal status was to try to give some power to the average consumer (shareholder) and diminish the overwhelming influence local municipalities exerted as both the largest shareholder and the regulator. As shareholder entities, it was one share, one vote. Under Bolivian law for cooperatives, essentially each juridical person or member of the cooperative, regardless of shares held, has one vote. In practice, the change in status has had little, if any, effect. Companies are still managed by people in theory "elected" by popular vote of the users. In practice, however, they have strong ties to the municipalities or major political parties and are far removed from the real needs of users or from matters relating to the quality and cost of services.

It remains necessary to purchase a telephone line in order to have service. During 1965–95, the price of a line oscillated around U.S.$1,500—this in a country with a 1991 per capita yearly income of approximately U.S.$845.

A small industry has arisen in La Paz in which companies do nothing more than buy and sell phone lines. The current official price for a phone line, sold by the co-ops, is U.S.$1,500, but the market price is closer to U.S.$2,000.

It is almost impossible in practice to transfer existing service out of a given telephone exchange. Instead, the customer has to purchase a line in the new exchange area, rent a line in the secondary market from an existing holder, or trade the existing line with someone seeking to transfer to the customer's exchange.

8.4 The Telecom Network

Bolivia's telecom infrastructure is currently underdeveloped, with only 4 lines existing for every 100 Bolivians; some new lines should come into service in the future, but this will still leave the country with a low per capita level of phone service. In 1992, Bolivia had only 207,823 telephone lines for an urban population of 3.69 million and a rural population of 2.72 million.

Almost 80 percent of subscribers are in the three largest cities (La Paz, Santa Cruz, and Cochabamba), and the next three largest (Tarija, Sucre, and Potosí) add another 10 percent. The remaining 10 percent are in eleven cities, each with its own local telco, and in six other population centers where ENTel provides local service. (All data are for March 1991.) In La Paz, Santa Cruz, and Cochabamba, the number of lines per 100 people in 1994 was 6.89, 7.63, and 7.16, respectively, according to statistics compiled by ENTel. In rural areas, on average, the number of lines was less than 1 per hundred people. In short, there are seventeen local telcos, plus the local service ENTel provides.

Local telcos in several major cities had significant expansion plans under way in the early 1990s, all using digital technology. La Paz was adding 70,000 lines to meet a waiting list for 23,266 lines, replace 13,660 lines dating back to 1941, and have some 33,000 lines for new demand. Santa Cruz was installing 50,000 lines, about half of which were for those on waiting lists, and Tarija was getting 18,000 lines, about a third for those on waiting lists. These projects, completed in 1994, largely eliminated waiting lists and almost doubled capacity in the three cities. At the end of 1994 there were about 243,000 lines nationwide.

The transmission systems consist of the southern analog microwave network, the analog and digital microwave network, the microwave link system between Santa Cruz and Puerto Suarez, the international earth link with Argentina and Peru, the UHF radio link (FDM/FM), the digital multiaccess national rural system, and signal transmission channels for broadcasting stereophonic radio and television systems.

The automatic telephone exchange system is digital for international traffic; national telephone operators are 60 percent digital. ENTel owns and operates two large ground satellite stations in La Paz and Santa Cruz, and thirteen small ground satellite stations throughout the country, all using the most modern technology. The telex and telegraphic automatic communications systems have 3,346 operational lines and 644 trunk lines. The data transmission network provides nontelephone exchange point-to-point (IBS) services between La Paz, Cochabamba, Santa Cruz, Orno, Potosí, and Sucre. Data verification is done with the magic-online system and a data transmission service of 64 kbps. Also, ENTel has recently completed the installation of a fiber-optic link for the telephone cooperatives of La Paz, Cochabamba, and Santa Cruz. The fiber-optic link will give users better quality and service. ENTel installed twenty-two small ground satellite stations throughout the country, which became operational by the end of 1993. Another five large remote stations were scheduled to be installed in Trinidad, Monteagudo, Bermejo, San Ignacio de Moxos, and Riberaha, along with seven other smaller remote stations. The Spanish government has provided financing to Bolivia in the amount of U.S.$27 million for new telecommunications equipment that will serve some 180 small villages throughout the country. The financing requires that Spanish suppliers be used, and Alcatel won the bid.

There is only one public data network. Operated by ENTel, it has been in service since 1988. Most of the customers are banks that use it to transmit files and transactions. In the early 1990s, there were only sixty-five subscribers, including twenty-eight in La Paz, twenty-one in Santa Cruz, and sixteen in Cochabamba. Subscribers must use modems supplied by ENTel. The network can operate at 50 to 300 bauds in asynchronous mode and 2,400 to 9,600 bauds in synchronous mode. Private data networks are provided to large users by Datacom. By 1995, these networks were also used for voice transmission.

Cellular phones are filling in some of the gap between supply and demand, and more growth is expected in that sector. In 1990, a concession was granted to Telecel to offer cellular telephone communications in the cities of La Paz, Santa Cruz, Cochabamba, Tarija, and Oruro. All long-distance communications between the cities necessarily will utilize ENTel's network.

Telecel, a joint venture between Millicon International and a U.S. company, and two local partners had invested U.S.$8 million by 1995. Telecel completed installation of the necessary equipment in the fourth quarter of 1991, and the system has been operational since then. By the end of February 1992 subscribers numbered approximately 5,000. At that time, tariffs were a fixed charge of about U.S.$5 per month plus a variable rate of about U.S.$0.35 for each minute on the air.

8.5 Television and Radio

Except for one government-owned television broadcasting station, all regional television broadcasting stations are in private hands and eight belong to the major state universities. About eighty-four stations existed in 1993. Only the government station is considered "national" because it alone reaches all areas of Bolivia. The other stations beam their signals only to major cities. All private regional and university television stations have to rent the interconnection system from ENTel to broadcast nationally.

Three private cable television systems exist in the cities of La Paz, Cochabamba, and Santa Cruz. One of them, Video Cable Universal, wholly owned by the U.S. company COMTECH Supply Inc., installed the latest fiber-optic technology in 1994. In 1996, a small-scale price war was going on in La Paz between Video Cable Universal and the UHF-based cable companies.

Cable television was introduced in the third quarter of 1991 with the granting of a license to Video Cable Universal (VCU) for operations in the city of La Paz. The packages offered to subscribers consist primarily of foreign programming received by VCU by satellite.

The industry is regulated by the Direccion de Telecomunicaciones (Telecommunications Directorate). The Directorate regulates hours for broadcasting but not price controls.

As in the case of the television stations, all but two of the 234 radio broadcasting stations were in private hands in 1993 (one of the two belongs to the military, the other to the government). Radio stations are popular in Bolivia in part because radios are cheap and can bring entertainment and news to the vast majority of the population, which cannot afford television. In the mid-1990s there was a large increase in new FM radio stations throughout the country. By 1993, there were 118 AM stations, 56 FM, and 60 SW.

8.6 Regulation

8.6.1 The Preexistent Legal Framework

Regulation had originally been entrusted by the government to the Ministry of Transportation, Communications and Civil Aviation (now Secretariat of Transportation and Communications). More specifically, regulatory powers resided with the General Directorate for Telecommunications (DGT), except for rural telecommunications, which was handled by the Directorate for Rural Telecommunication (DITER). Both agencies were at the same level in the ministry hierarchy and reported to the undersecretary for communications, who had direct responsibility to control all actions of the DGT and the DITER.

The organizational structure of telecommunications was rather complicated because the ministry that regulates the sector was also responsible, in the final analysis, for operating the state-owned long-distance company, ENTel. Both the minister and the undersecretary for communications were members of ENTel's board, together with representatives from the Ministries of Finance, Planning, and National Defense.

The DITER both regulates and operates the rural telecom system. For local telcos, a similar conflict exists, as the municipalities still participate in their operations and effectively control their tariffs. The local telcos were members of FECOTEL, the Federation of Local Telephone Cooperatives.

8.6.1.1 General Directorate for Telecommunications (DGT)

The DGT regulates, coordinates, authorizes, and controls all activities in the telecom sector not specifically excepted, and it participates in the design and execution of telecom policy. It has a long list of specific functions:

1. Manage the frequency bands for the various forms of radio communication.
2. Oversee licensing and permits within the sector.
3. Oversee concessions for systems, services, and media.
4. Suggest charges and tariffs and oversee their application.
5. Harmonize, evaluate, and coordinate telecommunications plans.
6. Participate in the execution of national telecom policy.
7. Control and coordinate the activities of all the companies in the sector—state-owned, private, and joint—in order to maximize performance of the systems while optimizing their efficiency.
8. Propose legislation for the sector.

9. Establish standards for material and equipment, including their installation and operation.
10. Encourage research and technical assistance, including the development of a local equipment industry.
11. Carry out and coordinate censorship and the like in cases of internal commotion or war.
12. Sanction those violating the General Law for Telecommunications and the corresponding regulations.

In practice the DGT has concentrated most of its efforts on carrying out the first four duties. Regarding tariffs (item 4), the DGT and the Secretariat have approved only the tariffs for domestic and international long-distance services provided by ENTel. Approval for charges by the local telcos was given by the municipalities, which continue to have regulatory powers. The DGT has done very little in the remaining areas for various reasons, including lack of funds and staff.

8.6.1.2 Directorate for Rural Telecommunication (DITER)

The main functions of the DITER are limited to rural telecommunications. They are mostly operational and very little, if any, work is done to maintain and expand the network. Services are offered by the private company Radio Serrano.

8.6.2 Problems

Telecommunications in Bolivia faced a number of technical, economic, and administrative problems. The problems were often interrelated and can be summarized as follows.

1. Lack of coordination between local telcos and ENTel, which resulted in incompatible plans.
2. Inefficiencies and defective tariff practices that limited the companies' ability to maintain and expand services.
3. Excessive government intervention and other bureaucratic procedures, as well as outdated and inflexible internal organization and practices in the companies.

8.6.2.1 Technical Problems

The main technical problem was lack of coordination between ENTel and the local companies in development of the network. This has resulted in imbalances. For example, in the late 1970s and early 1980s while ENTel was aggressively increasing capacity on its long-distance network, the local companies did little to install equipment to interface with ENTel. In the early 1990s, the completion rate within ENTel's network was at 82 percent. Completion rates were only 37 percent for calls originating in or made to La Paz, 46 percent for Santa Cruz, and 52 percent for Cochabamba.

These types of imbalances increased after the new digital trunk network linking La Paz, Cochabamba, and Santa Cruz became operational in August 1991, as the electromechanical switches then still serving 20 percent of the nation's subscribers had serious difficulties interfacing with the new microwave network.

In 1990 a major contract was awarded to Siemens (of Germany) and Oki (of Japan) to expand the telephone systems in La Paz and Santa Cruz, installing 102,310 new telephones lines. As late as 1994, lines were being installed. Pending governmental approval and availability of foreign financing, another 17,000 new telephone lines in other circles were planned for the near future.

Long-distance companies AT&T, Sprint, and MCI are now providing phone-card international long-distance service. All billing comes from the United States. Global Communications, also a U.S. company, is offering callback services in Bolivia, apparently with some success. Its lower rates may cut into ENTel's revenues. This service is available only to holders of major credit cards, so its numbers are relatively small.

Until the third quarter of 1991, only 10 percent of subscribers could dial international calls directly. However, by using a double tone, all but the 20 percent of users on the old electromechanical exchanges could have direct dialing.

While ENTel's digital network is capable of handling expanded value-added services, the local companies are doing little, if anything, to offer similar services, thus placing all responsibility for their development with ENTel or private-sector companies. Because the local telcos have a de facto monopoly within their operating areas, it is difficult for private companies to compete.

Seventeen cooperatives own 90 percent of the urban telephone system and a small part of the rural system. By 1994, 44 percent of the co-op system was digitalized. Cotel from La Paz, Cotas from Santa Luz, and Comteco from Cochabamba are, in that order, the largest telephone cooperatives. All the cooperatives must utilize ENTel's service for their national interconnection. Most of the rural system and the entire domestic long-distance system are wholly owned by ENTel, whose system was about 64 percent digitalized in 1994.

8.6.2.2 Tariff Problems

Regarding tariffs, although much has been done since August 1985 to eliminate direct subsidies from the government to telcos and to keep rates constant in U.S. dollar terms, problems remain.

In theory all tariffs must be approved by the government through the ex-Ministry of Transportation, Communications and Civil Aviation. The ministry has very little to say regarding charges by the local companies; rather, these are approved by the municipalities. ENTel and the DGT originate long-distance tariff proposals and submit them to the ministry for approval.

Since August 1985 tariffs for all public services were required to cover all expenses—operational and financial—and provide funds for the companies to invest in modernization and expansion. In practice, in the telecom sector, this is the case only with ENTel's tariffs for long distance.

ENTel's tariffs included the local telcos' participation, which was negotiated separately with each company and does not necessarily relate to the actual costs incurred by the local company. Also included was an amount negotiated between the ex-Ministry of Finance and ENTel, which was transferred each month to help balance the central government's budget. It is important to consider this practice, as these transfers are not considered taxes and are not a fixed percentage of the company's income. Rather, they are specified amounts of money, known to change depending on the requirements of the Treasury. Transfers were the equivalent of about 26 percent of ENTel's revenues for 1988, 24 percent in 1989, and 28 percent for 1990.

Accounting practices and the structure of ENTel had not permitted determination of costs for specific long-distance routes and services. There were no cost accounting systems until the mid-1990s: all company costs simply were added together and assigned to individual services in the same proportion as their participation in the overall traffic of the company.

An additional problem with tariff policy was that it presupposed that the level of efficiency at the company, both for operations and investments, was acceptable. If there were inefficiencies, they were transferred directly to the customer via the tariff. Mainly bureaucratic in nature and designed to control processes, with no emphasis on results, ENTel's structure, and the company's and government's mechanisms for control, did not contribute to improvements in the efficiency of the company.

Local companies' tariffs appeared to be artificially low. For various reasons, some technical companies, with the exception of Cotas in Santa Cruz, charged a flat monthly rate with no additional charges for the number or duration of local calls. In 1991 the average monthly charge for local service was U.S.$3.45, except in Santa Cruz. There, charges varied depending on the number of calls made. To this day the emphasis for local telcos seems to be on the onetime, up-front charge for purchasing a telephone line.

The local companies had problems with their accounting practices similar to those at ENTel. Most had not had cost accounting systems. One consequence of this was that the participations received from ENTel for long-distance calls undoubtedly did not reflect the real costs incurred by the local companies. Probably the payments exceeded the costs, in effect a subsidy from long distance to local services.

8.6.2.3 Administrative Problems

Although the government has little influence on rates, it does otherwise involve itself in the affairs of ENTel and the local telcos, many would say excessively. Particularly burdensome are the bureaucratic procedures that must be followed. They are aimed at such things as making sure the proper forms are being filled out and doing very little, if anything, to ensure that the actions of the companies yield the expected results. Government intrusion also has contributed to a state of confusion in the sector and added to the lack of direction in development, with the various players more often than not going their own separate ways. Even in the case of ENTel, the message from the government has not been clear most of the time, but rather has been a collection of requests and instructions that often are confusing if not contradictory in nature. In short, while the control of processes has been intended to improve efficiency at enterprises owned by the state or with state participation, it has been largely ineffective because very little or no emphasis is placed on results. A case in point is purchasing parts and equipment.

Essentially, all equipment is imported. The main suppliers have been Ericsson, Oki, ITT, NEC, Northern Telecom, and Siemens. The use of different suppliers has created problems of compatibility, but that is not the issue here. Under regulations still generally in effect in 1994, any purchase in excess of a certain amount (U.S.$50,000 in 1991) had to be channeled through one of three independent procurement agencies contracted by the government for this purpose. This was true even for the procurement of spare parts when there is only one supplier.

The three agencies are Crown Agents from Great Britain, UNDP/OPS from the United Nations, and C3D from France. Any enterprise where the state has a stake has to select one of the three to source equipment and supplies on its behalf according to technical specifications defined by the enterprise. The procurement agency is in charge of evaluating proposals and recommending the "best" to the enterprise. This often means the lowest initial-cost proposal, which of course is not necessarily the most cost effective over the life of the equipment. The agencies charge 2 to 3 percent of the value of the purchase for their services.

The average time required to complete this process, from the moment the company contacts the procurement agency to the moment an order can be placed, is twelve months. As a result, companies break up orders to stay below the threshold or maintain high parts inventories in order to be able to respond to technical emergencies. Neither of these tactics does anything to improve company efficiency or to allow flexibility to respond to a rapidly changing technology and marketplace.

The bureaucratic obstacles associated with procurement are only part of the problem. Consider the digital microwave network linking La Paz, Cochabamba, and Santa Cruz. The project was approved by the DGT on July 29, 1986. It was then decided that it needed to be approved by the government's Economic Council of Ministers (CONEPLAN). This approval was not granted until June 12, 1987. The next step was for ENTel's board of directors to authorize contacting a procurement agency; this happened on October 27, 1987. After the lengthy procurement process was complete, the company was authorized to award the contract on November 11, 1988. The award had to be ratified by the government; this was done on April 5, 1989. A few more steps had to be followed before the Central Bank issued the necessary Letter of Credit for the supplier to start manufacturing and installing the equipment. The Letter was issued in February 1990.

Installation was completed in August 1991, and the system has been operational since then. Bureaucratic procedures took over three and a half years from when the DGT granted approval. Manufacturing and installing the equipment required only one and a half years. An analysis of several other projects reveals a similar pattern.

8.6.3 The Actual Legal Framework

In order to resolve these administrative, technical, and tariff problems, three laws were enacted and now form the basis of the sectorial regulation: The Capitalization Law in March 1994, the SIRESE Law approved in October 1994, and the Telecommunications Law enacted in July 1995.

Bolivia enacted the Capitalization Law in a search for capital. It permits the state to transform ENTel (and other public enterprises) into corporations that are held by shareholders. Each corporation would consist of a major international investor, with the rest of the shares being given outright—not sold—to the pension funds of each Bolivian resident that was of legal age on December 31, 1995. The investor, with a controlling interest of about 50 percent, would manage the corporation. Instead of paying up-front for ENTel shares—as is the case with privatization—the investor would, instead, set aside a predetermined amount of capital to be expended on investments in the network.

The government shies away from use of the word "privatization" in good measure to placate parties such as the labor unions, which are antiprivatization, and to avoid the attendant connotations of downsizing and foreign ownership of precious resources. Bolivia, with its history of local cooperatives sharing power with a national operator, was perhaps destined to come up with a plan that would serve the interests of private capital and of social polity. In June of 1995 three power companies were capitalized for a total of U.S.$145 million. The telecommunications sector was the second to be capitalized, to be followed through 1996 by the state airline, railway, smelter complex, and the oil and gas company.

In October 1994, Bolivia passed another law, the Law of Sectorial Regulation (SIRESE). This law created a General Superintendency and several Sectorial Superintendencies to regulate many activities, including telecommunications. The Superintendencies are under the tutelage of the Ministry of Finance and Economic Development. The system acts primarily as a watchdog and is barred from dictating regulations, allocations of the spectrum, and granting concessions.

The Law of Telecommunications was enacted in July 1995, broadening the scope of the Superintendency of Telecommunications to include allocations of the spectrum and to establish technical standards for telecom services. The Superintendency is now allowed to grant concessions, approve tariffs, and approve contracts between telecom providers and users. It can also exact penalties, such as the modification or revocation of a license. However, the power to establish regulations resides only in the executive branch of government.

After capitalization, ENTel is granted six years of monopoly rights to national and international long-distance service. Additionally, ENTel is granted nonexclusive rights for a concession of forty years to provide other services, such as mobile cellular, satellite, data transmission, telex, telegraph, rural telephony, public telephones, and local service. The cooperatives also have temporary exclusive rights—for the same six years—to provide local service in their concessions. However, the local operators, like ENTel, must meet expansion and quality targets that are set forth in new contracts with the Superintendency. Local operators with more than 50,000 installed lines will lose 20 percent of their monopoly rights in each year that they fail to meet targets. Operators with less than 50,000 lines will lose 25 percent of their market in each year that they fail to meet targets. A cooperative's loss of exclusive rights will be taken up by ENTel or granted to another firm, via a new concession.

The 1995 Telecommunications Law permits ENTel and the cooperatives to merge or to buy or transfer shares among themselves. It is quite likely that ENTel will benefit by buying into cooperatives (and gaining market share) and will thereby create an entity that can more effectively block market entry by new competitors after its monopoly ends, in the year 2001. Competitive services will not be regulated, but operators must avoid anticompetitive practices, such as price fixing. Monopoly services will be priced according to the costs of providing them, adjusted for inflation. The executive body will oversee these prices, as well as prices for interconnection.

Three months after this last piece of legislation was passed, Stet International (Italy) won the bid for ENTel in October 1995, beating out both MCI and Telefónica de España. ENTel's revenues in 1994 were U.S.$16 million—Stet's bid valued it at U.S.$1.22 billion. Stet made a capital contribution to ENTel amounting to U.S.$610 million in November 1995. These funds must be invested by ENTel over a six-year period to satisfy demand in its concession area and improve quality of service according to preestablished goals. ENTel must also provide telephones for every community of more than 350 inhabitants and install 5,000 pay phones by May 1997.

8.7 Conclusion

The Capitalization Law in Bolivia has come under attack by critics who charge that Bolivia needs to address today's dire problems, such as illiteracy, rather than to provide for the future, in the shape of a pension fund. However, others believe that the only two choices available in Bolivia's politically charged and decentralized telecom arena might have been either capitalization or no privatization at all. Therefore, Bolivia's solution serves as an example of a creative way for cash-strapped embattled governments in other countries to attract foreign investment capital.

The government of Bolivia's total investment in telecommunications between the years 1989 and 1993 came to about U.S.$100 million. The number of lines per 100 habitants reached only 4. The telecommunications system had different problems (tariff, administrative, and technical) that made harmonic development in this sector impossible. The telcos in Bolivia represent a singular and an original case due to the role played by seventeen independent cooperatives without profit objectives and with a high level of monopoly power.

ENTel, a public-private enterprise, has provided the long-distance services for the country under a monopoly structure. In the past, the prices and tariffs of local services have been low and did not cover the installation, operation, and the maintenance costs. Also, it seems that cross-subsidies from long-distance calls did not exist. It became clear that greater infusions of capital were needed to bring the local telecom network up to a better standard. To do so, a new institutional body was established with three legal norms: capitalization, regulation, and a telecommunication law.

It is too early to conclude if this process has or will have good results, but all the conditions are in place to improve development of the telecommunications sector in Bolivia.

Note

Edgar Saravia is the primary author of this chapter, having written about developments up to 1992. The author wishes to acknowledge the contributions of Michael Chong Pineda and Sheryl Russell, who contributed the research and analysis of policy developments after 1992.

9
Colombia

MARGOT LISE HOOLEY

Colombia has seen significant growth since the mid-1960s, although the 1975–80 coffee boom contributed to inflation and slower growth, and its ending meant more inflation, even slower growth, and government deficits in the early 1980s. The collapse of the International Coffee Agreement in July 1989 cut the price of coffee in half. (Colombia is the world's second largest coffee producer after Brazil.) Reform measures beginning in 1990 have helped the economy recover. Discoveries of oil in the early 1990s doubled the country's proven reserves and further discoveries could double them again, which could help put the country on a faster growth path.

The population of 35.7 million (1993 census) is almost 75 percent urban and has been growing rapidly. (There were an estimated 25.8 million people, 60 percent urban, in 1979.) There are sharp regional disparities in the standard of living, and its overall level has been retarded by the high rate of population growth, particularly relative to productivity growth.

Colombia is on the northwest corner of South America, with both Caribbean and Pacific coasts, and covers about 1.1 million square kilometers. The western and northwestern parts are flat coastal lowlands. These give way to three cordillera of the Andes, the easternmost of which runs into Venezuela. These mountains make internal transportation difficult. The valleys on either side of the central cordillera contain many of the major cities, including Bogotá, the capital, which is at an elevation of over 2,500 meters. In the east are plains (*llanos*) that are part of the Amazon and Orinoco basins. The plains, which become tropical rain forest in the southeast, are about 60 percent of the area and have 4 percent of the population.

Colombia is a republic, with the executive branch dominant. The country is divided into thirty-two departments plus the capital district. Presidents serve four-year terms, as do legislators in both houses, although the elections are held a few months apart. The country has a history of civil wars and political violence dating from at least 1830 when Gran Colombia—which included modern Colombia, Panama, Venezuela, and Ecuador—disintegrated. Since the 1980s this instability has been exacerbated by drug traffickers. Ernesto Samper assumed the presidency in August 1994, having campaigned to continue the economic liberalization launched in 1990 but also to increase government spending on social programs.

9.1 History

From the first, telecommunications in Colombia has been marked by involvement by the state and decisive participation by the private sector, especially foreign companies, which have directed construction of much of the infrastructure and provided the technology.

In the mid-nineteenth century Colombia was at an incipient development level, with the extractive industries and agriculture as the foundation of the economy and political and social institutions inherited from the Spanish colonial period largely maintained. By then some industries had appeared utilizing the manual labor that became available after the abolition of slavery. Education levels were low, commercial activity limited, and communication difficult; the country was a patchwork of geographically isolated areas.

In this context the Revolution of 1850 took place. Set off by the governing Liberal Party, it generated a reformed economic structure. It was recognized that roads and communications media were needed in order to develop the nation's wealth. With the objective of promoting development and unifying the country, during the Liberal government of Manuel Murillo Toro, the first telegraph line was installed in 1865.

Built by the Compañia Anómina Colombiano de Telégrafo, a firm owned half by the government and half by private investors, the line linked Bogotá and Nare, a municipality 23 kilometers away along the Magdalena River. The private investors—Henry I. Davidson, William Lee Stiles, and William W. Woolsey, all from the United States—constructed the line at their own expense and were involved in the management. The initial concession was for thirty years. Soon after, it was decided to extend service to Medellín and construct additional lines, then to scale back plans and extend service only as far as Honda. Stiles was contracted by several state governors to build lines connecting to the main one.

In 1869 the state took complete control of the company on the grounds it had not fulfilled its contract to install a national network. Authority over telegraph service was given to the postmaster. Although subsequent installation was directed by the state, most of the actual construction was done through franchises or permits to individuals. Thus, in February 1870 the government contracted Stiles to extend the line from Honda through Manizales to Cartago.

Service was poor, with many long outages because of poor construction, including the use of wood poles in areas where they were unsuitable. As a result of this, in 1876 the government set standards for the construction, inspection, and maintenance of lines, as well as for government administration of the service, tariffs, and training. Private companies were reimbursed by the state for their work. By 1879 the network covered 2,690 kilometers, but service remained inefficient.

In 1879 the government contracted Fralick, Murphy & Company of New York to lay a submarine cable on the Pacific side beginning in Panama harbor, touching at Buenaventura, and ending at Callao, Peru. The firm was given an exclusive twenty-five-year concession. Service began in 1882. Later this concession was transferred to E. D. Adams and then to the Central and South American Telegraph Company. In 1881 Central and South American received a concession for a cable to connect Panama City to overseas countries and with commercial centers in Colombia. The concession, which was not exclusive, was initially for a term of twenty-five years. In 1903 it was extended to August 1924.

Also in 1881 the government contracted for telegraph lines to be installed connecting Colombia to Venezuela. The first lines were built in the department of Panama, using iron instead of wood poles, in 1888. By 1894 there were 675 kilometers of line in Panama.

In the wake of a post–civil war constitutional reform in 1886, under the principle "political centralization and administrative decentralization," forty new lines were built. In 1889 there were 100 posts linked to the telegraph service, and contracts were in place for further extensions and maintenance of the existing network. The system grew from 8,094 kilometers connecting 229 telegraph offices in 1890, to 9,614 kilometers in 1892, to 10,572 kilometers in 1894, and to 14,040 kilometers in 1898.

9.1.1 Early Telephone Service

Telephone service began in 1888 on a trial basis using equipment the government purchased from Mourlin & Company of Brussels. By 1892 Bogotá, Baranquilla, Cúcuta, and Medellín had service. That year, a law was passed (Number 98) authorizing the government to purchase the existing telephone companies and requiring government approval for construction of interurban lines. In 1894, by Decree 1294, the government spelled out procedures for private construction of interurban lines, which included receiving the approval of the municipal council of the districts. Contractors would receive concessions for specified time periods. By July 1898 there were 1,500 kilometers of interurban lines, including 200 in Panama. Still, there were few telephone customers before the 1910s.

9.1.2 1899–1919

The longest war in national history, known as the War of the Thousand Days (1899–1903), destroyed most of the interurban telegraph and telephone network, but this was only a temporary interruption in the sector's growth.

In 1910, under Decree 1130, the president became the regulator of telecommunications. An organization called the Intendencia de Telegrafos was created to manage maintenance of the telegraph plant and otherwise direct the industry. Construction of networks continued to be carried out primarily by private entrepreneurs under government contract. Domestic telephone service also was placed under the Intendencia.

Between 1910 and 1922 wireless telegraph stations were constructed in several of the more important cities. As part of this process, in 1911 Congress authorized the government to equip municipalities on the Caribbean and Pacific. United Fruit

Company (UFC) was contracted to install a wireless station at Santa Marta on the Caribbean and to transmit all government messages. UFC was given a twenty-year concession. Gasellschaft fur Drahtlose Telegraphie of Berlin received a contract in May 1912 to install a station at Cartagena with a thirty-year concession, after which the plant would become the property of the government. In January 1913 the company won a contract to install a station on San Andres island. The Cartagena station was closed after the outbreak of World War I but reopened in 1920.

In September 1913 Marconi Wireless Telegraph Company was contracted to install stations in Bogotá, Buenaventura, and Medellín with thirty-year concessions. Also in 1913, Colombia entered an agreement with Venezuela, Peru, Bolivia, and Ecuador to increase communication among these countries. Many telegraph lines—including those between Bogotá and Tunja, Tocaima, Girardot, Honda, and La Dorado—were able to transmit both telegraph and telephone messages by 1918.

In 1919 Marconi Wireless Telegraph was contracted to construct an international station in Bogotá and to repair and operate the system on San Andres. In April 1923, after repeated postponements initially because of World War I, wireless international service was inaugurated.

The 1910s also saw significant expansion of telephone service. By 1920 there were twelve private telephone companies. The largest was the Bogotá Telephone Company with 2,379 customers, equal to 38 percent of the country's total of about 6,300 lines. The next largest was in Medellín with 1,200 customers, triple the number in 1912. Founded in 1892 by the local government, the Department of Antioquia, Medellín's telco in 1915 became a private corporation, Empresa Telefonica de Medellín. J. P. Dieter of Chicago began telephone service in Baranquilla in 1890. The concession, which expired in 1916, was not renewed.

Each telco charged a rate deemed appropriate. For instance, the Bogotá company in 1920 charged U.S.$8 for installation and U.S.$36 a year for service. In Medellín in 1915 the monthly tariff was U.S.$2.50 for a business and U.S.$2.00 for a residence. Compañia de Telefonos de Baranquilla in 1918 charged U.S.$4.50 a month for a business and U.S.$4.00 for a residence line.

9.1.3 1920–1936

Communications development during the 1920s was closely linked to advice from foreign missions, particularly one from Belgium. That mission was in charge of extending the network and training domestic technicians to maintain it. The decade also witnessed rivalry among foreign companies seeking to provide services, both within the country and internationally. This participation and technological advice from foreign experts and companies left a highly satisfactory result: an increase in the telegraph network, creation of a technical training school, and improvement in long-distance communications.

The government provided various tax exemptions to the private companies in exchange for their maintaining low tariffs during 1914–28. After heated debates in the Congress, the exemptions were reduced and rates increased. The funds generated were used to finance the government deficit rather than left with the companies to invest in the system.

In 1929 the Compañía Telefónica Central (CTC) began operations. Owned by North Americans, it provided domestic long-distance telephone service. Marconi initiated the first international radiotelephone service in 1932.

During the 1930s the economic structure of Colombia changed as factory production increased and agriculture became relatively less important. The government continued to develop the communications system as part of unifying the country.

9.1.4 Nationalization

The government began a series of reforms in 1936 to institutionalize state intervention. These established that telecom services would be provided only by the central government directly or under franchises granted by it (Law 198, 1936), which was essentially the existing situation. Subsequently, there was a profusion of laws, almost always increasing intervention.

In 1943 the government of President Alfonso Lopez promulgated Law 6a authorizing nationalization of all communications services and formation of a single company to operate them. As part of this, in August 1943 the government purchased all the facilities of Marconi Wireless Telegraph, which had been operating in the country for twenty years. These were merged with other government-held telecom operations to create Empresa Nacional de Radiocomunicaciones. Two years later Law 83/45 became the basis for regulating the new company.

In 1947, ITT conducted a technical study at the request of the government of President Ospina Perez that made suggestions about network extensions and organizational changes in the Ministry of Postal Service. Soon after, ITT sold its Colombian network to the government and, under decree 1684 of 1947, Empresa Nacional de Radiocomunicaciones was reorganized under the name Telecom Colombia. At that point, just one foreign company, All America Cable, which provided international service, remained with a concession.

9.1.5 Telecom Colombia

Telecom Colombia was organized in 1947 as a public corporation with administrative autonomy, although it was required to follow the policies and plans formulated by the Postal Ministry. Its purpose was to monopolize provision of telephone, radiotelephone, and radiotelegraphic services. This meant taking over all interurban exchanges for long-distance service, being responsible for constructing lines, and providing telecom services to municipalities that lacked the financial or technical capacity to offer services. Notwithstanding Telecom's supposed monopoly, the Postal Ministry continued to provide some telecom services.

By the end of the 1940s it was realized that it made no sense to have two state entities providing service, so, in 1950, under Decree 1233, the operations were finally truly unified in a new company, although with an old name, Empresa Nacional de Telecomunicaciones. The new entity, called simply Telecom, was a public corporation with administrative autonomy and a monopoly on all services, although the Postal Ministry retained the power to inspect and control communications services.

During 1953–56 several regulations were issued reinforcing the coordination and control functions of what had in 1953 become the Ministry of Communications. These provided extensive definitions of the different services that could be offered, either directly or by franchisees of the state. The greater part of these regulations were still in force in the 1980s.

Telecom Colombia was partially decentralized in 1959, with the creation of regional management offices. These were intended to serve communities that were financially or technically unable to provide local telephone service.

9.2 1960–1990

All America Cable's concession expired in 1958 and the government purchased its Colombian assets in 1960. With that purchase, for the first time, all telecom services, domestic and international, were completely in Colombian hands—specifically, local and national government hands.

The Ministry of Communications was reorganized by Decree 3267 in 1963. Communications were centrally coordinated but functionally divided into specialized institutions attached to the ministry. The National Postal Administration (ADPOSTAL) was created for the postal service, while the Radio and Television National Institute (INRAVISION) was organized for radio and television. The National Telegraph service, which had been managed by the ministry, was merged with Telecom. Telecom also monopolized interurban and international communication, as well as telex (international telex service was introduced in 1965) and local service in some minor locations. In the wake of the decree, local service was significantly expanded by the creation of new municipal telcos. By 1975 there were fifty-four municipal companies and one regional company, Empresas Departamentales de Antioquia (EDA). EDA provides local and long-distance service within the department of Antioquia, except for the city Medellín.

In 1976 the Ministry of Communications was reorganized by Decree 129/76 to create a Division of Entities and Companies to oversee institutions that had their own infrastructure and the necessary human, technical, and financial resources to otherwise operate independently of the ministry. The reform distinguished policy making, regulation, strategic planning, engineering and research, and general aspects of commercial and financing management from operations. Operations, including network administration and maintenance, were handled by the telephone companies. These include Telecom and the municipal and departmental companies providing local service.

The other functions were performed by various central-level entities, primarily the Ministry of Communications. The National Planning Department took an economy-wide view of investment and financing plans and imposed priorities to assure efficiency in the use of external resources. The Ministry of Finance and Public Control examined projects in order to assure that the conditions of loans were satisfactory. In 1968 a Domestic Tariff Board was put in charge of setting prices.

Because of insufficient human and technical resources and the lack of strong political support, the ministry did not really have the operative and administrative capacity to fulfill the functions assigned to it. Staff were not always selected using technical criteria, partly because low salaries made the jobs uninteresting to those with the appropriate specialized skills. Strategic planning was not developed by the ministry, or by the National Planning Department, which was more concerned with macroeconomic planning and with credit and financial policies than with sectoral development planning.

One consequence of the absence of strategic planning and the failure of the central authority to establish clear technical standards during the 1970s and 1980s is a diverse mixture of switches throughout the country. Colombia depends on imported equipment for its telecom network. This actually can be advantageous, as the market for every major product line is highly competitive among a number of companies based in different countries. The significant enhancements to switches and the general move to digitalization in the 1980s meant that the country's failure to expand and upgrade service more during the 1970s and early 1980s was an opportunity to leapfrog a generation of equipment. Unfortunately, however, in the latter part of the 1980s, because of the lack of nationwide technical standards and the nature of the purchasing procedures required of state companies—which could take three or four years—the companies were buying what often, when finally delivered, was equipment made obsolete by continued rapid technological change. In addition, local telcos frequently bought particular solutions offered by a manufacturer that subsequently have prevented optimizing the total network as regards cost, operation, and maintenance.

Frequent changes in the minister of communications (and its predecessor, the Postal Ministry) have been a problem in regulating and promoting telecommunication. Ministers have served an average of just one year. In the 1930s this was ten months; in the 1950s, eleven months. Even within the same presidential administration, changes in ministers have meant there has been little continuity in policy.

9.3 Rate Structure

In 1936, under the administration of President López Pumarejo, the government began to regulate the prices charged for public services to ensure "fair profit margins and commercial morality." Any changes had to be announced in advance. The criteria used recognized financial factors such as costs but also included the ability of users to pay. In 1938 the Department of Public Service Companies was created to enforce the regulations. In 1955 a new Anti-Monopoly Law expanded explicit state involvement in setting prices, but only in 1960 was a government agency, the Economical Regulation Superintendency, created to exercise it.

The Ministry of Communications, under Decree 2848 of 1966, assumed the power to approve the rules and rates of local telcos. It also undertook to guarantee customer deposits, installation rights, and similar matters related to telephone service. However, the ministry had limited administrative capacity to perform these functions. Moreover, it was represented on the boards of directors of the companies, which created something of a conflict of interest. For these reasons, Decree 1765 was issued in 1972. It led to decree 3069 of 1978, which gave the National

Board of Public Services the power to fix, supervise, and control telephone rates. At the same time, the National Board of Tariffs, which is under the National Planning Department, was given an active role in tariff setting.

The Public Services board has been rather cautious, seeking to balance the sector's cash flow so that it is not being subsidized by the state but not running a surplus, which would indicate rates might be too high and thus repressing demand. Rates for telephone service since the 1970s have involved a fixed charge and a charge based on usage (time, duration, and distance of a call). In an effort to counteract the financial instability that occurred due to rapid inflation, steps were taken to index tariffs. The overall result was that for fifteen years, from 1977 to 1992, both local and domestic long-distance rates were fairly stable in real terms. In 1983, Law 14 provided for consideration of socioeconomic conditions in setting rates.

Notwithstanding the explicit formal legal role of the national government, historically, each telco has determined its specific rates, so rates for the same service can be different in different parts of the country. Seeking to reduce disparities, the government in 1988 issued Decree 189 setting guidelines for local charges, particularly usage charges. By the early 1990s usage rates were similar throughout the country, although Bogotá and Medellín have higher charges than most other cities. Since Decree 1900 was promulgated in 1990, tariffs, with the exclusion of connection fees, have decreased. The National Planning Department has established estimates of reasonable rates, and these have come to provide an upper limit to what regulators will approve.

Further movement toward a unified rate schedule was made in 1991 by the Cesar Gaviria Trujillo administration with Decrees 969 and 970, which provided municipalities with methodological guidelines and unified criteria for setting fixed charges. This included guidelines on socioeconomic factors used in determining rates. In urban areas the population (calling area) and external qualities of the individual customer's house are to be used. In rural areas, the internal qualities of the house are the criterion. In both areas, the better the quality of the house, the higher the cost of phone service. These guidelines were not immediately put into effect but rather were being tested in Bucaramanga in early 1995.

Local telcos receive little from Telecom Colombia for handling domestic and international long-distance calls, and they have requested greater compensation. Telecom has refused, maintaining that it needs the money to provide mandated deficit services such as telex, telegraph, and rural telephony. However, moves are being made to decrease the deficits of these services or to subsidize them in other ways. Thus, to fund the development of rural telephony, a tax has been imposed on cellular and mobile operators. However, the Ernesto Samper administration (1994–) has used the revenue to fund general government operations rather than to expand rural telephone service. In consequence, cellular operators have argued for removing the tax.

The disparity in the price of a call from Colombia compared to a call to Colombia is substantial, and the resulting recourse to callback services reduces Telecom Colombia's revenue.

In general, the telecom sector has operated under a system of cross-subsidies between type of service and socioeconomic status of customers. As the sector is reorganized, including requiring separate accounting for each service, the transparency of subsidies will increase.

9.4 The 1990–1991 Reforms

Telecom and the local companies have had almost unlimited power in their setting of administrative, financing, technological, and general policies. They have also generally been able to make their own development plans, following essentially only their own immediate interests. The result has been real but not always harmonic development, with technological choices and investment handled without long-term vision. In short, the network had developed as islands that could communicate with each other, but the concept of a unified domestic network had been lost.

To address this lack of unity, the first comprehensive evaluation of the sector was made in 1988 and the results published as the *National Telecommunications Study*. The objective of the study was to examine the principal aspects of the telecom sector—such as its organization, relevant legislation, and the demand for service—and to prepare a plan for extending the network and addressing its financial situation. The study thus excluded private networks, television, and other subsectors.

In the end, the study did not formulate clear objectives concerning the reorganization of telecommunications, nor was there a plan for the technological development of the sector. No consideration was given to administrative planning, sectoral management, or operations. The report expressed some feeling that a domestic microelectronic industry could be developed. It realistically looked at establishing assembly plants in the short and medium term and did not emphasize transfer of technology to local producers.

The 1988 study was fundamental in the government's decision to give the sector a new perspective, focusing on creating an environment conducive to the involvement of private companies in providing new telecom services. The government realized that, by itself, it did not have the administrative, financial, or technological abilities to face the accelerated development challenge that telecommunications present at a world level. Thus, in 1989 Congress passed Law 72 authorizing the government to issue standards to reorganize the sector under the principles that its planning, regulation, and control would stay with government bodies, but actual provision of services would continue to be through concession to particular companies.

The 1989 law was followed by Decrees 1900 and 1901 of 1990, which were implemented in 1992 after Congressional approval. These decrees somewhat restructured telecommunications. Although most of the institutional structure existing since 1976 was maintained, new rules made competition a principle, in particular by permitting private operators to provide value-added services. The Ministry of Communications was responsible for regulation, general policies regarding technological and institutional development, research and development, and promotion, as well as directly providing services or authorizing concessions under previously established standards. These macro functions were coordinated with the National Planning Department. The decrees spelled out three goals.

The first goal was to triple telephone density to a level of at least 25 per 100 people by the year 2000. This would bring Colombia to the low end of what international organizations consider developed. It was estimated that about U.S.$5 billion would be needed to achieve this goal, an amount substantially greater than had been invested in the previous eight years and beyond the capacity of the government to carry out without diverting funds from other endeavors. For this reason, privatizing telephone service was recommended.

The second goal was to increase the size of service areas—that is, merge municipal companies into larger units (regionalization)—as a way of obtaining economies of scale. A committee was formed to undertake this. Telecom's role would be somewhat reduced as intraregional long-distance calls that it handled under the old structure would be handled by the new regional companies.

The third goal was to increase the number of services offered and expand existing services into new geographic areas. All regions of the country were to have acceptable service levels.

Under Decree-Law 1900, the military and the government generally are allowed to have telecommunications networks for their exclusive use as part of defending and governing the country. Private parties can have networks for security or intracompany needs provided they are installed on private property.

9.5 No Privatization

After Congress approved Decree-Law 1900 in 1992, the Gaviria administration attempted to privatize Telecom Colombia over a period of ten months beginning in 1993. The employees, in response, went on strike, suspending all local, national, and international telecommunications service for a week. In the face of such intense opposition to privatization, which continues, the government has looked for alternatives.

A shared-risk joint-venture approach was developed as a way to install a large number of new telephone lines and replace old lines. This involves an exclusive concession to install equipment in a designated geographical area. The supplier must complete all necessary construction at its own expense. Telecom Colombia would operate and maintain the system, paying investors a percentage of installation fees and local, domestic, and international usage charges for a term of approximately ten years.

Since this type of agreement was not included in Decree-Law 1900, the government issued Decree 0533 on April 1, 1992, authorizing Telecom to enter such ventures with local or international organizations. The legality of Decree 0533 was challenged and the Supreme Administrative Court decided it was in conflict with Law 72 and thus illegal. In response, the government sought legislation explicitly allowing the arrangement. It did this by adding the necessary language to a bill concerning cellular mobile telecommunications then pending before Congress. Thus, Law 37, enacted on January 6, 1993, not only regulates mobile and cellular service, it also, under Article 9, authorizes Telecom to enter shared-risk joint-venture contracts, as well as other types of contracts.

9.6 Moving toward Competition

Overall, there has been a broad consensus among the political parties to opening telecommunications to competition. There also are ample legal grounds to introduce competition into domestic or international long distance: Decree Law 1900, Decree 2122 of 1992, Law 37 of 1993, and Law 142 of 1994. Still, for some time the government did not move. Then, in January 1995 the government outlined its intention to open long distance to competition on January 1, 1997. As it did in the cellular mobile telephone sector, the government is expected to divide the country into zones with two companies competing in each zone. Telecom is very dependent on domestic and international long-distance calls—they provided 93 percent of revenue in 1993 and 1994.

9.6.1 Cellular Service

In 1994 cellular mobile service was introduced in Colombia. The country was divided into three regions—east, west, and coast. In each region, two operators were awarded a concession, one a venture of a state company and a private company and the other a private company. The concessions are for five years, after which, in 1999, service will be evaluated to determine if the concession will be extended.

Celumovil and Comcel offer service in the east (61,865 customers in 1994), Cocelco and Occel in the west (70,661), and Celumovil de la Costa and Celcaribe on the coast (12,400). A study conducted by Economic and Management Consultants International estimated that there would be 24,210 customers in the first year of operations, 55,813 by the second year, and 94,638 by the end of the third year. Instead, the number at the end of the first year was 144,926, almost six times as many as predicted. In just one year Colombia had cellular penetration of 0.4 percent. Brazil, Chile, Argentina, and Venezuela took four years, and Peru took more than five, to reach that level.

The price of a concession ranged from U.S.$593 million to U.S.$624 million and, over the course of the first year, the companies spent between U.S.$100 million and U.S.$250 million each building their networks. Subscribers pay an initiation cost of approximately U.S.$650 and a monthly charge of some U.S.$150 plus between U.S.$1.00 and U.S.$1.50 per minute of usage.

The minister of communications regulates cellular service. Such service must be provided in urban zones, including low-income areas and areas in which access to wired service is difficult, thus helping to implement extension of the communications network.

9.6.2 Restructuring Telecom Colombia

In anticipation of competition in its key long-distance markets, Telecom has restructured the company in accordance with Decree 2123. Thus, in December 1992, Telecom changed from being a public institution to being a state-owned company, permitting it greater management flexibility and accountability. State-owned companies are regulated by the laws that govern private entities rather than those that govern public institutions. Day-to-day control is exercised by a board of directors appointed by the president of Colombia. However, the minister of communications has the authority to regulate, control, and plan the sector, making fundamental decisions about what Telecom Colombia may or may not do. Thus, the ministry would be involved in such decisions as building a fiber-optic network, launching a satellite, or abandoning the rural telephone program.

With its new legal status, the company's focus has been twofold. First, it is reducing operating costs. The telex and telegraph division, for instance, had 20 percent of employees but generated just 1 percent of net income in 1994. Union resistance prevented Telecom from reducing employment through layoffs. Instead, retirement packages were offered all employees except those with specialized skills the company wished to retain. This reduced the total workforce by approximately 15 percent.

Second, in Decree 2123 the minister of communications defined specific areas in which Telecom would have a competitive advantage. The company is charged with providing state-of-the-art telecom services within Colombia and to foreign countries. Therefore, the minister authorized Telecom to participate in association agreements with, or invest in, domestic telcos, as well as to enter association agreements with foreign companies. As a result, Telecom has shared-risk agreements with Nortel, Alcatel Standard Electrica de España, and Alcatel Bell Telephone (Belgium). Nortel Colombia also has provided Telecom with assistance in operating and maintaining the equipment.

Telecom has three goals: to achieve a higher level of service and technical support; to make local telephone service profitable; and to offer high-quality service. As part of this, it will administer local telephone service in a decentralized, regional manner. To achieve these three goals, Telecom intends to develop association contracts with third parties; expand the areas that associated companies cover; promote agreements for the development of local telephone service in areas not included in the company's own expansion plan; and develop and promote new services that complement local service.

Telecom Colombia was the local-service provider in nearly 500 of the country's cities in 1994. In over 2,800 small communities there are local companies tied into Telecom's national network, but there was no service at all in some 60 percent of rural communities. Of the twenty-five municipal and regional telcos in 1992, Telecom had a financial interest in eight. Of thirty-three in 1994, Telecom Colombia had a financial interest in thirteen.

9.7 The Mid-1990s

The network now consists of independent local telephone companies connected to a long-distance network operated by Telecom Colombia. The connections are not all automatic: indeed, an operator may need to go through another operator to reach the main network. For instance, TeleCartagena connects to TeleBaranquilla, which in turn connects to Telecom Colombia.

The three largest municipal telcos are La Empresa de Telecomunicaciones de Santa Fe de Bogotá (ETB), Empresas Públicas de Medellín (EPM), Empresas Municipales de Cali (EMCALI). ETB provides service to the city of Bogotá, whose population was 6.3 million (almost 18 percent of the national total) according to the 1993 census. ETB had 1.2 million lines in 1991 and almost 1.7 million in 1994. EPM provides service principally to the municipality of Medellín; it had 580,400 lines in 1991 and 718,420 in 1994. EMCALI principally serves the municipality of Cali, with 305,800 lines in 1991 and 302,474 in 1994.

Telecom Colombia serves areas of low population density and income not served by municipal companies. Such service is expensive relative to the revenue it generates. Often public telephones are installed to serve low-income segments of the population. A rural telephone plan has been announced to provide automated telephone service to 5,000 villages and 8,600 locations with populations of at least 250.

In April 1995 Telecom sought bids for a contract to build a 3,200-kilometer fiber-optic network extending from Barranquilla on the Caribbean to Buenaventura on the Pacific. Directly connecting twenty-six cities, it will link with international submarine cables, and some eighty other cities will be connected through secondary networks. Contracts will be awarded in September 1996 and the network is expected to begin operation in the third quarter of 1997.

9.7.1 Demand for Service

Other than in the 1988 *National Telecommunications Study,* there has been no analysis of demand. The study concluded that for each 1 percent increase in GDP the demand for local telephone service increased 0.65 percent and for domestic long distance, 1.32 percent. Although the study analyzed the ability of telcos to supply service, it did not address the ability of potential customers to pay for it. One indicator of unsatisfied demand is the willingness of customers to pay for service. Despite its very high costs, cellular service had rapid penetration: in 1995, after one year of operation, 0.4 percent of the population owned a cellular telephone.

Another method to characterize demand is teledensity measured in lines per 100 people. In 1994 this ranged from 0.067 in the department of Vicahada (tropical forest in the Orinoco River basin) to 27 in the district of Bogotá. Another method is the time required for a line to be installed. Official statistics published by the National Telecommunications Department indicate this ranges from one to forty-eight months. When Nortel began providing service, it was presented with lists showing people who had been waiting ten years. Nortel at first did not believe this. On ascertaining it was true, the firm began to advertise that anyone could have a telephone within a month. Customers began to submit applications for telephones, and soon the number of applications exceeded the number of lines Nortel had installed. Alcatel was presented with lists with names fourteen years old. Such waiting lists do not fully represent demand, since some potential customers have given up hope of ever receiving a telephone and consequently have not submitted an application.

9.7.2 Equipment Suppliers

The telcos depend on imported equipment and the producers are very competitive. Although there are two firms in Colombia that manufacture copper cable and one that manufactures telephone sets, operators prefer to import these items. The quality is better and, in spite of import duties, the cost is approximately the same. Duties on telecom equipment are approximately 6 percent, and there is a 14 percent value-added tax. Equipment that will be connected to the telephone network must receive import license approval from the Ministry of Communications, but there are otherwise no restrictions. The Institute of Technical Standards of Colombia (INCONTEC) establishes standards for products and equipment manufactured in or imported into the country.

The major equipment supplier in 1992 was Ericsson with a 42 percent market share, followed by Fujitsu with 12 percent. In 1993 Ericsson's percentage fell due to increased competition from Siemens and Alcatel. Ericsson, Fujitsu, and Siemens have long histories of supplying Colombia.

9.7.3 Regulation

Three bodies have important roles in regulating telecommunications. First is the National Council for Social and Economic Policy (COPNES), an advisory board to the government as a whole, which establishes broad economic and social policies that affect the industry. The Ministry of Communications has the ultimate authority. It provides guidelines for planning the network through its National Planning Department, assisted by the Ministry of Finance. The Telecommunication Regulatory Commission was created in 1991 to establish the tariff structure, oversee concessions for domestic and international long-distance service, promote competition, seek to improve efficiency and service quality, and otherwise regulate operations within the sector. To provide local telephone service in urban areas or to use spectrum, an operator must seek a concession or governmental authorization.

9.8 Conclusion

Having been foiled in privatizing Telecom Colombia in 1993, the Gaviria administration sought alternative solutions to meeting the country's needs for more and better telecommunications. The government decided to open the sector to competition gradually, preparing the labor force and Telecom for competition. Telecom identified and focused on certain core strengths and reduced its labor force through early retirement plans and attrition.

By comparison to many other Latin American countries, particularly Chile, Colombia has moved little and slowly in opening telecommunications to competition and reducing government ownership and involvement. When competition comes to long distance in 1997, Telecom will still be state owned and have had seven years to prepare. It will face only two new entrants. Other services that

Telecom offers such as basic telephony will continue to be provided without competition. Cellular, a completely new service when introduced in 1994, also has been limited in the number of participants in each region, and the state has maintained an ownership role in three of the six companies. Value-added services are more open to competition and have attracted participation by the private sector.

The technological, administrative, and financial development of telecommunications in Colombia has been uneven since the beginning. Administrative and financial bottlenecks have kept the system less extensive and less capable than it might have been. Tariff structures motivated more by political considerations than by recognition of the need to generate sufficient profit to finance the expansion and maintenance of the system have been part of the reason for this situation. In the 1990s Colombia has not used privatization or liberalization as a means of obtaining capital and expertise—particularly foreign capital—to expand and upgrade its telecommunications. At the same time, the innovative shared-risk ventures to include private, mostly foreign, partners in expanding service within a state-controlled context may prove to be a less traumatic alternative.

Note

This chapter draws on material provided by William Cartier and benefited from rigorous commentary by an outside reader.

References

"¿Aló, cómo vas?" 1994. *Semana,* November 8.

Beltrán, Fernando. 1995. *Monopolio y Competencia en Telecomunicaciones. Un Interno de Describir el Panorama Colombiano.* CINTEL, April.

Berthold, Victor. 1921. *History of the Telephone and Telegraph in Colombia, S.A.* New York: AT&T.

Colombia Telecommunications Funding Corporation. 1994. Northern Telecom and Telecom Columbia. Nomura Securities International, Inc., October 26.

Crow, John. 1992. *The Epic of Latin America.* Berkeley: University of California Press.

Estratificación Socioeconómica: Manual De Recoleccion Datos. 1994. Departamento Nacional de Planeacion.

Estudio Nacional de Telecomunicaciones. 1990. Departamento Nacional de Planeacion.

"Going Cellular." 1995. *U.S./Latin Trade,* March.

Headrick, Daniel R. *The Invisible Weapon: Telecommunications and International Politics. 1851–1945.* 1991. New York: Oxford University Press.

Jiméz, J. 1995. *Comunicaciones Rurales.* Alcatel Standard Elétrica, S.A. CINTEL, April.

Lay 37–6 Enero 1993: El Congreso de Colombia Decreat. 1993. Ministry of Telecommunication, January.

"Llamadas Calientes." 1995. *Semana,* April 25.

Ministerio de Comunicaciones. 1990. Diario Oficial: August 19.

Pisciotta, Aileen A. 1995. *Modelos Para la Regulación de Procesos y Procedimientos en Telecomunicaciones.* CINTEL, April.

"Se le cae el tono a la celular." 1995. *El Espectador,* March 15.

Swonkin, Sergio Regueros. 1995. *Análisis Crítico de la Legislación Colombiana en Telecomunicaciones.* CINTEL, April.

Telecom Markets in South America. 1993. Colombia: Pyramid Research, Inc.

Telecommunication Markets in South America. 1989. Office of South America International Trade Administration: Business America, June 5.

"Telecomunicaciones." 1995. *El Tiempo,* May 24.

Telefonia Local a Nivel Nacional, Planta Interna—Capacidad Instalada. 1994, 1993, 1992, 1991. Departamento Nacional de Planeacion.

"Termina guerra en celulares." 1995. *El Tiempo,* January 27.

Zuluaga, José Joaquín, Empresas Públicas de Medellín. 1995. *El Negocio do la Larga Distancia Internacional en Colombia: Del Monopolio a la Competencia.* CINTEL, April.

10
Venezuela

NATAN ZAIDMAN

Venezuela, the sixth largest country in South America, has an area of about 912,000 square kilometers and a highly urbanized population of almost 21 million (July 1994 estimate)—the twelve largest cities have about 75 percent of the population. Eighty-three percent reside in cities of at least 5,000 people. The population increased over 40 percent in the fifteen years from 1979 to 1994.

An extension of the Andes runs into Venezuela and mountains rise along much of the Caribbean coast. Several fertile valleys lie in these ranges. Caracas, the capital and largest city, with 20 percent of the population, sits at an altitude of about 1,000 meters. The northwest corner of the country, around Lake Maracaibo, is the traditional center of the petroleum industry. South of the mountains is a sparsely populated plain (*Llano*) of savannas and scrub. The southeast is part of the Guiana highlands and the largely tropical rain forest. The Orinoco River runs between, and drains, these last two.

10.1 History

Development of telephone service in Venezuela began in 1883 when a representative of Intercontinental Telephone Company of New Jersey, James A. Derrom, obtained authorization from the government of General Antonio Guzmán Blanco to install three telephones in Caracas, on a demonstration basis. In 1890, the English company Telephone and Electrical Appliances (TEA) became the assignee of the contract, by which time there were 400 subscribers. At the time, the economy was based on agriculture, a situation that continued until the beginning of petroleum exploitation in 1914.

In December 1894 American Electric & Manufacturing Company was contracted to install service for the government. The Venezuelan Telephone & Electrical Appliances Company Ltd. (formerly TEA) signed an agreement with the government on July 21, 1898, that regulated relations between the parties.

The Ministry of Transport and Communications (MTC) was created on February 25, 1936, and was originally responsible for administration of mail, communications, and air transport services of a civil and commercial nature. Subsequently it was split, with communications becoming a separate ministry. In 1977 the parts were recombined.

Since 1914 Venezuela's constitutions (1914, 1936, 1961) have embodied the principle that all matters related to telecommunications lie in the domain of the state. Thus, the constitution enacted July 20, 1936, conserved, without alteration, the provisions of the 1914 constitution that reserved to the executive branch "all activities related to the mails, telegraphs, telephones, and wireless communications." This has not, however, meant the state actually provided the service directly. Concessions were given private companies, generally foreign, to construct and operate domestic local and long-distance service, as well as international service.

On July 28, 1936, the Law of Telecommunications was enacted, superseding a 1918 law. However the 1927 Law of Overseas Cablegraphic Communications remained in force until 1940, when a new Law of Telecommunications was enacted.

10.1.1 Creation of CANTV

Compañía Anónima Nacional Teléfonos de Venezuela (CANTV) was organized and began operations in 1930.

In 1953, in the face of the private foreign sector's difficulty in undertaking the costly investments necessary to expand service at the national level, the government purchased all of the common stock of CANTV from Telephone Properties Ltd.

10.1.2 International Communications

On September 14, 1931, the Ministry of Development declared the international radiotelephone service it operated open to the public.

Venezuela became a part of Intelsat in December 1965 with a 1 percent participation. In August 1966 a submarine cable, co-owned by CANTV and AT&T, with a capacity of eighty channels, entered service. With this cable and with the irrevocable rights for use acquired in the Saint Thomas-Florida cable, the first modern international communications system of the country was completed.

10.2 Telecommunications Since CANTV's Nationalization

Venezuela's 1961 constitution, still in effect in 1996, establishes as a general rule that monopolies will not be permitted, but granting exclusive concessions is accepted for a limited time to establish and exploit services of public interest. The mails and telecommunications, among others, are thus within the domain of the central government. The constitution and several specific laws provide that ownership of telecom services resides with the state, but Congress is permitted by a two-thirds vote in each chamber to attribute to the states or municipalities specific areas of this national domain. As a consequence, in order to promote administrative decentralization, Congress can convert monopolistic national public services into state or municipal services.

Decree 782 of June 26, 1962, ordered reorganization of telecom services. This left the Ministry of Communications responsible for the administration and operation of national and international telegraph and radiotelegraph services, as well as control and supervision of television and radio broadcasting programs, control of the spectrum, and setting rates. It also granted CANTV the right to provide all telephone service, including international, as well as national and international telex, radiotelephone, facsimile, telephoto, data transmission, and facilities for the transmission of radio broadcasting and television programs. This decree was subsequently replaced by a 1965 law that confirmed the monopoly of the state, exercised through CANTV.

A subsidiary of CANTV, the Postal and Telegraph Institute (IPOSTEL), provided mail and telegraph service. Both services were slow. There were about 800 telegraph stations in 1988.

10.2.1 Network Growth before Privatization

Planning telecom services was initiated in 1958 with CANTV's first development plan, which covered 1958–64. The second was for 1965–70, and the third, 1971–75. The years 1965–75 gave rise to the most intense quantitative growth of the company, as during this period the change from step-by-step to common-control exchanges took place.

In 1976 the involvement of political parties and unions slowed CANTV's growth. Then, in 1979 and 1981, internal crises took place that led to the flight of many of the company's professional staff. These departures ended growth, and service seriously deteriorated as, among other things, congestion of the network increased substantially.

Demand continued to grow, producing a substantial bottleneck by 1980. In 1984 digital exchanges were approved. Political problems and the lack of resources—financial and human—compounded by internal problems at CANTV, meant their introduction was quite slow, however. Thus, at the height of the crisis of unmet demand in 1990, only 6,000 lines were installed. Demand was 300,000 to 400,000 lines per year. In 1991, CANTV regrouped somewhat and installed 180,000 lines.

It is possible to make CANTV's activities during the 1970s and 1980s look (superficially) favorable. During the debate over privatization, a former minister of Cordiplán noted that "population increased during the period 1970–89 from 10,762,000 to 19,369,000, that is, by 8,607,000, and during this period the large investments in telephone infrastructure by the State meant an increase in the number of subscribers from 276,834 to 1,462,885; that is, while the population increased by 80%, the number of telephone subscribers increased by 427%" (as reported in the newspaper *Diario El Universal* of November 20, 1991). Of course, this plays on the distortions possible when the base of one percentage change (telephone subscribers) is a small fraction of the base of the other (population). An increase of about 1.2 million subscribers against an increase of 8.6 million people yields an incremental teledensity of less than 14—a not particularly impressive level.

The history of CANTV is typical of the history of state telecommunications companies in Latin America: a period of enthusiasm, with growth stimulated by governments, then a period of decline, stagnation, and corruption that leads to calls for privatization. In Venezuela, privatization was carried out in 1991.

10.3 Change in the Political Environment

The government of Carlos Andrés Pérez, which took office in 1989, began to make profound changes in Venezuela's economic programs, reflecting a rethinking of the interventionism and protectionism of a bureaucratic (and inefficient) state that had characterized the country for decades. The principal political parties—Accion Democratica (AD), in power 1989–94, and Social Christian (COPEI)—have progressively broken with their original ideologies, which, to a greater or lesser degree, were "populist," to adapt to a "technological pragmatism" more in accord with the requirements of a country that claims "solutions" and not "flags."

There has been a movement toward competition, a market economy, and transfer to the private sector (with foreign participation) of activities and services that, in government hands, had generated large losses and otherwise been a major fiscal burden to the state. The need to refinance foreign debt, together with the policies of the International Monetary Fund, accelerated this process, from which telecommunications could not escape.

This shift has made it possible to achieve a consensus around the restructuring of the public services and other state-owned companies. All this led the government to establish guidelines for itself under which, among other things, it would minimize its role in providing telecom services. At the same time, the state would seek to broaden the coverage of services and increase the quality. It would also guarantee coverage of the support services fundamental to the social development and culture of the population, as well as the integrated and harmonic development of the network, particularly basic services. When these government enterprises are privatized, workers and other groups directly affected would be given an opportunity to acquire an equity interest in the new companies and, as appropriate, would also seek international partners with appropriate technical and administrative skills.

Other interest groups, such as the Federation of Chambers of Industry and Commerce (FEDECAMARAS), the national group of local chambers of commerce, and the Confederation of Workers of Venezuela (CTV), the federation of principal unions, have reached agreement on the proposed reforms in the telecom sector. CTV accepted the need to reduce employment at CANTV as part of the process of privatization.

Only some minor parties identified with socialism and intervention, such as the Movimiento al Socialismo (MAS), are opposed to this process. They argue that privatization of telecommunications leads to its denationalization, delivering it to transnational companies; that the technical conditions of the telecom network are inherently monopolistic; and that private providers will finance the system by charging users high rates. From this they conclude telecommunications should remain in the hands of the state.

10.4 Restructuring

A major consideration in the decision to privatize CANTV was the huge unmet demand; something simply had to be done to solve the problem. CANTV's own estimate was that obtaining service took an average of eight years from the time it was applied for. The goal at the time of privatization (1991) was to reduce this period at first to three years, and then narrow the interval to months, not years.

Related to this situation was the level of CANTV's foreign debt—some U.S.$600 million. Devaluations of the Bolivar (Venezuela's currency) exacerbated the state's problems servicing its debt, let alone making the investments necessary to meet demand.

Lack of investment meant entire segments of the market were going unserved, not just those wanting cellular phones, private networks, and other services taken for granted by subscribers in countries with well-developed networks, but also many trying to get basic service. There was a feeling it was necessary to introduce new actors into the sector to address these shortcomings, even though—actually, because—that meant ending CANTV's monopoly of service.

The government of Venezuela wants foreign investment to flow to the sector, along with the introduction of advanced technologies, the formation of more specialized human resources, and the availability of the greatest variety of services. I agree with those who say restructuring telecommunications is a prerequisite to attracting investors in all areas of the economy, because investors will not tolerate a backward and deficient telecommunications system.

10.4.1 The Legal Framework

After months of work, a draft law reforming telecommunications was put forward. It moved slowly through the Congress, acquiring amendments and spawning other laws relating to regulation of the industry. As an advisor to the Congress, I actively participated in drawing up the Law of Telecommunications that was finally passed and, in 1991, substituted for the one in force since 1940.

The new laws were a response to the need to update the legal framework that regulates this area and to define precisely the functions and responsibilities of the public and private sectors. A principal objective is to establish a system of equal access in the provision of different services, stimulating both national and foreign private investment in the context of free competition.

The October 1991 law, with a fundamentally technical nature, regulates the services that currently exist and provides for the incorporation of new ones. Services are classified as being for general use, for restricted use, and for broadcasting. Broadcasting (radio and television) is excluded from the coverage of this law; separate statutes deal with it.

The law establishes the rights and duties of users and provides for their participation in the design of policies. Among the rights, besides equal access to and use of services, there is to be timely attention to requests. Users will participate in the Consulting Council of the National Telecommunications Commission (CONATEL).

10.4.2 CONATEL

Regulation of broadcasting, television, telephone, telegraph, and mail services rested with the Ministry of Transport and Communications (MTC), through various renamings and restructurings, from the time it was created in 1936 until 1991.

Initially, MTC's General Dirección Sectorial de Telecomunicaciones was responsible for regulation and control of the sound and audiovisual media. This responsibility had two aspects: technical (regulation of utilization of the spectrum) and content. The division's jurisdiction was radically changed on September 5, 1991, when the Office of the President issued Decree 1826 creating CONATEL (the National Telecommunications Commission). The General Directorate of Communications retained responsibility for the content and programming of radio and television, and CONATEL became the regulatory body for technical aspects of telecommunications such as the use of spectrum and assigning frequencies.

More specifically, CONATEL had the authority to plan, direct, supervise, and regulate telecom services; recommend the granting of concessions, permits, and administrative authorizations; administer the rights of granting of concessions and permits; promote investment and technological innovation in the sector; apply administrative sanctions; watch over respect for users' rights; establish standards and other regulations for services; prepare criteria for setting rates; and collect fees and other income derived from the services.

CONATEL, autonomous in administration, finance, and budget, is assigned to the Ministry of Transport and Communications. At the time it was created, people assumed CONATEL would be temporary, necessary only until Congress approved a new law creating a regulatory agency of greater hierarchy and autonomy, with the presence of representatives of the legislative and executive branches.

One of CONATEL's charges is promoting competition in the telecom sector. This is also a responsibility of the Superintendency for the Promotion and Protection of Free Competition, a regulatory agency created as part of the Ministry of Development to cover all areas of the economy. My expectation is that CONATEL will have jurisdiction only on technical matters, with the exception of overseeing the concession contract between the state and the new CANTV. Other matters related to competition will be handled by the Superintendency.

10.5 Privatization

In April 1991, Fernando Martínez Mottola, president of CANTV, presented the "CANTV Proposed Privatization Plan." This document deserves quoting at length.

> Telecommunications require changes of enormous magnitude to promote national development. A wide national consensus supports this. The technological and organizational delay and the financial crisis the company is undergoing can only be corrected with very profound changes in its organization in order to undertake the anticipated growth and financing of its investments.
>
> Installed telephone lines increased from 1,150,020 in 1980 to 1,922,800 in 1990,

while the principal lines for each 100 persons rose from 5.13 to 7.38. In 1990, 45.46% of demand was met. The process of digitalization of the network [begun] with the purchase of 1 million digital lines in 1986 has certainly been restricted by the inability of the company to install equipment and put it into operation. The introduction of new services was limited to cellular mobile telephony in Caracas, with many deficiencies, starting in 1986.

A reasonable objective for the sector consists of reaching an acceptable level in regard to variety, quantity of supply, and quality of the services in a period of five years, and a good level in relation to international standards, in ten years.

To reach the objective implies attaining at least the following partial objectives or subobjectives: installing and putting into service 300,000 additional telephone lines per year, on average, during the next decade; refurbishing and improving the quality of operation of CANTV's installed plant, which included 1.9 million lines at the end of 1990, in a period of three to four years; creating an organization able to provide high-quality service in its different aspects, for a subscriber base that will double in five to seven years; introducing value-added services, providing them with a high level of quality, and expanding them according to the rhythm of demand. This expansion will require several hundred million dollars annually during the 1990s. (Martínez Mottola 1991, translation by Zaidman)

The plan was for an international operating company to become a minority partner, with a 30 percent interest. This company would have to commit to formulating a predetermined investment plan for expanding service; meeting specified quality levels similar to those of industrial countries; and doing this at tariffs established by the regulating body. CANTV workers would be transferred to the new operating company, with guarantees of their contractual rights and an option to purchase shares. This phase was to be completed within two years, after which sale of the government's remaining shares would be carried out in an international offering.

10.5.1 Selection Process

The initial plan was modified after discussions between the leading political parties (AD and COPEI) so that 40 percent of shares would be sold to the selected operator, 11 percent to company employees (who numbered about 22,000), and 49 percent would remain with the state until the company was able to command a better price, at which point shares would be offered to the public through the Caracas Stock Exchange. Each of these would be a different class of shares. The proceeds of these sales would become part of CANTV's equity.

Only bids from larger international operators were sought. This was done by establishing high minimum technical and financial requirements, such as at least 6 million installed access lines, 25 percent of local exchanges digital, and annual revenue of at least U.S.$5 billion.

On March 6, 1991, qualification documents were accepted from twelve bidders. Evaluation and analysis was carried out by a committee of the Ministry of Transport and Communications, the Venezuelan Investment Fund (a government agency that would hold the state's shares after privatization), and CANTV. In April, eight potential bidders were announced; five were U.S. companies (Ameritech,

Bell Atlantic, GTE, Southwestern Bell [since named SBC Communications], and U.S. West), plus Bell Canada, France Telecom, and Nippon Telephone & Telegraph. However, only two consortiums, one led by GTE and another led by Bell Atlantic and Bell Canada (BC), were interested in acquiring 40 percent of CANTV.

On November 15, 1991, the consortium led by GTE (51 percent), Venworld Telecom CA, was declared the winner, agreeing to pay U.S.$1,885,000,000 for 40 percent of CANTV. Other members are AT&T International (5 percent), Telefónica Internacional de España SA (16 percent), CA La Electricidad De Caracas (16 percent), and Consorcio Inversionista Mercantil (Cima) CA, represented by Venworld Telecom CA (12 percent). Citibank NA is the trustee of the employee shares (11 percent). The remaining shares were held by Fondo de Inversiones de Venezuela, the Ministry of Transportation and Communications, and the Bancó Industrial de Venezuela. Venworld is obligated to maintain ownership of all its shares until at least January 1, 1997, 70 percent until January 1, 1999, and 20 percent until January 1, 2001. In no case before 2001 may its shares be transferred to manufacturers of telecom equipment.

In January 1995 Venezuela's privatization agency announced plans to offer the public 32 percent of CANTV during the year's third quarter. This would reduce the state's holding to 17 percent.

10.5.2 The Concession Contract

CANTV's legal status prior to the beginning of the privatization process was that of a direct instrument of the state. It was thus necessary to formalize a concession contract between the state and CANTV, which was done on October 14, 1991. The concession runs thirty-five years and requires payment to the state of 5.5 percent of billings for all services. Importing of plant and equipment for use in the network requires prior authorization of the ministry. There will be limited competition in respect to basic services—local, national, and international—during a nonrenewable nine-year period (that is, through October 2000). Other services, including cellular and value-added, are open to immediate competition, and CANTV may participate in these markets.

Users basically had to accept CANTV service as it was when it was a state-owned and operated enterprise. There was essentially no recourse in cases of poor or no service. As part of becoming a responsible service provider, CANTV is obligated to provide equal treatment, prompt attention to claims, and compensation to subscribers when basic service is not restored within seventy-two hours of being reported. The privacy and inviolability of communications is also formally recognized.

10.6 Telephony in the 1990s

Nationwide, Venezuela had a density of 7 telephones per 100 persons in 1990, but the level in Caracas, with 1 million lines, was 25.

In the CANTV concession contract that took effect in October 1991, quality standards have been included using a detailed protocol of such measures as how long it takes to get a dial tone, an operator, and a repair, as well as the quality of billing. The private consortium controlling CANTV is subject to penalties such as newspaper announcements, fines, and the suspension of its concession if it fails to meet the obligations imposed by the concession.

It is assumed that in the year 2000, from 70 to 80 percent of demand will be met, compared to between 15 and 20 percent in 1992.

After CANTV's first year in private hands, a majority of Venezuelans still felt service quality was very poor, although CANTV had made some improvements. CANTV's problem in this regard was that things had been so bad, simply stopping further deterioration was a major task, and one the public would not directly perceive.

Demand for telecom services has been so great, it is almost inelastic: price increases have not significantly reduced demand.

By the year 2000, CANTV must be satisfying 90 percent of requests for a line within an average of five days. CANTV also is obligated to undertake an expansion program that will increase the number of lines from 1.8 million to 4.5 million in nine years, which will mean a teledensity of 14 to 15.

Rural service is open to competition in geographic areas with populations less than 5,000. Rates for these services will be higher than CANTV's in order to create incentives to make investments.

In July 1992 a program began to install 18,400 pay phones of state-of-the-art technology. They accept coins or intelligent cards. Services also improved. In 1991, 57 percent of public telephones were out of service. By 1993, only 10 percent of public telephones were out of service. In 1993, concessions for public telephone service were granted to three companies: Teleservicios VOZ/DATA (Venezuela), Telepub (Italy), and Smart Phone (Malaysia). Teleservicios was given the central coastal area and parts of Caracas. Telepub will cover Central Venezuela, and Smart Phone will cover the states of Amazonas, Nueva Esparta, and Miranda.

10.6.1 The CANTV Network

In 1992, in addition to the telephone network for voice, data, and fax, there was a telex network operating at 50 baud and a data transmission network (VENEX-PAQ). The telex network had 17,500 lines and 13,000 subscribers in 1988, over half of them in metro Caracas. Also, there were a large number of private networks for corporate purposes, such as those of the petroleum, steel, and banking companies. Tests of videoconferencing had been made in some petroleum networks.

At the time of privatization, the telephone system was overwhelmingly analog. Most telephone exchanges used electromechanical technology, but (in 1992) about 16 percent were digital, using the AXE 10 from Ericsson, NEAX 61E from NEC, and EWSD from Siemens. These companies had been the successful bidders in 1986 for what was until then the largest tender offer in CANTV history. The technological change in Venezuelan telecommunications contemplates the installation of 1 million digital lines, to accommodate 792,000 new subscribers, together with an important number of support centers including training and repair.

The purpose of this project is to establish an ISDN structure. In 1992 a 140 Mb/s backbone Radio Digital Interactive (RDI) project was completed, providing digital links among all major cities. A project called VENFOIN (Venezuela Interurban Optical Fiber) was begun at 1992 and due to complete in 1996. It was to link major cities and rural areas to the national network. In 1993, the RD-2 2 (Radio Digital) project was completed. Its main purpose was to increase transmission capacity. It links the main cities of Venezuela. The benefits of this network will be increased capacity, videoconferencing, and high-speed E-mail.

The principal bottlenecks in the basic network have been interconnections between local exchanges for domestic and international long distance. In practical terms, it has historically been much easier to call Venezuela from abroad than to call abroad from Venezuela. This is probably due to an old CANTV policy to facilitate entry of calls, which generates more income than outgoing calls.

10.6.2 Satellite Communications

Venezuela participates as a party, with CANTV as the signatory, to the Intelsat agreement. The privatized CANTV has remained the country's satellite communication provider. Growth of telephone traffic via satellite has been very great, primarily from international traffic. Intelsat introduced what has been called international business services (IBS) in 1987. These are totally digital integrated services handled by satellite at speeds of 64 Kb/s to 8,448 Mb/s. In Venezuela, state entities, such as the petroleum companies and national government, as well as multinational companies, have become IBS users.

CANTV is required to give access to private operators who want to use Intelsat directly. CANTV charges 40 percent above Intelsat rates for this service. The possibility of bypassing CANTV and dealing directly with Intelsat was being studied in 1992. This was already happening in the United Kingdom. Called cosignees, new users would not need to coordinate anything with CANTV. Intelsat wants greater traffic and thus is happy to cooperate in such arrangements. Profits are distributed among all the stockholders, which include CANTV.

In the late 1980s, orbiting of the PAS-1 satellite by Panamsat, a U.S. company, offered an alternative supplier of satellite communications services. Before deciding to utilize it, Venezuela studied the new system's impact on Intelsat. It is technically compatible with Intelsat until 1998, and utilizing the new system is not expected to adversely affect Intelsat economically, provided services are point to point and not interconnected to switched networks at both ends. It was thus decided to allow use of Panamsat, but only for transmission and reception of domestic and international television programs. This limitation will continue until the Ministry of Transport and Communications defines the available frequencies for other satellite telecommunications services (IBS, data, teletext, voice, fax, and the like). In addition, because Venezuela has obligations with the Simon Bolivar Andean Satellite System, in the sense that all domestic and subregional traffic must be through this satellite when it is in orbit, use of Panamsat will be by permits issued for one-year terms. Several television stations have been using Panamsat. In 1993, CANTV added two new digital earth stations for a total of four at Camatagua. One is used for domestic satellite traffic, and the other is used for international digital traffic. Another earth station was scheduled for installation in Maracaibo, the second largest city in Venezuela, in 1994.

10.6.3 Rate Structure

Before privatization, rates nominally were approved by the president of the country, although the actual exercise of this power was by the Ministry of Transport and Communications in coordination with the Ministry of Development, pursuant to an assortment of laws and regulations and the interests of the Treasury. As part of attracting private investors, rates are to be set more broadly and with greater flexibility. Three things are considered in setting rates: recovery of capital invested in equipment, operating expenses, and the need to generate a profit for the benefit of the National Treasury.

Before 1967, charges were based on the number of calls. Since then, time of day, duration, and distance are a factor in long-distance charges where equipment permits direct dialing. For local calls, duration charges are for 90-second increments (one pulse or unit).

As has been the case in most countries, long distance has been used to subsidize basic residential service. In comparison to the United States, which has gone the furthest in relating rates to costs, international and domestic long-distance rates are quite high, and local rates, both residential and commercial, are quite low. In 1990 the basic commercial rate was about U.S.$12 a month. Since privatization, rates are being rebalanced, which means residential rates will increase to reflect costs more accurately.

Venezuela has been using rate caps since privatization. This method is considered the most efficient from an economic point of view, as the service provider directly benefits from being more productive. The government desires universal service, understood to mean that all citizens have service at a "reasonable" cost.

10.6.4 Mobile Cellular Telephony

In 1988 Venezuela became the first South American nation to have cellular service. On May 31, 1991, a contract for a competing service was awarded to Telcel Celular CA, a consortium of Venezuelan investors and BellSouth, a regional operating company in the United States. It is able to offer service nationwide. CANTV was by then already serving about 9,200 subscribers in Caracas and along the central coast.

Telcel's initial system would serve 20,000 subscribers. It paid the government U.S.$100 million for the right to offer service. Telcel is the A-band operator and is using Motorola technology. In 1992, CANTV spun its cellular service, the B-band operator, into an affiliated company called Movilnet. By 1992, Movilnet served 21,000 subscribers. And by 1993, subscribers increased by 268.5 percent, to a total of 77,184. Movilnet provides cellular service with the technological support of GTE. By 1994, Movilnet served the following cities: Caracas, Los Teques, La

Guaira, Maracay, Barcelona, Punta de Mata, Maturin, Alto Guri, Ciudad Bolivar, Puerto Ordaz, Valencia, Barquisimeto, Cabudare, Araure, Ciudad Ojeda, Cabimas, Maracaibo, San Antonio, and San Cristobal. CANTV's cellular concession, purchased in 1992, is good for twenty years and can be expanded for another twenty years.

Given the congestion of the basic network, cellular phones are quite popular among those who can obtain and afford them. A wide assortment of mobile phones are available, including Radio Shack, with Motorola and NEC having the largest market share.

Quality of the cellular service has not been optimal in either band. Partly this is from topographical factors—Caracas is located in a valley surrounded by mountains—but it is also due to a scarcity of base stations. The presumed paralysis of the original plans for investments and expansion must be noted.

10.6.5 Data Transmission

Data transmission does not have a dedicated network. Despite this, the service has achieved noteworthy penetration. Data are carried on the telex network (limited to 50 baud), switched telephone network (RTC), and private circuits. While the RTC can technically support transmissions up to 4800 baud, CANTV did not promote use of the RTC for data because it did not have adequate means to manage it. Private interurban and international circuits provide only for the leasing of channels for speeds of 50 baud.

The fact CANTV did not offer greater facilities caused an anarchical expansion of private data networks. The private data networks were often used illegally for voice traffic. Aware of this, CANTV undertook several studies, concluding there was significant profit potential from establishing a switched public data network. In addition, once in operation, the network would contribute to establishing new informatics services and strengthening those already available.

The first study on a data transmission network for Venezuela was prepared by CANTV's Division of Technical Planning and Norms in 1979. It recommended initiation of tests of packet switching equipment, which were done, and a multiplexor network (named Venmux), which was not pursued. A 1981 study concluded packet switching would permit better utilization of the existing transmission media and facilitate the interconnection of equipment with distinct communications protocols.

As a consequence, at the end of 1982, a bidding process was opened for the acquisition of equipment and cable related to data, which would permit meeting demand for this service during 1983–86. The data network proposed for 1986 was based on a star-grid network with seven concentration nodes, twenty-one remote centers, connected to the nodes through statistical multiplexors, and a network control center (CCR). This would permit 10,957 users, including 25 percent not on dedicated lines (that is, accessing the system through the regular telephone and telex networks), located in forty-five cities.

By 1992 there were several data transmission networks.

VENEXPAQ. Begun in the early 1990s, this is a packet switching network in the eight most important centers of the country utilizing Siemens nodes and managing SDLC, BSC, X.25, X.28, and X.32 protocols. Put into operation by CANTV, its privatization is expected.

CONICIT (SAYCYT). At the end of 1982 the National Council of Scientific and Technological Investigations (CONICIT) contracted with GTE Telenet, a U.S. company, to implement a data network to facilitate access to national and international information centers, stimulate the development of new national databases, and reduce the cost of communications for scientists and other researchers in the country.

SWIFT (Society for Worldwide Interbank Financial Telecommunications). At the end of 1984 CANTV approved a request from the National Bank Association for operation of the SWIFT network for interbank financial communications. Venezuela became a party to SWIFT on March 17, 1988. The network has approximately twenty user banks, which connect their terminals by means of dedicated links to the local concentrator in Caracas. The concentrator is connected by two links with SWIFT's international operations centers, directly or through concentrators in other countries.

In April 1990, IBM de Venezuela SA offered CANTV the computer services of IBM Information Network (International Network of Applications) at the world level, and the proposal was still under study two years later. IBM de Venezuela has been supporting the idea of connecting all the libraries of the country and, subsequently, allowing connection to international academic networks. Moreover, IBM is supporting FEPAFEM (Pan American Federation of Faculties and Schools of Medicine) in providing Venezuela with a medical network that permits disseminating all kinds of medical and health information.

A study by the National Teleinformatics Council (CNT) paid special attention to the type of company that should administer the public data transmission network. It considered four possible options.

1. CANTV be the exclusive provider.
2. A privately owned organization be in charge of the global administration of the service.
3. CANTV associate with a private company, but have a controlling interest.
4. CANTV, through a new subsidiary, initially be in charge of the service to give time for it to be established, but later the new company would become independent.

10.6.6 Equipment Industry

Before the 1990s there was no electronic components industry in Venezuela, except for the manufacture of printed circuit boards. In consumer electronics, local industry basically has been dedicated to assembly. Motorola, which is providing a good deal of equipment to the expansion and modernization of telecommunications worldwide, announced plans to build a semiconductor plant in

Venezuela to supply South America, particularly other signatories to the Andean Pact and the Caribbean. The firm has some expectation of being treated as a national company. Motorola already carries out assembly of some telecom equipment, as do Ericsson, Alcatel, and national companies such as Maplatex. However, there is no "real" local manufacturing of such equipment.

10.7 Conclusion

There is no doubt in the minds of most Venezuelans that without adequate development of telecommunications, a takeoff into a real market economy through the promotion of financial, industrial, and commercial activity cannot be carried out successfully. This means the modernization of the basic telecom network, as well as providing value-added services—and hence, privatization with a foreign operating partner.

In the process of change, several question arise. Is there any purpose to privatizing a state company if it continues to be a monopoly? The answer is yes, if it is a step toward ending the monopoly. For Venezuela and most other Latin American countries, the capital and technology needed for the task are not going to be available unless the provider has reasonable assurance of a return on the tremendous investment necessary.

Although most political leaders and economists recognize the world is simply not going to give Venezuela a good telecom network—let alone a healthy and prosperous economy in general—and domestic resources are inadequate, there has been a backlash against foreign participation and implementation of reforms. The most notable of these were the protest and looting of February 27, 1989—after newly installed President Carlos Andrés Pérez announced a major economic restructuring program that included the doubling of the price of gasoline—and an attempted military coup on February 4, 1992. In November of 1994, the National Guard was called out to patrol Venezuela's big cities in order to control a nationwide crime wave that overwhelmed the resources of the local police.

Experience elsewhere—as in Mexico—has shown that when governments set a period, for example, two years, for a privatization program, it often takes longer, perhaps close to four or five years, to achieve the declared objectives. CANTV's history since privatization is a cautionary tale for investors there and elsewhere. Privatization of CANTV in 1991 benefited users, thanks to increased investments in infrastructure, but investors in the company did not fare as well. If timing, as the axiom goes, is of the essence, then investors couldn't have picked a worse time. In 1991, the following signs boded well for investment in the local economy: an increase of GDP growth from 6.5 percent to 10.9 percent, a decrease in inflation from 36.6 percent to 31.0 percent, and a decrease in unemployment from 9.9 percent to 8.7 percent. And then the economy took a nosedive.

In addition to political uncertainties, investors faced an increasingly hostile economic environment. GDP growth plunged from 10.9 percent in 1991 to –1 percent in 1993, while inflation grew from 31.9 percent to 40.9 percent within the same time period. In 1994 and 1995, inflation grew even more, hovering at 60 to 70 percent annually. In 1994, the local economy reeled due to bank failures. The government was forced to take over ten of Venezuela's forty-seven banks.

Meanwhile, CONATEL, the regulatory agency, presented yet another source of problems for investors. Often touted by the government as an autonomous agency, CONATEL began to look more and more as though it were in danger of compromising this autonomy and becoming politicized. CONATEL was legally entitled to decide upon purchases without the approval of Congress, but it still chose to consult with Congress regarding acquisitions. As late as 1994, the new administration of CONATEL considered imposing more restrictions on its own decision-making authority. Although CONATEL could legally grant concessions without restriction, its president chose to be open to the idea that all pending and new concessions should be approved by Venezuela's attorney general.

CANTV's profit potential, hobbled by the aforementioned economic and political crises, an increasingly antagonistic regulatory agency, and contractual commitments to invest heavily in infrastructure, faced yet another hurdle: an accounts receivable crisis. In 1995, government entities were, on the average, at least a year overdue in paying telephone bills. CANTV was also restricted—by CONATEL—from other potentially profitable activities, such as the delivery of video services. CANTV hoped to return to profitability in 1996, but dividends were not expected for yet another two years.

The lack of telecom infrastructure in Venezuela in the early 1990s was good news for the cellular services industry, which experienced burgeoning growth. By 1994, Telcel and Movilnet—the first two concessionaires in this industry—jointly served about 230,000 subscribers. Increasingly, cellular service emerged, for many users, as the only form of telephone service. And as CANTV invested in installation—expansion and modernization—at the expense of repair service, users began to view cellular service as the more reliable option. In response to demand, Movilnet plans for 1994 included doubling its 1993 investment in cellular infrastructure. Cellular became an attractive option even for public telephones in densely populated areas such as Caracas.

Note

The author wishes to give special recognition to the National Telecommunications Commission (CONATEL) in the person of José Gregorio González for his cooperation in collecting data and statistics for a previous version of this chapter and to Sheryl Russell for her contribution in assisting in the update of this chapter.

References

Antequera, Ricardo. 1989. "La Protección Jurídica del Software." *Actualidad Jurídica* No. 2. March–April.

Brewer, Allan R. 1981. Régimen Jurídico de las Empresas Públicas en Venezuela. Caracas.

CANTV. 1973. Libro de la. Caracas, Policrom. C.A.

_____. 1991. Documents on Privatization.

CANTV Consultoria Juridica. 1990. "Régimen Jurídico de las Telecomunicaciones en

Venezuela." Report presented to the Asociación Hispanoamericana de Investigación y Empresas de Telecomunicaciones (AHCIET).

Fuenmayor, Carlos José. 1990. "Desarrollo de la Industria de la Información en Venezuela." I.B.M. De Venezuela.

Fuenmayor Espina, Alejandro. 1982. "Régimen Jurídico de la Radio y la Televisión," Caracas.

Gatica, Raul. 1985. "Las Empresas del Estado como Instrumento de Planificación." (caso CANTV). Thesis, U.C.V., Caracas.

Lares Martinez, Eloy. 1965. "Manual de Derecho Administrativo."

Martinez Mottola, Fernando. 1991. "CANTV Esquema Propuesto de Privatización." April.

Ministerio De Transporte y Comunicaciones. 1988. "Manual de Organización."

"Modernización y Empresas de Telecomunicaciones de los Estados Miembros de la O.E.A." 1988. Arthur D. Little, Inc., Informe Final. Reference L-7509.

Ramos Martinez, José Antonio. 1985. "La Reforma de la Ley de Telecomunicaciones." Papers presented in the Primeras Jornadas sobre los aspectos Jurídicos de las Telecomunicaciones. CANTV.

Seijas, Felix. 1986. "La OCEI y la Ley de Informática Nacional." July 9–11.

Ungerer, Hebert. 1988. "Las Telecomunicaciones en Europa." Brussels, Luxembourg.

Vittori, Serafino. 1986. "Situación del Servicio de Transmisión de Datos en Venezuela." CANTV. July.

Zaidman, Natan. 1987. "Aspectos Jurídicos de la Informática." Speech given on May 27 in the Rotary Club of Caracas.

_____. "El Futuro Régimen Jurídico de las Telecomunicaciones." 1990. Revista "Actualidad Jurídica Empresarial" No.

_____. "El Nuevo Derecho de las Telecomunicaciones." 1990. Inaugural speech in the II Jornadas Derecho de Telecomunicaciones.

11
Argentina

ALEJANDRA HERRERA

Just before privatization, Argentina boasted a fairly well-developed network in relation to other countries with a similar gross domestic product (GDP). There were more than 10 lines per 100 people in 1989, a rate much higher than the Latin American average. However, the average concealed huge regional and social inequalities, poor quality, and lack of diversification of services. In short, there was significant telecommunications underdevelopment. As a state-run company, the principal operating telco, ENTel, engaged in chaotic investment planning and deficient selection of equipment providers, which increased operating costs and discouraged emergence of an efficient national equipment sector.

Privatization of ENTel in late 1990 modified not only the provision of services but also the possibilities open to the equipment industry. If the new private owners comply with the established goals, the public network will expand, quality of services will improve, tariffs will increase, and changes in the tariff structure will benefit commercial users at the expense of residential ones.

11.1 Background

Argentina lies at the extreme south of the American continent, facing the Atlantic Ocean. It covers 2.8 million square kilometers (excluding territory in Antarctica and the islands located on its maritime platform) and is inhabited by 34 million people (July 1994 estimate), mostly of European origin. Approximately 86 percent of the population lives in urban centers, and over 40 percent is in the province of Buenos Aires and the Federal District, which includes the city of Buenos Aires. Annual population growth is under 1.2 percent.

Since December 1983 the country has been governed by elected authorities, an unusual situation for a country characterized by political instability.[1] Before then, coups were the norm for decades. The military governed during twenty-two of the years from 1930 to 1983, and some of the civilian regimes can be fairly characterized as totalitarian.

The country is a republic divided into twenty-three provinces and a Federal District. The National Constitution, which dates from 1853 (although with many

131

amendments), establishes three branches: an executive, led by a president with fairly broad powers; a legislature comprised of a bicameral congress; and a judiciary, with a supreme court as its highest authority. The president is chosen by an electoral college for a six-year term. There are forty-eight senators (two from each province and the Federal District) serving nine-year terms, with one-third elected every three years. The Chamber of Deputies has 257 members serving four-year terms, with half elected every two years. The number of deputies representing each province is proportional to the population.

The Partido Justicialista, an umbrella organization of Peronist political groups, has controlled the Senate since 1983 and the lower house since 1989. The Radical Party, or UCR (Union Civica Radical), is the second major political force. The president, Carlos Saul Menem, a Peronist, was elected in 1989 and reelected in 1995.

11.2 The Economy

By the late 1920s Argentina's economy ranked with a number of European countries and was the most developed in Latin America. Growth up to then was based primarily on agriculture—first exploiting grazing land (cattle and sheep) and then, from the late nineteenth century, also crops such as wheat. Over half the country is in agricultural use, an extremely high percentage that reflects the fact so much of the country—including the famous Pampas—is suitable for grazing and farming. Industrial activity dates from the turn of the century, but the bulk of expansion came in the 1930s when import-substitution activities became the predominant mode of industrialization.

Slow growth and chronic macroeconomic instability—including several periods of hyperinflation—characterize the economy from the 1940s until the 1990s.[2] Beginning in the late 1940s the government expanded its direct role, becoming an increasingly important investor and a source of subsidies.

Protected from foreign competition, a heterogeneous manufacturing sector with a distorted evolution of technological innovations and structure, and oriented primarily to the domestic market, has emerged. Before 1987 most exports were commodities, while manufacturers needed to import intermediate and capital goods. This meant periodic crises related to balance of payments constraints, with disastrous consequences for economic stability and inflation.

In March 1976 a coup led by Lieutenant General Jorge Videla changed the path of Argentina's economic history. Between 1976 and 1981, the government abandoned long-standing protectionist policies and implemented a variety of economic measures that resulted in economic opening. Foreign direct investment, profit remittances, capital repatriation, and technology transfer were liberalized, and tariffs were cut. However, many old habits of state involvement continued. Thus, there were new industrial promotion programs that, among other things, allowed production of intermediate goods—in particular, paper, petrochemical, and iron and steel—to remain protected from foreign competition. The number of foreign firms shrank, and large, diversified domestic economic groups increased. The latter largely benefited as providers of goods and services to the state or through participation in industrial promotion plans. Funding these plans and covering deficits of state-owned companies became a major source of government deficits, which ranged between 6 and 18 percent of GDP during 1978–83, and thus of government debt.

The political background operating behind these economic policies was widespread repression of political opposition, including the slaughter of several thousand people. The government was thus able to impose a significant reduction in real wages.

Involution of the productive system, crumbling living standards, surging foreign debt, and Argentina's defeat in the Malvinas (Falklands) War contributed to the fall of the military regime in 1983. A weakened and divided junta allowed elections in October, and, in an upset, Raúl Alfonsin of the UCR was elected president and gained a majority in the Chamber of Deputies. The Peronists elected more provincial governors, and this allowed them to control the Senate, whose members are selected by the provinces.

The new government faced an external debt of U.S.$45 billion that the public sector had either incurred or assumed. Attempts to address the country's macroeconomic instability were belated. The Plan Austral of June 1985 sought to stabilize prices. It, as well as its successors, had brief periods of seeming success. The August 1988 Plan Primavera was the first attempt to link stabilization and structural reform.

A new surge in the already chronic inflation led to President Alfonsin resigning in July 1989, six months before the end of his term, in favor of the winner of the May 1989 elections Carlos Saul Menem (Partido Justicialista). The Menem cabinet adopted a tight stabilization program. As before, programs started well but then fell apart, and there were several changes of economic advisers. However, the government was steadily putting in place institutional and other reforms that would support stabilization and growth.

Two major elements of the new economic policy have had important effects on Argentine industrial structure, and the telecommunications sector in particular. First is implementation of the July 1989 Law on the Reform of the State, which is rooted in a privatization program for state-owned enterprises and state assets. Second is the decision to integrate Argentina in a regional common market—Mercosur—with Brazil beginning in 1995. Uruguay, Paraguay, and Chile subsequently joined. Mercosur has been developed in the framework of the country's adherence to the Brady Plan. (The foregoing summary draws in part on Chudnovsky 1989 and CEI 1992.)

In 1993 GDP was estimated at about 251 billion pesos (29 percent higher than in 1990, adjusted for inflation), exports were U.S.$12.7 billion (compared to U.S.$11.5 billion in 1990) and imports were U.S.$16.0 billion (compared to U.S.$8.0 billion). Foreign debt had increased to U.S.$74 billion in April 1994 from about U.S.$54 billion in 1990, reflecting both accrued interest on old debt and new lending based on renewed optimism about the prospects for the country.

11.3 Early Development

Argentina's first telephone company—Unión Telefónica del Río de la Plata—was created in 1886 by British capital. In 1929 the International Telephone and Telegraph Corporation (ITT) purchased it and, until 1946, provided telecom services in most of the country. That year the government bought the rights and assets of the company and created Empresa Mixta Telefónica Argentina. Then, in 1948, the government restructured the firm, creating Empresa Nacional de Telecomunicaciones (ENTel), owned completely by the state.

The state-owned ENTel, its predecessors, and its direct successors have supplied telecom services to most of the nation, including international service. The exceptions are the provinces of San Juan, Mendoza, Salta, Tucumán, Santiago del Estero, and Entre Rios, where the service provider is Compañia Argentina de Teléfonos (CAT), a subsidiary of L. M. Ericsson. Until the mid-1980s, Ericsson had two subsidiaries, CET (created in 1916) and CAT (created in 1927), both connected to ENTel's network for long-distance service. In 1989 CAT absorbed Compañia Entrepriana di Teléfanos (CET).

11.4 Service in the Late 1980s and Early 1990s

With 3.1 million lines in operation (and capacity for 3.5 million) in 1989, ENTel handled 95 percent of Argentina's total telecommunications traffic. Besides local, long-distance, and international telephone services, it offered telex, telephoto, fax, data transmission (Arpac), broadcasting of radio and television, leased circuits for telephone and telegraph, and leased fixed and mobile rural radio systems. The company also was a member of Intelsat and Inmarsat, and it provided earth-satellite links through stations in Balcarce and Bosque Alegre.

The Argentine telecommunications system has long been characterized by regional and social inequalities, technical heterogeneity, and poor service. Large portions of the population and most economic activity are concentrated in a few provinces and, within them, in large urban centers. Thus, in 1987, the Federal District had some 19 percent of the country's population, produced 27 percent of the country's GDP, and had some 32 percent of total telephone lines. Three provinces (Buenos Aires, Santa Fé, and Córdoba) collectively boasted 47 percent of the population, 48 percent of GDP, and 50 percent of lines. The rest of the country held 34 percent of the population but produced 25 percent of GDP and had only 18 percent of lines.

Taking network distribution by per capita income, the top 10 percent (annual average income over U.S.$9,000) had 55 telephones per 100 people, while those with incomes below U.S.$2,300, U.S.$1,300, and U.S.$750 had 13, 6, and 3 telephones per 100, respectively (CPU-FOETRA 1988).

The system run by ENTel combined at least eleven telephone technologies and three telex technologies that were operated with a variety of software. This network architecture obviously increased operating costs and impeded use of digital technologies for centralizing repair and maintenance operations (Herrera 1989).

There was a marked and persistent inability to respond to demand; unsatisfied demand remained high for several decades. During the years 1960 to 1985, when connection cost was marginal, demand remained constant at 45 percent of all lines in operation, according to ENTel data. Some customers waited twelve to fourteen years to have a telephone installed in their homes; others never got one. Believing they would never get one, many did not bother to sign up. After 1985, when connection costs increased to approximately U.S.$600, unsatisfied demand dropped to one-quarter of all lines in operation.

In terms of service quality, in 1989 ENTel had over 14 million requests for telephone repairs and other service deficiencies. This means the average telephone was out of order several times during the year. Extensive failures occurred in both the local and long-distance transmission systems (Petrazzini 1991).

11.4.1 Financial and Planning Problems

Investment and network expansion restrictions, coupled with a procurement policy that led the company to pay prices much higher than those offered in the international market, pushed ENTel to search for financial aid. Since the company was not allowed to borrow in the domestic market, its external debt rose steadily for a long time. During the 1980s, the length of loans was reduced and alternative sources of financing evaporated. This put further economic stress on the company.

In 1985, through a plan called Megatel, ENTel tried to overcome the situation. The main goal was installation of 1 million new lines. Purchasing the required equipment would be financed in advance by those requesting service. However, as a solution to the company's financial problem the plan was insufficient. Two estimates were used to establish the connection price per line: the number of potential customers and the price ENTel would pay for the needed equipment. As it turned out, the hardware was more costly than estimated and the number of users signing up for connections was lower than expected. The high prices resulted from the fact that the company agreed to pay extremely high interest rates on vendor-financed purchases. This complicated the financial situation of ENTel even further. In 1989 ENTel suspended tax payments to the central government, contributing to the government's already substantial deficit.

Ultimately, ENTel's financial problems related to the fact its tariffs were never paired with the "unreasonably" high level of its costs. The costs were related to two interrelated facts: a lack of investment planning, including the absence of control over work in progress, and the character of ENTel's relations with its equipment providers.

Lack of investment planning is evident throughout ENTel's history. Expansion of the public network came in spurts. For example, during the 1970s, delivery of lines was as low as 6,000 in 1975 and as high 200,000 in 1979. The degree of randomness in ENTel's works was so high that, even during the limited periods when an official Work Plan was in effect, the number of unplanned projects executed equaled 55 percent of planned ones. Further, the planned projects were only occasionally finished on schedule.

The company lacked controls to monitor implementation, physically and financially, of its Work Plans, nor did it have the means to assess the interaction among different projects. It was, therefore, unable to visualize how delays and problems in any one project affected the plan as a whole. The inability to predict bottlenecks meant a total lack of coordination between the pace at which ENTel received equipment from its providers and the time needed to incorporate it into the public network. This caused persistent difficulties in coordinating the connection of new users to the network when new switching systems were purchased or old ones expanded. Connections could be done only by ENTel until 1979, when new regulations allowed competition in construction of the local loop. Of course, lines not connected to a user had a negative economic effect because the equipment went unused and thus failed to earn its planned income.

11.4.2 Regulation

The legislative basis for regulation is the 1972 Telecommunications Law (19,298). The law grants the executive branch considerable power to control the development of telecommunications while leaving other branches—in particular, the Congress—with a secondary or marginal role.

The Communications Secretariat (SECOM) had direct control of ENTel. The main task of the agency was development and implementation of communications plans and control of service provision (Presidential Decree 2,483). In the state's hierarchical structure SECOM was part of the Ministry of Services and Public Works. The executive manager and other top officials of ENTel were appointed by the president of the nation. Therefore, the managerial structure of the company was tightly tied to politics.

Moreover, ENTel was subject to the decisions of seven or more government agencies, which usually had contradictory policies and projects for the company and for the sector in general. The Ministry of Economy, for example, oversaw ENTel's budget; the Ministry of Labor set the salaries of company employees; the Secretary of Industry decided the purchasing of equipment; the Ministry of Services and Public Works generated policies for public services and controlled their provision; and the Communications Secretariat crafted policies for the sector in general, and for the company in particular. Tariff rates were decided by the Ministry of Economy and by the country's president, based on the political needs of the moment.

"Unconsulted" decisions, meaning those taken at the company level, often upset or contradicted goals pursued by higher strata of the administration. Therefore, new institutions (such as the Directorio de Empresas Publicas) were created to mediate and exert some control over the performance of state enterprises. The result was complete chaos. The executive manager of ENTel had to manage the company on a daily basis while surviving in a loaded political environment (Petrazzini 1991). It is no wonder that in the thirty years before privatization there were twelve presidents and twenty-eight executive managers.

11.5 Procurement and the Equipment Industry

As a state company, from its creation in 1948 ENTel was subject to "compre nacional" (national procurement) requirements that granted preference to local providers. These were in fact a small, already-established group of transnationals in switching, transmission, and terminal equipment coexisting with a relatively marginal group of local firms that produced mainly for domestic private users. In 1978 employment by domestic equipment makers peaked at 8,000; it had fallen to 5,000 by 1984, the last year from which there are aggregate data.

The monopsonistic procurement power exercised by ENTel for most of its history contributed to the company having just two local suppliers of switching equipment and telephone sets. These were Compañia Standard Electric Argentina (CSEA) and Equitel, subsidiaries of ITT and Siemens. Ericsson also produced equipment locally. Its presence was relatively marginal, however, being limited primarily to supplying its subsidiaries, CAT and CET, which together operated about 10 percent of the Argentine network.

Ericsson and a predecessor of ITT began local production at the end of 1910. Note that ITT continued as a supplier even after its operating company, the predecessor of ENTel, was nationalized. Siemens entered the market as a domestic producer in 1954. Seven mostly European transnational firms dominated the public transmission equipment market.

Due to ENTel's practices there were significant barriers to the entry of new transnational firms and a marginalization of local companies as potential suppliers. No doubt this was a factor leading the latter to produce radio equipment for the private market. The status quo was justified by the government on the same grounds as regulatory and protectionist policies in developed countries: the existence of important economies of scale, the need to guarantee the continuity of repair and maintenance of the network, and the advantages that first entrants have in regard to network knowledge.

Despite state intervention on behalf of transnational providers, their position could not be characterized as secure. For example, in 1973, during a Peronist period, the telecom transnationals operating in the country had their contracts to provide equipment to ENTel revoked by congressional action (Law 20,743). This practically paralyzed the industry until the military coup in 1976. (Herrera 1989, pp. 114–26.)

For mainly political reasons, throughout its history ENTel concentrated most of its equipment purchasing in short periods of time, generating strong demand shocks in the local industry. These surges generally were followed by periods of contraction, which sometimes almost halted procurement initiatives. This boom-bust pattern had a strong influence on the nature and structure of the industry. Until the late 1970s, competition based on price or product differentiation was almost irrelevant. Rather, precedence, reduction of costs, idle production during long periods of time, and research and development focused on the adaptation of products and factory layout to local conditions were among the requisites to stay in the market.

Contracts between ENTel and its providers did not directly require technology transfer or high levels of local content. Despite this, during the period in which electromechanical technology dominated (that is, until 1979), there was an increase in local content in the production of switching equipment. This resulted mainly from high levels of competition. The firms tried to capture the externalities generated by the machine tool sector, which had highly skilled labor that could be used in the production of telephone equipment.

Between 1975 and 1978, twenty new firms with majority domestic capital entered the industry. Many oriented production to assembling PBXs. They were small and employed engineers working for relatively low wages, generally less than half what transnationals paid. These new firms produced a limited amount of PBX equipment, copied from foreign models two or three generations behind the technological frontier. They used mostly imported parts, so the level of local content was low. After 1979, several abandoned local production and disappeared or shifted into marketing imported equipment. They were unable to compete in a context of increasing technological innovation, lowering of tariffs, and sharp drops in foreign exchange rates.

11.5.1 The 1979 Policy Shift

Between 1979 and 1983, during the military regime, the government encouraged new foreign capital to enter the Argentine telecom market. As part of this move, in 1979, ENTel decided to take advantage of a favorable exchange rate and trade liberalization to purchase all kinds of imported equipment. In each case, ENTel agreed to buy the latest version of technologies that operating telcos in industrial countries were using only marginally and for testing purposes. This early incorporation of digital technologies from many different suppliers generated a very heterogeneous network architecture.

In 1979 provision of 660,000 lines was opened to international bidding. The companies ITT, Siemens, Philips, Fujitsu, Ericsson, Hitachi, NEC, Thomson, GTE, and Italtel all showed an interest. This led to real price competition among the equipment companies, something that had been absent, and it created instability among traditional equipment providers. In Argentina, as elsewhere, Japanese firms tended to offer the best prices. As a consequence, in 1981 a consortium of NEC and the local group Perez Companc, Pecom-Nec, won half the equipment market. The consortium committed itself to produce locally one-third of the equipment (by value).

Only because ENTel included nonprice criteria to justify retaining its two traditional providers were ITT and Siemens able to keep a quarter of the market each. The justification was that these companies had been operating in Argentina for more than sixty years, they were currently in full production fulfilling previous contracts with ENTel, and they knew the systems already installed very well, which was considered important for future installations. This action reestablished market precedence as an entry barrier.

The decision to favor Pecom-Nec at the expense of Fujitsu, which had offered equivalent terms, signaled foreign firms that it was important to make alliances with local capital to acquire lobbying capabilities. Indeed, the decree awarding part of the market to NEC states that Fujitsu was passed over because, among other reasons, Pecom-Nec had a majority of local capital and the company had previous contracts with ENTel (including providing repair services and the "digital belt" for Buenos Aires). Fujitsu's only relation with ENTel was an agreement to lend a switching system.

When an elected government took power in December 1983, the contracts derived from the 1979 bidding had not been completed, and a long process to renegotiate the terms for the delivery of equipment began. The Argentine authorities were unable to profit from the new competitive conditions in the international market. Instead, after several years of negotiations, the government ended up agreeing to prices well above the international market.

In 1985 the national switching equipment industry reverted to having just two firms. Siemens bought ITT's local subsidiary, CSEA, leaving the market divided equally between it and Pecom-Nec.

Between 1978 and 1983, five companies (Politronix, Ambil, DGT, Mocoreta, and Soldyne) took advantage of the low price of imported electronic parts to launch small and medium switching systems using local technology. These were generally "semi-electronic"—hybrids of integrated circuits and mechanical switches. Local content, equivalent to 50 percent of direct costs, was confined almost exclusively to circuits, power supplies, cabinets, and assembly. The firms were able to stay in the market with less sophisticated systems because of the pricing practices of the transnationals. The gap between the foreign firms' import and sale prices was so wide that local producers could find market niches for their low-priced products.

Politronix, founded in 1980 entirely with local capital, is a particularly interesting example of a new company. It started with forty employees, including a strong group of engineers. One of its first jobs was producing a round electronic keyboard for Equitel, which used the product in equipment sold to ENTel. The strategy was for Politronix to use the benefits obtained from the relationship with Equitel to finance research and development. Politronix expected that this research and development would allow it to enter the PBX market with products adapted to local demand and conditions.

11.5.2 Promoting a Domestic Electronics Industry

During the 1980s, government policies aimed at the electronics sector not only were adopted in an incoherent fashion, but they also lacked an institutional framework that would have turned them into an effective industrial development tool. In telecommunications, conflicts of interests within the governing UCR translated into instability and short tenure for government officials in charge of the sector.

In January 1985, the secretary of industry proclaimed Resolution 44, which offered financial benefits, primarily tax breaks, to firms undertaking development of a domestic electronics industry (see Azpiazu, Basualdo, and Nochteff 1988). Participants were selected by bidding, and some of the most important transnational informatics companies, most associated with local firms, were among the winners. Resolution 44 was followed by a number of poorly articulated and contradictory regulations that distorted the original spirit of the project. This was particularly true in regard to the role local capital was supposed to have.

In 1986 the team appointed to lead SECOM (the Communications Secretariat), which had participated in the elaboration of Resolution 44, conceived an integrated plan for the electronics sector based on the proposals of the 1983 National Commission of Informatics. ENTel's procurement power was used actively to promote the technological development of companies with domestic capital.

In March 1986, ENTel was authorized by Presidential Decree 428 to open bidding for the selection of local equipment providers, mainly in relation to the Megatel network expansion plan. A wide range of items from high-capacity electronic switching systems to terminal equipment for users was to be put out for bid. Also, SECOM defined the required activities related to research, development, and engineering, as well as the periods over which projects would be completed. The allocation of orders for each item was based on the price of the product, level of local content, and product and process technology.

Preference was to be given firms offering to meet the required levels of local content in shorter periods, or to achieve higher level of content than those required by the government. The companies had to be located in the country, with preference given to firms formed with majority local capital. The bidding was never opened. In July 1986, the secretary of communications who created the project resigned. Decree 428 was canceled. The newly appointed secretary and his team completely changed the policy, dropping local-company preference and reviving traditional arrangements.

11.5.3 The Mid- to Late 1980s

The Alfonsin government in 1987 established new criteria for the selection of providers in response to the "tied aid" policies of governments of industrial countries. They would lend money on favorable terms on condition the loan recipient used it to buy equipment from companies of the lender country. France was very aggressive in this regard, and in September 1987 the Argentine government publicly announced the possibility of including Alcatel Thomson as a third switch provider. Then, in December, the governments of Argentina and Italy signed an agreement that set the basis for a possible joint venture between companies of both countries to take over digitalization of the Argentine network.

Interestingly, the threat of a third company led Siemens and Pecom-Nec to do more than reduce prices. For a while the state emphasized price criteria, while the transnational companies argued in defense of the national industry and its labor market. The corporations went as far as to launch an advertising campaign declaring their intention to increase technology transfer far beyond what was required.

The agreement with Italy also brought about changes in the strategies of other suppliers. A cartel, Union Transitoria de Empresas (UTE), including most of the companies operating in the country, was formed. It designed a digitalization project for the national network and reached an agreement with the state on prices and market share. In fact, ENTel faced the rather bizarre situation of the initiative having been taken by the equipment providers, usurping from the state its role in defining the expansion and restructuring of the public network.

11.6 Privatization

The first steps toward privatization came in 1976, when, responding to directives from the Ministry of Economy, ENTel's managers started to transfer installation to the private sector. After 1983, the civilian government continued this transfer and started privatization of new services such as mobile telephony, telephone circuits, and data transmission in downtown Buenos Aires (where the national financial system is concentrated). The UCR administration also liberalized equipment provision.

The right to provide cellular telephone service in the Federal District was granted in 1989, through bidding, to the Compañia de Radiocomunicaciones Móviles SA, formed by three foreign and two national firms: Bell South, Motorola, Citibank, IECSEA (Macri group), and SICOM (BGH group).

11.6.1 The Circumstances

The spread of new technology and institutional changes occurring within the industrial countries—the United States, Great Britain, and Japan, in particular—were important in shaping Argentine telecommunications during the 1980s and especially influenced the nature of ENTel's privatization process. These factors have continued to affect its development in the 1990s.

The existence of substantial global idle capacity at large transnational equipment producers during the 1980s led them to increase exports and to apply pressure to seek changes in the sourcing policies of state companies that had protected a small set of local suppliers. At the same time, the appearance of new services, plus the lowering of barriers to entering equipment production and providing certain existing services, threw into question the existing institutional structure, which was designed primarily to regulate a monopoly whose basic function had been simple voice transmission.

The decision of the Baby Bells in the United States and of various European companies to respond to changes in the structure of their home markets by extending operations beyond their borders resulted in their having a serious interest in the privatization of telecom services in undeveloped countries (Herrera 1992).

Even though these circumstances—relatively internal to the telecommunications sector—were extremely important, one must recognize that in Argentina the privatization of ENTel was determined above all by other matters that were, in a certain sense, way outside the arena of the telecom industry.

Since the 1940s, the operations of many companies in Argentina had been linked to the ability to win state subsidies and privileges. This increased the country's fiscal imbalance, a process that was exacerbated when, in 1982, the government decided to "statize" the private debt that many of these companies had incurred. Argentina was unable to service this debt (Basualdo 1986).

The Peronist government that took office in July 1989 proposed a restructuring of the state apparatus that would allow simultaneously for near-term relief from the country's grave economic crisis and for payment of public foreign debt. These efforts provided continuity to similar strategies pursued in the 1983–89 period by the UCR government. Restructuring meant the government would reduce its direct and indirect roles in the economy, which included selling state-owned companies. Because the debt and fiscal crisis are closely tied together, the technique used for privatization involved the state trading equity in public enterprises for its external debt.

State-owned ENTel constituted the test case, and the government put great political importance on its success. Privatizing the telephone company would not only be proof of the government's willingness to honor foreign debt but also of its ability to actually make loan payments.

11.6.2 The Process

The Alfonsin government announced, in 1988, its intention to sell 40 percent of ENTel's shares to Telefónica de España (TEF). The plan was blocked in Congress by Peronist deputies—the same ones who later voted in favor of President Menem's privatization proposal.

Thus, in July 1989, just after Menem took office, Congress, with the support of Peronist and UCR legislators, approved the Law on the Reform of the State, which allowed privatization of state companies. It also gave the president extraordinary powers. All this aroused hostile protests. Unions, for example, started a mobilization against ENTel's privatization. In Buenos Aires, several telecom union leaders in favor of partial privatization were expelled from the union. Argentine equipment providers, in association with some groups from the financial sector, offered to replace TEF as a private partner of ENTel.

In response, Menem issued decrees that reduced the possibility of effective challenges to the privatization process (Petrazzini 1991). Measures included dismissing many of the ENTel workers who had struck in opposition to privatization.

In January 1990, the government sought tenders for 60 percent of ENTel's shares, with a base price of U.S.$214 million in immediate cash (U.S.$100 million for the northern region and U.S.$114 million for the southern region) and an additional U.S.$228 million paid over six years beginning three years after the takeover. The winner would offer the most Argentine foreign debt (counted at face value plus accrued interest), with a minimum of U.S.$3.5 billion (Presidential Decree 62/90). Just before the plan to privatize ENTel was announced, Argentine debt traded at 12 percent of its face value, with payment of capital scheduled for the twenty-first century. Subsequently, it rose to a plateau of approximately 30 percent.

Of the remainder of the company, 10 percent was reserved for employees and 30 percent was reserved for later sale to the public. In short, the government would completely, and fairly quickly, divest itself of its entire interest in ENTel, retaining neither a "golden share" nor even a minority stake. However, the employee shares are still under state control, and there is no agreement on who will be the beneficiaries, in what way they will be transferred, or when.

When ENTel was sold, it was discharged of liabilities and debt, except for commitments to employees and certain obligations to equipment providers and users. This meant the state retained U.S.$1.5 billion in debt, part of which was retired with the cash from the sale of the company. Of the debt, approximately U.S.$900 million was owed domestically. Certain assets, including those for services prior to the transfer and the capital contributions made to Intelsat and Inmarsat, also were kept by the state.

The decision to divide the network into northern and southern parts was a political one taken by the executive branch. It was made against the advice of the international consulting firm hired by the government to report on the most suitable privatization process.

The winning bidders, announced on November 8, 1990, agreed to submit debt of U.S.$2.3 billion (plus U.S.$100 million in cash and U.S.$177 million in promissory notes to ENTel) for the southern region and U.S.$2.7 billion (plus U.S.$114 million in cash and U.S.$202 million in promissory notes to ENTel) for the north within ninety days of ENTel being handed over. Note that all of the cash and debt were for the benefit of the government, none of it was new capital for telecommunications. The buyers were compelled to meet a set of requirements regarding expansion of the network, quality of service, and the like, which are discussed later.

11.6.3 The New Structure

Transfer of ENTel took place on November 8, 1990, and resulted in four new firms. Basic telecom services are offered by Telefónica Argentina (Telefónica) and Telecom Argentina (Telecom), companies formed as successors to ENTel's southern and northern regions, respectively. Although CAT renewed its license, it entered negotiations with the new companies to sell its system. This occurred in 1992.[3]

Telefónica and Telecom own equal parts of Teleintar, which provides international service, and of Startel, which offers "services open to competition," the most important of which are mobile radiotelephone, mobile maritime radio, telex, data transmission within the national boundaries of Argentina (ENTel's Arpac data packet-switching network became part of Startel), and value-added services.

Besides ENTel's assets, the companies acquired monopolistic rights for seven years (extendable to ten) to provide basic domestic local and long-distance service in their corresponding zones, as well as all types of international service through Teleintar. During the monopoly period third parties are allowed to install point-to-point private lines, but they cannot resell capacity and may install such systems only if Telecom or Telefónica do not provide the service within 180 days.

The companies will face a competitor in the cellular phone market, and there are no prohibitions on the entrance of new operators in value-added services. Independent companies are allowed to offer urban telephone service in areas located more than 15 kilometers from a central office if Telecom or Telefónica are not interested in providing service in the area within a year.

After their monopolies expire, Telecom and Telefónica will be eligible for licenses to provide, outside their regions, data transmission services and other value-added services in competition with other suppliers, as well as offering the services contained in their original licenses.

11.6.4 The Winning Bidders

The winning bidders are consortiums: Nortel SA won Telecom and Cointel SA won Telefónica. Nortel initially was held 30 percent by each of STET, France Cables et Radio, and the Perez Companc group; J. P. Morgan & Company owned 10 percent. Cointel was owned 33 percent by Telefónica Internacional (a wholly owned subsidiary of TEF), 57 percent by Citibank, and 10 percent by Techint. Note that each consortium comprises at least one telephone company, an Argentine conglomerate, and a U.S. bank. Citibank leads the committee of Argentina's creditors, and J. P. Morgan is among the country's largest creditors.

The firms STET, France Cables, and TEF are operating telcos with related companies that produce telecom equipment. Owned by the Italian state, STET holds the Italian Reconstruction Institute (IRI), which has 20 million lines in Italy and operations in Germany, the Netherlands, the United Kingdom, and the United States. Italtel, another subsidiary of STET, for years sold transmission systems to ENTel. France Cables et Radio SA, controlled by France Telecom and associated with Alcatel, has 28 million lines in France. During the years of UCR rule and with the support of the French government, it tried to make itself into a third ENTel equipment supplier. The Spanish government owns 40 percent of TEF, which operates 11 million lines in Spain. Telefónica de España has a very aggressive, expansionist policy in other European countries, as well as in the former Soviet Union and Latin America. Sintel, a subsidiary of TEF, sold ENTel the Arpac data transmission network.

The Perez Companc and Techint groups each include more than fifty companies, covering a wide variety of activities. For Perez these include naval construction, food processing, petrochemicals, construction, electronics, financial operations (two banks), and services. Techint operates in iron and steel, construction, and various other areas in the primary, service, and financial sectors. During the period of import substitution, both Perez Companc and Techint collected substantial state subsidies under various industrial promotion plans and as providers to the state, mainly in the construction sector. Both were responsible for significant amounts of debt that the government assumed in 1982. Subsequently, they have been involved in the debt-for-equity privatizations of various state enterprises—oil, highways, and railways, among others.

Perez is associated with NEC, which entered the Argentine market in 1978 by selling ENTel a digital network and later became one of the two providers of switching equipment to ENTel. Techint, besides having been one of the principal installation subcontractors for ENTel, has been collaborating with Italtel and Teletra on a project financed by a credit line of U.S.$135 million granted by the Italian government to digitalize the telephone network. This means Telefónica and Telecom are associated, through Italtel and Techint, respectively, on a project supplying transmission equipment.

11.6.5 Public Offering and Capital Structure

In December 1991 the government's remaining 30 percent interest in Telefónica was sold to the public in an international stock offering. A similar offering of Telecom stock was delayed until March 1992 because the company would not provide the information needed to produce a prospectus. The Telefónica offering brought the government U.S.$800 million, Telecom brought U.S.$1.2 billion. Both companies trade in the United States on the New York Stock Exchange (as American Depositary Receipts), as well as in Argentina.

Each company has three classes of shares. Class C shares, representing 10 percent of the equity, have been retained by the government to be distributed to company employees, although the procedure has yet to be determined. Class B shares, 39 percent of total equity, are fully transferable, as are the shares that trade publicly. The actual public float represents 30 percent of equity; class B shares, representing 9 percent, are held by the controlling consortium. All the class A shares (51 percent of equity) are held by the controlling consortium. They are transferable only with the prior consent of the regulatory body, Comisión Nacional de Telecomunicaciones (CNT). Each consortium thus owns 60 percent of the total equity.

11.7 Expanding and Improving the Privatized Network

The transfer contract requires meeting certain expansion goals in the area of basic services. It also establishes a requirement that Telecom, Telefónica, and Teleintar assure the continuance, regularity, equality, and availability of service delivery to the public in their respective areas. Thus, the consortiums cannot disconnect any town from the national satellite service. If there are other efficient telecommunications alternatives, they have to be approved first by CNT.

By the end of 1996, Telecom must install 609,500 lines and Telefónica, 623,920. To extend their monopoly to ten years (the end of the year 2000), the figures are 810,710 (about 33 percent higher) and 792,850 (about 27 percent higher), respectively. Connecting users to 205,000 lines bought by ENTel but not allocated to any particular customer counts as part of the installation requirement, as does connecting 90,000 lines already assigned and paid for by end users and connecting lines bought with credits from the Italian and French governments (U.S.$60 and U.S.$135 millions, respectively).

Each company must provide at least 13,000 public or semipublic telephones. The new lines must be distributed nationwide, with a specified minimum number in each province. The planned distribution (for a ten-year monopoly) assigns metropolitan Buenos Aires (the Federal District) 41 percent of the new lines, with the provinces of Buenos Aires, Santa Fé, and Córdoba receiving 34 percent. This could reduce regional concentration, given that the rest of the country began the period with only 18 percent of lines but will be getting 25 percent of new ones. However, growth greater than the expected level could result in regional reconcentration along the axis of Buenos Aires, Santa Fé, Córdoba, because there are no specific obligations regarding geographical distribution of any expansion above the minimum.

Certain quality goals also must be met. These involve efficiency in completing calls, speed of the response in services involving operators, reduction in the number of failures in external and internal plants, and reduction in delay time for repairs. (For public or semipublic telephones, these goals are suggested, not obligatory.) The transfer contracts stipulate that, year by year until 2000, these quality parameters will be met, and by truly imposing these guidelines a definite improvement will be seen in the Argentine network, even though it still will not have reached the average efficiency levels of networks in industrial countries.

By September 1994, Telefónica and Telecom had installed 2.2 million lines, of

Table 11.1. Basic Indicators of the Argentine Telecommunications Network Companies
Telefónica and Telecom, 1990–94

	Nov. 1990	Sept. 1991	Sept. 1992	Sept. 1993	Sept. 1994
Installed lines	3,471,283	3,629,939	4,256,643	4,967,588	5,637,837
Annual variation*		158,656	626,704	710,945	670,249
Lines on service	3,086,964	3,199,190	3,682,145	4,091,804	4,834,073
Annual variation*		112,226	482,955	409,659	742,269
Digital lines	460,284	559,000	1,189,499	2,270,390	3,488,923
Annual variation*		98,716	630,499	1,080,891	1,218,533
Public phones	22,549	25,690	36,500	47,254	56,844
Annual variation*		3,141	10,810	10,754	9,590
Network digitalization	13.26%	15.40%	27.90%	45.70%	61.88%
Working personnel	40,772	35,286	36,293	33,736	31,289
Annual variation		–5,486	1,007	–2,557	–2,447
Lines on service per employee	75.7	90.67	101.46	121.29	154.5

Telefónica installed 50.7 percent of the total new lines; Telecom installed the rest. (Regarding the lines already operational, Telefónica had 51.5% of the total.)

*The variation in 1991 was measured in relation to the privatization of ENTel (Nov. 1990).

Source: Own production based on data from the Comision Nacional de Telecomunicaciones (CNT), 1995.

which 1.7 million were in service (see table 11.1). Overall, by 1994 the companies had already exceeded the expansion goals for 1996. Parallel to the network enlargement was a process of modernization, including substitution of advanced technology, which is reflected in the increase in digitalization from 13 percent to 62 percent between November 1990 and September 1994. In October 1995, Siemens AG announced a contract to provide more than 1 million lines of its digital switching system and 5,000 kilometers of fiber-optic lines, to be installed by the end of 1997 by various Argentine telcos.

Combined with the layoff of more than 4,900 at Telefónica and almost 4,600 at Telecom, this modernization allowed for a substantial increase of efficiency: the ratio of lines per employee went from 75.7 to 154.5. The percentage of lines not in service fell from 4.91 to 0.19 percent, and the delay to repair a damaged line went from an average of twenty-three days to an average of three days. It has been difficult for CNT to collect suitable data on other aspects of service quality. Table 11.2 shows the amount invested by telecommunications companies during 1990–94.

Table 11.2. Investments of Telecommunications Companies, November 1990–December 1994 (in millions)

Telecom	$2,745.3
Telefónica	$2,728.9
Teleintar	$112.1
Startel	$33.4
Total	$5,619.7

Source: Comision Nacional de Telecomunicaciones (CNT), 1995.

11.7.1 Competitors and Interconnection

Since the early 1980s it has become progressively clearer that creating an environment fostering effective competition depends as much on the possibility of interconnection between networks as on the conditions under which potential competitors get access to the basic network (Noam 1988; Helm and Yarrow 1988).

During their monopoly periods (until 1997 or 2000) Telecom, Telefónica, Teleintar, and Startel are required to interconnect their networks, and they can arrange with independent local network companies and with the holders of domestic point-to-point connections the conditions and prices of the interconnection. Telefónica and Telecom are required to allow access to the public network for companies that want to provide services that create a competitive environment. And, in all cases, the cost of connection and the use of the network must be "normal," not "discriminatory," even though these terms are nowhere defined.

There were five point-to-point international data networks that had begun operating during the ENTel period. They are not allowed to connect to any national or international network during the period Telecom and Telefónica have monopoly rights. When Teleintar's right to monopolize provision of international data and voice transmission runs out, it must agree with its competitors on the conditions under which network connections will be made and rates will be set. If the firms involved do not reach an agreement, the regulatory agency will intervene.

Interpretation of the contracts signed by Telefónica and Telecom has generated an untenable level of confrontation between them and CNT over the issue of interconnection. The situation reached a decisive point in June 1995 when the Ministry of the Economy, Works and Public Services dismissed all of CNT's directors and its president.

The dismission was directly linked to controversy surrounding CNT Resolution 1197 of May 9, 1995, which rejected the October 5, 1993, agreement by Telecom and Telefónica regarding conditions for their provision of data services, telex, value-added, and other services to Startel. Among other things, CNT ruled that all agreements between Startel and the operating telcos regarding interconnection and basic services must be submitted to CNT for approval. Because Startel is owned by Telefónica and Telecom, the judgment emphasized the need for independent review. In intervening, the ministry indicated it felt CNT was overstepping its mandate.

11.7.2 Tariffs and Cross-Subsidies

The majority of countries modifying their telecommunications regulatory systems have sought to end most cross-subsidies on the grounds it is unfair for some users to subsidize others. Argentina generally has run counter to this approach. The only prohibitions established at the time of privatization relate to using earnings from basic services to subsidize international service and using monopoly services to subsidize competitive services (basically, domestic value-added services).

Indeed, the explicit objective of having international services provided by a monopoly owned by the companies that regionally monopolize basic domestic services was to allow expansion of the domestic network using revenue from international calls. In 1990 when Maria Julia Alsogaray, head of ENTel and in charge of its privatization, reported to the Communications Commission of the Chamber of Deputies, she stated "the reason not to deregulate the provision of international services at this time is the lack of maturity of the public network. The revenue drawn from international calls are needed to develop this network, which is still very inefficient. . . ." Similarly, Telecom and Telefónica are required to use the profits from Teleintar to achieve expansion goals and to improve their networks (Decree 62/90, Clause 7.8.5).

11.7.3 Tariffs

Under the privatization agreement, installation charges are up to 50 percent of the direct cost of the line for residential service and 100 percent for others. The concept "direct cost" is broad. It includes, among other things, land, buildings, switching equipment, energy nodes, and access to the long-distance network and urban switching.

The transfer contracts extensively cover tariffs. The procedures they establish have led to domestic and international long-distance prices that are quite high by world standards. This negatively affected not only companies—especially transnationals—that were intensive users but even families.

Tariff levels have been a source of conflict between the companies and the government since April 1991 when the Law of Convertibility was passed. This law tied the currency to the U.S. dollar, prohibited price increases, and required businesses to reduce prices to their August 1990 levels. However, the government could not impose the law on the new telephone companies. Although the pulse price (similar to message units) stayed lower than what the privatization agreement stipulated, it was 21.5 percent higher than it would have been if the law had applied, and the companies kept the right to raise rates (even retroactively) to the levels that the transfer contracts granted them.

A new agreement was ratified by decree on November 28, 1991, a year after privatization. The basic monthly charges for a commercial line were reduced about 40 percent and were increased about 50 percent for a residential line. Overall, this probably had a neutral effect on the telephone companies' earnings. To help offset the increases for users, the state reduced by five points (from 16 percent to 11 percent) the value-added tax charged on telephone tariffs.

One of the most important changes was dollarization of rates. Twice a year, on April 1 and October 1, rates are adjusted according to the Consumer Price Index in the United States, regardless of what is happening with inflation in Argentina. Amounts due are converted into Argentine pesos at the exchange rate on the billing date.

In 1995, London-based National Economic Research Associates conducted a study for the government on rate restructuring. A draft released in September called for increasing local and reducing long-distance rates while maintaining overall profits. The increases would be particularly high in metro Buenos Aires, where local service is substantially less than elsewhere in the country. The new rates would more closely link costs and rates, which is seen as a necessary step for opening the telcom market to competition.

Beginning in November 1992, installation charges have been reduced. In 1997 they are to be at a level not exceeding the average in countries with mature networks (estimated at U.S.$250), and the prices paid by residential and commercial users will be the same. In August 1995 connection costs were U.S.$750 for commercial users and U.S.$500 for residences, compared to U.S.$1,800 and U.S.$900, respectively, in 1992.

A few months after the new agreement, the companies and the state were again in conflict. This time the issue was the mechanism for awarding the second mobile cellular telephone band. The secretary of finance, against the wishes of Telecom and Telefónica, insisted that, like the first band, the award should be by competitive bidding. At the end of February 1992 an agreement was reached. The companies could have direct access to the second band—that is, without undergoing a competitive process—but they had to reduce, by an average of 3 percent, long-distance rates and speed up the timetable for reduction of installation charges. Reducing installation charges was something the companies had already decided to do anyway. They had estimated that maintaining the allowed levels would mean demand would soon be insufficient to sustain the expansion and modernization plans they had proposed.

11.8 The Equipment Industry in the 1990s

Liberalization of the supply of terminal equipment in 1988 and privatization of ENTel in 1990 imply significant changes that might upset the relative and the absolute positions of manufacturers with factories in Argentina. During the negotiations on the conditions of privatization, worried established suppliers looked for ways to assure their position vis-à-vis potential purchasers, who wanted to avoid imposed purchasing policies.

In January 1990 it was decided that ENTel's new owners would be required to honor existing work and service contracts and, though only for the first eighteen months after privatization, equipment purchase orders. From January 1990 until consummation of its sale, ENTel would not assume new purchasing debts or permit payables to accumulate.

The Italian and French governments mobilized to defend the interests of their equipment companies and succeeded in forcing the Argentine government to step back. Thus, in June 1990, the state allowed ENTel to sign contracts with Italian and French suppliers for up to U.S.$200 million in equipment, and the new owners have had to honor these agreements (Decree 1,130/90). These agreements ended up being an obligation to firms related to the consortiums. Thus, the Italian credit involved, among others, Techint and Italtel as suppliers.

Suppliers to ENTel were able to get the company to accept delivery of equipment and materials while privatization was being negotiated, without regard to the company's work plan. Two things made the suppliers realize the speedup was good business. First, the new owners would have to accept delivered equipment whether they wanted it or not; it could not be returned. Second, when payment was deferred, the interest rate ENTel paid greatly exceeded the market rate, so such debt constituted an excellent financial deal for the suppliers.

There had been an official declaration that the amounts earned with the sale of ENTel would be used to pay its debts. However, a Presidential Decree on March 30 rejected that position, saying that the money would be used for health, education, justice, and defense. But Siemens, in July 1991, was able to collect U.S.$60 million from the Argentine government against outstanding debts. The German chancellor personally lobbied President Menem for payment.

Although Telecom and Telefónica cannot build terminal equipment, they can buy it for lease or resale to their customers. All manufacturers whose equipment has been approved by the regulatory authorities have access to the terminal equipment market under nondiscriminatory conditions and can sell directly to users. Moreover, Telefónica and Telecom can provide installation and maintenance of terminal equipment only under competitive conditions.

The transfer contracts say that when the total cost of equipment purchases exceeds U.S.$500,000 per year, purchases should be undertaken by "bidding or other competitive processes" (Decree 62/90, Clause 15.6). When it does not involve a price difference greater than 10 percent, the companies are obligated to give preference to the existing national industry when selecting suppliers. A "national industry" is a firm with a minimum local content of 40 to 60 percent, the exact level depending on the item. Inputs of national origin include labor, research and development, product engineering (including quality control), and software. Although CNT is to define the levels, it had not done so and, in general, had failed to affect the conditions related to purchases of equipment from the national industry.

This section of the transfer contracts is, at first glance, quite shocking because of what it implies in terms of state interference in the purchasing policies of private companies. Designed to mollify the local business community, including subsidiaries of multinational firms with factories in Argentina, it is not necessarily effective. Years of experience by state corporations in dealing with national purchasing requirements show that there are ways to exclude those the company does not wish to buy from (Aspiazu, Basualdo, and Nochteff 1988).

Analyzing purchases by Telefónica and Telecom during 1991–94 shows a tendency to bring in at least a third supplier while continuing to purchase from the most important of ENTel's local suppliers, even where the suppliers are not related to the consortiums' owners. The continuation of purchases beyond the formal requirements agreed to with the government is probably related to two factors. First is the benefit of not confronting firms that have the capacity to lobby federal authorities. A struggle with equipment producers might provoke a backlash in a period of great vulnerability for the service providers because the regulatory framework is still unsettled. Second, it is likely that, for some time to come, economies of precedence will carry weight, as there really is a necessity to make equipment compatible, to have a detailed knowledge of the network, and the like.

Related to this is the possibly greater ability of companies already in the country to respond immediately to a significant increase in demand, partly because of otherwise idle capacity (Herrera 1992). In this view, it is likely that transnational manufacturers, going beyond what is strictly dictated by their cost structures, would keep factories in the country as a way to exert political pressure on the purchasing decisions of Telecom and Telefónica. This is being done elsewhere by large international equipment producers. For example, Siemens has joint ventures in Poland, the Czech Republic, Slovakia, Romania, Hungary, and Ukraine that grant it advantages in competing for contracts in public telephony.

Transnationals in Argentina also are producing in Brazil and sometimes in Mexico and other Latin American countries. For this reason, if one bets on the success of current government initiatives to create regional trading blocs (Mercosur, for example), it is possible to imagine a restructuring, consistent with the implementation of complementary production plans among subsidiaries installed in different countries. Or there might be closure of some plants considered redundant. After all, foreign direct investment for equipment production in Latin America was done only when the government required it for access to the market; the size of the local markets otherwise did not justify it (Herrera 1992).

Nevertheless, it is possible during the mid-1990s that there may be space for activity by small and medium local firms producing parts or items used as customer premises equipment—particularly telephone sets and PBXs. The advantages these firms can count on (besides geographic location and continued trade protection) are the costs outsiders incur developing software to adapt products to the Argentine network, as well as to the characteristics of the end user. Despite ongoing liberalization, tariffs of up to 50 percent remain on some items.

11.9 The Regulatory Authority

The conditions for the sale of ENTel were established prior to deciding some crucial aspects of the regulatory framework. Privatization anticipated promulgation of a telecommunications law, but it occurred while the law's content was still the subject of discussion in Congress as to what the mandate of the regulatory body was to be.

The president is in charge of setting the basic outline for sectorial development, with the regulatory body being in charge of supervising the carrying out of these plans. The regulatory body is the Comisión Nacional de Telecomunicaciónes (CNT), created in June 1990 by Decree 1,185/90. According to its statutes, CNT is responsible for regulating, controlling, and supervising the delivery of all telecom services (excluding radio); seeing that the quality and expansion goals established in ENTel's transfer contracts are met; and overseeing rates. The role of CNT regarding rates is limited to proposing a pricing framework to the secretary of communications, who makes the actual decision, and to supervising implementation by the companies of the decisions.

In the name of protecting the public good and the rights of consumers, CNT is the administrator of the electromagnetic spectrum (excluding radio); has control over licensing (although new licenses that grant monopoly rights can be given only by the executive); guarantees networks interconnectivity (by resolving conflicts within ten days); verifies there is no anticompetitive conduct against users of the satellite system; and is obligated to protect Teleintar's rights. Also, CNT has powers of confirmation regarding equipment purchases and in some cases will supervise the purchasing policy of a service company to verify that a competitive selection process is used.

The director of CNT is appointed by the country's president. A tax of 0.5 percent of earnings (net of taxes) from the provision of telecom services finances the agency.

The contrast between the size of the tasks assigned CNT and its lack of personnel and infrastructure is truly notable. Since the privatization of ENTel, CNT has been conspicuously absent from any defining of the principal issues involving national communications. None of the important disagreements that have arisen between the state and the private firms have involved CNT in their resolution. Essentially, this is because this regulatory body consists of an "unarmed police" assigned to oversee measures taken by policy makers that occur outside its area of control.

Nonetheless, CNT is in the midst of controversy. In November 1994 the secretary of communications, with the agreement of the minister of economy, tried to approve a price restructuring in which CNT did not have any participation and which was opposed by most CNT directors. ADELCO, a consumer advocacy group, also objected. The protests produced intervention by the courts. In June 1995, as discussed earlier, the executive removed all of CNT's directors and its president. That action also was appealed to the courts, who found for the existing directors, but the government has appealed. Both matters remain undecided as of July 1995.

In addition to this picture of management crisis and conflict among different government levels, CNT lacks the human and financial resources to make an independent evaluation of compliance by the companies it supposedly supervises. It does not even have the power to compel the firms to deliver the information necessary to make such an evaluation correctly.

In the first half of 1990, in anticipation of CNT's creation, the Secretariat of Communications, up until then in charge of the design and implementation of federal policies and of the control of companies operating in the telecommunications area, was downgraded to a subsecretariat. Some two months after privatization, on January 31, 1991, it was dissolved altogether and its approximately 400 employees were dismissed, with a large number of its laid-off technicians ending up in the private sector. With this, the state was almost completely emptied of technical personnel with telecommunications experience.

Subsequently, the Ministry of Economy and the Ministry of Works and Public Services were merged to create the Ministry of Economy, Works and Public Services. A Secretariat of Public Works and Communications was created and a Communications Subsecretariat was reestablished. This did not alleviate the situation. In fact, subsequent conflicts between the CNT and the newly created ministry resulted in the decision in mid-1996 to end the ministry's administrative authority over the CNT; it will be run directly by the president of the country instead. Meanwhile, the National Congress is discussing the possibility of giving the Senate complete administrative oversight of all regulatory bodies of public services.

11.10 Outlook

A look at the future of Argentine telecommunications must recognize that, in the context of structural weakness in the state's regulatory capacity, Telefónica and Telecom have been given monopolistic powers for as long as until 2001, not only for provision of basic domestic local and long-distance telephone services but also, through Teleintar, all types of international services. In addition, the two companies own Startel, which offers services in areas where competition is permitted. Further, subsidies from international to domestic service are required.

For users, the primary result of privatization has been higher rates. In compensation, the consortiums have expanded the network and worked to improve service quality. Additionally, it is hoped the new regulations will lead to the entrance of new suppliers of domestic value-added services.

Argentine equipment producers have benefited from privatization because of the substantial investment being made in new plants and equipment. Although free of the previous requirements to buy locally, the operating companies have in fact increased imports only somewhat. This is in part because from the first moment of the postprivatization period the new telcos have paid prices much lower than those paid by ENTel. For example, in 1991 Siemens and Pecom-Nec sold Telecom 25,000 lines at U.S.$240 each, in line with the international market, and much lower than ENTel had paid during the two previous years. To the extent these cost reductions do not translate into proportionately lower prices for service and the "extra" profits are only partially used to modernize and expand the system, there is a redistribution of resources favoring the companies themselves, in detriment to the end user and some equipment suppliers, who may be forced to undergo a complete restructuring.

11.10.1 Potential Instability?

In contradiction to the contention that privatization must be used to stimulate competition (which, in turn, brings benefits such as a lowering in the cost of international telephone service), in Argentina, if the present regulatory framework remains unaltered, it is very likely that there will be a tendency toward a consolidation of Telefónica, Telecom, and Teleintar.

As far as attracting new companies is concerned, a rate structure could emerge that, added to the award of the second mobile telephone band to Startel, creates an environment of discriminatory linkages against potential competitors in the delivery of value-added services. The possibility of consolidation relates to the existence of economies of precedence, the possibilities for cross-subsidies (see Helm and Yarrow 1988), and the absence of regulatory bodies with real supervisory powers (which includes, among other things, a lack of government control over the rate structure).

Indeed, some CNT directors assert it is obvious Telefónica and Telecom have been building a large fiber-optic network, using profits from monopoly services, to obtain an advantage in providing value-added services and entering the market for cable television when the period of exclusivity, during which they can provide only telephone voice services, ends.

Argentina never developed a system of controls on the cost structure of ENTel, and nothing indicates that the privatization process has changed this arrangement. On the contrary, CNT does not have the resources to independently evaluate the cost structures of the new private companies, which have been reluctant to provide information. This is important because, if the government intends to allow market entry to new service providers, CNT must have precise information on the cost structure for each service and know in detail the type of demand that the companies face in each segment of the market (Helm and Yarrow 1988; Noam 1988; OCDE 1988). From the fragmented information CNT has had access to, some of its directors infer that the internal rate of return on assets used of the basic services companies was above 40 percent during 1992–94. This is obviously higher than the 16 percent proposed as acceptable by the government in 1990.

If one thing characterizes the regulatory framework that emerges from the privatization of ENTel, it is its potential instability. Even though the weakness of CNT leaves the individual consumer in a virtually defenseless situation, some groups negatively affected by the Telefónica and Telecom monopolies are also very powerful. These groups can, in many cases, count on the support of the governments of industrial countries, and they are ready to do battle to obtain a regulatory environment that will permit them to operate under better conditions than currently exist in the Argentine market.

Among other things, they could succeed in imposing institutional changes that favor users of international data transmission services hurt by the current Teleintar rates; users who want access to services not offered by the system; companies that the legislation left on the margin of the Argentine market; cable television companies that want to get into international data transmission; and suppliers of equipment excluded by the purchasing policies of the private companies.

An example is the Supreme Court decision that, since December 1994, has allowed companies providing international "callback" services to enter the market. Teleintar argued that the decision damaged its monopolistic rights. In 1994 the U.S. telecom company MCI bought the largest Argentine cable television company (Cablevision) with the goal of competing against the local telcos, and MCI seems ready to contest the monopolies of Telefónica and Telecom when they end, probably not until 2000, given the companies' success so far in beating their mandatory targets for expansion and service quality. The discussions about the scope of the rights of Telefónica and Telecom, including pricing, have divided the Argentine government, as seen in the dismissal of CNT directors in June 1995.

Within two years of privatization, some major users and equipment suppliers had begun to exert effective pressure on federal officials. On the user side, a crucial example is that of the directors of the primary foreign news agencies operating in Argentina, which, in the name of the Associated Press, France Press, Agenzia Nacionale Stampa Associate, Deutsche Presse Agentur, United Press International, and Reuters, in 1992 delivered a document to the president of the Senate's Commission for Free Speech (Comision de Libertad de Expresion del Senado).

The document contends that "the privatization of communications in a monopolistic form and the lack of official regulation" limits freedom of the press because the license holders seem to be taking "restrictive and regulatory" steps in regard to journalistic activity and "are limiting and blocking the delivery of information to the media in Buenos Aires and the interior and limiting and blocking the international dissemination of Argentine news." It also claims "the Comision Nacional de Telecomunicaciones is not functioning, there is a failure to expedite licensing for operating antennas for private use, a rate structure for the IBS linkages is missing, there is no regulation for setting tariffs on the receipt of information of public interest on the part of the license holders, and there is discrimination in the use of international satellites for the receipt of public-interest information."

Domestic equipment producers, including the subsidiaries of multinationals, expressed themselves publicly in 1991 through the Argentine Chamber of Telephony and Related Fields (ACTRF) and the Argentine Chamber of Electronics Industries (ACEI). They spoke in "defense of the industry, of its technological qualifications, and of national sources of work." Further, ACTRF wrote CNT accusing the telcos of violating the decree obliging them to give preference to Argentine industry. Also, ACEI asked members of the Communications Commission of the Argentine Congress for legislation obligating the telcos to buy a major part of their equipment in the country. It obtained the support of the commissioner, who tried to gain the support of the minister of the economy. This mobilization is probably one reason the companies have continued to purchase a significant portion of their equipment from ENTel's politically well-connected traditional suppliers.

Given this outlook, the future of domestic equipment producers is uncertain. They have been benefiting from the modernization and expansion of the network, even though their sales are at lower prices than when imports were restricted. As the Mercosur agreement reduces trade barriers between Brazil and Argentina, transnationals may build or consolidate existing facilities in just one of the two countries. Brazil is the larger market, so regional consolidation may work to the detriment of an equipment-making industry in Argentina. In any case, as part of a regional economic market with Brazil, Chile, Paraguay, and Uruguay, Argentina can be sure its economic and technological evolution will have a strong influence on the development of telecommunications in Latin America.

References

Aspiazu D., E. Basualdo, and H. Nochteff. 1988. "La revolución tecnológica y las políticas hegemónicas." Buenos Aires: Editorial Legasa.

Basualdo, Eduardo. 1986. "Nuevas formas de inversión de las empresas industriales extranjeras en la Argentina." Documento Cepal No. 33, Buenos Aires.

Centro de Profesionales Universitarios de ENTel and Federación de Obreros y Empleados Telefónicos de la República Argentina (CPU-FOETRA). 1988. *Propuesta Quinquenal de Desarrollo de las Telecomunicaciones.* Buenos Aires.

Herrera, Alejandra. 1992. "La Integración Latinoamericana de la Industria de Equipos de Telecomunicaciones," en *Revista Integración Latinoamericana,* No. 178, Buenos Aires.

_____. 1989. "La revolución tecnológica y la telefonía argentina." Buenos Aires: Editorial Legasa.

Jones, Loroy P., Pankaj Tandom, and Ingo Voglsang. 1990. *Selling Public Enterprises: A Cost-Benefit Methodology.* Cambridge, Mass.: MIT Prcss.

Noam, E. July 1994. "Beyond Liberalization III: Reforming Universal Service," in *Telecommunications Policy.*

_____. 1988. *Network Pluralism and Regulatory Pluralism.* OCDE, "The Telecommunications Industry: The Challenges of Structural Change." Paris, mimeo.

Petrazzini, Benalfa. 1991. "Restructuring Telecommunications Policy in Argentina: Issue Beyond Domestic Concerns." University of California, San Diego, mimeo.

Vickers, J., and G. Yarrow. 1988. *Privatization: An Economic Analysis.* Cambridge, Mass.: MIT Press.

World Bank. 1991. *Informe sobre el desarrollo mundial 1991, la tarea acuciante del desarrollo.*

Notes

1. Between 1940 and 1980, the average tenure for ministers, secretaries of state, and governors was 13.7 months, 12.2 months, and 14.1 months, respectively. This pattern was even more pronounced at certain parastatal companies or regulatory agencies between 1970 and 1990: the average tenure of head officials was just 9 months (Petrazzini 1991).

2. Consumer price inflation for 1965–73 is estimated at over 26 percent annually. During 1973–80 the annual rate was over 182 percent and was over 328 percent during 1980–90 (World Bank 1991, p. 21). The 1989 rate was 3,080 percent, but it was only 7.4 percent in 1993 and 3.9 percent in 1994.

3. Telecom took the southern part of the Federal District and 5.8 percent of the telephones in Buenos Aires province; it has licenses for Catamarca, Córdoba, Corrientes, Chaco, Formosa, Entre Ríos,* Jujuy, La Rioja, Misiones, Salta,* Santa Fé, Santiago del Estero,* and Tucumán. Telefónica took the northern part of the Federal District and 94.2 percent of the lines in Buenos Aires; it is licensed for Chubut, La Pampa, Mendoza,* Neuquén, San Luis, San Juan,* Santa Cruz, and Tierra del Fuego. Provinces marked with an asterisk were served by CAT until 1992.

12
Uruguay

GRACIELA PÉREZ MONTERO GOTUSSO

Uruguay is the Latin American country with the highest United Nations human development index, an indicator of the quality of life based on education, earnings, and life expectancy. It is also considered one of the most politically stable, despite a quite turbulent history. Economic development has been retarded by heavy government regulation and high inflation. With some 3.2 million people (July 1994 estimate) and an area of about 176,000 square kilometers, Uruguay is a small country. Although the population is over 80 percent urban, agriculture forms the base of the economy, with large shares of industrial production and exports related to processing wool and beef.

Telecom services are quite good, at least by Latin American and developing country standards. The teledensity—17 per 100 people in 1994—has for some time been the second highest in Latin America (after French Guyana). About half the population lives in metropolitan Montevideo, the capital, and most of the modern equipment is concentrated there.

Elections in November 1989 brought Luis Alberto Lacalle of the Blanco party to the presidency, with a plurality but not a majority of seats in the General Assembly. Inaugurated in March 1990, Lacalle spearheaded broad economic reform, including plans to privatize many companies. However, a referendum in December 1992 overturned key portions of the legislation intended to achieve this. In regular elections held in November 1994, Julio María Sanguinetti of the Partido Colorado was chosen president, a position he had held from 1985 to 1989. A coalition of the Colorado and Blanco parties controlled the legislature.

The Partido Colorado favors continued state ownership of enterprises that offer a significant source of income to the state or are seen as strategic or natural monopolies. The new government is willing to transfer to the private sector activities that need a strong injection of funds to increase capacity or productivity, or that the state does not have the funds to support. As an example, in June 1995 private interests acquired 51 percent of PLULNA, the troubled national air carrier.

12.1 Early Telecommunications Development

The Constitution of 1830, the country's first, was based on a liberal and individualistic doctrine that confined state functions to protection of citizens and the

157

administration of justice. Thus the private sector initially freely participated in the provision of telecom services. However, as the nineteenth century came to a close, the state moved to a more activist stance, assuming the roles of banker, insurer, tradesman, and direct promoter of economic development. As a result, the state has come to be in charge not just of what were long considered natural monopolies, and thus appropriate for a state to operate—the post, telegraph, and telephones—but also electricity and public transportation, as well as port services (Schrumann and Coolighan 1966, p. 492).

12.1.1 Telegraphy

Telegraph service was inaugurated in Montevideo in 1855. In 1865 the Compañía Telegrafía del Río de La Plata, a joint Uruguayan-Argentine company, began providing telegraph service between Montevideo and Buenos Aires. A direct connection between the two cities—by submarine cable across the wide estuary of the Río de la Plata—was approved in 1883 and completed in 1884 by foreign contractors.

Other regional, private companies appeared, including Telégrafo Oriental, Compañía del Oeste, and Compañía Platino Brasilero (which initially provided service to Brazil and subsequently expanded with Uruguay). These companies were owned or financed by Argentine, Brazilian, British, and U.S. entities, as well as by Uruguayans. By 1910 most of the country had service, with the principal towns connected to Montevideo. By 1920 they were connected directly to each other.

Reflecting the shift toward government involvement, the National Telegraphy was incorporated under the General Director of Postal Services in 1892.

12.1.2 Telephony

In 1882 the Compañía Telefónica de Montevideo (CTM) was founded with British funds to serve the capital. By the end of the 1880s Montevideo had two companies providing telephone services, CTM and locally owned Cooperativa Telefónica Nacional, which had been created because CTM was not providing service as quickly as users wanted. Their service areas did not overlap. In 1889 there were 2,700 registered users.

The first company outside the capital, La Sanducera, was founded in April 1891 to serve the Department of Paysandú, in the western part of the country. It was owned by members of the local elite. Subsequently, other small, local companies were similarly formed. They generally had a single exchange and served only a few hundred or few thousand subscribers. They were not interconnected.

A government-operated telephone network for the police was established in April 1894, with the intention of its becoming nationwide. A year later, rules for construction of a national telephone network were approved. These rules were early steps in a process that had the publicly proclaimed purpose of converting telecommunications into a state monopoly.

In 1907 the government approved creation of a national telephone network, which took over the local private company in Paysandú. The next step in the government's move toward consolidating telephone service in state hands came in

1909 when a government commission was set up to study telephone service in Montevideo and explore ways to link the various telephone systems in the interior to the capital and to each other.

Finally, in December 1915, a law was passed creating a Dirección General de Correos, Telegráfos y Telefónos with domestic monopoly rights regarding the post, telegraph, and telephones. However, the law did not immediately or automatically extinguish any concessions made to private companies by special laws, so the existing private companies remained in business. Moreover, new concessions could be granted to private parties, including monopoly concessions for services in specific geographical areas. In other words, although the state was slowly creating a telecommunications system that it owned and operated, initially it was primarily asserting its right and power to determine who offered services. Service to foreign countries remained open to free enterprise (Resolution of September 24, 1918).

12.1.3 The First Monopoly Period: 1915–1974

The 1915 law called for a nationwide government monopoly of telephone service. Steps toward achieving this began with nationalizing, under decrees of March 1916 and October 1917, a number of the small, independent telephone systems in areas outside Montevideo. These were added to the police network. In other words, the police network was being used to form the backbone of a government-run system. The two private Montevideo companies were allowed to continue in business, but regulation of their operations, and those of the other private companies, was begun. The government, through the Dirección General de Correos, Telegráfos y Telefónos (DGCTT), issued them operating permits revocable at any time.

In December 1916 the private domestic telegraph companies were purchased by the government, becoming part of the DGCTT. International service continued to be provided by several mostly foreign companies: Western Telegraph, All America Cables, Río de la Plata, and Compañía Telegráfica y Telefónica del Río de La Plata. However, in October 1931, international service was taken over by the state.

At the end of 1924 there were twenty-nine privately owned telcos in Uruguay, including the two in Montevideo. There was no interconnection among them, except in Montevideo, so long-distance calling was not possible, except on the police network. (Police stations throughout the country were connected by radio and cable.) Subscribers to the private systems numbered 23,662, including 15,535 (66 percent) in Montevideo; average daily usage was 166,662 calls (Libro del Centenario 1925). For context, the population was about 1.6 million (45 percent in Montevideo).

From 1915 to 1930, parliamentary discussions abound regarding who would be awarded the contracts to construct the national network of trunk lines interconnecting the local companies. Finally, Law 8,767 of October 1931 gave Usinas Eléctricas del Estado (UEE) the job of constructing and operating the new telephone network, as well as the right to exercise a monopoly in wired telephone communications throughout the entire country.[1]

The Comisión de Obras Públicas, established by Parliament, reasoned there was an indisputable convenience in having a body of electrical technicians supervise installation of a communications system based on the applications of electricity. In November UEE changed its name to Administración General de las Usinas Eléctricas y Teléfonos del Estado, generally referred to as UTE.

Law 8,780 of October 20, 1931, allowed UTE to buy or expropriate the various telcos in the country. The Montevideo companies, which represented the vast majority of telephones, were promptly nationalized at negotiated prices, as was provision of international service, but the other private companies were not taken over because there were limited funds to buy them. Instead, the government, through UTE, continued to build a trunk network to connect the most important cities of the country. The remaining private telcos were allowed to add subscribers—although this was subject to revocation at any time.

In March 1932 UTE began installing cable and ten central offices for automatic service in Montevideo. The system had a capacity of 22,000 lines. A decree of December 1933 ordered government agencies to cease using the private companies when UTE's new exchanges became operational. Only in 1936 did UTE start buying the remaining private companies. Because internal funding, rather than debt, was used to finance the purchases, it was 1949 before the last one was acquired, unifying domestic telephone services in the hands of the government, where it has since remained.

12.2 ANTel

Telecom services—telephony and telex—were notoriously deficient during the UTE period. In 1974 there were almost 30,000 applications pending for service, compared to an installed base of about 188,000 lines. This was true even though there were enough central office lines—over 207,000—to handle a large percentage of the applicants.

Having a line did not mean having a working phone. For example, during 1974, on any given day as many as 17,000 of 140,000 subscribers had no working service. This was due to a number of factors, including lack of spare parts and obsolete equipment because of import quotas and limited repair budgets. In the face of this situation, the government proposed breaking up UTE and creating a new entity to be in charge of telephone and some broadcast services.

Thus, on July 25, 1974, under Decree-Law 14,235, Administración Nacional de Telecomunicaciones (ANTel) was created as a public company. It was formed by combining three entities that had had some control over telecommunications: the Dirección General de Comunicaciones, Dirección General de Telecomunicaciones, and the telephone division of UTE. The new company was placed under the Ministry of Defense, and all of its acts were made subject to approval of the executive branch. The Office of Planning and Budget (OPB) advises on tariffs, investments, and debt management.

As a monopoly, ANTel is responsible for the construction, provision, and management of local service, as well as domestic and international long distance, telex, and telegraph. Decree-Law 14,235 also gives ANTel the power to "intervene and control any activity related to telecommunications, either public or private, unless such activities are assigned expressly to another state entity." It also acts as the Uruguayan party to international telecom agreements, including Intelsat and interconnections. Except for the armed forces and police, private networks are not allowed unless approved by ANTel and the executive branch.

In the area of broadcasting, ANTel initially controlled allocation of some frequencies (television, but not radio) and had technical oversight and operations supervision of television transmissions. Radio was under the control of the Dirección Nacional de Comunicaciones (DNC), also part of the Ministry of Defense. In October 1984 control of television frequencies was transferred to DNC. Thus, DNC has general control of spectrum management and oversees radio communications (including paging) and broadcasting (television and radio stations, and cable television).

The 1984 law also made DNC responsible for Uruguay's relations with international communications organizations such as the International Telecommunication Union (ITU), the International Consulting Committee for Telegraphy and Telephony (CCITT), and CCIR. They previously had been functions of the Dirección General de Telecomunicaciones.

In addition, DNC is charged by the 1984 law with coordination and execution of the national communications policy approved by the executive branch. However, in practice it has done very little in this regard. Since DNC has not done any studies on service costs or tariff structure, it is unable to assess the reasonableness of ANTel tariff requests.

Decree-Law 14,235 of 1974 lacks a clear definition of what communications is. This has led to jurisdictional problems in assigning some services, especially the new value-added ones. For example, conflict arose in 1988 between ANTel and the private companies that offer facsimile equipment. In 1991, there was a problem with the utilization of international services by companies located in "free zones" (designated areas where productive activities are free of taxes other than the income tax). In the 1988 case, to induce customers to buy fax equipment from it, ANTel offered to waive connection charges. Both cases were resolved by OPB as the executive branch organ having authority over tariffs. To preserve fair competition among suppliers, ANTel was prohibited from waiving connection charges.

Creation of ANTel did not change the poor quality of the country's telephone service. The system remained so antiquated and unreliable that into the 1980s firms often resorted to courier service within downtown Montevideo.

12.2.1 Investment and Quality Improvements

Motivated in part by the government's feeling that Uruguay would be the financial center of the Southern Cone and a future regional customs union, ANTel finally initiated a strong expansion program at the beginning of the 1980s. The goal was overall improvement in the range of coverage and the quality of services. Investment during the decade was at a rate 5.1 times the depreciation on fixed assets in telephony. For 1986–91, average annual investment was U.S.$50 million; it reached U.S.$76 million in 1992 and U.S.$123 million in 1993.

There were 615,000 central office and 530,000 primary subscriber lines at the end of 1993, increases of 88 percent and 84 percent from 1985 and equal to 17 primary lines per 100 people. Over one-third of 1985 central office capacity had been replaced by digital switches by 1993 which, with the new lines, meant about 65 percent of central office exchange lines were digital (78 percent in Montevideo). From 1976 to 1990 domestic long-distance links grew at an annual rate of 13.4 percent and international links at 11.6 percent. A microwave network linking the country was completed in 1990. By 1992, 90 percent of domestic trunks were microwave, and 86 percent of international links were by microwave or satellite.

Despite the impressive numbers of lines being added each year, unsatisfied demand remains high. It equaled 19.2 percent of the 530,000 primary lines in 1993, compared with 15.5 percent in 1975. Even though central office capacity is in place to satisfy most of the unmet demand, ANTel has been unable to generate enough revenue from its operating activities to reduce the backlog, and there have not been sufficient government resources available in the face of the public sector's need to reduce its deficits.

Still, the investment there has been has permitted ANTel to improve its service quality, although difficulties with digitalization led to increased problems during 1989. In Montevideo, the average number of subscribers with faults decreased from 12 percent (over primary lines) in 1975 to just 0.3 percent in 1990. The average time without service decreased from twelve days (thirty-two days maximum) in 1981 to two days (ten days maximum) in 1993. These improvements notwithstanding, a large number of faults continue to exist in the network, primarily because of inadequate operations support and maintenance by ANTel.

Unfortunately, ANTel has not kept statistics on such quality indicators as what percentage of the time a subscriber does not get a dial tone or is otherwise unable to complete a call, or how long a new subscriber must wait to have a phone installed. Public opinion polls have shown a steady increase in those saying they thought ANTel service was "good" or "very good": from just 26 percent in 1988 to 32 percent in 1989, 40 percent in 1990, 45 percent in 1991, 65 percent in 1992, 70 percent in 1993, and 80 percent in 1994.

12.3 Services and Rates

Subscribers can receive the basic package of telephone services from ANTel, along with some value-added services. Digital technology was first incorporated into the system in 1985. The first household telephone set must be from the telephone company, but additional sets and other equipment can be obtained from other sources. Direct lines, including analog lines for data (Urupac) and voice transmission, as well as specialized services such as background music, are provided only by ANTel. Urupac includes electronic mail without additional charge.

Value-added services available by the 1990s include packet-switched data transmission, electronic mail, electronic information services, and electronic fund transfers (EFT). There are providers other than ANTel for all of these except packet switching.

In December 1990 ANTel put mobile terrestrial service up for bid. The winning bidder was Movicom Cellular Service (MCS), owned by Uruguayans and Argentines. Bidders were competing for the right to construct the infrastructure (including obtaining transmission sites). Movicom Cellular Service provides service directly to users and is required to provide capacity to ANTel's cellular subsidiary (ANCel) under a ten-year leasing arrangement. Then ANTel acquires ownership of the equipment. Service, available in the department of Montevideo and part of the coast, including Punta del Este, began in December 1994 with about 15,500 subscribers.

12.3.1 Rates

Proposed tariffs are submitted by ANTel to the government's executive branch for approval. Because the company does not have cost accounting and demand studies were not undertaken until 1991, its tariff structure is somewhat arbitrary. Since 1974 tariffs have been adjusted based on recommendations by the International Consulting Committee for Telegraphy and Telephony (CCITT) and the Conferencia Interamericana de Telecomunicaciones (CITel).

As in most countries, residential users pay less than others for establishing service and then for basic monthly service. The exception to this is that rural subscribers are generally charged substantially more for installation than urban ones, generally because these lines are radiotelephones. Thus, in 1995 (compared with 1992) the charges were U.S.$4,210 (U.S.$3,655) for a rural line, compared with U.S.$395 (U.S.$260) for an urban nonresidential line and U.S.$260 (U.S.$160) for an urban residential line. There is also a surcharge, refunded with interest when service is discontinued, of U.S.$50 (U.S.$120) for a residential line and U.S.$120 (U.S.$240) for a nonresidential line.

Local calls are charged on a message-unit basis. Where central office equipment allows, rates vary by day and time of day, with peak (11:00–18:00), shoulder (7:00–11:00 and 18:00–22:00), and night rates (22:00–7:00) on Monday through Friday. Saturday from 7:00 to 15:00 the shoulder rate is applied, and the night rate is in effect during all other times. Typically, in 1995 (compared with 1992) residential subscribers received 50 units as part of a U.S.$6.30 (U.S.$4.00) monthly rate, while others paid U.S.$14.40 (U.S.$10.00).

As small as the country is, until January 1993 there were seven area bands for long distance. There are now three bands. Rates are high and, for most calls, have increased from their levels of the early 1990s when they ranged from U.S.$0.045 per minute (0 to 25 kilometers) to U.S.$0.60 per minute (over 400 kilometers). In 1995 per minute rates varied from U.S.$0.12 (to 50 kilometers) to U.S.$0.40 (over 100 kilometers). There is a 60 percent reduction for off-peak calls.

International long-distance rates historically have had little to do with physical distance. Thus, in 1992, while rates to immediate neighbors Argentina and part of Brazil were the lowest, it cost less to call the United States, Australia, and the United Kingdom than to call most of the rest of Latin America. Charges have been reduced since 1990, but calls originating in Uruguay still generally are more expensive than inbound ones. In 1995, calls to Argentina and the Brazilian state of Rio Grande do Sul were U.S.$1.50 per minute; to the United States, U.S.$1.50

plus U.S.$1.00 per minute; U.S.$2.00 to Chile and Paraguay, U.S.$2.50 to Canada, Australia, New Zealand, the United Kingdom, and Spain; U.S.$3.00 to the rest of the Americas; and U.S.$3.50 to the rest of the world.

12.4 Changes in ANTel

Midway through 1987 ANTel began to redefine its mission and philosophy, as well as the company's management style. The new mission and philosophy were approved by the board of directors on May 15, 1988. Even though the overall policy of the government is for the company to continue to operate as a monopoly, there are now plans to develop and use some services from private companies. These include electronic information services (such as Reuters, Delphi, Telerate, and CMA), international electronic messaging services (such as AT&T Easylink), and teleprocessors (such as Infonet). In addition to provision of cellular phone service, private companies are already performing support services such as cleaning and security.

This change was partly in response to the policies of the government of President Julio María Sanguinetti (1985–89), which considered telecommunications a basic component of creating a more open and internationally oriented economy. Management also recognized a need for change, in part reflecting the relatively young ages of the managers—averaging around forty—compared to other public companies.

The company's self-image was to be modified from that of an engineering firm to a company oriented to the customer and to service. In that sense the philosophy changed to "the client is the reason for the existence of ANTel." Management style was to change accordingly. Three basic principles were incorporated: delegation of authority, decentralization, and management by objectives within a centrally determined global plan. Operations were decentralized in 1989, creating five zones—Montevideo (with half of the population), Periphery, East, Center, and West)—divided into thirty-two regions and (for Montevideo) four districts. Still, a technology focus has continued to predominate because most of the managers, including all the general managers, have been engineers, not marketers or administrators, by training.

The proclaimed customer orientation has not changed the fact that in case of a controversy over billing or service problems, the burden of proof still falls on the customer, not the company. Credit is not given customers without service until the tenth consecutive day.

12.5 Conclusion

Although attempts to privatize ANTel have been rebuffed, some political leaders are trying to build a consensus for more competition and reform of state-owned enterprises. Since returns on investment in telecommunications are high, the future is promising for the availability of funds to make the investment necessary to improve quality, expand service, and lower prices.

Notes

1. Usinas Eléctricas del Estado was the government-owned successor to the private company that had been created in 1885 by Marceliano Díaz y Garcia to provide Montevideo with public lighting and electricity. Banco Nacional gained control in 1889, the year electricity was first provided, because of the financial problems of UEE's owner. Banco Nacional restructured the company as Compañía de Alumbrado a Gas y Luz Eléctrica SA. The government gained ownership in 1896 when Banco Nacional was liquidated because of its financial problems. Renamed Usina de Luz Electrica de Montevideo in 1906, the company in 1913 began to expand into the interior of the country. Until 1913 the only other town with an electric utility (established in 1900) was Paysandú. Initially privately owned, that utility was taken over by the state company in February 1919. The electric utilities had 3,000 subscribers in 1905, 12,700 in 1910, and 26,500 in 1915. In 1920 the enlarged UEE served 47,700 subscribers and in 1925, 75,000.

References

ANTel (Administración Nacional de Telecomunicaciones). Memorias Anuales.

Ayub, A., and O. Hegstad. 1988. "Public Industrial Enterprises: Determinants of Performance." Industry and Finance Series, vol. 17. Washington, D.C.: World Bank.

Basco, J., and C. Givogri. 1988. "Situación Actual y Alternativas para el Reordenamiento de las Telecomunicaciones en la Argentina." *Revista Estudios* 47 (Julio–Setiembre).

Partido Nacional. 1989. "La Respuesta Nacional." Editorial *El País*.

Pérez Montero Gotusso, G. 1990. "El Monopolio de las Telecomunicaciones." Serie Descripción e Indices. CERES (Centro de Estudios de la Realidad Económica y Social).

_____. 1991. "Hacia una Nueva Conceptualización de las Empresas Públicas Uruguayas." *Revista de Derecho Comercial y de la Empresa* 49–50. Montevideo, Uruguay: Fundación de Cultura Universitaria.

"Privatization in the U.K." 1990. Background briefing. H. M. Treasury, United Kingdom, March.

"Restructuring and Managing the Telecommunications Sector." 1989. A World Bank Symposium. Washington D.C.: World Bank.

Saunders, Robert J., Jeremy Warford, and Bjorn Wellenius. 1983. *Telecommunications and Economic Development.* Baltimore, Md.: Johns Hopkins University Press (for the World Bank).

Vickers, J., and G. Yarrow. 1988. *Privatization: An Economic Analysis.* London: The MIT Press.

13
Mexico

KATHLEEN A. GRIFFITH

The call for modernization has been the single most important factor in bringing telecommunications into the forefront of policy attention in Mexico since the late 1980s. This point was made clear when Carlos Salinas de Gortari stated, very early in his 1988 presidential campaign, that "telecommunications will become the cornerstone of the program to modernize Mexico's economy." Salinas followed through on his campaign pledge by restructuring the telecom agencies, reinterpreting the legal framework, and reprivatizing the telephone monopoly. He thereby implemented a liberalization strategy for accelerating modernization of the telecommunications sector.

It is commonplace that modern economies require access to extensive and sophisticated communications networks, and Mexico has undeniably lacked the requisite infrastructure. Thus, enhancing the competitiveness of the economy became another major theme driving the telecommunications agenda during the Salinas administration, especially during the North American Free Trade Agreement (NAFTA) campaign. The implementation of NAFTA codifies and clarifies specific telecom issues, such as access to and use of public networks, standards-related measures, and technical cooperation. It also eliminates restrictions on enhanced services, protects intellectual property rights, and, perhaps most significantly, liberalizes trade in services.

Liberalizing trade in data services, in particular, opens new opportunities for Mexico's industrial development, supporting both the growing service sector and the more traditional manufacturing sector. Jaime Serra Puche, the former secretary of trade and industrial development and Mexico's chief architect of NAFTA, observed that "Mexico has a great future in data services. Mexico has more engineers per capita than the U.S. and can offer sophisticated data services, such as software programming, as well as low skilled services, such as data entry" (Griffith 1992, p. 55).

For Mexico to be able to develop, market, and support data services adequately in a competitive international marketplace, the country's information infrastructure must rapidly merge the full capabilities of telecommunications and computers in the context of global networks. This is the challenge for President Ernesto Zedillo Ponce de Leon's administration, which took office in December 1994.

Joint ventures and other strategic partnerships are being formed by major international communications companies and deep-pocketed firms owned by Mexican billionaires. Indeed, five of Mexico's ten billionaires on the 1995 *Forbes* listing of the world's richest people are communications magnates. These ties may well position Mexico to lead Latin America in the Global Information Infrastructure (GII) and to attain a competitive advantage in the global economy through the use of cutting-edge information technology and services.

Mexico's challenges of achieving modernization and competitiveness are shaping the national telecommunications industry. This chapter looks at the roots of these challenges by first outlining the history of telecommunications in Mexico, identifying aspects of telecommunications unique to the country, and then describing the present situation and possible scenarios. A review of the legal framework affecting the industry and the organizational structure of the sector complete the background for an analysis of the policy-making process and the players involved. This analysis is presented in the context of how Mexico can better prepare for sustainability in the wake of the economic crisis of 1995.

13.1 Background

Mexico is the second most populated Latin American country. During and immediately after World War II, the country underwent rapid industrialization, accompanied by rapid urbanization and explosive population growth. The population was slightly over 14 million in 1920, about what it had been at the beginning of the century (there had been a decline during the 1910s because of violence associated with the Revolution), about 70 percent of whom lived in communities of fewer than 2,500 people. There are now over 92 million (July 1994 estimate), only 30 percent "rural." Slightly more than half of the population is considered economically active, defined as age twelve or older and available for work.

Mexico's almost 2 million square kilometers are diverse terrain: desert, mountains, canyons, and jungles. Almost half the country is covered by the Mexican Plateau, over 2,100 meters in elevation, which is bordered by mountains that parallel the coasts. Mexico City, the nation's capital, sits at an elevation of 2,240 meters and, with a metropolitan-area population of over 20 million, is the world's largest urban conglomeration.

Mexico's economy has been based on petroleum, which was originally developed by foreign interests and nationalized in 1938. Mexico has decreased its dependency on oil substantially since the 1982 collapse of oil prices. That year, oil accounted for 75 percent of exports; its share had fallen to below 32 percent in 1992. (For more on Mexico's state-owned oil company, Pemex, see Aspin 1995.) During the early 1980s, the *maquiladora* industry emerged as Mexico's second most important source of export income.[1]

A federal republic with a strong executive branch, Mexico has been dominated by the Institutional Revolutionary Party (PRI) and its precursor since 1928. This date marks the achievement of political stability, through a consolidation of political interest, after eighteen years of bloodshed and disruption during the Mexican Revolution. The political unrest of the 1990s has facilitated the increased influence of an opposition party, the National Action Party (PAN). As of 1997 the PRI has lost any placement in the Mexican Governement and currently has no political power.

13.2 Early Development

Modern telecommunications in Mexico begins with the Spanish immigrant Juan de la Granja, who, on May 10, 1849, obtained an exclusive concession to introduce telegraphy. On November 5, 1851, de la Granja and his associate William George Stewart began service between Mexico City and Nopalucan, Puebla, a distance of 180 kilometers. In 1852 a line between Mexico City and Veracruz, on the Gulf of Mexico, was completed, and by 1854 the first Mexican telegraph operators had been trained. International service was initiated on November 16, 1867, by a concession granted to an affiliate of Western Union Telegraph. (A comprehensive history of telegraphy in Mexico is in SCT 1987.)

During the decade 1877–87 Mexico achieved significant communications growth. Major developments included extension of the telegraph network from 9,000 to 40,000 kilometers and construction of an average of 700 kilometers of railroad a year.

The first telephone connection, between Mexico City and Tlalpan, a distance of 16 kilometers, was made on March 13, 1878. Nine months later telephone service was officially established by Alfred Westrup and Company for six police stations, the Office of General Inspection, the Mayor's Office, and the Ministry of Interior.

Western Union Telegraph continued to aggressively pursue opportunities in Mexico, and in 1896 agreement was reached for its subsidiary, Compania del Cable, to function as the intermediary dispatch for international traffic. A year later a contract was signed between Compania Telegrafica Mexicana and Western Union for the operation of Mexico's international telegraph service. By 1901 the country's telegraph network had grown to comprise 47,828 kilometers owned by the federal government, 12,036 kilometers by the railroads, 6,917 kilometers by state governments, and 3,942 kilometers by private enterprise (SCT 1987, p. 263).

In 1903 radiotelegraph stations were installed in Baja California for communication across the Gulf of California (Mar de Cortes). Other stations were subsequently built in various coastal regions of the country until 1911, for radiotelegraphy developed rapidly in response to national security matters related to the eruption of the Mexican Revolution in 1910. In 1919, as the Revolution's violence ebbed, development intensified again with the modernization of the national radiotelegraph network, including the addition of new stations and the exchange of messages with Germany and Chile. Radiotelephony and other radio communications services, such as mobile land services, also were initiated.

13.2.1 The Role of the State

Within the first few years of the introduction of telegraphy, the state began taking an active role in the development of domestic telecom policy. President Benito Juarez was interested in accelerating construction of telegraph lines and in 1855 and 1861 expedited decrees to promote their development. On November 3, 1867, tariffs for telegraph lines appeared in the Mexican government's *Diario Oficial* for the first time and, the same year, its Rules on Railroads established the intimate relationship between the train and telegraph systems. By 1869 the Rules for Telegraph Offices were established. On July 1, 1891, the secretary of communications and public works was created and took over control of the federal telegraph lines from the secretary of development. the director-general of Federal Telegraphs facilitated the expansion of communications infrastructure, negotiating contracts for the construction of new federal lines. Mexico participated in the 1906 International Radiotelegraphic Convention and began to play a role in international telecom forums and regimes as well.

The 1917 Mexican Constitution declared telegraphy and other means of communications a monopoly of the state, including the exclusive management and control of facilities. This did not, however, mean private parties could not participate: for example, private broadcasting was allowed at designated frequencies under rules setting limits on power and establishing fees. The 1926 Law of Electrical Communications required permits or concessions from the government for use of channels and radio frequencies.

The 1938 Law of General Means of Communications requires the national telecommunications industry to be under the control of the SCT (Secretaria de Comunicaciones y Transportes) for national security purposes. The SCT formulates and conducts policies to promote a modern telecom system and establishes supply, coverage, and rates that are adequate to the country's needs. In addition, it has the authority to plan, administer, and control the utilization of the radioelectric spectrum and the media in which electromagnetic waves are broadcast. Also, under the 1938 law, it had the exclusive power to provide a wide range of public telecom services. As discussed later, since 1992 SCT has been reorganized into the telecom regulatory agency, with operating responsibilities transferred to a separate state enterprise called Telecomunicaciones de Mexico (Telecomm).

13.2.2 Early Telephone Service

In 1881 the U.S. businessman M. L. Greenwood was granted a concession to install a telephone network in Mexico City. The next year he acquired new concessions to expand the services of Compañia Telefonica Continental. The first company on national territory was called Mexican National Bell Telephone, but it never provided service because of conflicts among several diverse interests. Mexico had become a favorable place for foreign investment under the Porfirio Diaz regime (1877–1911), and many investors were vying to provide telephone service. Their conflict was resolved by the formation of a new company under Greenwood and three other foreign partners on July 18, 1882. Their firm was called Compañia

Telefonica Mexicana (Mextelco), and it was technically and financially supported by Western Electric Telephone Company. By the end of the year long-distance service was established between Veracruz and New York City, and by 1883 subterranean routes and ducts were being constructed in Mexico City.

In 1903 Mextelco was granted a new contract to continue service in Mexico City, and by 1905 it had increased its capital and modified its name to Compañia Telefonica y Telegrafica Mexicana. Also in 1905, L. M. Ericsson was granted a concession. It began service with 500 subscribers under the name La Empresa de Telefonos Ericsson in 1907.

The telephone played its first historic role in the nation's political life during the "tragic ten" days (*decena tragica,* February 9–18, 1913) of the Mexican Revolution when President Francisco I. Madero was informed by telephone that General Bernardo Reyes had gone with his troops to the National Palace with the intention of taking it over and denouncing the government.

The Revolution adversely affected the advancement of telephony in Mexico because of the physical destruction it caused and because U.S. capital was unwelcome at a time when Woodrow Wilson's regime was meddling in Mexico's internal affairs.[2]

By 1915 Compañia Telefonica and Telegrafica Mexicana was operating under government intervention. The company also began having serious problems with its workforce. In the meantime, Ericsson worked normally and was able to inaugurate the first automatic central telephone, known as Rome central, in 1924. Within two years, Ericsson had the capacity to connect 10,000 lines.

By 1924 government intervention had ceased and Compañia Telefonica y Telegrafica Mexicana was acquired by International Telephone and Telegraph (ITT). The deal was even more attractive for ITT after the secretary of communications and public works modified the company's concession, including an extension of fifty years. Under ITT control the company was able to regain its position in the market vis-à-vis Ericsson.

By 1936 the government acknowledged that, in the public interest, the two incompatible phone networks needed to unite and expressed this desire to the competing companies. To advance the process, the 1940 Communications Law legally obligated the companies to comply. The precedent set by the oil expropriation of 1938 and the leftist populist rule of President Lazaro Cardenas beginning in 1940 provided further impetus. The following decade witnessed intense activity by the Telephone Workers Union and restrictive pricing policies by government regulators. Thus, the two companies ultimately were sufficiently motivated to collaborate on a unification package that would appeal to the government, as well as adequately compensate their parent companies.

13.3 Telmex

Telmex (Telefonos de Mexico, SA de CV) was officially established on December 23, 1947, by the merger of the country's two telephone systems. The new company was 51.24 percent owned by Continental Corporation, 48.75 percent by

Ericsson, and the remainder by three Mexican companies. The agreement stipulated that between 1948 and 1957 Telmex would pay Ericsson 2.5 percent of gross annual income and 3 percent afterward. Between 1950 and 1958 Telmex was consolidated and capitalized as the principal telephone company in the country. It was also "Mexicanized," becoming majority Mexican-owned in 1958, although foreign capital remained welcome—in 1960 a stock offering was held in the United States. (The company's official history is recounted in Telefonos de Mexico 1991; Szekely 1995 is a publication subsidized by Telmex that provides a history of the company since privatization for potential investors.)

The 1956 rule of priorities for capitalization of the company included the provision that those who bought shares in Telmex received priority for installation of new service. (During its early days, AT&T had a similar policy in the United States.) In effect, this meant one had to buy shares in order to acquire a line. This practice explains the huge growth in the number of shares of the company and remained in effect until late 1990.

In 1972, by acquiring a 51 percent equity holding, the government gained control of Telmex's development strategy. The secretary of communications and transportation presided over the board of directors until reprivatization in December 1990 and then participated as a board member from 1991 to 1994. The 49 percent of shares remaining in private hands traded publicly on the Mexican Bolsa and the New York Stock Exchange (as ADRs).

In 1976 SCT increased Telmex's value by extending its concession by thirty years to 2006, with a possible twenty-year extension after that.

Telmex has a regional affiliate, Telnor (Telefonos del Noroeste), which covers the state of Baja California and the northeast of Sonora up to Sonoyta. Service in the area had been provided by a private concessionaire who was operating a racket selling lines on the black market. He quickly discontinued investment in the company when it seemed likely to be taken over by the government. Consequently, the region fell greatly behind the rest of the country in telecom development during the mid-1970s. Expropriation came in 1978.

In response to the region's industrial development needs, including the growing *maquiladora* industry, the government began an aggressive investment program. After great success in digitalizing the region, Telnor evolved into a model for Telmex to follow for its management style and more flexible labor contracts. Relative to Telmex, Telnor has higher productivity and faster response times, in part because of its better labor relations. The companies have remained separate because of differences in their labor contracts.

13.4 System Development from 1948 to 1985

By the late 1940s the Mexican government had determined that the nation's telecommunications infrastructure and service were insufficient. Hence, the government implemented the Miguel Aleman Plan during 1947–1952. The SCT built new land telegraph lines, modernized twelve radio transmission stations, and completed ten radio stations for transmission and reception. Further, it undertook plans for direct communications with Europe, completed arrangements for radiotelegraph and radiotelephone service with Central America, Venezuela, Colombia, and Ecuador, and initiated similar measures with Chile, Uruguay, Brazil, and Argentina. Among the achievements, the number of federal telegraph, telephone, and radiotelephone offices reached 1,236, staffed by 6,800 employees.

Telmex's creation spawned a rapid expansion of telephone service, as well as competitive systems within the government. The SCT controlled the telegraph and its microwave network and competed with Telmex's public telephone system. In 1952 Telmex installed a microwave link between Mexico City and Puebla with twenty-three telephone channels. To facilitate domestic manufacture of telecom equipment, in 1956 Telmex created Industria de Telecomunicaciones SA (Indetel) with capital from Ericsson and ITT. Telex was introduced between the capital and Acapulco in 1957.

After the initial microwave station had operated on an experimental basis, additional stations were installed to improve the transmission system. Mountainous terrain made installation and maintenance very costly. The first network covered the southern part of the country. By 1959 there were 1,500 kilometers of microwave links in Mexico, including Telmex's public network and a government network used by Pemex & CFE (Comision Federal de Electricidad, the state-owned electric utility). Pemex and CFE eventually operated their own private networks.

Telmex installed a microwave system in 1962 to enhance its automatic long-distance exchange service. By 1963 Telmex's microwave system extended from Mexico City through Monterrey to San Antonio, Texas. Also in 1963, for the first time, live broadcasts were made via SCT's national microwave network: the trip of President Adolfo Lopez Mateos to Europe and the launching of astronaut Gordon Cooper into space. These transmissions illustrated the capabilities of global communications and thus provided an impetus for accelerating technological change for the XIX Olympics, scheduled to be held in Mexico City in 1968.

In the mid-1960s the government was motivated to initiate a National Telecommunications Program, including establishment of a National Microwave Network and a plan to eventually install its own satellite system. Telephone density in Mexico in 1965 was comparable to Spain and Korea. Over the next three years Telmex installed DDD (direct distance dialing, *Lada* in Spanish) on a national level, and by 1968 the microwave network linked the principal cities, primarily on routes radiating from Mexico City.

The Olympic games were broadcast to more than 700 million people in almost seventy countries by radio, television, telegraph, and radiotelephone. Satellite transmissions were provided by Intelsat and Domsat. Mexico's dependency on these foreign-owned satellites strengthened the pressure from the powerful media conglomerate Televisa on the government to finance a national satellite system.

In 1968, ten years after Mexicanization, there were 725,000 operating telephones in the country. In 1970 Mexico inaugurated its Lada 95 service with a call to Washington, D.C. In 1979 Telmex introduced digital systems into Mexico and also its Integrated Digital Network (RDI), an overlay network for the traditional telephone network. After 1983 the first digital lines were functioning and represented a major step in the modernization of the system. Lada 800 service was introduced in 1988 and facilitated the first electronic videoconferencing, utilizing RDI. In the mid-1980s Telmex was allowed to provide data services.

Telmex restructured during the late 1980s, splitting into six regions in an effort to decentralize the company. In 1993 it restructured into three regions—north, central, and south—as Telmex's first reaction toward competition. However, the regional operation structure was paralyzed by central investment decisions. Without the power to commit resources, the regions lacked real independent marketing and management. The organization of Telmex has reflected a basic lack of marketing focus since its inception.

The development of telecommunications was severely restricted after 1982 because the economic crisis limited resources. Many structural problems arose from the catastrophe of the 1985 Mexico City earthquake. By 1990 Telmex had debt equal to 23 percent of its capital.

13.4.1 Satellites

In December 1982 a modification of Article 28 of the Constitution designated satellite communication as a strategic area under the exclusive charge of the state. This was President Miguel de la Madrid's response to his predecessor's contract with Hughes Communications International for a new satellite system and private media conglomerate Televisa's increasing pressure for more control over the system.

In 1985 the Morelos Satellite System was launched by Hughes for the Mexican government. The Morelos System consisted of two geosynchronous satellites, each with twenty-two transponders using both Ku-band and C-band. Although the government accomplished a speedy implementation of satellite technology to meet the growing demands of the two primary users, Televisa and the telecom agency DGT (Direcion General de Telecomunicaciones), it did not adequately utilize or develop the social applications promised in the promotional campaign for the project, nor the commercial applications offered by the technology. Indeed, for over half its working life, Morelos I did not operate at capacity. In mid-1995 Morelos II was still not filled to capacity, even though its life may end during 1997–98. Morelos was underutilized for three reasons: tariffs were high, the regulatory framework was restricted, and the technology of the earth stations was not well developed. VSAT (very small aperture terminal) technology allowed more access.

A reinterpretation of the Mexican Constitution ultimately allowed the emergence of private VSAT networks as a popular solution for intracorporate telecom needs and for governmental commercialization of the underutilized bandwidth on Morelos. A precedent was set when the first private cross-border VSAT network was established to connect Honeywell's Tijuana plant with a corporate office in Gardena, California, in 1989. Subsequently, VSAT networks became very popular along the border and in rural areas of Mexico. Also during 1989, privately owned ground stations were allowed for private-sector use of the Morelos satellites. International links with foreign satellites still had to donate ground stations to the government. Sharehops and teleports were authorized on the condition they *not* be used to transport public switched service.

13.5 Pressure for Change

Many factors have influenced the changes in Mexico's telecommunications policies since the mid-1980s, not the least of which are external forces. Mexico's adherence to the General Agreement on Tariffs and Trade (GATT) in August 1986 led to such measures as lowering tariffs to a maximum of 20 percent, removing import license requirements for telecom equipment, eliminating official import reference prices on all but fifty-three categories of goods, and eliminating a 5 percent surcharge on imports. The pressure for free trade in services within GATT motivated price restructuring for telephone service and allowed entry of alternative international carriers in 1989. Thus, the Secretariat of Trade and Industry (SECOFI) facilitated importation of information technology and enhanced Mexico's competitiveness even before NAFTA.

Telmex's ability to build up communications services had reached its limit by the early 1980s. The company's investment program was affected because demand became overwhelming and the government began to lose favor. With over 1.5 million telephone applications pending and a significant deterioration in the quality of service, the company was forced to undergo massive reorganization and decentralization. Until the late 1980s the government had not made Telmex's growth a clear objective, since there was not an awareness of telecommunications' role in economic and social development.

Telmex employees faced negative publicity as the media launched a direct attack on the company's inefficiency. A public opinion poll—conducted by Telmex, SCT, the Secretariat of Labor and Social Prevision (STPS), and the telephone workers' union and first reported as an advertisement in a leading newspaper (*El Financiero,* October 16, 1987)—found that general corruption among Telmex employees was widely seen as having exacerbated the company's inability to give adequate service. It was commonly believed that the union had been instrumental in handicapping the growth of the company through prolonged strikes, personal political battles, and sabotage. At the same time, rumors circulated that many nonunion employees engaged in sabotage and blamed it on union employees.

Unable to forestall or prevent privatization, the union ultimately negotiated a 5 percent equity position in the deal and has provided strong political support for the company since.

Users emerged as aggressive demanders of change in the system in the late 1980s. Their role as key players in defining policy was unprecedented; previously their interests usually had been subordinated to those of government agencies, the telephone workers' union, and the service and equipment providers. In fact, one of the most important users, Pemex, was allowed to construct its own private network. Due to the pressure exerted by users, not least by various governmental secretariats, the government finally acknowledged that priority had to be given to telecommunications for the country's modernization and competitiveness (Griffith 1989b, p. 552).

Three factors influenced the decline of Telmex before privatization. First, during the financial crisis of the 1980s, the government reduced investment in

Telmex. Prior to the oil and debt crisis of 1982, 50 percent of revenue from the telephone tax was obliged to be reinvested in Telmex. This policy ceased under crisis. Second, an historic decision of 1981 positioned Mexico as one of the first countries to digitalize its telecom system. However, this plan was complicated by the technological failure of the digital system introduced by ITT (System 12) through an international bid. The software did not work and ITT could not meet the deadline. Subsequently, ITT sold its telecom equipment business to Alcatel and Ericsson, which ultimately replaced ITT. Third, the 1985 earthquake in Mexico City caused the loss of all long-distance capability in the capital city and much of the country due to the dependency on the central switch.

Since the late 1980s the growth of the *maquiladora* industry has led to rapidly growing demand for improved services along the border with the United States. Telmex's large-user department initiated the company's first efforts to commercialize services, with a focus on this booming industry. By 1989 special services offered in the border cities of Ciudad Juarez, Nogales, Reynosa, Nuevo Laredo, and Matamoros included digital Pulse Code Modulation (PCM) systems, digital microwave links, and fiber-optic systems for local and national use, as well as international connections. Points of connection originated in industrial parks and manufacturing plants.

Cellular phones and CB radios became another popular solution for voice communications during the late 1980s. Although expensive, cellular phones were desirable because of the long delays in otherwise acquiring phone service. Many operations actually found cellular systems more cost efficient for international connections, even though cellular systems were originally deemed illegal for transborder communication. In 1992, eight agreements regulating telecommunications along the border were signed between the United States and Mexico, as discussed later.

In 1980 the country's second digital exchange was installed in Tijuana, and the regional operating telco, Telnor, successfully digitalized much of the local telephone system in Baja California during the following decade. By 1989 Mexicali and Tijuana each had over 76 percent of their local area networks digitalized. In fact, Telnor's early regional success prompted its parent Telmex to decentralize into three regions in an attempt to improve service. By 1993 Telnor had completely digitalized telephone plants in the urban zones parts of its service area. Telnor's region boasted a density of 13 lines per 100 inhabitants by mid-1995, having increased the number of installed lines by 64 percent and the number of lines in service by 51 percent since the beginning of privatization (de Murguia 1995, p. 7E).

13.6 Regulation and Policy Changes

Until the late 1980s telecom regulation in Mexico had been pursued to achieve several goals, each of which implied a different role for the state. These goals sought to limit profits, allocate resources efficiently, maximize the size of the networks, and maximize government revenues (Griffith 1989b, pp. 548–49). Subsequently, a radical departure from this formula has occurred.

By 1987 Telmex was reversing the government-imposed populist approach to service by increasing local and medium-range service rates about 16 percent faster than long-distance rates. Previously, Mexico's local rates were among the cheapest in the world, subsidized by long-distance rates that were among the most expensive.

An early initiative of the Salinas administration (1988–94) was to restructure the government agencies involved in telecommunications as a precursor to deregulation and privatization. Until 1989 SCT had divided telecommunications into telephone service, primarily provided by Telmex as a monopoly, and all other types of communications. The latter were controlled by an agency of SCT called the General Directorate of Telecommunications (DGT). Under this structure, DGT and Telmex were the two policy-making forces that influenced SCT in defining telecommunications in Mexico.

After restructuring, SCT continued to regulate telecommunications, granting concessions and permits, as well as providing telecom services such as operating the national satellite system. Three undersecretariats were established to fulfill its mandate: (1) Transportation and Infrastructure, (2) Communications, and (3) Technological Development. There are also two autonomous agencies that SCT uses to provide telecom services: Telecommunications of Mexico (Telecomm) and Navigational Services in the Mexican Air Space (Seneam). The Mexican Institute of Communications (IMC) serves in an advisory capacity for communications issues.

Quite important was the removal of a constitutional obstacle. Mexican policy makers changed the legal framework through a reinterpretation of the law, rather than the lengthy process of amending the Constitution. For example, in March 1989 SCT's restrictions on transborder satellite communications links were withdrawn. International links were reinterpreted to refer only to cross-border satellite connections using systems *other* than the national Morelos Satellite System. This allowed Telecomm to issue domestic permits to anyone using Morelos for private, intracorporate networks. Technically, the law provides for government control over all satellite use, and all ground stations belong to the Mexican government. Satellite users have to purchase hardware for their networks, donate it to the government, and then lease back 50 percent of the capacity—the government retains the other half.

Mexico's previous protective policies had hindered the development of satellite services because the government did not invest in earth stations, nor would it allow the private sector to have ownership rights. Consequently, Morelos operated below capacity for years. Once Telecomm began to commercialize services under new rules allowing private ownership, full capacity was reached within a short period. In particular, VSAT usage in the border region became popular for establishing private intracorporate networks.

The 1995 Telecom Law has provided an even broader interpretation, including a provision for the privatization of the Solidaridad Satellite System launched in the early 1990s. Privatization will allow for more efficient utilization and management of the satellite network, space segment, and value-added services.

In connection with the Telmex privatization, President Salinas issued the Regulations for Telecommunications in 1990, which defined for legal purposes many of the services and technical terms used in the field. Also, these new regulations (published in the *Oficial Daily* on October 29, 1990) authorized SCT to grant competitors of Telmex concessions for public telephone networks, either for specific regions or specific services. The regulations protect Telmex's monopoly over long-distance service until August 1996 and classify providers into two categories: concessionaires of public telecom networks and licensees of private networks, value-added services, and other services that utilize public networks.

Policy makers responded to the rapidly growing demand for compatibility along the border with the signing of eight U.S.-Mexico Border Telecommunications Agreements in 1992. These were designed to better coordinate operations and assign radio and cellular frequencies on a reciprocal basis in the region. They also provide for new services and thus include technical specifications for cellular telephones, data transmission, communications services for highway and railroad transportation, television via microwaves and satellite, and high-definition television. Cellular telephone subscribers gained legal permission to use their phones on either side of the border. Also, an administrative agreement protects frequencies used by the International Boundaries and Waters Commission (IBWC). This is designed to prevent radio interference.

Mexico's most significant economic policy decision of the twentieth century has been to establish a regional trade partnership with the United States and Canada. The North American Free Trade Agreement (NAFTA) is a model agreement for its unprecedented opening of trade in services and its substantial contribution to competitiveness. Implementation of NAFTA on January 1, 1994, immediately opened additional opportunities for U.S. and Canadian exports of telecommunications equipment to Mexico and improves opportunities for U.S. and Canadian companies to provide enhanced services in Mexico, a market expected to have grown from U.S.$22 million in 1991 to over U.S.$100 million in 1995. Prospects for Mexican exports of enhanced services, which totaled U.S.$27 million in 1990, also improve under NAFTA. The agreement eliminated investment restrictions in most enhanced services immediately and eliminated all investment and other restrictions on videotext and packet-switched services in July 1995. (See Griffith 1994 for more on telecom trade issues; see De la Calle 1994 for a discussion of improved market access and prospective benefits.)

Mexico's Foreign Investment Law places certain restrictions on investment in common carrier services by limiting foreign investment to 49 percent equity ownership. Although NAFTA generally lifts this foreign ownership restriction and requires national treatment, basic telecom providers are exempt from NAFTA.

The 1995 Telecommunications Law replaces the previously prevailing legal code. The law outlines the introduction, beginning in 1997, of full competition in all segments of telecommunications. The SCT must confront difficult regulatory issues concerning universal service, access charge levels, and equal access as it moves to a fully competitive multicarrier environment.

13.7 Partial Privatization

In 1987 the government decided to partially privatize Telmex. It was a very controversial decision and was not immediately announced to the public. The telephone workers' union, which represented more than 90 percent of Telmex employees in 1989, was the greatest source of opposition to privatization, which it saw as a threat to its overwhelming power within the company. A rapid deterioration of labor relations ensued, but immediately before privatization, relations had improved and President Salinas lauded the company's labor contract as a model for reaching productivity goals.

Although the union failed to stop privatization, it did gain a 5 percent equity position to appease its leaders. The union has subsequently grown to 52,000 members industrywide and remains a significant political force in the development of telecommunications policy. At the end of 1994, the company employed 48,810, approximately 82 percent of whom were unionized. There were 5.9 employees per 1,000 lines in service, an improvement of 10.6 percent from 1993.

Since private-sector interests took control, Telmex no longer has a role in the regulatory process. However, it is commonly understood that the company continued to influence policy during the Salinas administration due to the long-standing relationships established when the company was part of the public sector and the close friendship of President Salinas and Telmex's president, Carlos Slim Helu, the head of Grupo Carso who became a billionaire under Salinas. The sweetheart deal under Salinas is increasingly coming under public scrutiny.

13.7.1 The New Telmex

In December 1990 the government sold control of Telmex to a consortium of Grupo Carso, Southwestern Bell (now SBC Communications), and France Telecom for U.S.$1.76 billion. At that time, the secretary of communications and transportation ceased being board chair but remained a board member until 1994. The government sold almost all of its remaining interest in global stock offerings in May 1991 and May 1992, taking in almost U.S.$1.8 billion; it disposed of its final stake in a privately placed convertible bond offering in May 1994.

Telmex's capital structure reflects the need to have access to large amounts of foreign equity capital even while retaining voting control in the hands of Mexican nationals. Thus, the company has three classes of common stock, each with different voting rights but otherwise the same. Two of these were issued in connection with the 1990 privatization: the AA (sold to the consortium and thus having full voting rights and representing 22.11 percent of Telmex equity) and the L series (sold in the global offerings and having limited voting rights, representing 74.25 percent). Series A shares (representing 3.64 percent), which also have full voting rights, are those that were previously in private hands.

In 1996, Telmex posted earnings of $1.476 billion and sales of $6.708 billion. Telmex's earnings were the second highest of any company in Latin America, behind only Telebras de Brasil. Telmex continues to operate the largest local and long-distance network in Mexico. It has $6.6 billion in annual revenues and serves nearly 9 million residential and business customers. In spite of losing monopoly control in January, Telmex has been able to hang onto the majority of Mexico's long-distance market. Although many users are choosing AT&T and MCI alliances on local ballots, most telephone users have not voted and will therefore remain with Telmex. The company's executives claim 90 percent of Mexico has opted not to switch carriers. Telmex believes it is keeping customers because of its lower rates, national coverage, and quality service. In early 1997, Telmex charged 53 cents a minute for the access fee to use its lines. Industry analysts expect long-distance prices to drop 20–30 percent.

Grupo Carso is the biggest single owner of controlling shares with 20.5 percent of the voting rights (while SBC holds 10 percent and France Telecom holds 5 percent) and 40 percent equity ownership, mostly through holding AA shares. The remaining majority of voting power is held primarily by other Mexican nationals, as of year-end 1995.

Telmex Series A and L shares trade publicly in Mexico and the United States as ADSs (American Depositary Shares). In 1994 the ADSs representing L shares were the most actively traded issue on the New York Stock Exchange, with over 1 billion changing hands, a record for any company. The AA shares are restricted by the original terms and cannot be traded before 2001.

13.7.2 The Concession

The concession remains effective until March 10, 2026, and allows Telmex to provide voice, data, text, sound, and video transmission services. It also required that telephone service reach several goals by 1994, including: basic services in all communities with more than 500 inhabitants; automatic switching services for all communities with more than 5,000 inhabitants; and two public (pay) telephones for each 1,000 persons (and five per person by 1998). The company also must have provided regulators with its four-year working plan. Since 1996 automatic switching must be provided in all communities with at least 100 requests for it and improvement must be made in the quality of service, particularly as regards responding to reported failures.

The company is allowed to offer additional services such as cellular telephony, radiotelephony, and television signal distribution and to manufacture telecom, computer, and electronics equipment. Telmex is allowed a monopoly of long-distance service until 1997, when new firms will be allowed to compete with it. As discussed later, cellular service was open to competition in 1989. The federal microwave network was sold to Telmex in 1991 as part of the concession for domestic long distance.

13.7.3 New Investment, Large Profits

Telmex's capital spending has increased dramatically since the partial privatization. In 1989 it invested less than U.S.$500 million; in 1991, the year after privatization, the figure was over U.S.$2.75 billion. For the six years 1991–96, the total was U.S.$12 billion, including U.S.$1.3 billion for telephone equipment, U.S.$2.7 billion for transmission equipment, U.S.$3.9 billion for switches and power equipment, and U.S.$3.7 billion for outside plant. Most of this has been to work off the backlog of requests for new service at the time of privatization and otherwise meet the requirements of the concession.

The privatized Telmex spent $12 billion laying more than 18,000 miles (28,000 kilometers) of fiber-optic cable, increasing the number of telephone lines in the country by 66 percent, from 5.3 million lines to 8.8 million. It extended phone services to 25,000 small towns and boosted the extent of the network's digitalization—compression of sounds into high-speed transmissions—from 30 percent to 90 percent.

Density has reached 9.6 lines per 100 inhabitants, up from 6.5. As a result, the wait for a new line dropped from three years to less than three months. The number of public (pay) phones has tripled, to approximately 240,000, with at least one in every locality with more than 500 inhabitants except in the area of conflict in Chiapas.

Revenue (in pesos) increased over 115 percent from 1990 to 1993. Aided by tariff schedules designed to allow it to generate cash for improving and expanding the system, in 1993 the company had a U.S.$2.7 billion net profit on U.S.$7.9 billion in revenue. Telmex's operating margins of over 50 percent (before the 1994–95 economic crisis) were among the highest in the world, which originally motivated some forty firms to seek to compete with Telmex in 1997, when its monopoly is terminated. By year-end 1994, debt was just 15 percent of Telmex's capital compared with, for example, AT&T's 39 percent, Telecom Chile's 44 percent, and Telefónica de España's 54 percent.

The economic crisis that began in December 1994 negatively affected the company. Telmex raised rates 12 percent in March 1995, but increases are not expected to catch up with the accelerated pace of inflation in its costs. Revenue actually declined in the second quarter of 1995 compared with 1994. The peso's 1994–95 devaluation meant higher debt and debt-service costs measured in pesos—about 60 percent of Telmex's foreign debt is in U.S. dollars and 25 percent in Japanese yen—leading to a reported U.S.$65 million loss in the first quarter of 1995.

In October 1994 Telmex made a major statement of its intention to compete in multimedia services by announcing plans to acquire 49 percent of Empresas Cablevision SA, a subsidiary of Grupo Televisa SA. Cablevision began operations in 1969, offering transmission of point-to-point television. In mid-1995 it had some 210,000 subscribers for its twenty-four-channel basic service; the company also offered seven premium channels. With about a 20 percent share of the domestic cable market, it was much smaller than market-leader Multivision.

The controversial deal was approved in June 1995, despite questions by senior legislators in all three major political parties and challenges raised by companies planning to compete against Telmex in 1997. As a condition, Cablevision must give access to other telephone companies if its cable network (more than 7,000 kilometers) is open to telephone service.

Media conglomerate Televisa controls more than 85 percent of Mexico's television market and is the primary producer of Spanish-language programs in the world, with concessions for distribution rights in fifty-two countries, including China and the former Soviet Union. It is owned by the Azcarraga family, led by Emilio Azcarraga, who also dominates Direct-to-home (DTH) television, music, film, magazines, and advertising, as well as owning a newspaper, two football (soccer) teams, the Aztec Stadium, and an equity share in Panamsat. During the early 1990s Televisa and Venevision acquired the majority participation in Univision that is allowed for foreign investors in the United States.

13.8 Other Players

In March 1992 SCT signed an agreement with Hughes for the construction of two satellites to replace the Morelos system. Solidaridad I was launched in November 1993 and Solidaridad II in October 1994. The government leases space to users. Each has eighteen transponders in band C, sixteen in Ku, and two in L for mobile telephony. Band C will be used for television, voice, and data; Ku, for digital data networks and DTH satellite television. Introduced in Mexico for the first time, band L is expected ultimately to have 50,000 mobile users and 20,000 stationary users. The Solidarity system has a life of fourteen years, and its footprint includes the major cities of the American continents. Solidaridad's two goals are to spur television, trade, and industry and to provide communication to all rural areas. The May 1995 Telecom Law provides for privatization of the system. Under privatization, nonsatellite services such as telegraph, telex, and wire transfers will likely be linked to the post office, similiar to the European experience.

13.8.1 Telecomm

Telecomunicaciones de Mexico (Telecomm) is a key operator of telecom activities in Mexico. It was created in November 1989 as a decentralized government agency to provide diverse services, including telegraph, radiotelegraph, public fax, satellite services, a satellite data network called Infosat, a packet-switched data network called Telepac, and an electronic mail service called Infonet. It thus took over many of the functions of DGT. Regulations reserved telegraph and satellite transmission services to the state, while opening other services to the private sector and competition. Telecomm has continued to strive for increased autonomy and financial self-sufficiency through commercialization of its services.

As the second largest user of equipment, Telecomm is responsible for the telegraph network with 1,600 offices. In 1994, over 5 million telegrams were sent, and the number of wire transfers increased to contribute 25.6 percent of telecommunications revenues. Money wire transfers provide 90 percent of revenue for telegraph service, which is available in 1,500 cities. Telex is available in 120 cities connected by 82 central offices with 24,663 lines. In 1990 Telecomm initiated a program to renovate installations offering services that include public telephone, fax, and telex.

In 1994 Telecomm had revenues of U.S.\$267 million, 43 percent from satellite services (Valerdi 1995). Now that the 1995 Telecom Law allows privatization of the satellite system, the future of Telecomm is unclear. Included in the privatization is Morelos II (which is being considered for repositioning to extend its life beyond the current 1997–98 limit); Solidaridad I and Solidaridad II, with lives extending to 2007–9; orbital slots for direct broadcast satellite (DBS); transmit/receive (T/R) ground stations in Mexico; landing rights in Latin America and the United States; and agreements for interconnection with U.S. teleports, low earth-orbiting satellites (LEOs), personal communication service (PCS), and Ka-band, which is primarily for television. Another agreement with Hughes provides for the manufacture of another satellite, Morelos III, to be launched in 1998.

The primary domestic companies interested in bidding on the satellite system include Multivision, Televisa, Avantel, Alestra, and Redsat. Among the U.S. operators forming U.S.–Mexican teams and bids for various holdings are Lockheed Martin Corp. (teamed with Televisa), Hughes Electronics Corp. unit of General Motors Corp., Loral Space Communications Ltd., and the GE Americom unit of General Electric Co. Some assets will be sold by late summer 1997, and others will be sold by the end of the year. The DBS license could climb as high as $500 million, while the remaining assets could attract an equal amount.

13.8.2 Grupo Iusacell

Telmex's most serious competitor, and one of the most dynamic players in Mexico today, is Grupo Iusa, headed by the powerful Peralta family. Since 1965, when the Mexican government granted Iusacell a fifty-year concession to provide basic telephony service for select rural and suburban areas throughout Mexico, the company has been aggressively staking out markets in Mexico and the rest of Latin America.

Iusacell is the second largest cellular operator in Mexico, after Telcel, a Telmex subsidiary. Its franchises cover more than 70 percent of the population and it holds a nationwide 450 MHz license for unspecified services. The company operates a switched data company, Iusanet, and offers private line bypass through Satellitron. Microwave facilities and fiber-optic capacity leased from the CFE (Comision Federal de Electricidad) support its operations. In 1993 Iusacell had an estimated 150,000 cellular subscribers, spending an average of U.S.$200 per month. The group had net income of U.S.$40 million from telecom revenues of U.S.$400 million, as part of a U.S.$1.7 billion industry group.

In 1994 Bell Atlantic purchased 42 percent of Iusacell in a transaction valued at almost U.S.$1.04 billion. Consistent with Mexican law, voting control remains with the Peralta family. However, Bell Atlantic has been promised it will be able to participate in key business decisions based on its economic interest in Iusacell. Grupo Iusacell completed an international initial offering of 9 percent of its stock in 1994; shares trade on the New York Stock Exchange as well as in Mexico. The new long-distance concession is called Iusater, SA de CV.

During the same year, Iusacell entered a partnership with equipment manufacturer Northern Telecom for joint education and training. The program calls for more than 6,000 Iusacell staff members to receive management, sales, marketing, and distribution training in preparation for growth in communications markets.

13.8.3 Sprint

Sprint has been a player in Mexico since 1987 when it sponsored a forum at the University of California's Center for U.S.-Mexican Studies that challenged Mexican policy makers to privatize the phone company. Sprint initially maintained a low-key role, but it has been very effective in negotiating numerous contracts with Telmex and its regional subsidiary Telnor. Illustrating their excellent rapport, Sprint and Telmex formed a joint venture in late 1994. The agreement was actually a major coup for Telmex because Sprint withdrew from an alliance with Iusacell-Bell Atlantic to form the partnership. The alliance allows Telmex to compete as a global player, offering seamless cross-border products and services to corporate accounts.

Sprint's other clients in Mexico include AeroMexico, Banamex, Bancreser, Cecoban, Cifra (Mexico's largest retailer), Compania de Luz, Grupo Autrey, Pemex, PMI Comercio Internacional, and Telecomm. Sprint began offering service in late 1989, and in 1995 included IDDD, operator services, Sprint Express, Mexico Directo, Meeting Channel, ITFS, IVPN, and private lines.

Ongoing facilities, product, and service quality development programs are in place with Telmex. The Sprint-Telmex network includes over 2,000 circuits at four fiber-optic border crossings: Tijuana-San Isidro, California; Reynosa-McAllen, Texas; Juarez-El Paso, Texas; and Nogales-Nogales, Arizona. The Sprint partnership will allow Telmex to leverage the common platform of technology products and services as part of preparing for future competition. Telmex also has an option to align with and benefit from the Sprint alliance with Deutsche Telekom and France Telecom and with Call-Net of Canada for development of a global telecommunications network known as Global One. The Sprint joint venture will allow Telmex to compete as a global player offering seamless cross-border products and/or services to multinational corporate accounts.

In February 1997, Telmex and Sprint announced another joint venture to market long-distance service to the growing Hispanic market in the United States. The newly formed company filed an application under Section 214 of the Communications Act with the FCC for authority to carry international traffic to and from the United States. It plans to cater to the special needs of the large and influential Hispanic population by offering conveniently packaged calling plans and products.

13.8.4 Others

Although its position may be eroding, AT&T remains one of the most significant international forces in Mexico. It was the sole provider of international long-distance telephone service until 1989, but it has since been under pressure from the other common carriers allowed to provide service, including Sprint, MCI, and LDDS. As a strategic move to better position itself to face this competition, AT&T Telecom Mexico Inc. joined forces with two large Mexican firms, including Alfa Telecom S.A. de C.V. of Monterrey, to form Alestra S.A. Grupo Alfa is a powerful industrial conglomerate with major interests in steel.

In preparation for the opening of the domestic long-distance market, Grupo

Financiero Banamex-Accival, Mexico's largest financial group, became the first company to apply for and receive a long-distance license. In October 1994, it entered a joint venture with MCI Communications Corporation. The new company, Avantel S.A., is 55 percent owned by Banamex. Based in Mexico City, the venture expects to have much of the necessary infrastructure in place by 1997 and to have invested U.S.$2 billion in the new network by the year 2002. During 1995–96 Avantel spent U.S.$650 million on the first stage of a fiber-optic network. An additional U.S.$1.15 billion will create a 19,200-kilometer fiber-optic network, focusing on corridors from Mexico City to Monterrey and Guadalajara. In early 1997, Avantel was granted a $481 million 13-year loan by the Export-Import Bank in the United States and the Export Credit Development of Canada (EDC) to support its telecommunications investment plan. Avantel launched its service with Ahorrafacíl program, featuring highly competitive rates for domestic long-distance calls. Avantel also offers special rates for international calls made within a strip along the border (50 miles south and 55 miles north of the border). Within the next five to seven years, Avantel expects to capture 20 percent of the market with its fiber-optic network. Since 1975 Banamex has been creating Infratel (Infrastructura de Telecomunicaciones), Mexico's largest private telecom network, which serves 250 cities. Banamex has a permit to offer as much as 30 percent of its network capability for private services.

Bancomer, Banamex's most serious banking competitor, joined forces with the holding company Valores Industriales, S.A. (Visa) in 1994 to form Unicom Telecommunicaciones S. de R.L. de C.V. They are launching a firm to offer value-added services not available from Telmex, such as interconnections and videotext transmission. The company will also build infrastructure for long-distance telephone service. Bancomer and Visa already have a private infrastructure utilizing satellite, microwave, and public networks.

Two other concessions have been granted, to Marcatel and Investcom, to foster competition with Telmex. Marcatel is the consortium made up of Radio Beep, Western International, and IXC Communications. With at least six companies investing over U.S.$800 million each, SCT anticipates a total investment in telecommunications of U.S.$5 billion over a five-year period, 1996–2000.

Arthur Andersen won the contract to handle the complicated accounting of all telephone traffic between the United States and Mexico. The number of calls between the two countries is probably the highest worldwide. For example, there were 2.4 billion minutes of calls between Mexico and the United States in 1994. U.S.–Mexico traffic is a $4 billion annual long-distance market that could grow to $11 billion within the next five years. To allow competition to reach its full potential, an accurate account of calls made to Mexico through AT&T, MCI, Sprint, and the more than 400 smaller operating companies in the United States is vital to ensure that the calls will be assigned proportionally to the eight Mexican competitors.

13.8.5 Equipment Suppliers

Domestic producers of telecom equipment include Alcatel, AT&T, Ericsson, GPT (a Pleussy marketing arm), Mitel, Northern Telecom, Siemens, TPS (a Phillips subsidiary), and some small Japanese and Korean firms located along the Baja California border.

Grupo Ericsson is the longest surviving telecommunications company in Mexico, with operations dating back to 1907, when it initiated telephone service. Ericsson became a major shareholder of Telmex when it was formed in 1947 by merging the country's operating companies. It subsequently disposed of its stake but continued to be Telmex's principal supplier. Ericsson produces central office switches, power equipment, and transmission equipment and also assembles radio equipment for Telcel. It is developing software for both the Mexican market and common applications for Ericsson worldwide, in particular for the U.S. market. This is significant because of the importance of software in modern central office switches. Approximately 70 percent of Grupo Ericsson's sales are to Telmex (1993 data). Exports to Central America account for 12 percent of total sales; another 3 percent go to the United States and Europe. A little over 10 percent of Telmex's purchases are from L. M. Ericsson and its affiliates, and 10 percent of L. M. Ericsson's worldwide sales are to Telmex.

Imports, almost half from the United States, accounted for about 60 percent of Mexico's U.S.$2.5 billion equipment market in 1993. The overall market was expected to grow at 10 percent during 1994–96, with import growth projected at just 8 percent as a larger share was served by domestic production. Equipment made in the United States has been highly regarded due to its quality, price, delivery time, and high technology. Strong technical assistance to the client has been an additional factor for U.S. product popularity (Gutierrez 1994).

13.9 Nonbasic Services

Rights to offer cellular telephony were first auctioned in 1989, and the response has been overwhelming due to the lack of adequate basic phone service. Mexico has been divided into nine cellular regions. Each has two providers, Telcel and a competitor. Estimates for the end of 1994 indicate 400,000 subscribers in over 85 cities, with Mexico City having at least 60 percent of them. Much social status is associated with having a cellular phone.

Paging has been available since the early 1950s and had approximately 77,000 subscribers in 1993. As elsewhere, paging is popular among the medical profession and companies providing maintenance service. In 1991 Televisa entered a joint venture with Mobile Telecommunications Technologies Corp. (MTel), offering satellite paging services.

Value-added services (VASs) are defined by the 1995 Telecom Law as "services that employ a public telecommunications network and that affect the format, content, code, protocol, storage, or similar aspects of the information transmitted by any user, as well as provide users with additional, different, or restructured information, or involve interaction of a user with stored information."

Enhanced services have generally come to be interpreted to include VASs and information services. In Mexico, both are regulated as value-added services. The VASs usually comprise telex (with store and forward features), e-mail, voice mail, protocol conversion, videotext, packet switching, and video conferencing. Information services include databases, on-line computer services, information brokers, and the like. Enhanced services such as e-mail and voice mail are among the fastest growing sectors of the telecom industry.

Some private networks, such as CFE and Banamex, have been granted permits to share their network with other users. Private networks have been established by Televisa, Cifra, Electronic Data Systems (EDS), and the Mexican Petroleum Institute (IMP).

Beginning in 1995 U.S. and Canadian investors have been able to own 100 percent of a Mexican enterprise that provides value-added services, including videotext and enhanced packet-switching services.

13.10 Looking Ahead

Mexican telecommunications have undergone significant liberalization since the late 1980s, and more is planned. One aspect of privatizing Telmex has been the breakup of its monopolies. Telmex's long-distance telephone monopoly ended in 1996, and its general monopoly will be completely terminated by 2026. Telecomm's monopoly of the national Solidaridad Satellite System is being eliminated in 1997 as well. Competition has already been allowed in cellular services, paging, videotext, radio, voice mail, cable television, and value-added services through the granting of concessions to new entrants.

The terms of deregulation will define how the industry will look as the century ends, and it will influence overall foreign direct investment in Mexico. In fact, the *Wall Street Journal* observed, "Telmex is so important to Mexico that how the government decides to deregulate will be the most important policy move since the decision to proceed with the North American Free Trade Agreement" (Torres 1994). As of June 1994 approximately U.S.$18 billion of foreign money had been invested in Telmex. At that time, the company's stock made up 18 percent of the Mexican stock market's total capitalization and 23 percent of daily trading volume. By the end of 1996, Telmex had been the most actively traded stock on Wall Street for the previous two years. It accounted for about a quarter of the value of the Mexican stock exchange and has spawned the maxim, As Telmex goes, so goes the economy.

The economic crisis that began with the devaluation of the Mexican peso on December 19, 1994, devastated Telmex's share price. Series L shares traded in New York fell to a low of U.S.$23 on March 11, 1995, less than their initial offering price of U.S.$27.25 in May 1991 and 76 percent below their high of U.S.$75.50 on February 8, 1994.

Yet, the crisis did not lead to a major reprioritization of the terms of deregulation. Before the devaluation, SCT had announced interconnection guidelines favorable to new entrants as regards open markets entry, number of interconnection points, and ability to bypass. Legislation in 1995 revealed the ultimate two objectives: to motivate the participation of the greatest number of businesses of various sizes in existing markets and subsequent spin-off markets; and to rapidly pass on the benefits of modernization in the sector in the form of new services at competitive prices for all consumers.

To meet the challenges of an accelerated modernization process and enhanced competitiveness in the global economy, companies will continue to make a huge financial investment in the telecommunications industry, at least until the end of the 1990s. In fact, in a study made public in mid-1995, Northern Telecom estimates the market will reach U.S.$31 billion by the year 2000 (including equipment, service, and infrastructure) and that more than 230,000 people will be working in the sector. The estimates assume 20 telephone lines for every 100 people, more than twice the number in 1995. As with AT&T in the United States, even though Telmex will lose market share as a result of competition, it is expected to continue to grow.

In response to competition, Telmex is raising issues such as reciprocity on the part of the United States for entry into its markets. As a result, Telmex won the right to provide direct long-distance service to clients in the United States. This is especially significant because 65 percent of Telmex traffic with the United States is to SBC territory. Also indicative of the increasing global competitive pressure, the president of Telmex, Carlos Slim Helu, argues that the controversial Telmex-Televisa deal between specialists in telecommunications and production "represents a necessary strategic alliance of two Mexican companies that are preparing to compete in improved conditions with the major transnationals that are coming to Mexico because of globalization and could easily take over the domestic market" (*El Financiero International* 1995).

What originated as the cornerstone of the Salinas administration's drive for domestic modernization may well emerge as the gateway for Zedillo's team to position Mexico in the vanguard of those exploiting the infobahn, leading Latin America in the Global Information Infrastructure (GII). Initiatives evolving from the Summit of the Americas held in Miami in December 1994 indicate that there is growing interest in coordinating a Latin American agenda for information infrastructure. The broad themes of the event—hemispheric economic integration, sustainable development, and reinventing government—will all be more easily attained via an efficient and well-coordinated information infrastructure. Mexico is well positioned to set a national technical and political agenda to serve as a model for the region.

Regional model or not, information infrastructure is considered essential for the social reforms demanded of the Zedillo administration. Zedillo strategists are mapping out a game plan for intragovernmental networks linking directly into the GII. In particular, widespread access and participation could be attained through establishment of a national satellite network within the country's 260-campus technical training institute, Conalep. Conalep provides students with a competency-based education in computers and therefore offers a vehicle for the concept of networking to be integrated at both the administrative and educational levels.

Entering the twenty-first century with widespread GII access and participation will further domestic reforms in other sectors. The opening of the telecom monopoly in January 1997 and the expansion of value-added services provides more competitive prices and services for the growing economy. For example, Telmex has acknowledged that it will have to cut long-distance rates up to 25 percent to compete in the open market. The 1994 elections showed the sophistication of the extensive automation of PRI's campaign headquarters, as well as the Federal Electoral Institute's (IFE) reliance on information technology for a more accurate and accountable election.

13.11 Conclusion

Several interrelated domestic factors, intensified by competition in the international economy, spawned a radical change in telecommunications policy in Mexico after 1988. The inability of the government-controlled public telephone monopoly to provide even basic service, let alone accommodate demand for new and improved telecom infrastructure and services, exacerbated by inefficient management of the government-owned national satellite system, were key factors providing impetus for change. The desire for accelerated modernization created a momentum that led to restructuring telecom agencies, reinterpreting and rewriting communications law, reprivatizing the telephone company, and now privatizating the satellite system. In fact, the political impetus behind revolutionizing Mexico's marketplace over the past two years stems from the deep belief that without boosting the telecommunications sector, NAFTA would never take off. Furthermore, the deregulation of equipment and liberalization of value-added services arising from NAFTA provides an additional catalyst to Mexico's participation in the information revolution. Perhaps most important, the 1995 economic crisis awakens Mexican policy makers to the need for a development plan that is sustainable. In the words of Telmex Director-General Jaime Chico Pardo, "You cannot run a country just on economic models: you must respond to social realities." There is no doubt the role of telecommunications will be important.

Notes

The author wishes to thank Carlos Casasus, Mexico's former Undersecretary of Communications and Technological Development and Jaime Chico Pardo, Director-General of Telmex, and Carlos Mier y Teran, Director-General of Telecomm, for comments.

1. *Maquiladoras,* or "in-bond" industries, are assembly plants operating under a program that permits duty-free entry of parts and supplies into Mexico. Most of the output is exported to the United States, which charges a duty only on the value added in Mexico— generally only the labor cost of assembly. Relatively inexpensive and plentiful labor makes this setup appealing for certain types of operations. Exports from these plants soared from just below U.S.$2.5 billion in 1980 to over U.S.$26.2 billion in 1994. The program will ultimately become obsolete due to NAFTA, and the sector will disappear by the year 2001.

2. When Madero attempted to correct the illegal situation of giving certain foreign investors favorable exemptions, such as a minimal obligation to pay taxes, representatives of these interests joined with the Porfirian army and the Mexicans defeated by the Revolution to assault the government and, on February 22, 1913, assassinate Madero. The U.S. Embassy served as a headquarters for the foreign interests.

Bibliography

Aspin, Chris. 1995. "Privatization: Road to Recovery . . . or Ruin?" *Mexico Business,* May, pp. 40–48.

Casasus, Carlos. 1994. "Privatization of Telecommunications: The Case of Mexico." In *Implementing Reforms in the Telecommunications Sector,* edited by Bjorn Wellenius and Peter A. Stern. Washington, D.C.: The World Bank, pp. 177–84.

Cowhey, Peter, J. Aronson, and G. Szekely, eds. 1989. *Changing Networks: Mexico's Telecommunications Options,* Monograph Series, 32. San Diego: Center for U.S.-Mexican Studies, University of California, San Diego.

De la Calle, Luis. 1994. "Telecommunications and Other Competitiveness Enhancing Aspects of the North American Free Trade Agreement." *Interchange '94,* Washington, D.C., October 12.

de Murguia, Gilberto. 1995. "Telnor: Facing the Competition." *El Financiero Special Supplement: Telecommunications,* pp. 7–8E.

Flores, Javier. 1993a. "The Telecommunications Equipment Market in Mexico." USDOC, U.S. Embassy in Mexico City, January.

_____. 1993b. "Industry Subsector Analysis -Computer Peripherals." USDOC, U.S. Embassy in Mexico City, June.

Frischkorn, A. 1993. "Why NAFTA Will Benefit U.S. Telecommunication Equipment Manufacturers." *Telecommunications Magazine,* 26(January):1.

Griffith, Kathleen A. 1987. "Mexcom '87 Telecom and Computer Update." *Transnational Data and Communications Report,* 11(April):4, 10.

_____. 1988. "Opening Mexican Telecom Options." *Transnational Data and Communications Report,* 11(January):1, 10.

_____. 1989a. "Communications Options in Mexico." In *Mexico's Maquiladora Guidebook,* edited by Jay Hyde and J. Peters Hyde. San Diego: HPH Partners, Inc., pp. 139–42.

_____. 1989b. "Mexican Teleconnectivity." In *PTC '89 Proceedings,* edited by L. S. Harms and D. J. Wedemeyer. Pacific Telecommunications Council, January.

_____. 1991. "Telecom Maximizes Cross-Border Relations." *Telephone Engineer and Management,* June 15, 51–52.

_____. 1992. "An Interview with Dr. Jaime Serra Puche, Secretary of Trade and Industry of Mexico." *Columbia Journal of World Business,* 27(Spring):1, 55.

_____. 1994. "NAFTA and Telecommunications Opportunities in Mexico." *Pacific Telecommunications Review,* 15(March):3, 23–28.

Gutierrez, Maria Aydelia. 1993. "Industry Subsector Analysis—Electronic Components." USDOC, U.S. Embassy in Mexico City, June.

_____. 1994. Telecomunicaciones en Mexico." Paper delivered at Latcom '94 Conference, Mexico City, January 26.

Kauachi, Carlos, J. Perez Bonilla, P. Cerisola y Weber, and A. Cerezo. 1994. "Telmex." Presentations made at the Telmex Investor's Meeting, Mexico City, February.

Levison, Andrew, and H. Reynel Iglesias. 1993. "The Online Industry in Mexico." *Online,* May, pp. 116–19.

Malkin, Elisabeth. 1993. "Telmex Gets Its Wires Crossed." *Cover,* August 29, pp. 20–23.

Mier y Teran, C. 1992. "Telecommunications for the Modernization and the Social Development in the Americas." *Americas Forum '92: Toward the Next Millennium.* Acapulco, Mexico: ITU.

Secretaria de Comunicaciones y Transportes (SCT). 1987. *Historia de las Comunicaciones y los Transportes en Mexico: El Telegrafo.* Mexico City: SCT.

Szekely, Gabriel, and Jaime del Palacio. 1995. *Telefonos de Mexico: Una Empresa Privada.* Mexico City: Grupo Editorial Planeta.

Telefonos de Mexico. 1991. *Historia de la Telefonia en Mexico: 1878–1991.* Mexico City: Telefonos de Mexico.

Torres, Craig. 1994. "Future Is on the Line for Mexico's Telephone Company." *Wall Street Journal,* June 29, p. B4.

Valerdi, Jorge. 1995. "Privatization of the Mexican Satellite Business: Options and Issues." Working Paper, IDM Satellite Division, pp. 1–14.

Acronyms

AT&T	American Telephone and Telegraph
BANACCI	Holding company for Banamex
BANAMEX	Banco Nacional de Mexico
BANCOMEXT	Banco de Mexico (Mexico's import/export bank)
BANOBRAS	Banco Nacional de Obras Publicas (Mexico's infrastructure bank)
CEICO	Telmex's telephone attention centers providing custom service and sales by phone
CEPAL	Comision Economica Para America Latina y el Caribe
CETES	Certificados de la Tesoreria de la Federacion
CFE	Comision Federal de Electricidad
COMPEX	Comision para la Promocion de las Exportaciones
DID	Direct inward dialing
FCC	Federal Communications Commission
GATT	General Agreement on Tariffs and Trade
ITT	International Telephone and Telegraph
NADBANK	North American Development Bank
NAFINSA	Nacional Financiera (Mexican finance bank)
NAFTA	North American Free Trade Agreement
OECD	Organization for Economic Cooperation and Development
PEMEX	Petroleos Mexicanos (Mexico's state-owned oil company)
PFIC	Programa de Fomento de la Industria de Computo (Computer Industry Industrial Development Program)
PMIC	Programa de Modernizacion de la Industria de Computo (Computer Industry Modernization Program)
PRI	Partido Revolucionario Institucional (Mexico's Institutional Revolutionary Party, in power for almost seventy years)
RDI	Red Digital Integrada (Integrated Digital Network)
SCT	Secretaria de Comunicaciones y Transportes (Secretariat of Communications and Transportation)
SECOFI	Secretaria de Comercio y Fomento Industrial (Secretariat of Commerce and Industrial Development)

SHCP	Secretaria de Hacienda y Credito Publico (Secretariat of Finance and Public Credit)
SPP	Secretaria de Programacion y Presupuesto (Secretariat of Programming and Budget)
TELECOMM	Telecomunicaciones de Mexico (Mexico's agency for commercializing telecom services, such as satellite and telegraph)
TELMEX	Telefonos de Mexico, S.A. (Telephones of Mexico)
UNDP	United Nations Development Program

14
Puerto Rico

RAMÓN MORALES CORTÉS

Puerto Rico has made great strides in the development of its infrastructure and telecommunications facilities. With over U.S.$3.8 million invested since 1974, the island, a territory currently under U.S. congressional jurisdiction, has modernized its central office systems and has built an extensive digital fiber-optic network. Puerto Rico is on a par with respect to access of telecommunications services to its population of over 3.6 million people. The local telecommunications industry is poised for major growth with the advent of new technologies and wireless services such as personal communications systems, Integrated Services Digital Network (ISDN), and frame relay.

14.1 Background

Puerto Rico lies at the eastern end of the Greater Antilles, the major island chain of the Caribbean that also includes larger and geographically more diverse Cuba, Jamaica, and Hispaniola (Haiti and the Dominican Republic). Puerto Rico, including the neighboring islands it administers, covers about 9,100 square kilometers and has a population of 3.8 million (July 1994 estimate). The island is mostly mountainous, with a coastal plain belt in the north. Although San Juan is one of the biggest and best natural harbors in the Caribbean, most of the coastline is relatively smooth and fringed by many small islands and cays, especially in the south and east. The island is roughly rectangular in shape, stretching 180 kilometers from east to west and averaging 56 kilometers north to south.

Christopher Columbus set foot in Puerto Rico in 1493 on his second voyage. Within a hundred years the occupants he encountered, the Taino, had been largely decimated by war and disease. In recognition of Puerto Rico's strategic location, the Spanish built major fortresses. The island quickly became a thriving commercial center, exporting sugar, coffee, and other agricultural products while importing finished manufactured goods from Spain and Europe. By the late 1870s the bulk of the island's trade was with its North American neighbor, the United States.

14.2 Early History

Telegraphy came early to Puerto Rico because Samuel F. B. Morse, inventor of the electromagnetic telegraph, had a daughter living on the island. In 1858 Morse connected the hacienda of his son-in-law Edward Lind to the small beach town of Arroyo. The first telegraph lines were formally registered and authorized by the Spanish colonial government on March 1, 1859. On that day Morse transmitted the prophetic lines "Puerto Rico, beautiful jewel! When you are linked with the other jewels of the Antilles in the necklace of the world's telegraph, yours will not shine less brilliantly in the crown of your Queen!"

The island's colonial ruler, Spain, was one of the first countries to introduce telephone service. In Puerto Rico, the government sought to implement service by commissioning franchise licenses to local businessmen, in much the same way as in Spain. Thus, in 1880 Alfonse XII signed guidelines and policies for establishment of concessions. These included the following: each telephone network would consist of a central station with no individual line exceeding a distance of 10 kilometers; each installation would be completed within thirty days; network operations could not start until formal recognition by a regulatory body, Cuerpo de Telégrafo, composed of appointees of the Spanish Crown in Puerto Rico; the board would determine rates; and the franchise owner would be responsible for the repair and maintenance of all lines and equipment. The franchises were for specific geographical areas that, in rural areas, were coterminous with haciendas.

In 1882 Preston C. Nelson, a U.S. national, approached Governor Miguel de la Vega Inclán with a plan to build an interconnected network covering the island's three largest municipalities—San Juan, Mayagüez, and Ponce. Nelson represented the West Indies Telephone and Telegraph Company, based in New Jersey and controlled by the Continental Telephone Company of Massachusetts. Nelson was so confident of the viability of the network that he proposed to have his company assume all of the construction and equipment costs. In return, the Spanish colonial government was asked to grant exclusive rights.

A major debate among members of the colonial government ensued. San Juan's newspaper, *El Buscapié* (The Firecracker), took a favorable view of the proposal, but several of the governor's advisers pointed out dangers in accepting the offer. Key among their objections was that the system would be completely under foreign control and would not be subject to any local laws or regulations, as none had been enacted. The advisers also wanted assurances of ultimate control to maintain military security.

In 1883 Vega nonetheless agreed to permit Nelson to develop a pilot network connecting San Juan with the La Marina sector of the capital. However, three months into the project, before any major work had begun, the government canceled the trial.

In 1884, the same year Alfonse XII by royal decree ordered establishment of a telephone network under a government monopoly in Spain, the colonial governor in Puerto Rico ordered a phone network for use by the government, its dependencies, and the military. By 1885 a network of thirteen local stations and a central station at La Fortaleza in San Juan formed one of the most advanced telecommunications infrastructures in the Spanish empire.

In 1890 the colonial government gave concessions to various entrepreneurs to set up local monopoly telephone service, as had been done in Spain in 1886. These were given to Rafael Fabián y Fabián for San Juan in the northeast, Pedro Juan Rosaly for Ponce in the south, and Alfredo L. Casals in Mayagüez on the west coast.

By 1897 lines connected San Juan, Ponce, and Mayagüez. The principal users were commercial and government entities. The island's commerce and trade expanded significantly as the advent of telecommunications services permitted easier transactions between the agricultural centers of Ponce and Mayagüez and with the civilian and military government apparatus centered in San Juan.

In 1898, as a result of the Spanish-American War, Puerto Rico was ceded to the United States. The island became a protectorate, subject to U.S. control of its government, laws, currency, and foreign policy.

In 1901 La Compañia de Ferrocarriles de Puerto Rico was given permission by the local Interior Commission to build and maintain telephone and telegraph lines along its route and to contract to provide services on behalf of local franchise holders. The company provided service between San Juan and Ponce and fifteen towns along the way, a distance of over 175 rugged kilometers, generally stringing both telegraph and telephone lines on poles placed along the railroad right-of-way.

The telecommunications industry at the beginning of the twentieth century saw the transformation of the Spanish system of franchise holders into modern corporate entities. In November 1902 the San Juan Telephone Company, established six months earlier as a New Jersey–based corporation, changed its name to Porto Rico Telephone Company, with Rafael Fabián y Fabián as president. In December, the company was awarded a franchise to build and manage a telephone network centered in San Juan and extending throughout Puerto Rico.

Three years later, the South Porto Rico Telephone Company (incorporated in Maine) was awarded a franchise to operate a network centered in Ponce in the south and providing service to various towns on the west coast. Its president, Pedro Juan Rosaly, was one of the original franchise holders for the city.

Porto Rico General Telephone Company was formed in October 1906 (as a Connecticut corporation) to purchase the Porto Rico Telephone Company, which it did the next month. This gave the new company control of the network in San Juan.

In 1907, a law was passed giving the Interior Commission the right to build, maintain, and operate telephone and telegraph systems between the cities of San Juan and Ponce. Additionally, it allowed formation of local telephone centers for the expansion of service to smaller towns and municipalities. These would be government-owned concerns under the control and jurisdiction of the Interior Commission, operating alongside the privately owned telecommunications companies.

14.2.1 The Birth of ITT

Puerto Rico is part of the beginnings of one of the largest early international conglomerates and innovators of telecommunications technology, International Telephone and Telegraph (ITT). The company's founders, the brothers Hernan and

Sosthenes Behn, were born on the Caribbean island of St. Thomas (then a Danish possession). They began experimenting with telegraph technology in 1901. In 1906 a stepfather left them extensive land holdings in San Juan in what is today a major tourist center called the Condado. The Behns immediately began to build a telegraph network and a bridge, which became known as the Puente Dos Hermanos (Two Brothers Bridge), connecting the Condado with San Juan.

In December 1906 Sosthenes Behn became president of the Porto Rico General Telephone Company. Hernan became a corporate officer in 1907. In July 1911, flush with U.S.$25,000 in cash from the 1910 sale of their bridge to the city of San Juan, the Behns purchased the company outright. In September 1913 Sosthenes, who was the creative entrepreneur and merger genius of the two brothers, initiated a merger with South Porto Rico Telephone. The next June, the brothers formed Porto Rico Telephone Company (PRTC) as a Delaware corporation and, with the approval of the U.S. government, concluded the merger of the Ponce- and San Juan–based companies. The new company had an extensive network connecting the island's major arteries of trade and commerce and approximately 1,800 telephone users. It also had formal approval to construct, manage, and maintain telecommunications services throughout the island except for a cluster of towns around the municipality of Caguas in the northeast and the islands of Culebra and Viegues, where service continued to be run by the Interior Commission.

The Behn brothers were also given the authority to form a long-distance network and provide telephone services to local towns not under government control. The authorization provided for a twenty-year limit whereby the island's legislature retained the right to extend or terminate the agreement.

In 1914 Puerto Rico became one of the first places in the world to have coin public telephones. Operator assisted, the calls cost 5 cents. The same year, PRTC published the first telephone directory, listing all the telephone numbers in its network.

In 1917 the Jones Act gave Puerto Ricans U.S. citizenship. The same year, the island legislature passed Law 70 establishing a Public Service Commission to regulate utilities, including the telephone system. The law also reinforced the role of the local government as a direct provider of telecommunications services.

Puerto Rico was hit by a terrible earthquake in 1918. It caused devastation throughout the island, including destruction of most of the telephone and telegraph cabling. Reconstruction began quickly but was significantly hampered by materials being in short supply because of World War I. By 1920 PRTC had reestablished services and expanded its system to 6,500 users.

In 1920 the Behn brothers incorporated the International Telephone and Telegraph Corporation (ITT) in New York City. This company became their corporate flagship for expansion into Cuba and into Europe. Also in 1920, they formed a telephone company in Cuba and supervised the construction of a cable connecting Cuba with New York. The Behns acquired all the shares in Compañía Telefónica de España, which had just been granted the right to operate the Spanish telephone system, in 1924. Their company gained another major foothold in Europe with its purchase of American Telephone & Telegraph's European manufacturing subsidiary. This also gave ITT new muscle for its worldwide expansion.

The experience of the early mergers and the formation of PRTC had given the

Behns the experience they needed to operate a telephone company. Moreover, PRTC's rapid growth provided a revenue stream and a solid base from which to launch their global efforts.

14.2.2 Destruction Leads to Modernization and Improvement

In 1928 Puerto Rico was hit by another major natural disaster. Hurricane San Felipe wreaked havoc from Ponce in the south to the northeast, where the telephone infrastructure was most concentrated. The hurricane devastated PRTC's operations, leaving the island without telephone service for several months. San Felipe also brought great destruction to the coffee industry, already suffering from intense competition from other Latin American–based growers and a higher, U.S. dollar–based, price.

Once again, PRTC's creative efforts produced a successful reconstruction. Legions of installers went to work to rewire the island zone by zone, building by building. This task was all the more difficult because already rugged terrain was made virtually inaccessible by thousands of trees felled by the hurricane. Carrying materials in horse-drawn carts, PRTC crews worked tenaciously for long hours to get the island's phones ringing again. The 1930 decision by the Plant Department to use trucks advanced the rewiring effort and permitted the company to respond more quickly to repairs and new installations.

Destruction of the old phone system led to its modernization and improvement. For example, decaying galvanized wire gave way to more durable copper wire. In addition, the company modernized its inside plant. Over a sixteen-year period PRTC transformed Puerto Rico's telecommunications infrastructure. Long-distance service between San Juan and Ponce was improved with new cabling that passed through Arecibo and Utuado. Rural public telephone service was introduced in 1940, beginning with the town of Naranjito, located in the central mountain range. Over 19,000 telephones were in service by 1941.

In 1945 PRTC introduced its first fully automatic central office, with a capacity of 8,000 lines, in Santurce, a sector of San Juan. The company also adopted the first of a series of multiyear plans to expand central office capacity, using forecasting tools to determine the number of new subscribers.

14.3 Telephone Service as a Universal Right

Beginning in the 1910s, Puerto Rico's phone system was operated by two entities, the private Porto Rico Telephone Company and the Interior Department, based on the 1907 law. The major cities and long-distance service were in the hands of PRTC. A Communications Authority was formed by a series of laws during 1942–45 to provide service to the cluster of towns in the eastern part of the island that were not within PRTC's franchise. These laws further formalized the dual system and provided a mandate for the government to act as a direct service provider through a subsidized phone company. The laws also transferred the telegraph system from the Interior Department to the Communications Authority.

These laws are the root of the current telecommunications system and reflect its traditions. The Puerto Rican government recognized the need to extend telephone service as a universal right to all of its constituents and was willing to actively undertake the role of service provider to achieve that goal. These themes have played continuously over the subsequent decades as the system was nationalized and then almost privatized.

14.4 A Quantum Leap

In 1952 the U.S. Congress gave Puerto Rico free associated-state status, permitting Puerto Ricans local governance under their own constitution while remaining within the jurisdiction of U.S. federal laws that covered a broad range of areas, including trade, foreign policy, and telecommunications. (The Federal Communications Commission has authority over Puerto Rico's telecommunications, as well as radio and television.) Puerto Ricans elect local officials and have an elected official with nonvoting observer status in Congress.

Attracted by the "American dream" and pushed by the employment crisis generated by the transformation of the island from an agricultural to an industrial economy, the Puerto Ricans began a decade of great migration in the 1950s. Puerto Ricans moved to the United States by the hundreds of thousands. Nearly a third of the population left, primarily for low-wage and farm jobs in the northeastern United States that had been created by the postwar expansion. The demand for long-distance phone service between the new arrivals and their island relatives grew substantially.

The 1950s saw installation of 41,000 lines, increasing the number of lines by some 117 percent, to 76,000, by the end of 1959.

With the rapid expansion of the Puerto Rican economy in the 1960s and early 1970s, phone demand was at an all-time high. There were a number of developments to meet this demand. An underwater cable connecting Puerto Rico with Florida was constructed in 1960, and microwave links were established between San Juan and Ponce in 1961 for intraisland long distance. Direct dial service (DDS) within Puerto Rico and between the island and the United States was introduced in 1968. By 1969 PRTC had over 276,000 subscribers, a 231 percent increase over 1959. Despite its expansion of lines and facilities, the company's efforts did not keep up with demand, and there was a dramatic deterioration in service.

Long waits and down time were common for those seeking new service or reporting a repair problem during the 1950s and 1960s. The island had good phone coverage in urban areas but very low penetration in rural areas. Part of this situation was inherent in a business model based on amortization of capital costs over a highly concentrated urban subscriber population. In Puerto Rico, as everywhere, populations dispersed in the countryside are expensive to reach with poles and copper wiring.

14.5 Nationalization

By 1973 PRTC had U.S.$75 million in gross revenues and over U.S.$6 million in earnings. It also had acquired a notorious reputation. In October 1973 the Public Service Commission slapped it with U.S.$219,000 in fines and refused to grant any rate increases. Additionally, the company was forced to pay damage claims in excess of U.S.$114,000 to customers. In February 1974 PRTC had a backlog of 32,000 orders, with many having waited over two years to get a phone installed. The situation affected expansion of U.S. and Puerto Rican-owned businesses, many of which found themselves without access to basic phone service.

International Telephone and Telegraph was seen as making a handsome profit from its Puerto Rico operations and milking PRTC through equipment purchases from other ITT subsidiaries. For example, ITT Caribbean Manufacturing was accused of selling obsolete equipment at extremely high prices. The company's personnel policies came under assault as well. Some non–Puerto Ricans were paid nearly four times the highest paid Puerto Rican executive, whose salary was U.S.$30,769 in 1973. Mandated cuts by ITT in maintenance and staff training programs were seen as being at the root of PRTC's service problems.

As the situation became more chaotic, editorials called for quick action and leadership. Under Governor Rafael Hernández Colón, the commonwealth government responded with Law 25 creating the Puerto Rico Telephone Authority on May 6, 1974. Through this entity the government purchased PRTC from ITT for U.S.$168 million. International Telephone and Telegraph remained the provider of overseas service.

The Communications Authority, the second largest telephone provider and already under government control, was also put under the Telephone Authority but not merged with PRTC.

Three factors can be seen as contributing to the nationalization of PRTC. These were the company's poor service image among residential, business, and corporate customers, large and small; a new administration aggressively pursuing a public mandate to provide universal service and improve the quality of telecommunications as vital to the island's long-term economic viability; and ITT's involvement in Chile in the early 1970s.

14.5.1 PRTC as a Government Entity

With the takeover of PRTC complete, the government set its sights on turning the company around and winning back the confidence of customers. The first step was to invest in plant and network expansion. In 1974 the government created a U.S.$500 million modernization fund. By the end of 1974 PRTC had over 241,200 telephones in service, equal to 8.3 per 100 inhabitants. The next twenty years saw a complete overhaul of PRTC, creating a major diversified telecommunications entity with state-of-the-art technology.

Independent of ITT, PRTC no longer had to depend on ITT Caribbean Manufacturing as its exclusive supplier. The company now used competitive bids, and major manufacturers, including AT&T and Northern Telecom, competed for contracts.

In 1976, PRTC inaugurated use of electronic switching systems (ESS); the same year AT&T began introducing them in the United States. With ESS, maintenance became more manageable and efficient. The company also set about augmenting its infrastructure, including building an islandwide microwave network. To provide much-needed training to its over 5,500 employees, PRTC also expanded its telecommunications school.

In 1977 the FCC ruled that the long-distance network between Puerto Rico and the United States should be converted from an international to a domestic service. Puerto Rico would thus enjoy long-distance costs comparable to domestic interstate traffic within the United States. The first impact of this ruling was a lowering of rates by nearly 73 percent across the board.

By the end of the 1970s PRTC was positioned for major growth, having overcome the service and expansion limitations it had experienced under ITT ownership. There had been success in three key areas: the growth of infrastructure able to support expansion and use of sophisticated switching systems; development of a trained Puerto Rican managerial and technical force competent in the new technologies and loyal to the PRTC mission; and creation of a diversified purchasing strategy implemented by a staff that had the ability to identify and acquire advanced technologies at competitive prices.

In 1980, after six years as a government entity, PRTC could boast that the number of lines installed had grown from 242,100 to 413,200, a 71 percent increase, and lines per 100 persons had increased from 8.3 to 12.9. To achieve this, PRTC had invested over U.S.$500 million.

Expansion of U.S. corporations and major island-based banks fueled both the need and the demand for advanced communications during the 1980s. This demand was first addressed through expansion of PRTC's microwave network, creating line-of-sight delivery systems in the early 1980s. The company undertook digitalization quite early as well, installing its first Northern Telecom Digital Multiplexing System (DMS) 100 switches in 1981. This allowed a suite of new services, including call waiting, call forwarding, and call conferencing. Also, PRTC installed its first X.25 packet-switching equipment in 1981, although full deployment did not occur until 1989.

Keeping pace with technological advances, PRTC commenced installation of a U.S.$1.2 billion fiber-optic network in 1984, and in 1987 it established an advanced satellite communications system interconnected with its land lines. In 1986 the FCC gave the company permission to begin cellular telephone service based on establishment of five major regional markets.

In 1984, PRTC decided to challenge ITT in the overseas calls market. The Puerto Rico Telephone Authority, the PRTC's holding company, proceeded with the incorporation of a new subsidiary called La Telefónica de Larga Distancia (TLD), which was planned to be the official overseas long-distance provider (U.S. and international calls) of the PRTC. Then AT&T purchased ITT's overseas network in 1987, including its underwater cable system, in 1986. Although AT&T continued ITT's opposition to allowing PRTC into the overseas market, the 1984 breakup of AT&T and the introduction of competition into long-distance service in the United States changed the situation significantly. The argument made by AT&T

was that allowing PRTC to be the local and intraisland long-distance telephone monopoly while a subsidiary (TLD) was a provider of overseas calls was inappropriate. Nonetheless, in 1989 the FCC approved TLD's application. Sprint and MCI were also allowed to provide overseas long distance in 1989. The FCC required PRTC to provide the other three carriers equal access with TLD to its network.

Although AT&T had vehemently objected to PRTC competing against it, the two companies agreed to build a new underwater fiber-optic cable between the island and the United States. The cable, called the Taino-Carib, was completed in 1994.

In September 1989 Puerto Rico was hit by Hurricane Hugo. Although the island suffered major damage, telephone service was minimally disrupted and service outages were quickly restored. Most affected were the rural areas in the northeast served by the Communications Authority. This contrasts with 1928's San Felipe, which brought down the entire system for an extended period.

14.6 Privatization, Almost

On February 20, 1990, Governor Colón, in his last term, proposed the sale of the Porto Rico Telephone Company. The major reasons given were to use the proceeds to better the island's educational system and to improve the island's infrastructure. The government was well aware of the need for continued massive investment in telecommunications to meet the competition that loomed on the horizon. The sentiment of officials facing budgetary shortfalls was that for years to come such investment would drain Puerto Rico's coffers of much-needed capital that could be better used to overhaul the education system.

The sale, estimated to bring in U.S.$2 billion, would include Telefónica Larga Distancia, the Puerto Rico Communications Authority, and the mobile cellular services unit.

The proposal created a tremendous debate and thunderous opposition from consumer groups and unions, which warned of major layoffs. On March 28, 1990, over 3,800 telephone company employees went on a one-day strike. They were joined in a march to the capitol by over 150,000 people, making it one of the largest protest rallies ever in Puerto Rico. The future of the telephone system became a regular news item and talk-show topic.

The sale never happened. In spite of a massive campaign launched by the Colón administration and the support of the business sector, the sale became a symbol of the uncertainty and reluctance of a people unwilling to forgo the benefits of a government-sanctioned monopoly. The major suitor was Bell Atlantic, one of the regional companies created by AT&T's breakup. It was represented by Miguel Lausell, PRTC president during 1985–86 and a highly respected member of one of Puerto Rico's best-known entrepreneurial families. Bell Atlantic retreated from discussions without ever making a formal offer.

The aborted sale of PRTC did not, however, stop the sale of one of the company's parts, its overseas-call subsidiary La Telefónica Larga Distancia (TLD). It was acquired by Telefónica Internacional de España, the Spanish telephone company's global arm, for U.S.$141 million in 1992. The FCC approved the deal only after the commonwealth government convinced the commissioners that all of the infrastructure would remain owned by the Puerto Rico Telephone Authority (PRTA). This was done by the PRTA holding 20 percent of the equity in the new company. With TLD spun off, PRTC merged with the Puerto Rico Communications Corporation on May 5, 1994, finally consolidating all local service under the PRTC umbrella.

14.7 Conclusion

With an array of modern technology, highly skilled engineers and technicians, and a management well versed in the most advanced forms of telecommunications, PRTC is well positioned for future growth and expansion. In 1994 it had over 1.3 million lines in use, for a teledensity of 34.9 lines per 100 inhabitants. With over U.S.$3.1 billion invested in plant and equipment during 1974–94, PRTC had one of the most advanced telecommunications networks in the world, including a 100 percent digital plant with a fiber-optic backbone.

In 1995 PRTC launched ISDN service for both commercial and residential customers, offering integrated delivery of voice, data, and video conferencing at speeds up to 128,000 bits per second. The company is testing video dial tone in an experiment to deliver video services to Puerto Rican households. It also is preparing to offer personal communications service (PCS), the wireless technology expected to replace cellular phones, sometime in the next five years. Deployment of these services, as well as other advanced telecommunications technologies, will continue to make PRTC one of the most advanced telecommunications companies in the Caribbean and Latin America.

15
Chile

JOSÉ RICARDO MELO

Chile pioneered restructuring and privatizing telecommunications in Latin America, and although the motivations and circumstances for this are perhaps unique, the opportunities and problems that have followed are of interest to others less far along the path of liberalization.

The country stretches more than 4,200 kilometers along the Pacific coast of South America and averages only 177 kilometers in width. The Andes form the eastern border, and there are mountains along much of the coast, creating valleys between. It is in the valleys in the middle of the country where most—some 70 percent—of the population of 13.4 million (July 1994 estimate) live, although this is only some 20 percent of the country's 757,000 square kilometers. The three largest cities—Santiago, with 4 million people, Valparaíso and Concepción, each with 700,000—are here. The northern part of the country is one of the driest deserts in the world.

Chile's political and social history since the 1960s, and earlier, has been turbulent, as is discussed later. The legal system is based on the Code of 1857, derived from Spanish law, and subsequent modifications with French and Austrian influence. A Supreme Court can review legislative acts. Since the return to civilian rule after the 1989 elections, presidents serve six-year terms. Members of the lower house of Congress serve four-year terms, eight years in the upper house.

The economy historically was very dependent on copper, and the mineral remains the principal foreign-exchange earner, but there has been significant growth and diversification. Chileans in general are prosperous, especially by Latin American standards; national product per capita on a purchasing-power basis was estimated at U.S.$7,000 for 1993. The country is considered well along the road to developed status, although poverty and income disparity are concerns.

15.1 Early Development

By the mid-nineteenth century Chile was a nation well established in terms of political institutions. The post-colonial government, established in the 1820s, had been stabilized by the 1830s with a constitution that would last a century. The centralist regime, with a strong executive branch, organized the state at an early stage. The population was about 1 million in 1835 and 1.44 million in 1854. Although mining was already important, agriculture was the core of the economy and was owned by established families who provided political support to the government. The intellectual class was strongly influenced by European thinking, especially from Britain and France. The 1840s saw something of a cultural revolution as new political theories—as well as new ideas in the arts, sciences, and technological development—flowed in from Europe.

15.1.1 The Telegraph to 1930

Telegraph service between the two most important cities, Santiago and Valparaíso, was started on April 23, 1851, by a private company under a license awarded by the government. Although its first response had been licensing private parties, the telegraph's success drove the government to participate in, and ultimately seek to monopolize, the service. This followed the pattern of European countries, especially France.

Thus, in 1854 the government started building a line south from Santiago to Talca, the most productive agricultural region of the country. This service started in 1857. In 1865 service was extended north of Santiago, reaching La Serena, 500 kilometers away; in 1866 the network had 2,000 kilometers and stretched from Caldera and Copiapó on the north to Lota on the south.

In 1857 the first law regarding telegraphy was enacted, covering tariffs. Others followed, including the 1866 Rules and Regulations of State Telegraphs.

Several private companies, as well as the state railroad, offered limited services. These included Telégrafo Eléctrico Americano, which extended from Santiago to Casablanca and San Antonio, about 100 kilometers away. International service began when the Compañía del Telégrafo Trasandino installed an underground cable through the Andes in 1872, uniting Chile and Argentina. In 1875 the service was extended to the United States and Europe via Brazil. The same year, the West Coast of America Telegraph Company Ltd. joined Valparaíso with Callao, the principal port of Peru, with a submarine cable. At the end of the century, Central and South American Telegraph used a submarine cable to link the United States to Lima and Valparaíso. It connected with Telégrafo Trasandino's line to Argentina.

The state telegraph company also continued to extend its reach. The 1879–84 war with Peru and Bolivia led to lines being extended to Antofagasta, and later to Iquique, Arica (the country's northernmost town), and into the Peruvian towns of Tacna and Tarata, which were the battleground. On the south, a submarine cable was installed to Chiloé island. In 1904 a new underground cable was pushed through the Andes. These and other expansions and upgrading in the late nineteenth and early twentieth centuries, despite their high investment and maintenance costs, were undertaken because the country was experiencing rapid economic development. But soon the service was in a crisis.

Tariffs were determined more by political criteria than by financial ones, and for several decades service depended on government subsidies. Receipts were insufficient to maintain the service level attained earlier, as renovations (such as changing from iron to copper wire) and plant improvements were costly for a shrinking state budget.

In 1928 licenses were awarded to the Chilean Society of Transradio and the International Radio Company (CIRSA) to provide radiocommunication services and communications with the exterior using the recently discovered phenomenon of ionospheric propagation.

15.1.2 The Telephone to 1930

In 1880 Thomas Alva Edison permitted a U.S. citizen resident in Valparaíso to utilize the patents on telephones, and later that year he was named Edison's representative in Chile. After watching a demonstration, the president of Chile signed a decree allowing a telephone license to the Compañía de Teléfonos de Edison on April 26, 1880.

In 1881, 250 telephones were in service. New capital was needed to develop the company, which was sought in the United Sates after a failed attempt in Europe. The company name was changed in 1884 to the West Coast Telephone Company, which operated until 1889. During those eight years, the company extended operations, offering local service in Santiago, Valparaíso, Concepción, and San Antonio (on the coast near Santiago). It also experimented with long-distance telephony between Santiago and San Fernando (100 kilometers away) using the state railroads' telegraph lines.

Valdivia National Telephone was formed in 1893. Valdivia, 800 kilometers south of Santiago, was heavily colonized by Germans in the second half of the nineteenth century. The government recognized the establishment of the company in 1894 when it opened with fifty-five telephones.

West Coast was acquired by Chile Telephone Company in 1889. This new company started activities with 2,907 telephones (1,804 in Santiago, 466 in Valparaíso, and 637 in other localities). The population of Chile was 2.5 million at the time.

Over the next thirty years, various small telephone companies using private capital were started to offer local services in various areas, including in and around the many important mining (nitrate and copper) and agricultural (wheat, timber, and stock breeding) centers. Most of these ultimately were absorbed by Chile Telephone, which also expanded by introducing service in new areas. By 1927 service, provided primarily by Chile Telephone, existed in most cities from Arica (the north of Chile) to Puerto Montt (1,000 kilometers south of Santiago). The company had 26,205 telephones in service, primarily in the central region. However, the company had not established a network. Interurban communications continued to be very difficult even between two cities managed by the same company. The exception was between Santiago and Valparaíso.

Unlike telegraphy, telephony received little government attention other than the granting of the necessary licenses. In 1925 the General Electric Services Law was passed, creating General Electric Services Management to oversee the development of electricity. The law also established the general principles for government concessions, establishing that electrical and telecommunications services "demanded significant attention of the public authorities." It thus provided the legal basis for government regulation, as well as for direct government participation through private businesses. The system lasted until 1982, when the first general law for telecommunications was passed.

In 1927 the International Telephone and Telegraph Corporation (ITT) acquired the stock of Chile Telephone. A telecom equipment maker as well as service provider, ITT was acquiring telecom companies throughout Latin America. Other equipment manufacturers were following similar strategies around the world, but ITT was the only significant player in Chile.

Between 1927 and 1930, turbulent years in Chilean political and economic history, ITT contemplated how to organize the company and run its business in Chile. The goal was to find the best approach to assure stability and, of course, profitability. In 1930 a special agreement was signed with the government. The agreement was formally enacted as a law, something absolutely exceptional compared to other operators and economic sectors.

15.2 Disruption and Change

World War I disrupted the country's export markets and deprived it of many imports. As a consequence of this, and then of the worldwide economic crisis, the belief that the government was responsible for the promotion of development of basic infrastructure in all sectors began to spread and develop as a new political agenda. This infrastructure had to be capable of creating the necessary conditions for industrialization sufficient to replace many imports.

In 1925 President Arturo Alessandri had pushed through a new constitution. It provided for direct election of the president, as well as separation of church and state. The resulting political crisis carried into the next decade. Thus, the 1930s began badly. Economic and political problems were having serious effects on public order, on the development of the country, and on the living conditions of the population, which was about 4.3 million in 1930.

In order to achieve the new political agenda, the Chilean government created a special ministry-level institution in 1939, Corporación de Fomento de la Producción (CORFO, or Increased Production Corporation). Along with this institution, several other government businesses established themselves as independent corporate entities. They had government capital but a notable independence when it came to operations. One of the more prominent was the National Electrical Company SA, created in 1944, which successfully developed an electrification plan employed by the entire country. This company later served as a reference and an institutional model in telecommunications.

15.2.1 The Telegraph, 1930–1960

Even before 1930, the state-owned Telégrafo del Estado had made the government aware of the need to renovate and modernize. The government, however, was unwilling to commit much in the way of financial resources to telegraphy, nor was it willing to allow tariffs to be high enough for the service to be self-financing. Despite these limitations, the number of telegrams continued to grow.

Several private companies gained importance. One of these was Trans Radio Chilena—Compañía de Radiotelegrafía Ltda (forerunner of VTR Telecommunications)—which was founded in 1926 as a joint venture of several foreign companies including RCA and Siemens. It began providing international telegraph service in 1928 and added international telephone circuits in 1941. Compañía del Telégrafo Comercial established a physical network from Los Andes to Puerto Montt. In 1951 it had 68 offices and dispatched 627,000 telegrams; Telégrafo del Estado had 497 offices that dispatched 6.3 million telegrams.

Use of the telegraph started to decline in the 1950s. Although it continued to be important in remote rural areas, it was being replaced by telex. In 1954 5,845,000 public telegraph messages were sent; in 1969, the number was 4,887,000. By comparison, 954,000 minutes of domestic telex and 315,000 minutes of international telex were transmitted in 1969.

In 1959 a law declared that domestic public telegraph service would be subject to government monopoly, operated by Telégrafo del Estado. However, the government permitted existing companies to continue operating until the end of their concession periods. The government applied the same principle in a new law for postal and telegraph services, promulgated in 1960. This law provided that telegraph and telex services within national territory would be centralized under government monopoly, but private businesses could compete with Telégrafo del Estado in international telegraph traffic.

15.2.2 The CTC Concession

In the early 1930s it was believed that Chile's development should be based on government action. Nonetheless, it was during this time that a private, mostly foreign-owned enterprise, Compañía de Teléfonos de Chile (CTC), rapidly became one of the most important companies in the sector, and it remains so to this day. Indeed, it has been the central pivot around which Chile's subsequent telecom history has revolved.

A subsidiary of ITT and successor to the Chile Telephone Company, CTC executed a contract with the Chilean government, promulgated on January 23, 1930, by Law 4,791, that provided radically different terms than those usually applied to concessions for telecommunications companies. At the time, CTC provided service to 37,687 telephones.

In essence, this statutory contract granted a concession for fifty years, subject to renewal every thirty years thereafter. Initially the entire country was covered, but the concession did not stipulate an obligation to provide services in any particular area. The company also had no obligation to interconnect with other concessionaires. Its only obligation was a general one: to "provide the public with a modern and efficient system" based on available technology. Moreover, CTC was permitted to keep its own accounting, only "subject to the systems established by the most advanced telephone companies."

The CTC management also was allowed to set its own tariffs. However, these required approval by two of the three government-selected members of the company's board of directors. This system was structured to provide a return of 10 percent on net investment, plus 2 percent more for unspecified "reserves." The amount of net investment was to be ascertained by accountants and valued in gold on a monthly basis. This was to protect the company from inflation. Disputes could be taken to the Supreme Court, which had the power to authorize termination of the concession, but in that case the government was obligated to acquire the company for its estimated value in gold according to the financial accounting of CTC.

In the mid-1950s the Compañía Nacional de Teléfonos de Valdivia was the second largest telco. It served approximately 40,000 square kilometers from Loncoche to Puerto Montt, but (in 1954) had only 5,246 lines, of which 47 percent were automatic. It handled 6.2 million local calls annually, and 470,000 interurban calls. By comparison, CTC had 97,475 lines in service (with 1.45 telephones per line), 68 percent on automatic exchanges. In 1953 it handled 371 million local and 23 million interurban calls.

15.3 DFL 4 of 1959

The legislative framework was completely revamped by DFL 4 on July 24, 1959. This was similar to the General Electric Services Law, but it also covered telecommunications. It confirmed the principle of granting licenses to establish, operate, and exploit public and private telecom services. It also provided that there would be no monopolies, except for the national telegraph service. Public service concessions could run for thirty to ninety years, and the public telephone service concession zones could include obligatory areas. Concessionaires would be required to pay the government an initial, and then an annual, tax for the opening and operating of their systems, and they had to interconnect with each other.

As for tariffs, they were to be set to provide an annual 10 percent return on fixed assets, but a company could solicit a tariff adjustment before the annual report was due if operating costs increased significantly over 10 percent. The accounting methods used had to comply with regulatory standards. In January 1970 long-distance tariffs were set using seventy-five distance bands. By July 1972 this had been reduced to thirty-five, and to sixteen by July 1973.

Finally, the General Directorate of Electric, Gas, and Telecommunication Services, answerable only to the Interior Ministry, was formally established to supervise and inspect companies. This group performed tariff analysis and represented Chile in international organizations, among other duties.

However, CTC continued to manage itself pursuant to its 1930 enabling statute. This statute had been generally upheld, but it was affected by judicial interpretation during the 1940s in connection with disputes over its compatibility with other laws. The 1959 law could have modified the precepts of the 1930 statute but did not do so. This meant that CTC maintained various privileges and that the government still expected the telephone situation to be resolved through this private company.

The 1960s was a time when the country tried to establish a development strategy that would permit greater access to service. Even the middle class had trouble getting a phone, as investment in expanding service was lower than needed to keep up with demand. Many people became convinced that the government had to intervene directly in businesses in various sectors, particularly those related to infrastructure. With this political agenda, successive governments created and operated various kinds of businesses. In the case of telegraphy, the government kept the same service that had been running for a long time but allowed competition from private enterprise, particularly in the lucrative field of international communications.

In the more sensitive case of telephones, national opinion changed gradually. As a newly created private company, CTC had successfully obtained a very favorable contract in the 1930s. For various reasons it never managed to satisfy the demands of the government or of consumers, which created growing tension. The government gradually made known that it thought telephony management also required intervention. This initiative resulted in the creation of a new and powerful company called ENTel and in a partnership between the government and the shareholders of CTC.

15.3.1 ENTel

In 1960 a major earthquake in central Chile made the government realize the scarcity and poor quality of long-distance communications. In fact, the sole link in good working condition was the one between Santiago and Valparaíso. In 1963 the Interior Ministry solicited CORFO to put a long-distance plan into effect. In June 1964, in order to do so, CORFO agreed to create a subsidiary called Empresa Nacional de Telecomunicaciones S.A. (ENTel), which was authorized by a decree of December 1964. The new subsidiary was financed mostly with government funds.

Using a microwave system, ENTel quickly built a trunk network throughout the country. In 1967 the Santiago-Concepción section was inaugurated. It was built with equipment purchased by CTC for this route but transferred to ENTel after government intervention. By 1971 the system in the north, and the extension of the southern system to Puerto Montt, were completed.

In 1965 ENTel applied to become part of Intelsat. By 1968 the first ground station for communications via satellite from South America had been established.

With the creation of ENTel and the 1967 agreement with CTC on the microwave trunk, it was clear that the government had fundamentally changed its policy regarding the regulation and management of telecommunications. The government was no longer confining itself to regulation but was becoming an owner-manager and operator.

15.4 The Rise of the Government

As the 1960s ended, Chile was facing a difficult political crisis that brought radical changes in the patterns of social and economic development. There wasn't a sector of national life left unaffected.

During the presidency of Eduardo Frei Montavala (1964–70) the government began to buy the U.S. copper companies operating in Chile and to expropriate land, which had been concentrated in the hands of a small number of holders, for redistribution. By the end of the 1960s the government had become the principal economic actor, particularly in the sectors responsible for infrastructure.

Despite all the efforts to promote local production and instigate self-sufficient development through import-substitution policies, increased demand outpaced solutions. In the face of the increased activity by the government, private businesses started acting defensively, which reduced their access and willingness to become involved in projects they otherwise would have participated in. The political situation became increasingly radical.

The 1970 presidential election offered a choice between the relatively conservative Frei and an avowed Marxist, Salvador Allende. Allende narrowly won with a plurality. During the three years of his regime, large segments of the government and of the opposition adopted radical viewpoints, as each side became more intent on destroying the other than on promoting its own beliefs. Several foreign businesses with investments in Chile supported those opposed to the government. One of the businesses anxious about its investments was ITT. The government accused ITT of contributing to destabilization and sedition. Numerous private businesses were nationalized, including basic services like telecommunications, but not CTC.

15.4.1 Taking Control

The 1967 contract with ITT seemed more a truce in the dispute over the control of the sector than an agreement. Those advocating nationalization of foreign businesses and basic service companies were obviously not pleased with it. Probably ITT was also dissatisfied, even more so after a Marxist government took power.

In September 1971, the Allende government accused CTC of serious technical problems in its operation of telephone services, whereupon the Electric, Gas, and Telecommunications Services Directorate took over administration of the company. The government also compelled the owners of Teléfonos de Valdivia (which had about 12,000 lines) and Teléfonos de Coyhaique (with only 500 lines) to sell participation rights, which were then purchased by CORFO. Through ENTel, CORFO already controlled long-distance service, as well as some local service. In Arica, the service provider, Empresa Telefónica Municipal with 4,000 lines, was already indirectly under government control.

The Allende government tried to present a political agenda for the sector that would achieve several goals. These included integrating existing interurban and international networks (excluding military ones); forming independent government businesses for the operation of the sector; centralizing sectorial planning in CORFO; and creating a domestic equipment-manufacturing industry. However, these intentions never went into practice. Centralizing planning at CORFO became enormously complicated because the idea was to make it responsible for coordinating all strategic sectors. This was too ambitious. In spite of these setbacks, CORFO made some progress, such as concluding a contract for new equipment for CTC, signed with SESA-España, another ITT company, in 1972.

In February 1973, to complete the transfer of control from CTC to the government, the 1930 enabling statute was formally revoked and all contracts affiliated with it were terminated. The governing statute became DFL 4 of 1959.

15.4.2 Promoting a Domestic Equipment Industry

Before the 1970s, local manufacturing of telecom equipment had been all but nonexistent. A subsidiary of ITT, Standard Electric, had a plant in Santiago that provided some items to CTC. In 1971 CORFO created a subsidiary, Empresa Eletrónica Nacional (ELECNA), that built a semiconductor plant in Arica. The objective was to supply both the national and Andean regional markets. Shortly after it was completed a radiocommunications equipment factory was built with the same objectives.

However, these expectations were frustrated; the factories were not completely developed because demand for their output was not as large or sustained as had been projected initially. When CTC was nationalized, Standard Electric lost its assured contracts and ITT was no longer the sole equipment provider for CTC. In the face of rapid technological changes and uncertain markets, Standard did not have the resources to upgrade its plant. Because of this, the company remained primarily a commercial representative. The plant was acquired by Alcatel when ITT exited the telecom equipment business. The 1973 military coup affected business adversely, as it contributed to the distancing of Chile from it neighbors, causing those markets to be lost.

During the 1980s, when digitalization and other technological innovations swept telecommunications, Chile had essentially no national equipment manufacturing. Custom rates were low, and no effort was made to protect any emerging domestic companies. Thus, equipment was almost entirely imported.

15.5 The Tide Turns Again

The 1973 coup that installed Augusto Pinochet Ugarte as president completely changed the telecommunications situation. The new regime sought to reorder government involvement in businesses and the economic system in general. State-run businesses faced profound restructuring and were seriously affected by the loss of qualified personnel, and the management staff allied with the previous government. Moreover, in 1975 the government implemented a painful contractionary policy that drastically reduced demand in many sectors.

Once the severest years of the crisis had passed, the Pinochet government had to develop a policy to deal with the large number of state-owned businesses. The government had chosen open-market policies but had not resolved the ownership issue. In 1974 in the Declaration of Government Principles (Declaración de Principios del Gobierno) it was proclaimed that there should not be a government business where there is private business interest.

A large number of small government businesses were privatized quickly, but it was not until 1977 that privatization was seen as a solution for larger businesses in strategic sectors, including public utilities. This conclusion was reached by many economic officials in the government, but privatizing utilities was opposed by many in the military and by almost all of the political opposition. In the field of telecommunications, the differences and problems took several years to resolve.

15.5.1 Regulation and Policy, 1973–1977

With a military junta in charge of the government, telecommunications became beholden to the National Defense Ministry. The ministry worked with the advice of the Telecommunications Management Directorate on matters concerning tariff, technical, legal, and concession regulations. While CORFO continued to hold the government's interest in the companies, the directorate had administrative control of the companies. In 1974 the government decided to resolve the situation regarding CTC through expropriation of ITT's 80 percent interest, under Law 801. The purchase took place the same year, with the shares going to CORFO.

The government decreed some important changes to improve the status of companies and make the public sector more efficient. Thus, in 1974 service to the public sector was suspended if bills were not paid, and in 1975 government-owned companies had to charge delinquent customers 150 percent of the current interest rate for a delay in settling an outstanding bill.

Although DFL 4 of 1959 and CTC's enabling statute provided for a 10 percent return on fixed assets, inflation had been outpacing rate increases since the mid-1960s, so the statutory return had not been earned. The company had been able to offset this problem somewhat by systematically overestimating its fixed assets. After 1973 the theory was that tariffs should be based on costs, but very little was known about the structure and level of CTC's costs. Another problem with this approach was that its application took an inordinate amount of time. However, from 1975, lower inflation and more frequent tariff adjustments allowed the sector to lose less ground.

The government kept investment at such a low level that it was not possible to catch up with demand—there had been a long waiting list for some time. In some cases, such as ENTel, companies used credit with providers or multinational companies, but companies without that option were especially hard hit by the 1975 economic contraction.

During the 1970s the two main telcos, CTC and ENTel, were completely under government control—and unable to overcome the distance between them. Their origins were too different; their technical and economic practices came from very different sources. The companies had frequently attacked and long mistrusted each other. To merge under a single owner would not be easy.

Both companies wanted to control the long-distance network because of the greater profit margin, as well as the ambition to be the leader in Chilean telecommunications. To achieve this end, ENTel counted on ownership of most of the long-distance transmission networks, whereas CTC counted on the fact that the structure of this network required interconnection. Interconnection was CTC's area of expertise and where investment would be cheaper if it were combined with local exchanges. This conflict continued into the 1980s.

15.5.2 SUBtel

In 1977 the group in charge of regulating the telecommunications sector was restructured as an undersecretariat (Subsecretaría de Telecomunicaciones, or SUBtel) within the Transportation and Telecommunication Ministry.

This new regulator, SUBtel, was made responsible for several things. These included preparing policy proposals and coordinating telecommunications in the country; setting technical standards and overseeing their implementation; formulating and updating the principal technical plans; administering the spectrum; representing the country in international organizations and agreements; processing applications for concessions and licenses; and applying administrative sanctions. However, the sector continued to be formally controlled by DFL 4 of 1959, which had not been revoked. Even though the creation of SUBtel was significant progress, the substance of DFL 4 left the situation confused, as the spirit of the regulatory system it involved was quite different than that animating SUBtel.

In some ways, regulation had been designed so that technical aspects were supervised by SUBtel and economic aspects by the antimonopoly tribunals created in 1973. Consequently, regulation resided partly in the administrative authority of the executive power and partly in the judicial power. This setup made proceedings exceedingly slow, ambiguous, and unpredictable.

15.5.3 Telephone Service, 1977–1990

For a long time, CTC has supplied basic telephone service to over 90 percent of the population. A municipal company also provided service until 1977, when it was incorporated into CTC. Compañía Nacional de Teléfonos (CNTV) and Compañía de Teléfonos de Coyhaique (CTCoy) have operated in Regions X and XI where CTC has no license to operate. (Chile is divided into thirteen regions, which, while they have names, are commonly referred to by numbers, except for the metropolitan Santiago region. Regions X and XI are in the extreme south of the country.) In December 1975, CTC had 434,000 telephones in service; CNTV, 14,334; Arica, 5,272; and CTCoy, 907. In 1977 total CTC telephones in service had increased to only 466,000, and growth at the other companies had been practically nil. As ever, a backlog of people wanting service persisted. In 1977 the waiting list equaled 46 percent of installed phones, and it normally took years to get a line. Many people did not even bother to register, others used friends or political influence. Still, and even though it was a time of economic crisis in the country, the number of lines installed and in service increased.

Local and long-distance calling also continued to increase, particularly after introduction by CTC of direct distance dialing (DDD) at reduced rates in 1980. As with the old manual service, the new DDD service was provided jointly by ENTel and the local telcos. By 1989 more than 70 percent of long-distance calls were DDD.

15.5.4 Mobile and Cellular Service

In 1981 the government granted mobile and cellular telephone concessions to Telefonía Móvil CIDCOM, a private company of local and North American investors. Using International Mobile Tracking System (IMTS) technology, the company installed and started operating mobile systems that same year in Santiago, Valparaíso, and Concepción (the three largest cities). Shortly thereafter, service was extended to include the highway between Santiago and Valparaíso, and from Santiago 80 kilometers south to Rancagua.

In order to exploit the high-power coverage, CIDCOM offered fixed wireless service (private and pay phones) in rural areas within its service areas that wireline networks wouldn't reach.

In 1988 CTC decided to establish a cellular system in Santiago and Valparaíso, and it went into operation in early 1989. A few months later CIDCOM established its own cellular service in this area. By the end of 1991 there were over 25,000 subscribers on the two systems. Most large cities in Chile obtained cellular service in 1991 when two other companies began operations. At the end of 1994 there were some 120,000 cellular phones in the country.

15.6 The Economic and Political Context, 1977–1993

In 1977 the Pinochet government was past the phase of political and institutional self-affirmation and was ready to try to redesign government and policy. From the beginning, the new government had been favorably disposed to an economy that gave a fundamental role to open markets and competition. This produced reactions from political and social groups that felt their well-being was threatened; these protests were immediately stifled.

A fall in the price of copper (Chile's principal export) combined with rising oil prices and interest rates during 1979–81 exacerbated imbalances in the economy. In addition, there had been an enormous increase in external debt. The government decided to devalue the currency in June 1982 and to introduce a strong contraction in expenditures. The ensuing severe recession of 1982–83 drastically reduced per capita gross domestic product and many companies went bankrupt. To avoid a collapse of the nation's financial system, the government guaranteed private foreign debt and assumed the private banks' bad debts.

In the following years the economy recovered, and by 1987 it had regained its 1981 level. But political opposition also grew stronger. By 1988 the government made public its desire to extend its leadership but was defeated in a plebiscite. This led to elections in December 1989.

Paticio Aylwin (Christian Democratic Party, PDC) was elected president with a majority of the vote cast, and the PDC formed a coalition in Congress. The new government took office in March 1990. Although while in opposition the PDC and its allies had opposed many of the previous regime's economic policies, including privatization, they have basically continued almost all of them—but have placed more emphasis on social issues. In 1993 Eduardo Frei Ruiz-Tagle, also a PDC member, was elected president.

15.6.1 National Telecommunications Policy

Overall, during 1967–77 the telecommunications sector was particularly frustrated. Three different political regimes tried their formulas on the sector and none was satisfactory, although the approaches of 1967–70 and 1970–73 can be considered unconsummated because external factors interrupted them. Telephone demand increased beyond supply and the quality of basic services deteriorated on several occasions. A number of problems appeared, including the adequacy of tariffs and deferral of maintenance. A profound renewal would be needed to solve these problems.

The 1977 law creating SUBtel was a significant step. However, it was not enough to ensure development of the sector. In 1978 the general principles for development were formally laid out through the issuing of a national telecommunications policy. In general terms, the government wanted a competitive system with strong participation by the private sector. Interconnection was obligatory so as to allow for an integrated system, possibly of many companies. As to the electronic and telecom equipment industries, the policy was succinct, announcing only security standards for the people who used the equipment. Tariffs were not mentioned at all.

Among the characteristics of the Chilean telecommunications regulatory system were that it barred legal monopolies or exclusivity periods and it did not require payments from concession holders, except for a modest amount for spectrum usage. In principle, any license requested would be granted if it complied with the technical standards. Where there were limitations, such as spectrum availability, the law used the date of the request for a license. A holder could transfer a license for a profit.

Two new private telephone companies—Compañía Telefónica Manquehue (CTM) and Compañía de Teléfonos (CMET)—obtained licenses for local service in 1981. To allow these companies to develop, the government stopped new CTC investment in their service areas, which were high-income sections of Santiago where lack of supply had brought willingness to pay very high sums for a telephone line. This paved the way for operations with high initial profits.

In 1977 a complaint was filed demanding that CTC be compelled to modify Article 17 of its General Regulation, which said that only equipment managed by the company could be connected to its network. The Comisión Preventiva, a government antimonopoly tribunal, found for the complainant. This promoted growth of a market for equipment that previously had been controlled exclusively by CTC. Users could now buy or lease equipment from companies other than CTC.

In 1979 CTC was required to accept an open market in telephone lines with only technical restrictions. Until then, CTC had had the exclusive right of connection for each subscriber, who could not sell or sublet a line. This system had been severely criticized because many felt CTC administered a shortage it had created for its own benefit. The result was an increase in economic efficiency in the assignment of scarce telephone lines. An active market for lines was established in areas where there were significant shortages.

15.6.2 The General Telecommunications Law of 1982

In 1982 the General Telecommunications Law was promulgated, providing a formal legal basis for the 1978 policy principles and effectively repealing DFL 4 of 1959. This document, with a few amendments, continues to be the main judicial basis for telecommunications in Chile. Also in 1982, the law giving the government a monopoly on domestic telegraph and telex service was repealed.

The new law provided for the classification of service: public, private or limited, broadcasting, amateur radio, and intermediate services (added later). It also established procedures for obtaining licenses and concessions and specified there would be no exclusive concessions; operators would have to meet a set of technical standards, including allowing interconnection between systems.

Again, mention of tariffs was minimal, establishing only the principle of free tariff setting and indicating as exceptions cases in which "market conditions or regulations were insufficient to insure free competition." In these instances, the government would set the tariffs for the respective services.

There were areas the law did not deal with clearly. One was the nature of the act of granting a concession. There had been a debate as to whether it was necessary to maintain a government concession-granting system or whether it could be replaced by a system of registered areas of operation. Finally, the concession system was maintained, although some people thought the government might use this power to raise unjustified barriers to entry.

Network interconnection between companies was another point of legal dispute. The procedures the National Telecommunications Policy had established as obligatory were not sufficiently detailed in regarding how costs should be assigned. From the start in 1981 this situation provoked ongoing conflicts between the new telephone companies and CTC that ultimately were taken to court. This was the first time a conflict had not been solved within the sector's regulatory framework.

It was generally agreed that monopoly services should have rates set at costs. A restructuring of tariffs gradually occurred as cost studies were made. Ongoing inflation meant rates were rising steadily in nominal terms; rebalancing was done by adjusting the relative increases. Thus, long-distance rates were increased less than local service tariffs, and commercial services received smaller increases than residential services. Unexpectedly, consumers accepted these modifications without much protest.

15.6.3 CTC and ENTel in Government Hands

Although there was no explicit legal requirement to do so, until the 1970s the government granted new concessions only to CTC and ENTel. There were a few private companies, such as CNTV, operating under prior concessions.

In 1982 separate managements were designated for each company, but both depended on a specially created office in CORFO called Holding de Telecomunicaciones CTC-ENTel. It was responsible for "defining and orienting the coordinated development of government companies." The same year, the government considered whether to merge the two companies, and yet another commission was formed to "study telecommunications policy, the necessary modifications that needed to be introduced, and to establish the permanent coordinating standards required for the organization of the sector." This organization also did not succeed in functioning: the differences and tensions between the companies were too strong.

In 1984, CORFO tried to coordinate the activities of both companies by assigning clearly separated types of services in specific areas to each. These efforts were challenged and opposed by various parties, among them the private shareholders of CTC. In October 1987 the Anti-monopoly Commission ruled CORFO could not do this.

Then SUBtel issued a technical developing plan in 1984 suggesting CTC install interurban centers at the primary level (as defined by the ITU), while ENTel could do it at the secondary and tertiary levels. Although this seemed appropriate for a time, eventually it became insufficient because there was no way to guarantee an adequate distribution of traffic (and income) in the interurban network.

From 1985 both companies realized how difficult it was to establish a stable long-term development plan when it was clear they would soon be privatized, and until then the government would not allow additional debt. Long-term decisions would necessarily need the new owners' approval. As a result, CTC staff proposed a plan with limited objectives. This so-called Link Plan involved adding 117,000 digital lines; the winning bidders were NEC, Telrad (an Israeli company), and Ericsson.

15.6.4 Modifications

A 1985 amendment to the 1982 law was intended to clarify the old problem of the obligation to grant concessions if there were no technical objections, but the problem persisted. Another amendment introduced an "intermediate services" category. This referred to those providing services to other telecom companies but not the public. It specifically singled out long-distance carriers that offered services to telcos and others.

The most innovative legislation came in 1987. In the text of 1987 DFL 1, several important tariff and financing changes were introduced. Users were told that they had to pay periodically for the right to use the spectrum. Probably the most important section was devoted to tariffs. A detailed system was developed in the law for determining how the regulated services would be identified and their rates set; other services would have rates set by the market. Tariffs would be determined for each service, each operator, and each geographic zone. The rates would be for five-year terms, including a formula indexing them to variations in costs. Costs were those for a hypothetical efficient company, which would be allowed to earn a specified return on invested capital. International services were excepted, as their tariffs were fixed differently, taking into account the tariffs of the correspondents.

Telephone companies were obliged to provide services to any potential subscriber in urban areas within two years of the request for service. There was a transition period of ten years before this was to be completely enforced. Telephone companies could require a refundable fee equal to the average cost of installing an additional line. Issuing company stock to the subscriber could be used to satisfy the requirement of the fee being refundable.

The 1987 amendment solved the tariff problem very practically by setting tariffs for public telephone service, including ENTel's long-distance services. The policy went into effect on January 10, 1989. During the initial five-year term it was expected that cross-subsidies between services would be eliminated. The obligation to provide basic service in urban areas gave the companies incentive to push their development plans to preempt competition in their concession area.

Various impediments kept companies from collecting the refundable fee the law had granted them. These consisted of legal obstacles and difficulty establishing values for the stock. Eventually the process was abandoned. In any case, privatization had opened new financing resources to the companies.

15.7 Privatization

The original government plan emphasized liberalization and privatization. Liberalization meant promoting market growth and facilitating entry of companies bringing new, private capital. But the prospect of additional capital did not move the government to start selling existing small and medium companies to bidding until 1982, and large companies until 1986.

Several things were done to pave the way for privatization. Under the military government, Decree-Law 600 established attractive conditions for foreign investment with guarantees regarding remitting profits and capital. Importantly, Chilean foreign debt could be used at face value to buy companies being privatized. Because such debt generally sold at a discount, this was a substantial benefit for investors. In addition, the government used several methods to promote "capitalismo popular"—the participation of workers in privatization. One of these was subsidized credit to workers to acquire interests in the government companies where they were employed, and even in others. A mechanism frequently drawn on was the advancing of retirement or severance pay to employees for the acquisition of shares.

15.7.1 Beginning the Process

In 1982, CORFO decided to sell its interests in the two regional telephone companies it controlled: Compañía Nacional de Teléfonos (CNT; later renamed Telefónica del Sur), operating in region X; and Compañía de Teléfonos de Coyhaique (CTCoy), operating in region XI. The country's long-established international telex operator, VTR Telecommunications, acquired the government's interests in both companies in public bidding. Five foreign telecom companies owned VTR.

15.7.2 Selling CTC

In the early 1980s the government studied dividing CTC into regional companies, but potential investors were not interested in pieces, and there was also the matter of existing private shareholders, who still held 8 percent of CTC. To determine a selling price, the government had several estimates done valuing the company on the basis of its growth potential. The method was similar to the one defined in DFL 1 in 1987 for estimating a value for shares that consumers were to have been required to buy to get a new phone line.

The first sale of CTC shares was during April and May 1985. This sale placed just 0.04 percent of CTC shares. It was more a symbolic step to test the mechanism for a significant transfer. Additional stock was sold during 1986 and 1987 and, by the end of 1995, 25 percent of CTC shares were in private hands.

In August 1987 CORFO invited international bidding for 30 percent of CTC, with the opportunity to acquire an additional 15 percent. Australian investor Alan Bond, through Corporación Bond, bid slightly higher (U.S.$118 million) than Telefónica de España, but because of administrative objections by the General Comptroller's Office, the offer had to be rejected. However, CORFO sold shares to Corporación Bond in January 1988 on Bond's terms. This gave Corporación Bond 50.13 percent of the company's shares, but the company's statute permitted any one shareholder to hold only a maximum of 45 percent. In October, Bond agreed to reduce its holdings within four years and to vote no more than 45 percent of the total shares.

Then, in January 1989, Bond agreed to sell its entire participation in CTC to Telefónica Internacional de España for U.S.$392 million. Control was transferred three months later. By July, CTC was trading a new issue of nonvoting shares on the New York Stock Exchange as an American Depositary Receipt (ADR). In 1990 CORFO continued to sell shares, reducing its holdings from 2.9 percent at the beginning of the year to less than 0.1 percent by December, which concluded the process of privatizing CTC.

15.7.3 Selling ENTel

The privatization of ENTel was handled differently; a controlling interest was not sold and there was no issue of new shares. In November 1985 CORFO, which then held 99.97 percent of ENTel, agreed to sell 30 percent of the company within five years. This was done to meet the requirements of Law 3500, which reformed the pension system by making it private. The new private pension funds had the ability to buy ENTel shares if they were available.

During 1986 CORFO reduced its interest by the full 30 percent. The buyers were mostly pension funds, no one of which could hold more than 5 percent of ENTel's shares. A further 3 percent was sold during 1987, and CORFO reduced its holdings substantially during 1989, so that by the end of the year it held just 1.11 percent. Two large buyers were Telefónica de España and a local subsidiary of Banco Santander, a Spanish commercial bank. Each held 10 percent, and they informed the authorities they intended to coordinate their holdings. In the last months of the military government, some of CORFO's holdings were transferred to the military, so at the end of 1989 it had a 10 percent interest. In 1990 the military sold its shares to Telefónica de España, and the coordination agreement with Banco Santander was ended.

15.8 The New Era, 1988–

By the end of 1990 the government had no significant telecommunications company properties except for Televisión Nacional de Chile (TVN), which was the national television channel. It owned several ground links, as well as satellite and broadcasting systems employed for its exclusive use as a means of mass communication.

In 1988, soon after Corporación Bond took control, CTC announced plans for several new businesses, including cellular telephones and long-distance transmission (not only exchanges). Later ENTel indicated an interest in opening calling centers with public phones and other services, information services, and cellular telephones, among others. Soon, other companies, such as Telex-Chile and VTR, entered data services and began providing domestic and international long distance. Clearly, liberalization and privatization had created a competitive environment for many services. The only exception was local telephone. Two small companies founded in 1981—CMET and CTM—operated networks that partially overlapped with CTC's, but generally, although there were no legal restrictions against new entrants, local service was still considered a natural monopoly.

A new problem emerged from all this: how to regulate relations between incumbent companies and their new competitors. More particularly, how could anyone control CTC, which had a virtual monopoly on local services and thus an edge on other companies?

15.8.1 The Internal Structure of the Companies

The two major companies, CTC and ENTel, adopted new internal structures, creating wholly owned subsidiaries to offer specific services. For CTC these were CTC-Cellular (September 1988) for cellular telephones; CTC-Negocios (December 1988) for marketing equipment and services, especially to large clients; and CTC-Regional Transmissions (April 1989) for providing signal transmission services (basically, long distance).

Subsidiaries of ENTel include Global (March 1989) for marketing services and equipment, and leasing equipment, and ENTelDATA (December 1988) for information and telematic services, and marketing associated equipment. In September 1989 ENTel-International was formed to provide international consulting and investment. In addition, ENTel joint ventures include Telecom Chile (August 1988) for cellular telephone throughout the country, except metro Santiago and region V (Motorola holds two-thirds); SATEL (March 1989) for satellite communications such as IBS and VSAT (COMSAT owns half); and Buenaventura (October 1990), a cellular telephone equipment owner owned equally with VTR Cellular (both have licenses in the same geographic area).

In 1990 VTR Telecommunications was established to hold VTR's interest in several other companies. These were Compañía Nacional de Teléfonos, or Telefónica del Sur (91 percent owned), Compañía de Teléfonos de Coyhaique (88 percent), and VTR Cellular (50 percent). By 1991 the group had restructured to become a financial holding company, VTR Investments, with diverse subsidiaries. Shares of the subsidiaries were spun off to the owners of VTR.

15.8.2 System Expansion

When control of CTC went to Corporación Bond, there was a notable change in the approach to development plans. They were both more carefully and more ambitiously formed, with well-defined quantitative objectives, such as entering businesses previously not considered by the company. In the words of the company's new president, CTC stopped being "a technical operating company and turned into a private service-oriented company focused on development and results." From 1988 on, the development plans expanded. Each year the number of lines scheduled for installation increased, with contracts signed with NEC and Alcatel. When control of CTC was transferred to Telefónica de España, some modifications were made to the contracts and administration of plans, but progress was not interrupted.

In 1989 CTC developed a satellite transmission project for public communications between interurban stations and VSAT networks. That June, CTC acquired a transponder on Panamsat's PAS-1 satellite and the appropriate ground station equipment from Scientific Atlanta. The company also designed a fiber-optic system between Valparaíso, Santiago, and Temuco, 600 kilometers south of Santiago.

There was substantial progress for CTC's projects, such as cellular telephones and diverse services for commercial consumers. By the end of 1991 there were 18,500 cellular lines in service, 17,952 private lines, and 17,049 pay phones, all free of government tariff regulation. In terms of personnel, the proportion of technician and professional staff increased in the late 1980s and early 1990s.

In 1988 ENTel started to digitalize its microwave trunk network, a task finished in 1991. The company also digitalized certain national and international satellite networks. In 1990 it installed its first urban fiber-optic network. Then ENTel decided to install fiber optics in the national trunk network, a task begun in 1991. In 1992 ENTel invested in international fiber-optic cables.

15.9 Government-Company Relations

After privatization there were three areas in which government-company relations adopted a more formal quality. These were tariff setting, license granting with corresponding interconnections, and the supervision of technical and economic operation of the companies, particularly in the cases of monopolistic services.

The regulator SUBtel remained in charge of setting the technical standards for the quality of telecommunications services and supervising their execution. It adopted recommendations from countries with more developed systems as norms for quality, although in some instances the norms were slightly lowered. Historically, SUBtel and its predecessors had few resources with which to do their job. Moreover, its power to impose fines and penalties had been reduced, replaced by judicial proceedings.

Regulating power was vested primarily in SUBtel, which is under the Transportation and Telecommunication Ministry, but a number of other parts of the government have important roles. Thus, the Ministry of Economics is involved in tariff setting and subsidies for rural services; the Antitrust Commission, more closely related to the judicial than to the executive branch, has strong powers in matters dealing with competition; and Congress has become an important arena for discussion of some issues.

15.9.1 Tariffs

Until the 1982 General Telecommunications Law had been promulgated, tariffs had been regulated by DFL 4 of 1989. This set tariffs to provide a 10 percent return on fixed assets. Given that the companies were in government hands, the process consisted of each company presenting proposed tariffs to the Ministry of Economics. The ministry would either modify the tariff or accept it. Regardless of calling volume, subscribers paid a flat monthly charge that discriminated by type of subscriber: residential, basic (offices, professional studios, small businesses), commercial, and trunk PABX.

In March 1981 measured local service was begun in the public telephone system, initially by adding the appropriate equipment to automatic exchanges then in service in the three largest cities, and then in other locations. Each call was charged a fixed amount plus an amount determined by the origin, destination, day, time of day, and duration of the call. The structure of calling charges was modified frequently according to its impact on the volume of traffic. The fixed component became increasingly less important.

In early 1989 tariffs set under DFL 1 of 1987 went into effect. In general, local rates kept their previous structure—that is, a basic monthly rate plus a charge for each call based on its duration and time (of day and of the week). Local rates increased markedly, as eliminating the subsidy between local and long-distance rates was one of the goals of the new tariffs. In early 1994, when a new five-year term for tariffs began, the monthly basic rate was about U.S.$12, local calls cost about U.S.$0.03 per minute during the day and U.S.$0.005 at night. Installation was about U.S.$250, but it has been reduced since.

As for long distance, during 1989–94 rates were fixed for ENTel, and the local telco would add an access charge. In 1994 a competitive, multicarrier system was introduced for both domestic and international long distance with rates set by the carriers, except for local access, which is regulated. As of April 1996, eight companies were offering service. Subscribers can choose the most convenient one for each call by dialing a prefix, or by dialing direct they automatically use their specified carrier.

15.9.2 Concessions and Interconnections

Two aspects of concessions have been especially complicated: the technical and economic specifications of the interconnections and the prevention of monopolistic practices.

From the perspective of the two dominant companies, additional subscribers at another company can be beneficial if they could not have otherwise provided them service and if the cost of interconnecting them does not exceed the incremental revenue from doing so. This was not always the case, though; as a result, the new companies frequently complained that the networks they were legally entitled to use were not in optimal condition. These small companies obviously depend on CTC's and ENTel's networks to do business.

The most difficult obstacle for the new companies has been setting the economic conditions of the interconnection. In a few cases where agreement was not reached, the matter was taken to court. The courts have not known how to deal with these conflicts, which has meant that the cases have been subject to long delays and verdicts that did not leave either party satisfied. More broadly, the courts have received many accusations of inappropriate conduct on the part of the major telecom companies, and verdicts have largely been in favor of the complainants.

In 1988 CTC had studied the possibilities for expansion into new areas of business. Among these was long-distance communications, which led to acquisition of equipment the following year. In 1989 SUBtel consulted the antimonopoly courts before granting CTC permission to offer long distance. Both the Comisión Preventiva and the Comisión Resolutiva considered the problems posed by having CTC participate in long distance. On the one hand, it was argued that because CTC practically monopolized local service, it would be able to offer a service preferable to its competitors. In short, it would be impossible to have real competition. On the other hand, it was argued that with adequate protective measures, competition was possible.

In 1989 the Comisión Preventiva ruled CTC and related phone companies could not participate in the long-distance market where it offered local service. On appeal, the Comisión Resolutiva overturned the ruling, deciding CTC could operate its system on condition it was a separate subsidiary and that subscribers actively select it as their carrier, which is known as multicarrier dialing. The Supreme Court subsequently ultimately upheld this action. While the Court was considering it, the matter was investigated by the Congress, which came to the same conclusion as the Court. The process took about five years.

Simultaneous ownership in competing companies has been another important issue. Telefónica de España was the indirect owner and controller of over 40 percent of CTC and 20 percent of ENTel. The antimonopoly courts held this illegally undermined the pattern of free competition and ordered Telefónica to sell its interest in one of the companies. Telefónica appealed to the Supreme Court, but the lower court decision was upheld. Telefónica disposed of its interest in ENTel in 1994.

From January 1989 to May 1994 the rates for regulated services in Chile were governed by Decrees 135 and 136, which set tariffs for a five-year period. On

March 10, 1994, Law No. 19302 amended the existing telecom law, allowing providers of local service, through either an affiliate or subsidiary company, to provide long-distance and international services using their own equipment. At the same time, long-distance network operators were allowed to compete in local markets on the same terms. Now CTC competed through its subsidiary CTC Mundo. Eleven concessions to run long-distance and international traffic were awarded. Only eight are operational, and they include ENTel, CTC Mundo, Chile Sat, VTR, BellSouth, CNT-Carrier, Iusatel, and Transam. Only three of these have their own long-distance networks.

Maximum market shares were laid out by the Ministry of Telecommunications as follows for July 1995:

CTC	Long distance, 35%
	International, 20%
Others	Long distance, 80%
	International, 70%

Actual average 1995 market share for long distance for the top four carriers, ENTel, CTC Mundo, Chile Sat, and VTR, was 37.36 percent, 28.9 percent, 21.89 percent, and 7.92 percent, respectively.

The competition for long-distance and international service has continued and resulted in rate decreases. Rates for both services have decreased by roughly 50 percent from August 1994 to January 1996. Competition is fierce, with price wars common. In the first six months after competition started in August 1994, prices dropped by 80–90 percent, but they quickly rebounded as companies realized that they were losing money.

As of June 1996, there were 13.6 lines per 100 inhabitants, with 1.754 million telephone lines in the country, with 100 percent digitalization. It is estimated that by the year 2000, there will be 3.016 million lines in the country, with penetration of 21.90 lines per 100 inhabitants. In 1996, there were seventeen authorized providers for telecommunications services, six for local and eleven for long distance, of which eight are currently offering service. As an example of the increase in service, new line requests are fulfilled in less than thirty days on average. Rates have been rebalanced so that business customers no longer subsidize residential service, and long distance no longer subsidizes local service.

Cellular service was provided by four companies, two of which have subsequently merged. The companies CTC Cellular and VTR Cellular merged and currently control more than 50 percent of the market. BellSouth Inversiones and Telecom Chile are the other two competitors in the market, but as of this writing, they were studying the possibility of merging to better compete with the CTC Cellular-VTR Cellular company. Cellular serves 200,000 subscribers, with a penetration of 1.4 lines per 100 inhabitants, with 350,000 subscribers estimated by the end of 1996.

Cable providers have also been investing heavily in infrastructure to provide more services. Four cable providers—TISA, VTR, Telefe, and Video Cable Communications—are competing to be the first to offer multimedia and interactive television services. Cable companies have been laying down fiber-optic and hybrid fiber-coaxial networks. Video-on-demand systems have been tested by Intercom in Santiago, and Intercom plans to go commercial with the service by the end of 1996. Cable companies are also planning to provide local telephony services over their networks, although launch dates for the service have not yet been announced.

15.10 Taking Stock

The era of liberalization and privatization began in 1977, and the process continues. There have been three phases: establishment of the formal foundations for liberalization (1977–85); privatization of CTC and ENTel (1985–88); and repositioning of the private companies in new areas of business (1989–).

The positive aspects are undoubtedly the tremendous developments made in the quantity, quality, and variety of services. Since the late 1980s, the spread of basic telephone coverage has been noteworthy. Several services not available at the beginning of the period have spread quickly. Although substantial foreign capital and technology have been involved, the process has been planned and directed primarily by Chileans.

A difficult point has been establishing tariffs and competition. Under the old system, tariffs were way under costs and, on occasion, even unrelated to costs. There was the kind of cross-subsidization found in most countries when service is provided by a state or otherwise regulated monopoly: individuals, rural areas, and local calls benefited relative to businesses, urban areas, and long distance. In Chile, low-income individuals had particularly benefited from low rates. Tariffs based on marginal costs have eliminated much of the subsidy, a result acceptable for economic efficiency but not necessarily good social policy.

This leads to an important negative result of liberalization: the limited capacity of the government to promote projects that are beneficial socioeconomically unless they also are profitable. Rural telephone service is one of many examples in telecommunications. Since the telcos are not interested, it has been left to the government to develop it. But liberalization has left the government without effective tools for promotion of such projects.

A possible solution is to auction grants to companies interested in taking on the projects. This mechanism was utilized in Chile with funds from the central government, but it was intended to cover only the costs of installing rural pay phones, not private phones. Regional and local authorities were assigned the task of determining the geographical areas needing subsidizing and formulating projects. However, the ability of local authorities to formulate projects was limited, the cost-benefit methodology used for determining the necessary subsidies was complex and imprecise, and no supervision was provided for project operation.

The era of liberalization has, overall, brought substantial net benefits to Chile. However, there are numerous unresolved problems. Some of these have carried over from earlier times, others have been precipitated by liberalization.

15.11 Decree 95 of May 1994

Law No. 19,302, issued by the Chilean government on March 10, 1995, allowed CTC the right to compete in the long-distance and international markets. Previously CTC was forced to use ENTel for long-distance service. The new Decree 95 also permits CTC to circumvent ENTel's access charges and high tariffs.

Law No. 19,302 permits long-distance carriers to compete in the local network—clearly, a blow to CTC, the traditional provider of basic service. The Decree 95 provided yet another blow. A new tariff—based on an index including the Wholesale Price Index, the peso-U.S.$ rate, and overall Chilean salary levels—had the effect of giving CTC a lower rate of return. Cutthroat competition and the aforementioned change in accounting methods helped to account for CTC's 5.5 percent revenue decline by 1995.

However, other benefits of the new decree might allow CTC to stay the course. The company is no longer limited to billing by the flat rate method, as opposed to measured service. It can bill more for "peak hours." The new law permits more hours to be defined as "peak hours." Also, CTC can, for the first time, charge higher line rental fees if fewer lines are in service (and where it is unable to benefit from economies of scale).

15.12 Conclusion

When the telegraph and telephone first emerged in the nineteenth century, the concept of directing the development of a sector in an organized fashion for the nation's benefit was only being initially formulated. By the turn of the century, the governing circles of Chile had adopted the idea that they should oversee development of telecommunications, although actual operations would be by companies holding concessions. By the 1930s, many people had become disenchanted with this strategy. They believed the government should be more active and should accelerate expansion and availability of telecommunications and other public services. From then on, almost all important national activities, including telecommunications, were subject to direct government involvement and support. In a notable exception, a special concession was granted to a private company, Compañía de Teléfonos de Chile (CTC), to operate the country's telecommunications.

In the three decades following this grant, the gap between its proponents and opponents was maintained and even increased. Finally, the government created a company of the same stature: ENTel was made responsible for operating long-distance services. Ultimately, the government assumed the responsibility of ensuring telecom development. This was a failed effort. Paradoxically, as it became more evident that national telecommunications needed to intensify its progress, it was recognized that the advances were insufficient, and new paths were tried, unsuccessfully.

In the mid-1970s yet another new path was taken, with initiative for development given to private companies. This change was terribly exciting for the sector, although it required significant adjustments. Services grew considerably more widespread and improved in quality. For the first time in decades, it seemed that Chile had hit on a successful road.

Finally, in the 1980s and 1990s, Chile's telecom markets moved toward even more open competition. By 1994, traditional operators of local and long-distance services were allowed to cross over into each other's turfs.

However, there are unresolved questions. What role should the government take in strategy and policy? If telecommunications are increasingly indispensable for everyone, how does one guarantee no one is without access within a market framework? How does one organize a market in which there is such a range of size and power among the participating companies? What are the prospects of the present strategy of development of the sector? Or are we condemned to continue the tradition of changing strategies after a few years?

16
Brazil

ANTONIO JOSÉ J. BOTELHO, JOSÉ ROBERTO FERRO,
LEE McKNIGHT, AND ANTONIO C. MANFREDINI OLIVEIRA

Brazil is a large country in terms of both area (with 8.5 million square kilometers, it is slightly smaller than the United States) and population (over 160 million in 1995). Its telecomunications infrastructure is one of the most advanced among industrializing nations, although at the same time teledensity and accessibility is low. Brazil's telephone system deteriorated considerably during the 1980s and early 1990s due to a prolonged economic crisis, and it has been recovering over the past few years.

In the early 1980s, Brazil entered a democratic period following decades of authoritarian rule. The inauguration of the Collor administration in March 1990 promised to propel Brazil toward a neoliberal political economy. Collor's removal from office by impeachment proceedings in 1992 was viewed by some as demonstrating the strength of national democratic institutions. Others saw it as demonstrating the extent of political corruption and economic uncertainty.

In any case, the economic policies of the Collor administration represented a break from the past and have continued to influence policy during the current administration of President Fernando Henrique Cardoso. Pressured by federal budget deficits and high inflation, the Collor administration set out, as part of its economic liberalization campaign, to radically reform telecom institutions and markets. The relaxation of laws regarding private and foreign participation in Brazil's constitutionally mandated state monopoly in telecommunications was a cornerstone of the reform. Much of the reform was derailed, but President Fernando Henrique Cardoso revived the discussion of plans for telecommunications reform in 1995 and 1996. In January 1995, the Communications Ministry announced it was again preparing legislation to reorganize the phone companies and allow competition from private firms. Since then, the legal groundwork for liberalization and privatization has been laid, although as yet there has been little change in the monopoly position of the dominant public telecommunications service providers.

Nonetheless, privatization and legal reform promise to radically transform Brazil's telecom landscape by the next millennium. A more open economy is certain to emerge, but it is difficult to anticipate how long the transition will take and how open the markets will ultimately become. There is, however, little doubt that the emerging political economy will be quite different from the previous one based on import substitution.

16.1 Historical Background

Modern communications in Brazil dates to 1851, when the Ministry of Justice decided to replace the optical telegraph with an electric one. The first public telegraphic network was inaugurated in Rio de Janeiro, then the capital, a year later. By 1855, the network had 20,000 kilometers of lines, and a year later, the first long-distance line connected Rio to Porto Alegre, the southernmost state capital, a distance of over 1,100 kilometers. In 1874, a submarine telegraphic cable was completed connecting Rio to Salvador, Recife, and Belém—all ports along the coast to the north.

A maintenance workshop was created by the government telegraphic agency in April 1865, and by the 1880s there were efforts to make replacement parts, but until 1917 there was no communications equipment production in Brazil. Father Landell de Moura performed experiments with radiotelephone, reportedly several years before Marconi. In 1900 he obtained a Brazilian patent for a telephone with and without wires, and he received three patents in the United States covering a wave broadcaster, wireless telephone, and wireless telegraph (Capellaro 1989).

In the 1920s ham radio operators began assembling the first Brazilian radio equipment based on international designs. In 1926–27, Radiobrás, controlled by RCA International (Paris) installed the first shortwave transmitter. During this period, the first fifteen radio stations were built, mostly foreign and with imported equipment. This created incentives for the emergence of a local radio industry. In 1927 Radio Record was the first nonforeign radio station to use equipment built locally, although from imported parts.

The growth of the Brazilian economy in the first decades of the twentieth century created a market for equipment that was addressed in the early 1930s by at least a dozen local manufacturers, including Standard Electric SA (SESA) and the Companhia Marconi Brasileira. Standard Electric SA was controlled by ITT, which also controlled the International Standard Electric Corporation (ISE), charged with technical support of the automatic switching exchanges of the ITT European group in Brazil. Other major foreign firms included Ericsson and Companhia Brasileira de Eletricidade, controlled by Siemens, which in 1913 installed several radiotelegraphic stations at Army forts. In the late 1930s the Army began to manufacture its own field telephones, radiotelegraphic stations, and small telephone switching stations. Small national private companies also manufactured communications equipment for several other government agencies.

Actual and potential disruptions of imports during World War II created conditions for the development of a local electronics equipment industry, including communications equipment. Military fears of supply interruptions led to the development of a few communications projects in cooperation with academic institutions and the upgrading of the manufacturing capabilities of military research and development and maintenance centers.

During the second Vargas government (1951–54), mounting incentives for import substitution were successful in attracting (or forcing) international firms to establish equipment assembly operations using imported kits.

16.1.1 Early Postwar Operating Companies

In the two decades following the end of World War II, the communications system expanded rapidly, in conjunction with the growth of the Brazilian economy. However, this expansion was constrained by the power of local and state authorities to grant communications services franchises. These franchises led to an incredibly fragmented market, with over 800 national and foreign private concessionaires. Unrealistically low tariffs also contributed to reduced investment and sluggish growth of telegraph and telephone traffic. Thus, in 1957 Brazil's teledensity of 1.3 per 100 inhabitants was just over a third of the world average of 3.7.[1]

In 1960 there were around 1 million telephones for 70 million people. Two-thirds of the equipment and traffic were concentrated in the states of Rio de Janeiro and São Paulo, where most of the economic activity and population have been centered, and which thus accounted for the majority of the traffic. Foreign firms dominated the key markets, with Companhia Telefônica Brasileira (CTB), controlled by a Canadian holding company, Brazilian Traction Light and Power, servicing around 70 percent of the 1.5 million telephones in the country and handling 80 percent of the traffic in 1968.

The telegraph sector was dominated by Western Telegraph & Telephone. Cable & Wireless, based in the United Kingdom, was the other major company. After 1947 telegraph operations gradually came under state control, foreshadowing the state's greater involvement in the communications sector in the 1960s.

International telephone service was split among four firms—Radional/ITT, SUDAM/Alcatel, Radiobrás, and Italcable. Their concessions expired between 1970 and 1973, when international service came to be monopolized by the state company Embratel.

16.2 A New Order

In 1962 Law 4,117 (Brazil's Telecommunications Code) was decreed as the basis for the evolution of a new institutional regime and reorganization of the system. The code granted the state a monopoly in the operation and regulation of telecom activities. It also created the National Telecommunications Council (CONTEL) to develop a National Telecommunications Plan aimed at unifying and modernizing the system by reducing market fragmentation and rationalizing equipment supplies. Important provisions included setting more realistic tariffs and the approval, in November 1963, of a National Telecommunications Fund (FNT) financed by a 20 percent surtax on local calls and a 30 percent surtax on long-distance calls.

The Brazilian Telecommunications Enterprise (Embratel) was approved at the same time, but perhaps because of the political instability generated by the 1964 military coup, Embratel was not actually established until September 1965. It is a mixed-economy enterprise whose shareholders initially were the federal government and large public enterprises, including the national oil company (Petrobrás).

Embratel's initial objectives, to be financed from the FNT, included implementing and operating domestic and international telecom trunk operations, developing linkages enabling the integration of the country's northernmost region (the Amazon) into the national system through a microwave trunk network, and regulating telecom services.

In 1967 the regulatory function was transferred to the recently created Ministry of Communications (Minicom). Minicom's mission was to solve the significant problems that continued to limit the development of Brazilian telecommunications, such as the large number of concessionaires, outdated and incompatible equipment, and congested lines. These problems had continued to plague the system in spite of efforts made in the 1960s, including a doubling of the number of telephones.

As part of a Minicom-led rationalization effort, in 1968 the federal government acquired the largest foreign telephone concessionaire, Companhia Telefônica Brasileira (CTB), and gradually took control of most telecommunications operators in the country.

16.2.1 Telebrás

Telebrás was created in November 1972 to plan and manage the development of the national telecommunications system. As part of this plan, most of the federal government's ownership of Embratel, and hence the task of coordinating its activities, was transferred to Telebrás. To rationalize the supply of equipment, create scale economies for local production, and standardize networks for national integration, Telebrás was given a monopoly in the purchase of telecom equipment, which it allocated to the operating telcos, generally called pole companies. Telebrás was also assigned the task of developing a national telecom research and development strategy, centered in the Centro de Pesquisas e Desenvolvimento (Center for Research and Development, CPqD) created in 1976, and in three training centers.

Established as a public enterprise, Telebrás was initially 80 percent owned by the federal government; by mid-1992 about half of its stock, which trades on the São Paulo exchange, was in public hands as a result of sales of shares to purchasers of telephone lines as a way of financing the system's expansion.

By 1973, through a series of purchases and mergers, Telebrás had drastically reduced the number of firms operating telephone networks to thirty-seven major companies, about one and a half for each of Brazil's states. Telebrás often held a majority interest in these consolidated firms. State governments had substantial control over management of the majority of the pole companies. For convenience, this chapter will speak of Telebrás owning or controlling pole companies, although limits on both, because of other owners and the management interest of the state governments, have made the pole companies more independent than, say, the predivestiture Bell operating companies were of AT&T.

In 1982 the number of pole companies affiliated with Telebrás was thirty-six. The number of independent private service providers, about 1,000 in 1972, had been reduced to 150, with only 250,000 telephones. In 1992, Telebrás accounted for over 90 percent of total telephone lines through its control of twenty-seven pole companies.

16.2.2 Financing Expansion

In the early 1970s, with the mission of expanding the country's telephone system, the newly established Ministry of Communications devised a scheme to make up for Telebrás's lack of investment funds. The final user was, and still is, required to provide the cash for network expansion. Typically, to get a telephone, the prospective customer signs up with the local Telebrás affiliate and pays (in 1992) the equivalent of U.S.$4,000, which could be financed. Within a year, the customer is to receive Telebrás stock equal in value to the payment. The local telco has up to two years after final payment to actually install the telephone line and give the customer a telephone set. This approach compares to that used in Japan, where subscribers were required to buy bonds in the government-owned telephone company.

16.2.3 Embratel's New Role

In this new regime, Embratel was charged with the implementation and operation of the system, including the sale of a variety of trunk services in data, voice, and image communication for regional companies, television networks, naval communications, and so forth.

The growth rate of new capacity jumped from 3 percent per year in 1965 to 15 percent in 1969. By then, all major cities were connected through a microwave network, and the Amazon region was linked to the rest of the country by a tropodiffusion (microwave) trunk system. The international calling system was revamped in 1969 with the installation of an Intelsat earth station in Rio. After 1974, Embratel partially replaced its shortwave radiotelephone system with a line-of-sight system of microwave towers, and then with terrestrial satellite stations using a leased Intelsat transponder. International communications were greatly improved when new submarine cables were installed to expand connections to Europe (in 1973 and 1983) and the United States (in 1980).

By the late 1980s, Embratel's major activities were operating the terrestrial microwave network linking Brazil's major cities and the domestic and international long-distance satellite network, which consisted of two national satellites and thirty-eight earth stations. There are also terrestrial links with Uruguay, Paraguay, and Argentina. Since 1984 employment has been around 12,000.

16.2.4 Promoting a Domestic Equipment Industry

Through its monopoly purchasing power, standardization rules, and with a long-term strategy for acquiring technological capability, Telebrás promoted development of domestic equipment manufacturing. Initially, its research and development activities centered on training personnel and defining promising research areas, implemented from 1972 with the selection of five university groups to conduct research in areas relevant to future telecom systems. These mission-oriented contracts included pulse code modulation (PCM) and stored program control (SPC) technologies, as well as fiber optics and microelectronics. In early 1972 the Planning Ministry (Miniplan) had asked government agencies to propose sectoral research and development projects for what would become the first National Basic Plan of Scientific and Technological Development (I PBDCT). Telebrás took over the telecommunications programs plans when it was created.

Ericsson had started local manufacturing in 1955 after the largest operating telco, CTB (although foreign owned), sought to promote domestic production with the assistance of a government executive group. The availability of cheap labor and the possibility of an almost captive market provided great incentive for the venture. Other major foreign firms followed: NEC (1968), Siemens (1970), and Philips (1974).

Shortly after it was created, Telebrás ordered about 1 million lines, divided among Ericsson, SESA, and Plessey. Ericsson was rewarded for having started local manufacturing well before the others. It received the award for modernizing the São Paulo system, the largest market.

In the mid-1970s, with an eye on technological changes in the telecom equipment market and with the objective of protecting its research and development investments, Minicom reserved, through a series of regulations, half of the market for SPC exchanges for the TDM/PCM technology being developed by CPqD. The remaining half was allotted to analog technology, which could be imported or manufactured by the foreign firms that had recently been required to take on Brazilian partners for their local operations. Until a domestic technology was developed, however, the market was to be divided among the "localized" firms led by Ericsson and Standard Electric (ITT), which together accounted for 70 percent of installed telephone lines in 1979.

Import restrictions on computers and other high technology products, a vestige of the import-substitution industrialization strategy of an earlier era, began to fade in the 1990s, although remnants remain. The more competitive local market has accelerated the introduction of new networking products, to the benefit of diverse sectors of the Brazilian economy.

16.3 Telecommunications under the Second National Development Plan

In 1974 when the Geisel administration came to power, a very ambitious telecom strategy was defined within the broader Second National Development Plan (II PND). One of the goals was to increase by almost 200 percent the number of telephones in use by the end of the decade.

At that time, the institutional structure of regional operating companies controlled by Telebrás was consolidated. This gave Telebrás greater leverage to launch a more aggressive import-substitution policy, drafted in 1975, which aimed to reserve the market to national producers of equipment.

In the task of formulating industrial policy for the sector, Minicom was aided by the Executive Group for the Devices and Materials Industries (Geicom), an interministerial think tank charged with industrial studies for the development of a domestic communications equipment industry. Geicom's task was to coordinate and promote domesticizing production through studies and contacts with manufacturers and suppliers. At first Geicom sought to identify and organize the demand for inputs and components, and then it sought to influence other government institutions to provide incentives for the development of a network of national suppliers.

Under its five-year investment plan, begun in 1975, Telebrás was charged with providing authorization for all imports and public procurement orders for telecom equipment and with promoting the domestic industry. However, under pressure from foreign firms already established in the country, a compromise was found in the localization of foreign firms through their association with Brazilian financial groups: Siemens-Equitel, Ericsson-Matel, ITT (SESA)-Unipec; and NEC-Brasilinvest.

Under Minicom's executive order 622 of June 1978, in order to qualify for bidding on Telebrás projects, foreign firms had to cede 51 percent voting control to national groups and develop effective technology transfer mechanisms for their partners. The local partners were given preferred shares with the requisite voting power, but they contributed only 17 percent of the actual capital. Despite earlier import-substitution efforts, until this step, practically all high-tech and large equipment was imported. But from 1978, local production began to take off.

In the end, the association between Ericsson and Matel, controlled by the industrial holding company Monteiro Aranha, was the only one that effectively achieved the transfer of digital technology. This partly explains its selection for the manufacture of the digital exchange AXE in 1979 (the first of which was installed in 1982) and its enduring close relationship with Telesp, the pole company in São Paulo, which comprises about 40 percent of total Brazilian telephone traffic. Ericsson provided over 58 percent of the 1.2 million lines contracted by the National Telecom Plan.

Siemens, whose Brazilian operations mostly involved assembling crossbar-type exchanges, was not selected as a manufacturer of electronic exchanges in the 1978 competition. However, it was selected in 1981 when it associated with the Brazilian industrial group Hering. In 1979, SESA, with Plessey technology, was selected along with Ericsson in the National Telecommunications System bidding for digital exchange equipment. Then ITT sold SESA to a Brazilian investment firm, Brasilinvest, in 1981 as part of an overall divestiture strategy and in the face of additional Brazilian rules. Rights to crossbar, but not electronic digital technology, were included in the sale. Also in 1981, Brasilinvest took control of NEC do Brasil. Later, SESA was renamed Telbra and then Standard Electrônica.

Minicom's policy succeeded in the 1970s in expanding the network significantly, particularly in the last half of the decade. The number of lines in service more than doubled from 1973 to 1977, and it more than tripled by 1980, when it reached 4.7 million. During the five years 1976–80, over 500,000 lines a year were being placed in service.

16.4 Continued Promotion of Domestic Equipment Makers

Just a few years after the beginning of its research and development program in the early 1970s, Telebrás began transferring technology to local firms, which also became involved in the development phase of several projects. For example, in 1975 a firm was contracted to develop a satellite parabolic antenna, and a few years later another was selected to develop a push-button telephone set.

Throughout the 1970s Telebrás had gradually reduced dependence on international suppliers in a context of rapidly growing demand, the emergence of new services, and a technological discontinuity in production (from electromechanical to digital). By the end of the period, the Brazilian telecom system had attained a level of service sophistication and quality without par among developing countries.

Localized foreign firms in association with Brazilian partners accounted for over two-thirds of sales in Brazil's telecom market in 1981. They were followed by several smaller local companies that produced peripheral equipment and small exchanges, often with technology developed by Telebrás's research and development center, CPqD. In 1982 domestic communications equipment production reached U.S.$776 million. Imports were about U.S.$100 million, just one-third their all-time high in 1975. Aided by Geicom's gradual nationalization and import-substitution policy, by the mid-1980s localized foreign manufacturers could count on a network of some 1,200 domestic suppliers of parts, components, and materials.

By the end of the 1980s, the market share of equipment developed by CPqD, representing about 40 percent of the total purchase of domestic equipment by the Sistema Nacional de Telecomunicacoẽs (SNT), was U.S.$200 million, at competitive prices. For example, about 20 percent of the telephone lines contracted out by Telebrás in 1987 were based on the CPqD-developed Trópico system. By the end of 1991, there were at least four Trópico-RA digital exchanges in operation, manufactured by STC (Sharp group), Standard Eletrônica, Elebra (Alcatel), and PHT (Promon). In microelectronics, a dialing circuit to be used in the Brazilian standard telephone set was developed for a potential market of 1 million chips a year.

Incentives to domestic companies led several large industrial, media, and financial groups to enter the telecom market during the early and mid-1980s. Among these were the Globo media conglomerate, which owns Brazil's largest television network, in association with NEC do Brasil, and Bradesco, Brazil's largest private bank. Several other groups also sought to profit from the growth opportunities in the market, so that by 1990 a large number of national telecom firms were part of diversified conglomerates or holding companies.

All this has contributed to a declining degree of concentration (measured as the share of the market held by both the four largest and the ten largest firms). Moreover, small firms have been gaining important niches. At the same time, the ten largest local producers (those at least 70 percent owned by Brazilians) have gained share. It should be noted that the four largest firms are all affiliates of foreign companies (Ericsson, NEC, Siemens, and ITT).

16.4.1 The Heyday of Telecommunications Research and Development

Virtually all basic telecommunications research and development in Brazil is conducted by or in association with Telebrás, mostly at its center, CPqD, which opened in Campinas (São Paulo) in 1979. In 1992, CPqD employed 1,300 people, 70 percent of whom worked for Telebrás or university-based foundations involved in joint projects, and 30 percent for domestic firms involved in joint development projects with CPqD.

In the early 1990s the Telebrás System was investing 2.5 percent or more of its net operating revenues in research and development. Since 1985 the CPqD has by law received 2 percent of revenues, and the rest is distributed among the research and development centers of the pole companies. Under a 1988 ministerial order, at least 5 percent of Telebrás's annual research and development budget has to be spent at university research institutes or on small- and medium-enterprise-initiated projects.

In 1990 CPqD's budget was U.S.$60 million, distributed among fifty-three different projects for new equipment production in cooperation with twenty-two firms and thirteen academic research teams. Projects include the creation of a smart telephone (Intelitel) for the ISDN network under development; a large telex text exchange (Cetex) (equivalent foreign products cost three times as much); a multifrequency data communications system via satellite based on Time Division Multiple Access (TDMA) technology (Samsat); and optoelectronic devices for fiber-optics communications. Over 100 local firms take part in CPqD's Product Technology Program, which gives them preferential access to technical reports, qualified components lists, and updated packaging norms.

By 1993, CPqD had generated over 350 patents and contributed to about 400 smaller projects at the pole companies. Many of these developments were transferred to domestic firms, helping them take a 50 percent share of the local telecom equipment market in the early 1990s. Also, CPqD developed seventy-nine products in its laboratories and transferred them to sixty-six local firms, generating about U.S.$1 billion in revenue for them. Despite this local preference, Brazil's telecom equipment market was relatively open to imports compared to those of such developed nations as Japan, France, and Italy.

Telebrás's flagship project is the Trópico family of digital exchanges employing stored program control (SPC) technology. In 1990 tenders, Trópico equipment outsold the equivalent Ericsson system four to one. Moreover, Trópico brought down the average price per line from U.S.$670 for a digital exchange (Ericsson's AXE with 4,000 lines) to U.S.$450. Between 1976 and 1990, U.S.$37 million was invested in the development of the Trópico-RA central digital exchange, and total development costs for the entire family of exchanges was on the order of U.S.$237 million, including training personnel at the University of São Paulo. The Brazilian development cost was less than half that of the cheapest other digital exchange, the AXE, developed in the 1980s by Ericsson.

16.5 The Crisis of the 1980s

The crisis that hit Brazilian telecommunications in the 1980s had its roots in the mid-1970s. Maintaining successful development of domestic firms and research capacity required a continuous effort to keep up with the rapid technological change characteristic of information technologies.

In 1975 the FNT, the pool of money collected as surtaxes on telecom services, which had financed a sizable share of investment in the sector between 1965 and 1975, was removed from the direct control of the Minicom. As a result, public procurement, which until then had accounted for 80 percent of foreign firms' revenues, was drastically reduced. The FNT was finally abolished in 1982.

Still, over the seven years 1974–80, the number of telephone lines increased over 18 percent a year, and local production capacity reached 1.1 million lines in 1980.

However, after reaching a demand of 1 million equivalent lines as measured by the number of requests for telephone services in 1975, the public network's expansion was slowed by a succession of economic problems, including the second oil crisis, the debt crisis, and finally a galloping and persistent inflationary spiral through the 1980s. These problems were reflected in the fall in demand to 700,000 equivalent lines in 1976, followed by a further slide to only 450,000 for the next decade, less than half the level of 1980. In 1986 and 1987, demand experienced a slight recovery to 635,000 and 987,000 equivalent lines, but the following year it fell again to 630,000.

The number of new lines installed reached a peak in 1978, and there has not been a sustained telecom investment program since. Around then, the Telebrás system began to decline due to repeated government raids on its cash and revenue to help offset the mounting state deficit. Although in the early 1990s investment levels have equaled those of the mid-1970s, the market had continued to expand. It is estimated that in 1990 there was a U.S.$2.4 billion gap in the Telebrás system budget, representing the funds necessary to install the 1.2 million lines sold but not yet delivered. System growth in the 1980s was uneven, and telecom investment as a share of gross domestic product, just over 1 percent in 1976 and 0.73 percent in 1978, was in a 0.4 to 0.5 percent range during most of the decade.

16.5.1 Telebrás in the 1980s

After the consolidation of the 1970s, Telebrás fell prey to the politics of the early 1980s, which increased the power of state governments and the federal Congress. Little by little, the professional management and technical staff of Telebrás, already threatened by imposed short-term financial management, became victims of widespread clientelism, with high levels of inefficiency and mounting bureaucratization (traditional public service agencies). This pressure intensified after 1985, when the Sarney government replaced top-level professional management with political appointees, part of a larger game of political maneuvering.

The stagnation and decline of Telebrás in the 1980s was part of a larger deterioration of the government and its policy framework, reflecting the difficulties of fashioning a functional democratic system, with effective checks and balances, out of what had been a military-authoritarian system (Stepan 1989).

Telebrás became unable to keep pace with demand, and the quality of its services declined. This was exacerbated by the ongoing economic crisis and by the persistent lag of rates behind inflation: during the 1980s tariffs declined 80 percent adjusted for inflation.

16.5.2 Price Distortions

The requirement that a new customer make a lump-sum payment to fund network expansion is a critical part of the distortion in telecom service pricing in Brazil. In the early days, it was considered innovative, as Telebrás could count on an urban and increasingly affluent population to provide cash for expansion. However, low-income users generally were unable to gain access because of their lack of capital. The inflationary environment of the 1980s limited the ability of even the middle class to pay, reducing the rate of subscriber growth.

Prices for most services have remained extremely low by international standards. Although charges for international calls have been high relative to other nations (in early 1992 it cost about four times as much per minute to call from Brazil to the United States as from the United States to Brazil), tariffs for local calls and basic subscription are underpriced and heavily subsidized. As a result, the number of lines desired by customers but not yet installed continued to increase, jumping from 6 million in 1987 to 9 million in 1988.

Rates have been repressed as part of price control programs to reduce inflation. For example, in 1984 the average price of Embratel service, adjusted for inflation, was 42 percent lower than in 1981. For Telebrás, tariffs dropped 45 percent in real terms between 1985 and 1991. These declines were due not to improved efficiency and lower operating costs but rather to political constraints. As a result, investment capacity declined precipitously. When the brief recovery of the mid-1980s increased Embratel's traffic by 30 percent, the system quickly became congested. Embratel revenues from long distance and international calls are usually transferred to pole companies at the rate of 90 percent for the former and 120 percent for the latter.

16.6 Television and Radio

The majority of the VHF television band has already been allocated to the existing national networks (Globo, Manchete, SBT, Bandeirantes, and public educational channels). In the UHF band there are still about ninety channels available, which will be distributed through a lottery.

Because of very high levels of illiteracy and semi-illiteracy, television and radio have much larger audiences than newspapers and magazines. Television reaches more than 35 million sets, with more than 100 million viewers, or 75 percent of the population, and radio extends even further. Television advertising volume is among the top five in the world, with the state accounting for 40 percent of it (Perrone 1992).

Brazil's unique *telenovelas* (soap operas) are exported to over 100 countries, demonstrating the technical and commercial quality of this product (see Duarte, Straubhaar, and Stephens 1992). Programs from the United States may be more appealing to the middle class and elite, but *telenovelas* serve the cultural and entertainment needs of the majority, with their variety of themes, ranging from romantic affairs to historical dramas.

The diffusion of television and radio among low-income groups, as well as in the most remote areas of the country, gives these media significant political importance. For the majority, the means of being informed is limited to television and radio. Their potential to serve as political weapons is well known and is alleged to be responsible for radically transforming power structures, as in Eastern Europe. Quite conscious of this, the Brazilian elite has been attempting to use television and radio to maintain the status quo.

Radio stations generally have only a regional political impact. The granting of radio concessions is frequently the subject of intense disputes among local authorities and political leaders, which are managed by political factions through a bargaining process and coalition building.

The television market is dominated by the Globo network—the fourth largest television network in the world—with interests in television, newspaper, printing, electronics, and cellular franchises, as in Rio and São Paulo. Its television arm has the most advanced technology, enabling its stations to reach even the most remote parts of the country with a strong signal, and the most sophisticated programs, including prime-time *telenovelas,* news programs, variety, and comedy shows. These help give it a 60 to 80 percent audience share and 70 percent of total advertising revenue (Straubhaar 1991). The group's original success can be traced to efficient management, which combined professionalism, decentralized decision making, technology transfer from U.S. networks, and a market strategy that enabled it to reach all audience segments. Stable control by the Marinho family has enabled Globo to plan for the long term.

Globo has substantial political influence because of its economic strength. Indeed, it is reputed to have influenced election outcomes and even social movements. Even when there was a mass movement calling for presidential elections in 1984, with enormous numbers of citizens taking to the streets, Globo news coverage—the sole source of information for many millions of Brazilians—ignored the demonstrations. Globo paved the way for Collor's 1990 election as president by portraying him as a young, energetic governor who was aggressively confronting the traditional political elite and corruption.

More recently, Globo entered into alliances with Grupo Televisa of Mexico and Denver-based TCI, as well as with AT&T and Bradesco, Brazil's largest private bank, to enter the direct-to-home satellite television business and to bid in the coming privatization of the Brazilian telephone system, respectively.

16.7 The Emerging Telecommunications Regime

Brazil plans to have 25 million lines installed by the year 2000, 75 percent of which are to be digital. In the period 1992–95, Telebrás plans to invest U.S.$3.5

billion and install 4.2 million new lines, for a total of 13.5 million. However, in light of the 6 to 9 million line backlog, critics say the number of installed lines will have to reach 20 million just to eliminate the backlog. In 1991, 310,000 lines were installed.

During the second half of the 1980s the quality of telephone service declined considerably. Failed local calls, already above average by international standards in 1980, increased to 25 percent of all calls in 1990. Crossed lines—jokingly referred to as free conference calling—and wrong numbers also continued to increase. At the end of 1990, 30 of 100 calls between Rio and São Paulo did not complete. Overall, the direct dialed long-distance call completion rate fell from 49 percent in 1986 to 41 percent in 1990, and the chance of even getting a dial tone fell from 95 percent to 88 percent.

In 1990, installation of a line in Brazil cost U.S.\$4,570 against an international average of U.S.\$2,500, partly due to the higher prices of telecom equipment in Brazil (Hobday 1990, pp. 184–85). The cartelized manufacturers of telephone exchanges argue that the cost per line is high because they are forced to buy a number of inputs and components locally, such as copper.

The Collor administration used such evidence to call for a revolutionary liberalization of the sector, which would include a complete opening of the market to foreign companies, breakup of the state monopoly, and privatization of Telebrás and Embratel. Supporters of a nationalist view replied that the existing institutions had been quite capable of meeting the market, technological, and industrial challenges until their investment capacity was undermined by the tandem of spiraling inflation and tariff adjustment lag. They claim that had it not been for the nationalist policy, geographic coverage would not be as widespread as it is, a domestic equipment and service industry would not have emerged, and the technological capability for domestic production would not have grown over the past two decades.

16.7.1 Opening Procurement

Liberalization and deregulation have affected public procurement of telecom equipment. In June 1990 the market reserve for large switching systems was terminated. Since the early 1980s this market had been divided between NEC, Brasil, Equitel, and Ericsson. They benefited from a reserve of over 2 million lines. However, in 1991 AT&T was awarded a U.S.\$85 million contract by Embratel to install a new submarine cable between Brazil and the United States, with a digital switch located in Rio.

The Collor administration implemented decisions to import optical fibers and to allow foreign firms to manufacture in the country, threatening the future of domestic producers of fiber, which use technology developed by Telebrás's CPqD. Until 1988 Brazil had only one manufacturer of fiber cable, ABC Xtal. However, because of strong demand, Telebrás had authorized imports from Philips during 1988–89. The market was opened in 1990 when fiber optics was removed from the defunct Special Secretariat of Informatics (SEI) list of products to be protected by a market reserve until October 1992.

Another noteworthy development is the emergence of regional cooperative projects, particularly the Mercosur agreement to create a Southern Cone Common Market among Brazil, Argentina, and Uruguay. The Mercosur agreement was ratified by the Brazilian Congress in 1991. There has since been substantially increased trade, particularly between Brazil and Argentina, the two largest economies of South America, which heretofore had had quite low levels of interaction. As part of the agreement, the three countries have agreed to build a U.S.$92 million fiber-optic submarine cable to link them by 1994.

16.7.2 Aborted Reform

The Collor administration, inaugurated in 1990 with a liberalizing ideology, set out to effect profound changes in Brazil's political economy. Pressure for change came from the challenges of dwindling investment capital, the state's fiscal crisis, rising repressed demand, and declining quality of services generally, as well as the administration's recognition of telecommunications as a key infrastructure that must be enhanced for the government's economic strategy to succeed. The administration advanced its strategy for the sector in its March 1991 National Deregulation Program.

Any proposal for change in the existing structure must confront the state monopoly over basic telecom services. This is decreed by the Brazilian Telecommunications Code of 1962 and by the 1988 Constitution, which has been in the process of revision in 1995.

One of the linchpins of Collor's liberalizing strategy toward telecommunications was Decree 99,179 of March 1990, which allowed private capital to provide information services, private telecom exchanges in residential and business buildings, community telephone programs, and cellular mobile phone services. The same month, the administration abolished the Ministry of Communications (Minicom) and created the National Communications Secretariat (SNC) under the Ministry of Infrastructure. (The SNC was reestablished/renamed Minicom after the collapse of the Collor regime in 1992.) Then, in mid-1990, the government issued, as part of the so-called Collor Plan I, a provisional measure (Medida Provisória 151) stating the following objectives:

1. Regionalizing management of the Telebrás system, with the creation of seven (versus the current twenty-eight regional pole companies) regional operating companies, resembling the Baby Bell institutional model.
2. Opening telecom services markets—including long-distance service, cellular mobile phones, paging, cable television, telecom infrastructure development, and private data services—to private domestic and foreign companies.

The basic services monopoly was preserved, and state companies were allowed to compete in the value-added services market.

Opponents argued that the measure contravened the state monopoly over telecommunications embodied in the 1962 National Telecommunications Code and 1988 Constitution. The Collor administration chose to interpret these legal provisions liberally. In its view, there is no link between the concession of a right to operate a telecom service and the ownership of equipment or network used.

Thus equipment and networks can be installed, leased, franchised, or operated by the private sector. The government expected the liberalization measures to attract upward of U.S.$1 billion in new foreign investment for the sector.

Despite strong opposition from the center-left political bloc in Congress, the measure was approved, although with the suggested creation of two regional companies in the northeast instead of one and preservation of the status quo regarding Embratel. However, because the management and operation of local operating companies is a clientelist bonanza for local politicians, implementation never took place.

16.7.3 The Possibility of Privatization

In the first two years of the Collor administration (1990–91), sensitive sectors such as oil (Petrobrás) and telecommunications (Telebrás) were excluded from the privatization program. They were considered sacred cows not to be touched, lest opposition from nationalists derail the entire liberalization agenda. By early 1992, however, a new public attitude appeared to emerge, and the debate over privatization of telecommunications began in some earnest, although political instability slowed it down and gave it muted tones.

Because Brazil's 1988 Constitution does not allow for outright privatization of public utilities such as Telebrás and Embratel, a constitutional amendment is required.

There is also the problem of how to value a company like Telebrás, which practically controls Brazil's national and international telecommunications. In 1989, strapped for investment capital, Telebrás sold U.S.$450 million in debentures convertible into stock equivalent to 75 percent of the capital of the company. In mid-1992 estimates were made that privatization could fetch U.S.$10 billion in international stock markets, but the market value of its stock was only U.S.$600 million. At the time, Telebrás had fixed capital estimated to be worth upward of U.S.$8 billion.

The agency then in charge of telecommunications privatization, the National Bank for Economic and Social Development (BNDES), pushed for a revaluation of Telebrás's capital, not including its debt, with the objective of making it more attractive to foreign investors.

Some critics have suggested a mechanism for the government to recoup part of the U.S.$5.5 billion "loss" resulting from the 1989 debentures sale. They propose privatizing the pole companies without revaluing their capital base, so that the difference between the historic value and the sale price would be taxed, bringing into the government coffers a considerable sum of money.

16.7.4 The Regional Companies

At the local level, emerging entrepreneurial companies and state governments are already taking advantage of opportunities created by the regime changes. The regional (pole) companies, particularly the larger ones in the southeastern region (Telesp, Telerj, Telemig, and Telepar) have sought a role in determining policy. Traditionally, the pole companies have provided private residential and business lines. Since 1988, they have also installed point-to-point networks within their geographic areas.

In the emerging institutional regime, the regional operating companies are likely to acquire considerable managerial and budgetary freedom from the holding company. Already in 1989, the declining investment capacity of Embratel and the deregulation trend had wrested away Embratel's monopoly over telex maintenance service and modem supply, which were taken over by private companies.

Telepar, the operating company in Paranástate, just south of São Paulo, is investing its own funds to set up new transmission lines, promote data communications services, and otherwise renovate the system. Some of this will be done in partnership with the private sector, as a way of bringing in needed investment funds. The large state operating companies are also busy setting up their own packet switching and data communications local networks.

Telesp, the São Paulo state pole company, has fought for radical changes in the policy giving Embratel a monopoly on data services. Telesp argues that under the current system Embratel keeps a disproportionate share of operational revenues. It wishes Embratel to became a mere wholesale service provider, or carrier's carrier, to local telcos, which would market services directly to customers within their areas. To this end, it has signed an agreement with Sprint to design a data communications project for its service area.

The city of São Paulo considered legal action to recover control of the management of telephone service from Telesp.

16.7.5 Embratel

Embratel, which operates the basic long-distance and international networks, has been preparing to face competitive challenges. However, its investment budget to upgrade and expand the network (U.S.$650 million in 1991) has been limited by government pressure to reduce the public deficit.

The economic crisis and the emergence of new services (fax, low-speed data communications, public data packet network) threatened Embratel's profitable telex services. In 1989, with 135,000 terminals, Brazil had the world's third largest telex network. As of 1990, telex was responsible for 23 percent of Embratel's total revenues. That year telex traffic growth was just 4.7 percent against an average of 13 percent for the previous five years. Still, the price per minute of telex transmission is about fourteen times smaller than the equivalent cost of a telephone line for a fax transmission. Telex traffic began to fall more recently.

In order to respond to technological and market trends, and to prepare for competition in the value-added services segment of the market, Embratel increased its investment in the development of an intelligent network and related services. In the early 1990s, Embratel invested U.S.$1.2 billion to modernize its long-distance network in an attempt to triple the number of long-distance lines by 1993. In 1990, on total revenues of U.S.$1.4 billion, Embratel spent U.S.$900 million for five main services: packet data transmission, private data communication, telex, electronic mail networks, and VSAT. The company plans to install a fiber-optic cable between Brazil and the United States by July 1994 and a long-distance fiber-optic network linking Rio and São Paulo by the end of 1992.

In satellite markets, Brasilsat B1 is scheduled to be launched in May 1994 and Brasilsat B2 seven months later. The U.S.$300 million satellites will expand transmission capacity from 48 channels to 104 in order to meet the rising demand created by the growth of new information services and fax traffic.

Embratel has also been restructuring. The company pictures itself as a trunk service provider, leasing lines to more specialized firms in areas as diverse as financial information systems, mobile communications, transportation companies, and cable television. At the same time, Embratel plans to compete in those areas in which it has accumulated experience over the past decade, such as data communications, where it will compete with the pole companies. Its competitive advantage lies in its national network, an important point for large customers with widespread geographic markets (banks, retailing, transportation).

16.7.6 Telebrás

Telebrás had almost 100,000 employees in 1990. During the 1980s it undertook administrative reforms to increase productivity. Between 1985 and 1990 the company reported the number of employees per 1,000 installed phones fell from 14.2 to 10.0.

In 1990, Telebrás began experimenting with alternative financing sources for the installation of new lines. It now allows regional affiliates to contract out construction of public telephone networks to private groups, including municipal and state administrations. An example of this practice was the provision of 8,500 lines in two condominium complexes in the São Paulo area. The deficit of 1.1 million lines sold but not delivered was reduced to 300,000 lines.

Telebrás has also been expanding its links with the private sector. One example is its efforts to promote private investment in the Community Telephone Program (Procom), seeing it as a way to reduce the unfulfilled demand for 6.5 million telephone lines. Under this scheme, the company would be able to expand the network while reserving free cash flow for value-added services and modernization. Private firms would install regional trunk lines, sell the lines to subscribers, and collect user payments through monthly installments from Telebrás subsidiaries.

16.7.7 Research and Development in the 1990s

Telebrás's research arm, CPqD, pressured by a shift in industrial policy toward competitive integration into international markets and in order to align itself with the prevailing strategy of similar research and development centers elsewhere, underwent a sharp reorientation in the early 1990s. This included shedding the remnants of import substitution that had informed its strategy for the previous fifteen years. The major philosophical change involved moving away from tailoring the telecom system's specifications to the products of CPqD's applied research projects. Since 1991 CPqD objectives have been as follows:

1. Target technological development to the needs of the national public network, such as technical specifications, network architecture definition, and so on.
2. Be more selective in the development of new products.
3. Provide wider and more direct technological support to industry.
4. Develop software jointly with operating telcos and other members of the national public network for the automation of operations, planning, and evolution of networks.

Consequently CPqD now concentrates on development of basic technologies in optoelectronics and microelectronics, technical assistance services to private equipment manufacturers, and improvement of automation routines. Product development projects have become much more selective (Graciosa 1991) and industrial partnerships have become tighter, with participating firms now paying a larger share of research and development costs. An administrative reform had reduced the CPqD's direct staff to 530 employees by 1992.

16.8 Wireless Systems

A key market that has been in the forefront of the privatization debate is the mobile cellular phone market. Planning began in the early 1980s. However, by 1991 only Rio and Brasilia had service, with 10,000 and 2,500 lines, respectively. Since then, cellular telephony has expanded rapidly throughout most major cities in Brazil and has become a popular substitute to the expensive and limited terrestrial systems. Curitiba, capital of Paraná, was the third city in the country to have public mobile telephone service. In the first phase, 10,000 users were expected to use the service, with an investment of U.S.$18.3 million. The second phase, completed in 1995, involved U.S.$63.8 million for 50,000 sets. By the end of the decade, 220,000 users are expected in Paraná.

Political and bureaucratic delays prevented Telebrás's forecast of 91,000 cellular subscribers by 1992 from being realized. Nevertheless, the market has attracted a great deal of business attention domestically and abroad and in the 1990s became one of the largest in the world. As of October 1996, there were 1.6 million cellular subscribers, with another 1.5 million waiting for connections. With a population of 160 million, this gives a penetration of mobile telephony of 1 per 100, higher than that of some third-world countries.

Following the model adopted in many other countries, Telebrás will have two firms in each market. Band A is allocated to local pole companies, and band B is assigned to the private sector. For the latter, Telebrás makes a technical preselection, and the local pole company makes the final decision based on financial criteria. For example, in the October 1989 preselection for the Brasilia market, three companies qualified, and Elebra Telecom, using Northern Telecom technology, was selected. The bidding rules stipulate that the winner in one state cannot have more than a 10 percent share in a consortium in another state. The rules also emphasize a low service price as the most important criterion.

Critics have pointed out that Telebrás, which in other areas has carefully selected technology in accordance with standards set by the International Telecommunications Union, has approved outdated and incompatible technologies for several regional systems.

Foreign firm participation is limited to 49 percent, although supply and installation of the system can be contracted out. To this end, joint ventures have been established between foreign technology providers and Brazilian service providers, including some of Brazil's largest industrial and financial groups.

The prize market is São Paulo. Such market size attracted competition for the license from the heavyweights of Brazilian business, from finance to construction. Curiously, although in Rio and Brasilia, the local pole company started service before the private concessionaire, Telebrás attempted to prevent Telesp from directly competing, raising protests from local political forces. The São Paulo mobile cellular market reached 250,000 subscribers by the end of 1994, growing from 0 in 1993. This rapid growth illustrates the extent of unmet demand for telephone service, a result of the regulatory and structural weakness of the Brazilian telecommunications system prior to the reforms begun in 1995.

Local and foreign equipment and service suppliers are likely to profit from the market. For example, in 1991, NEC participated in a U.S.$64 million contract to install Rio de Janeiro's cellular system. The system has a capacity of 10,000 subscribers and is operated by Telerj, Rio's state pole company. The contract was awarded to a joint venture between NEC and the Brazilian conglomerate Globo Group, which extended a supplier's credit to Telerj for installation.

16.9 Political and Economic Imperatives

The terms of the debate on the institutional transformation of telecommunications in Brazil, and in Latin America in general, have been mistakenly cast in terms of privatization or, in more general terms, as liberalization. One cannot talk about privatization—selling the controlling share in a government-owned entity—without also talking about deregulation, loosening government control of a market. However, deregulation can occur without privatization. Latin American countries can transform their telecommunications with the benefit of industrial countries' experiences with deregulation and privatization.

Despite all the talk of deregulation, full privatization and elimination of barriers to entry has thus far occurred only in New Zealand and a few other countries. The World Trade Organization's 1997 agreement on trade in telecommunication services will accelerate reform and liberalization, but its effects on many developing nations may be delayed for a decade. Most European countries so far have preserved a mixed-market institutional model, while countries like Mexico, Chile, Venezuela, and Canada still limit foreign ownership of telecom carriers. (Rubsamen [1989] is a good review of the issues involved.)

The good performance—given the economic and political constraints of the last decade—of Telebrás and Embratel is worth noting. It should also be stressed that Telebrás has accumulated significant technological capability and has contributed to the creation of a domestic equipment industry. This notwithstanding, the financial and technological needs of the sector require an infusion of new funds and new management strategies.

In 1989 Telebrás was charging the final user U.S.$2,000 for a line it had spent U.S.$4,000 to install. That year, this resulted in U.S.$300 million in costs not immediately recovered from users.

By 1992 productivity gains through rationalization and personnel reduction had reduced costs, and the reduction in import tariffs, together with liberalization of public procurement, should bring costs down further through the mid-1990s. It is, however, questionable whether the system's persistent deficits can be dealt with from the cost side, as some have argued, without harming the expansion of basic service and overall service quality. The critical problem remains the tariff structure. To start on any path toward reform, a tariff increase in 1992 of at least 30 percent above inflation would have been needed to align revenues with costs. However, in August 1992 the Ministry of Economy authorized an average increase of only 16.54 percent. Thus, tariffs continued to lag behind inflation, limiting the investment capacity of the public network.

If by the year 2000, when the population is expected to reach 180 million, Brazil aims to have a telephone density close to that of the newly industrializing economies (Spain, Taiwan, South Korea), today around 30 per 100 citizens, versus Brazil's 6, some 41 million new phones are needed (more than four times the number currently installed). This would take an investment on the order of U.S.$127 billion, or U.S.$15 billion a year during the period 1993–2000 at a cost of U.S.$4,000 per phone, the average for 1989–92. If cost-reduction efforts succeed in bringing this amount down to the international average of U.S.$2,000, the necessary investment would be halved. But even U.S.$7.5 billion is well over twice the average invested for 1990–92 of about $3.3 billion. The tariff lag and financial transfers out of Telebrás revenues in the 1980s and 1990s reduced funds available to the system by an estimated U.S.$10 billion.

About 80 percent of residential users pay a tariff of less than U.S.$1 per month, but a jump in basic tariffs risks depressing potential demand. Also, increases in charges for long-distance, international, and value-added services—already relatively expensive in Brazil—which could provide a cross-subsidy to basic service, risks driving business customers away from the public network as competition emerges in these areas. In view of this situation, it is unlikely that privatization and a reduction in barriers to entry will solve the gap in investment.

One might argue that adjustment of basic service rates to account more adequately for inflation is, in the long term, unavoidable. Development of a lifeline service for the many millions of very low income households is possible, and it has been done successfully by the admittedly more advanced U.S. telecom sector. But what rate level is within the means of the 32 million Brazilians with incomes of less than U.S.$30 a month? Long-distance and international tariffs could be reduced but still include a modest premium to provide some subsidy. Such tariff adjustment would help Brazil compete for foreign investment by reducing the disincentives created by the current tariff imbalance and the limitations on network and service expansion.

Tariff adjustment plus liberalization and (partial?) privatization may still not be enough for Brazil to overcome the obstacles created by extreme income inequality. Nevertheless, a balanced program to encourage foreign direct investment, extend basic service to additional households, and promote national technological capabilities and industrial expansion in new markets for information and communication products and services may be the only strategy capable of addressing the myriad problems—and numerous opportunities—for Brazilian telecom policy on the eve of the twenty-first century.

16.10 Conclusion

Following a long history of leadership in telecommunications among developing countries, Brazil lagged in the 1980s and 1990s. The Collor administration promised to initiate a privatization program in 1990, only to find the program blocked and the president impeached. These actions understandably slowed the pace of reform in this vital economic sector. The Cardoso administration of the 1990s reaffirmed in 1996 its intention to proceed with privatization and liberalization. Privatization in other economic sectors such as electricity and mining are proceeding, and it appears to be only a matter of time before the national telecommunications system is reformed. Already, competitive broadcasting, cellular telephone, satellite and cable television, Internet service, and equipment markets are demonstrating the potential benefits to Brazilian society of more aggressively striving to improve Brazil's relative position in the electronic markets of global information economy.

Notes

The research for this chapter would not have been possible without the kind cooperation of several public officials and telecom professionals in Brazil. Participants in the electronic discussion group Brasnet provided a wealth of information and valuable viewpoints that helped frame and develop the issues. We would particularly like to thank Celina d'Avila Samogin, Rodney F. Carvalho, and especially Marcelo Alencar, who provided valuable comments on earlier versions of this chapter. The editorial assistance of Elizabeth Yoon, Laura Grillo, Jill Humphrey, and David Jull is gratefully noted. Views expressed by the authors are not necessarily shared by the institutions with which they are affiliated.

1. Note that the Brazilian data sets are contradictory and incomplete. The data presented represents the authors' best judgment on which numbers to believe—even if admittedly the data are not entirely internally consistent.

References

Antonelli, Christiano. 1991. *The Diffusion of Advanced Telecommunications in Developing Countries.* Paris: OECD (Development Center Studies).
Anuario Brasileiro de Telecomunicações. 1983–84. São Paulo: Talebras.
AT&T. 1990. *The World's Telephones—A Statistical Compilation as of January 1989.* New York: AT&T.

Boletim da Associação de Funcionários do CpqD (AFCPqD). Several issues.

Capellaro, Jorge José V. 1989. "História da Indústria de Equipamentos de Telecomunicações no Brasil: Dos primórdios atéa segunda metade da década de 70." In *História da Indústria de Telecomunicações no Brasil* (História Geral das Telecomunicações no Brasil—Cadernos da TELECOM I), Lins de Barros, Henry British, organizador. Rio de Janeiro: Associação Brasileira de Telecomunicações-TELECOM, pp. 11–46.

Crandall, Robert W., and Kenneth Flamm, eds. 1989. *Changing the Rules: Technological Change, International Competition, and Regulation in Communications*. Washington, D.C.: The Brookings Institution.

Delaunay, Anne Marie. 1989. "Transfert de Technologie et Maîtrise Locale: les firmes d'équipement de télécommunications et le cas du Brésil." Thèse présentée à l'Université de Québec à Montréal, Doctorat en sociologie.

Derthick, Martha, and Paul Quirk, eds. 1985. *The Politics of Deregulation*. Washington, D.C.: The Brookings Institution.

Dias, Leila Christina. 1989. "Les Enjeux Socio-Spatiaux du Développement des Réseaux de Télécommunications au Brésil." *CREDAL—Documents de Recherche*, no. 204, pp. 28–44.

Duarte, Luiz Guilherme, Joseph Straubhaar, and Joseph Stephens. 1992. "Audiences, Policy, Technology and 'Cable' TV in Brazil." Paper presented to International Communication Association, annual meeting, May 21–25.

Duch, Raymond M. 1991. *Privatizing the Economy: Telecommunications Policy in Comparative Perspective*. Ann Arbor: The University of Michigan Press.

"El hilo de la modernidad." 1992. *Vision* (Bogota), March 25, pp. 6–7.

Embratel. 1990. *Relatório Anual*. Rio de Janeiro.

Felix, David. 1992. "Reflections on Privatizing and Rolling Back the Latin American State." Paper presented at the workshop on The State, Markets, and Development, Kellogg Institute, University of Notre Dame, April 24–25. Mimeographed.

Freeman, John R. 1989. *Democracy and Markets: The Politics of Mixed Economies*. Ithaca and London: Cornell University Press.

Graciosa, Hélio Marcos M. 1988. "Telecommunications Research and Development in Brazil." Mimeographed.

———. 1989. "Pesquisa e Desenvolvimento na Telebrás—O CPqD." In *História da Indústria de Telecomunicações no Brasil* (História Geral das Telecomunicações no Brasil—Cadernos da TELECOM I), Lins de Barros, Henry British, organizador. Rio de Janeiro: Associação Brasileira de Telecomunicações—TELECOM, pp. 137–148.

———. 1991. "Evolução da Forma de Atuação do CPqD." Versão 1, March 21. Mimeographed.

Graciosa, Hélio Marcos M., Luiz Del Fiorentino, and Robert S. Goodrich. 1991. "Strategic Management of Telecommunications R&D in Brazil." Mimeographed. Submitted for publication to *International Journal of Technology Management*.

Griffith, Victoria. 1991. "Brazil Rings the Changes to Telecoms Market." *Financial Times* (London), August 2.

Guerra, Sílvio B. 1991. "Privatização e desenvolvimento econômico." *Conjuntura Econômica* 45(July):83–85.

Hills, Jill. 1986. *Deregulating Telecoms: Competition and Control in the United States, Japan and Britain*. Westport, Conn.: Quorum Books.

Hobday, Michael. 1984. *The Brazilian Telecommunications Industry: Accumulation of Microelectronic Technology in the Manufacturing and Service Sectors*. Rio de

Janeiro: Instituto de Economia Industrial, Universidade Federal do Rio de Janeiro (Texto para Discussão No. 147).

———. 1986. "Telecommunications—A 'Leading Edge' in the Accumulation of Digital Technology? Evidence from the Case of Brazil." *Information Technology for Development* 1(March):32–40.

———. 1990. *Telecommunications in Developing Countries: The Challenge from Brazil.* London and New York: Routledge.

ITU. 1989. *Yearbook of Common Carrier Telecommunications Statistics.* 16th ed. (Chronological Series 1978–1987). Génève: International Telecommunication Union.

Kay, John, Colin Mayer, and David Thompson, eds. 1986. *Privatisation and Regulation: The UK Experience.* Oxford: Clarendon Press.

Lerner, Norman C. 1988. "Formidable Aspirations Lead Brazil Forward." *Telephony* 218(October 24):58–63.

Lins de Barros, Henry British, organizador. 1989. *História da Indústria de Telecomunicações no Brasil* (História Geral das Telecomunicações no Brasil—Cadernos da TELECOM I). Rio de Janeiro: Associação Brasileira de Telecomunicações—TELECOM.

Matos, Gustavo. 1991. "País une iniciativa privada e tecnologia sofisticada para modernizar telecomunicações." *Indústria e Produtividade* 24(September):5–10.

Medeiros, Armando L. 1989. "A ITT e a Indústria Brasileira." In *História da Indústria de Telecomunicações no Brasil* (História Geral das Telecomunicações no Brasil—Cadernos da TELECOM I), Lins de Barros, Henry British, organizador. Rio de Janeiro: Associação Brasileira de Telecomunicações—TELECOM, pp. 184–87.

Morgan, Kevin, and Douglas Weber. 1986. "Divergent Paths: Political Strategies for Telecommunications in Britain, France and West Germany." *West European Politics* 9(October):56–79.

Nassif, Luís. 1992. "A privatização da Telebrás." *Folha de São Paulo,* May.

Noll, Roger G. 1986. "Telecommunications: A Challenge to the Old Order." In *Europe and the New Technologies,* edited by Margaret Sharp. London: Frances Pinter, pp. 87–133.

———. 1989. "Telecommunications Regulation in the 1990s." In *New Directions in Telecommunications Policy.* Vol. 1, *Regulatory Policy: Telephony and the Mass Media,* edited by Paula R. Newberg. Durham, N.C. and London: Duke University Press, pp. 11–48.

Perrone, Fernando. 1992. "Communication Systems in Latin America." Paper presented to the International Communication Association annual meeting, May 21–25.

Pilagallo, Oscar. 1992. "Fusão de consórcios esquenta a disputa." *Folha de São Paulo,* April 26, pp. 1–6.

"Privatizing Communications in the Third World: Miracle or Mirage?" 1992. MIT Communications Forum Seminar Notes, April 23.

Rubsamen, Valerie. 1989. "Deregulation and the State in Comparative Perspective: The Case of Telecommunications." *Comparative Politics* 22(October):105–20.

Snow, Marcellus S., ed. 1986. *Marketplace for Telecommunications: Regulaion and Deregulation in Industrialized Democracies.* New York: Longman.

Stepan, Alfred. 1989. *Democratizing Brazil: Problems of Transition and Consolidation.* New York: Oxford University Press.

Straubhaar, Joseph. 1991. Beyond Media Imperialism: Assymetrical Interdependence and Cultural Proximity. *Critical Studies in Mass Communication* 8:39–59.

Tapia, Jorge Ruben B. 1984. "A Política Científica e Tecnológica em Telecomunicações." *Revista de Administração* 19(January–March):101–11.

Telebrás. Various documents.
Telecommunications Market Review. 1990.
Teleguia-O Guia Completo das Telecomunicações. 1984–85. São Paulo: Telepres.
UNESCO. 1976. *Latest Statistics on Radio and Television Broadcasting.* Paris: UNESCO.
Wajnberg, Salomão. 1989. "A Indústria de Equipamentos de Telecomunicações no Brasil:
    Da segunda metade da década de 70 até hoje." In *História da Indústria de Teleco-
    municações no Brasil* (História Geral das Telecomunicações no Brasil—Cadernos
    da TELECOM I), Lins de Barros, Henry British, organizador. Rio de Janeiro:
    Associação Brasileira de Telecomunicações—TELECOM, pp. 47–81.
World Telecommunication Forum. 1988. Geneva: The Union. Organized by International
    Telecommunication Union (ITU).

17

The Brazilian Way
of Telecommunications Reform

MÁRCIO WOHLERS

Until the mid-1990s, Brazil's attempts at modernization and change in telecommunications differed from those in other Latin American countries. The Brazilian approach was not to engage in privatization but rather to maintain control by a government monopoly. But in 1995, the new Cardoso government began transforming telecommunications, starting with the removal of the legal monopoly of the Telebrás companies. The government's priority was the liberalization of cellular telephony, satellite telecommunications, data transmission, and value-added services.

In November 1995, the government proposed a "minimum law" that was approved by both houses of the Brazilian Congress in 1996. This law regulates only four services: (1) cellular telephony (to operate on the B-band); (2) satellite communications; (3) data transmission (to closed user groups); and (4) value-added network services. The administration did not propose privatization (sale of assets) as a short-term objective, except for public operators who provided cellular telephony on the A-band. The government ordered that sales of assets would take place only after the implementation of other reforms, including tariff rebalancing, mergers of operators into regional groups, and establishment of management autonomy. The government also repeatedly stated that it did not seek to replace a public monopoly with a private-sector monopoly but rather to introduce competition.

17.1 The Lead-up to the Present Brazilian Reforms

A public-sector monopoly in Brazilian telecommunications developed in the late 1950s and early 1960s. The growing need for telecommunications in Brazil at that time exposed the technological and institutional fragility of the existing telecommunications system. A chaotic system of concessions was in force, in which foreign-controlled operators served the networks in the country's main capitals but hardly invested in expansion and modernization of their lines and equipment. This practice resulted in serious points of contention with the authorities granting the concessions. In the interior of the country, the situation was even worse; the networks were operated by 800 concession holders, including local city halls, cooperatives, and small-scale private-sector companies. This fragmentation prevented expansion of service in Brazil, which had only 1 million telephone lines in 1960 (representing a line density of 1 line per 100 people). The system was also crippled by high pent-up demand and extremely bad quality of service; it was normal for a customer to wait several hours for his booked domestic long-distance or international call to be connected. Also, the governments of individual states and town halls exercised their power to grant concessions without effective means of estimating the major foreign company operator's costs. This exacerbated the political impact of new tariff negotiations.

Resolution of this impasse began in the early 1960s in two ways. One was the National Telecommunications Code (Law 4,117 of 1962). The other was a growing movement to nationalize the operating companies, which was first expressed when Governor Brizola, of Rio Grande do Sul state, decreed that the ITT subsidiary, CTN (Companhia Telefônica Nacional), should summarily become state property.[1] Soon afterward the government of Guanabara state and the federal government decreed intervention in CTB (Companhia Telefônica Brasileira), which was owned by the Brazilian Traction, Light and Power Company of Canada and served the nation's capital, Rio de Janeiro.[2]

The National Telecommunications Code of 1962 was the foundation of the Brazilian telecommunications system. On the technical level, an inspection and planning agency, CONTEL (Conselho Nacional de Telecomunicações), was charged with imposing national technical standards. A countrywide state-controlled operator Embratel was also created. In addition, the code laid down a surcharge on tariffs to fund the FNT (Fundo Nacional de Telecomunicações), designed to obtain extrabudget funding for the future state company. The system was completed by the creation of a regulatory Ministry of Communications (under Decree-Law 200) and of the holding company Telebrás, in 1972 (Law 5,792 of July 11, 1972).

Telebrás took over centralization, planning, and coordination of all the country's telecommunications activities, including the control of the long-distance carrier Embratel and the so-called hub companies—one in each state—that were formed by the acquisition of various existing smaller-scale concessions.

Between 1960 and 1970 several main players emerged in planning and implementing a telecommunications policy centered on development of the public monopoly. They were (1) the government (including managers of Telebrás); (2) the suppliers of telecommunications equipment; (3) the scientific community; and (4) the labor unions (though with a limited level of autonomy). The scientific community and the equipment suppliers were only strengthened when the state-driven development policy of import substitution in telecommunications equipment was put into practice, starting in the mid-1970s. The telecommunications labor unions, in turn, were extremely limited in terms of activities and attitudes by the restrictions imposed on the country by the military government (from 1964 to 1985).

At the end of the 1980s, the main features of Brazilian telecommunications were a small-scale telephone network; excessive regional imbalances in distribution of telephone lines; insufficient quality of service and an excessive congestion ratio;

insufficient supply of advanced telephony and value-added services; the high cost of lines, the long wait for installation of new lines and the consequent formation of a speculative secondary market in telephone lines (with prices from three to five times the value of lines as sold by the hub companies); an unbalanced tariff structure; irregular and insufficient investment; a healthy financial structure, with a reasonable net margin of profitability, in spite of the low tariff; a good outlook for funding from the international financial market; a lack of incentives and adequate regulation for private-sector investments in the industry; absence of a consistent medium- and long-term planning system; a manager selection process based on political influence rather than technical criteria; spare capacity in the telecommunications equipment producing industry (especially in the large companies); and the absence of an industrial policy oriented toward competitiveness in this segment.

17.2 The Period from 1988 to 1994—the Sarney, Collor, and Itamar Franco Governments

During the second half of the 1980s, Brazil carried out its transition to a democratic regime after decades of authoritarian rule. In the macroeconomic area, there were several attempts to stabilize the currency (such as the Cruzado Plan of 1986), but practically all of them failed. In the political arena, the most important event for the consolidation of democracy was the approval of a new Constitution in 1988. Under this law, the legislature adopted exclusively public-controlled models for basic telecommunications operations—including telephony, telegraphy, data transmission, and the other public services in the area (Article 21, Subsection XI). In terms of regulation, the basic law of 1962 remained in effect. Thus, at the end of the 1980s, while other Latin American countries such as Argentina, Mexico, and Chile were preparing plans for privatization of their operators, Brazil reaffirmed—through its Constitution—the public monopoly on telecommunications. This meant that the recovery and modernization of the system (expansion of digitalization and the offer of new services) continued to be carried out under the aegis of the previous organizational model: a public monopoly.

One of the most important indicators of the progress of Brazil's system recovery was the rising level of investments, which rose to a level of U.S.$2.5 billion annually from 1988 to 1993 (a growth of 127 percent in comparison with the period from 1983 to 1987). Another measure of great impact was the commencement of trading of Telebrás stock on the country's stock exchanges in 1989. These shares rapidly began to play an important role. Their trading today represents more than 50 percent of the stock exchanges' daily "spot" trading volume. The rise in the value of Telebrás PNs (nominal preferred) stock was a phenomenon of great significance, with the price rising from U.S.$5 per thousand shares in mid-1990 to over U.S.$35 per thousand shares one year later, in 1991.

The stock of Telebrás and the other public-sector holding companies (Petrobrás, CVRD, and the electricity companies) now account for the greater part of trading on the stock exchanges. From September 1994 to March 1995, the price of Telebrás stock declined (accompanying the fall in the stock exchanges of all Latin

America), from U.S.$62.44 per thousand shares to U.S.$27.04 per thousand shares. In March 1995, the price of Telebrás stock—now also traded via ADRs (American Depositary Receipts) on the New York Stock Exchange—began to rise again and reached U.S.$64 in May 1996 and U.S.$79 in July 1996.

As of 1996, the holding company, Telebrás, had both private-sector and public-sector stockholders, with the federal government holding 52 percent of the voting stock but only 24 percent of the total capital. This meant that, although the control of the voting capital was held by the government, the overall financial composition of Telebrás's capital was eminently private sector; it had already been privatized in fact, but without transfer of stockholding control.[3]

Telebrás, the world's twentieth largest operator, had 6.5 million stockholders in 1996, including people who received shares with their lines under the subsidiaries' expansion plans, as well as foreign investors who either bought shares on the local stock exchanges or bought ADRs. There was no legal limitation on foreign participation in Telebrás's capital, but the law required that the federal government maintain control over 51 percent of the voting capital. As of mid-1996, foreign investors held 36.7 percent of Telebrás's shares.

During the Collor government (1990–92), the initiative to privatize and deregulate telecommunications was very strong. The Collor government had a wide-ranging effect in acquiring equipment by eliminating the "reserve" of the market in geographical terms and opening the Brazilian economy, which extended to telecommunications equipment. In the transition government (1993–94) of Itamar Franco (the vice president who took over after Collor's impeachment) this theme was also extremely controversial, especially during the period of revision of the Constitution from the end of 1993 to early 1994. This period of revision ended in May 1994 without any decision having been made on telecommunications.

17.3 After 1994—the Cardoso Government

The Cardoso government ushered in a redefinition of the institutional organization of Brazilian telecommunications centering on opening the market and implementing privatization. In February 1995, the government put before Congress an amendment to the 1988 Constitution abolishing the state monopoly on telecommunications. This proposal, approved by the lower house in May 1996, was interpreted as a "flexibilization" of the telecommunications monopoly, as distinguished from a privatization (sale of assets) of Telebrás. The privatization per se was still in the political discussion phase.

In 1996 Telebrás subsidiary companies began planning a widespread restructuring (mergers, rebalancing of tariffs, etc.) as a preliminary step before privatization. Under consideration was a divestiture of the Telebrás system into perhaps five regional local companies, plus the long-distance carrier Embratel. New carriers could enter, and the Telebrás successor firms might enter each other's territories and services if their performance was satisfactory. Otherwise, a regulatory agency would supervise the system, regulate prices in monopoly services (by price caps), and oversee some redistributive mechanism for universal service.

In addition to the elimination of the monopoly, in 1995 the government also put into effect other important measures:[4]

- An overall plan for telecommunications (Program for Recovery and Expansion of the Telecommunications and Postal system—PASTE). This plan envisages investments of U.S.$75 billion (from both public and private sectors), of which half is to be invested in the first period of the plan (1995 to 1999) and the other half in the second period (2000 to 2003). The targets for service indexes are shown in tables 17.1 and 17.2.
- Tariff rebalancing. In 1995, the federal government adjusted telecommunications charges, including a reduction of the cross-subsidy. The basic residential subscription was increased by 513 percent, the price of the local meter unit by 67 percent, and the price of domestic long-distance service by an average of 21.3 percent. The government began a realignment of public-sector prices during a period in which inflation was relatively low and the economy less heated. The adjustment in telecommunications prices came shortly after the correction of electricity tariffs.
- Minimum law. In 1996, Congress approved a law to allow the rapid introduction of the private sector not only in cellular telephony (where there was great pressure from the private sector) but also in satellite transmission, data transmission, and value-added services. During the first three years after this new law, concessions for cellular telephony will be granted only to Brazilian companies, that is, those in which at least 51 percent of the voting capital is directly or indirectly owned by Brazilians. This limits foreign stockholdings to 49 percent of voting capital and 83 percent of total capital.[5] Regarding privatization, the new law gives the present concession holders two years to spin off their A-band cellular divisions into independent companies which may be privatized.

In the short term, the major effect of these measures will be in cellular telephony. Ever since this service was initiated (later in Brazil than in other countries of the region), it has witnessed an astonishing expansion, with 2.0 million lines in 1996, expected to increase to 9.6 million lines in 1999. This field promises opportunities for a wide range of operators. Since 1995, foreign operators have been working with strong local partners in preparation to bid for the ten regional cellular licenses. These institutional changes were important and also necessary, but they were implemented without a clear definition of goals or an analysis of the financial, social, and regional impacts. This situation led some legislators to complain that they were giving a "blank check" to the executive.

Change was in the air. But in 1997, Brazilian telecommunications services were still provided by Telebrás, which is a holding company through its twenty-eight subsidiaries: twenty-seven local operators plus the long-distance carrier Embratel. Telebrás is responsible for overall planning to coordinate the operations of all these subsidiaries, but they are, in practice, more independent than the former Bell operating companies from the predivestiture era. The subsidiaries have specific

Table 17.1. Targets of PASTE Expansion Plan

Service	Units	1994	1995	1996	1997	1998	1999	2003
Fixed telephony	million lines	13.1	14.3	16.5	18.9	21.7	24.7	40.0
Mobile telephony (total)	million lines	0.8	1.9	4.8	6.8	8.2	9.6	17.2
Virtual telephony	million voice boxes	0.05	0.4	1.5	3.0	4.6	6.0	12.6
Public use telephony	thousand phones	360	400	460	540	660	800	1650
Data communications	million subscribers	1.0	1.5	2.5	3.8	5.2	6.51	6.1
Pay TV	million subscribers	0.1	0.7	2.0	3.7	5.5	7.0	16.5
Paging	million subscribers	0.2	0.4	0.7	1.0	1.2	1.5	3.9
Trunking	thousand subscribers	70	80	100	150	210	290	800

Source: PASTE plan (1995).

Table 17.2. Service Indexes—PASTE Expansion Plan

Service	Units	1994	1997	2003
Fixed telephones	lines/100 population	8.46	15.0	23.2
Mobile telephones (total)	lines/100 population	0.52	5.83	10.0
Public telephones	lines/1000 population	2.3	4.9	9.6

Source: PASTE plan (1995).

local concessions in individual regions, and Embratel operates nationally and internationally. Telebrás's basic role is to plan and coordinate financing, technology, and operations of the subsidiaries on a national level. It is the majority stockholder of all of them and is thus responsible for providing the necessary investment and technology for their growth.

The services offered by the Telebrás companies include local, domestic long-distance and international, cellular mobile, public telephone, and data and video communications services, as well as the previously common services such as telex and telegraph services, and new services such as rapid dialing, automatic redialing, toll-free numbers, paid intelligent-network ("900") service, and card-operated public telephones. In December 1996 the Telebrás group of companies had 17.7 million lines, of which 14.9 million were fixed lines and 2.8 million were cellular lines, as shown in table 17.3. Telebrás has 91 percent of the total telephone lines in Brazil; a small percentage is still in the hands of four independent local operators (one of which, CTBC, is private).

The Telebrás group's two largest companies are the long-distance carrier Embratel and the São Paulo state operator Telesp. The local service operators (subsidiaries of the Telebrás group) are restricted to operating in specific geographical areas, and their operational performance varies as greatly as their economic indicators. Quality telephone service is concentrated in the southeastern and southern regions of the country. The revenues from the five subsidiary com-

Table 17.3. Aggregate Figures for the Telebrás Group of Companies

Service	Units	1972	1995
Fixed lines	millions of lines	1.4	14.9
Total mobile lines	millions of lines	—	2.8
"Virtual" lines	millions of voice boxes	—	1.5
Public telephones	thousands	10.3	433
Localities served	thousands	2.5	20.9
Data transmission	million users	—	1.5
Telephone companies			
Telebrás	No. of companies	9	29
Others	No. of companies	927	4
Pay TV	million subscribers	—	0.7
Paging	million subscribers	—	0.4
Trunking	million subscribers	—	80

Sources: Telebrás "Blue Book" (1994) and PASTE (1995).

panies in these regions plus the revenue from Embratel represent 73 percent of the total income from services of the entire system.

Telebrás offers high technology in telecommunications equipment, material, and software developed by its research and development center (CPqD). This research center is considered to be the largest in the southern hemisphere. It provides knowledge and technical support to the company and to the domestic telecommunications industry. The most important research and development projects include the Trópico central switching system, fiber optics, and inductive system phone cards. In 1996, 47 percent of the Brazilian telecommunications system used digital equipment, and this percentage is increasing rapidly. The main suppliers of Telebrás are multinational companies (with manufacturing plants in Brazil) such as Ericsson, Siemens/Equitel, NEC, Alcatel, and Pirelli, and numerous domestic firms such as Promon, Inepar, and others.

The outcome of the ongoing transformation of Brazilian telecommunications is not yet clearly defined. It is not certain how Brazil will emerge in the global telecommunications market, but the country possesses several key strengths that would allow it to respond to foreign competition. These strengths include the size of Brazil's domestic network as the eleventh largest in the world, the potential for applied research at CPqD, and the existence of a significant telecommunications equipment manufacturing plant. Brazil could use its existing resources to internationalize its public operators by fostering partnerships with similar companies in other countries or with other public-sector companies in Brazil. Such a move would certainly support Brazil's advancement into the international arena.

At the end of 1996, a proposed Brazilian General Law of Telecommunications would reform the telecommunications sector of Brazil. A regulatory body would be established (Agencia Brasileira de Telecomunicações), the twenty-seven operating companies would be merged into four or five regional companies, and these operators and Embratel would then be privatized. The final step would be to open the market to competition in basic services, but no decision has been made yet to implement all of these measures.

Notes

1. The expropriations of telephone companies at this time were approved by the respective regional military commands. The National Security Council (Conselho de Seguranca Nacional) issued a note in December 1961 in which it made quite clear its support for federalization of the telecommunications networks (Maculan 1981, p. 39).

2. In addition, CTB provided the telephone service in the states of São Paulo, Minas Gerais, and Espirito Santo—operating, in total, some 70 percent of all the country's telephone lines.

3. In comparative terms, the financial structure of Telebrás is more "privatized" than the financial structure of NTT of Japan (which was officially privatized in 1985), since the government of Japan still held (in July 1994) 64.8 percent of the total capital of NTT.

4. The new directives for the activities of CPqD, the research arm of Telebrás, were established in 1995 and result from reactions in the 1990s to the previous situation. These directives no longer refer to import substitution, as they did in the 1970s, but to applied research projects. These include: targeting technological development to the needs of the

Brazilian public network, in terms of technical specifications, network architecture definitions, and so on; selecting the development of new products; providing wider and more
direct technological support to manufacturers; and developing software jointly with operating telecommunications companies for the automation of operations, planning, and development of networks.

    5. Under Brazilian law, a minimum of one-third of a company's capital must be in com-
mon shares (with the right to vote), and a maximum of two-thirds must be in preferred
stock (without the right to vote).

References

Beca, R. 1991. *Privatization, Deregulation and Beyond: Trends in Telecommunications in
    Some Main Latin American Countries.* Santiago de Chile, ECLAC.

Bitran, E. C., and Saavedra, E. P. 1993. "Algunas Reflexiones en Torno al Rol Regulador y
    Empresarial del Estado." In G. Oscar Munõz (Ed.), *Despues de las Privatiza-
    ciones: Hacia el Estado Regulador.* Santiago de Chile: Collección Estudos
    CIEPLAN.

Costa, M. C. 1991. "Telecomunicações no Brasil: A Trajetória de uma Política Tecnológica
    (1962–1987). Campinas, IFCH/UNICAMP, Dissertação de Mestrado. Mimeo-
    graphed.

Herrera, A. 1992. "La Privatizacion de la Telefonia Argentina." *Revista de la CEPAL* 47
    (agosto).

Maculan, A-M. 1981. *Processo Decisório no Setor de Telecomunicações.* Rio de Janeiro:
    IUPERJ, Dissertação de Mestrado.

_____. 1992. "Telecommunications Policy and New Forms of Globalization in Latin
    America." Paper presented at "VI CLAIO," México, October 5–9.

PASTE. 1995. Programa de Recuperação e Ampliação do Sistema de Telecomunicações e
    do Sistema Postal. Ministério das Comunicações. Brasília.

Petrazzini, B. A. 1995. *The Political Economy of Telecommunications Reforms in Develop-
    ing Countries.* London: Praeger.

Petrecolla, A., A. Porto, and P. Gerchunoff. 1992. "Empresa Nacional de Telecomunica-
    ciones (ENTel)." In *Las Privatizaciones en la Argentina,* edited by P. Gershunoff.
    Buenos Aires: Instituto Torquato Di Tella.

Quandt de Oliveira, E. 1992. Renascem as Telecomunicações—Construindo a Base. Edi-
    tora Editel, São José dos Pinhais, Paraná.

Telebrás "Blue Book." 1994. Sistema Telebrás. Vice Presidência. Brasilia.

Wohlers, M. 1993. *Serviços de Infra-Estrutura de Telecomunicações e Competitividade.* In
    "Estudo da Competitividade da Indústria Brasileira." Campinas, Relatório Téc-
    nico, Consórcio UNICAMP-IEI/UFRJ-FDC-FUNCEX.

_____. 1994. "Reestruturação, Internacionalização e Mudanças Institucionais das Teleco-
    municações: Lições das Experiências Internacionais Para o Caso Brasileiro." Tese
    de Doutoramento apresentada ao IE/ UNICAMP.

Index